Education & Jobs

Education & Jobs
Exploring the Gaps

EDITED BY D.W. LIVINGSTONE

University of Toronto Press

Copyright © University of Toronto Press Incorporated 2009

www.utphighereducation.com

All rights reserved. The use of any part of this publication reproduced, transmitted in any form or by any means, electronic, mechanical, photocopying, recording, or otherwise, or stored in a retrieval system, without prior written consent of the publisher—or in the case of photocopying, a licence from Access Copyright (Canadian Copyright Licensing Agency), One Yonge Street, Suite 1900, Toronto, Ontario M5E 1E5—is an infringement of the copyright law.

LIBRARY AND ARCHIVES CANADA CATALOGUING IN PUBLICATION

Education and jobs : exploring the gaps / D.W. Livingstone (editor).

Includes bibliographical references and index.
ISBN 978-1-4426-0050-8 (pbk.). — ISBN 978-1-4426-0052-2 (bound)

1. Labor supply—Effect of education on—Canada. 2. Underemployment—Canada.
3. College graduates—Employment—Canada. I. Livingstone, D.W., 1943–

HD5709.E38 2009   331.13   C2009-901584-6

We welcome comments and suggestions regarding any aspect of our publications—please feel free to contact us at news@utphighereducation.com or visit our internet site at www.utphighereducation.com.

North America
5201 Dufferin Street
Toronto, Ontario, Canada, M3H 5T8

2250 Military Road
Tonawanda, New York, USA, 14150

ORDERS PHONE: 1-800-565-9523
ORDERS FAX: 1-800-221-9985
ORDERS EMAIL: utpbooks@utpress.utoronto.ca

UK, Ireland, and continental Europe
NBN International
Estover Road, Plymouth, PL6 7PY, UK
TEL: 44 (0) 1752 202301
FAX ORDER LINE: 44 (0) 1752 202333
enquiries@nbninternational.com

This book is printed on paper containing 100% post-consumer fibre.

The University of Toronto Press acknowledges the financial support for its publishing activities of the Government of Canada through the Book Publishing Industry Development Program (BPIDP).

Designed by Daiva Villa, Chris Rowat Design.

Cover Image: "Emergence #1" by Angela Livingstone

Printed in Canada

Contents

List of Tables and Graphs *vii*
Acknowledgements *xi*
Key Acronyms *xiii*

Introduction *1*
D.W. Livingstone

PART ONE PRIOR RESEARCH PERSPECTIVES

Chapter One Prior Concepts and Theories of the Relationship between Workers and Jobs *11*
D.W. Livingstone and K.V. Pankhurst

Two Prior Empirical Research on Education-Job Matching *33*
D.W. Livingstone

Three Starting with *The Education-Jobs Gap* *51*
D.W. Livingstone

PART TWO SURVEYING THE GAPS

Four Education and Jobs Survey Profile I: National Trends in Employment Conditions, Job Requirements, Workers' Learning and Matching, 1983–2004 *67*
D.W. Livingstone and Milosh Raykov

Five Education and Jobs Survey Profile II: Employment Conditions, Job Requirements, Workers' Learning and Matching, by Employee Class and Specific Occupational Group, 2004 *103*
D.W. Livingstone and Milosh Raykov

PART THREE EXPLORING THE GAPS: CASE STUDIES

Six Elements of an Integrated Theory of Work and Learning *137*
K.V. Pankhurst

Seven   Continual Learning, Autonomy, and Competency among High School Teachers *157*
Meredith Lordan

Eight   Staying Current in Computer Programming: The Importance of Informal Learning and Task Discretion in Maintaining Job Competence *185*
Johanna Weststar

Nine   Clerical Workers: Work and Learning in Fragmenting Workplaces *211*
Marion Radsma

Ten   Auto Workers' Learning in Lean Production *237*
D.W. Livingstone and Olivia Wilson

Eleven   Struggling to Remain Employed: Learning Strategies of Workers with Disabilities and the Education-Job Match *257*
Sandria Officer

PART FOUR   CONCLUSIONS

Twelve   The Relationship between Learning and Work: Empirical Evidence from the Case Studies *285*
K.V. Pankhurst

Thirteen   Education and Jobs: The Way Ahead *309*
D.W. Livingstone and K.V. Pankhurst

Appendices   Appendix 1: EJRM Case Study Interviewee Profiles *327*

Appendix 2: Economic Class and Specific Occupational Group, by Intentional Learning Activities, 2004 *334*

Bibliography *337*
The Authors *367*
Index *369*

List of Tables and Graphs

TABLES

2.1 On-the-Job Training Time Required to Perform Job (SVP), Employed US Labour Force, 1940–90 37
9.1 Changes in Clerical Occupations, Canada, 1991–2001 215

GRAPHS

4.1 Economic Sector Distribution, Employed Labour Force, Canada, 1983–2004 (%) 70
4.2 Economic Class Distribution, Employed Labour Force, Canada, 1983–2004 (%) 72
4.3 Job Demands "Great Deal" of Thought and Attention, by Employee Class, Canada, 1983–2004 (%) 74
4.4 Design Work "All or Most of the Time," by Employee Class, Canada, 1983–2004 (%) 74
4.5 Workers Reporting a Supervisory Role in Their Workplace, by Employee Class, Canada, 1983–2004 (%) 75
4.6 Employee Input into Organizational Policy Decisions, All Employees, Canada, 1983–2004 (%) 76
4.7 Input into Organizational Policy Decisions, by Employee Class, Canada, 1983–2004 (%) 77
4.8 Self-reported On-the-Job Training Time Required to Perform Job, All Employees, Canada, 1983–2004 (%) 79
4.9 Training Time by Credentials Required for Jobs, All Employees, Canada, 1983–2004 (%) 80
4.10 Educational Entry Credential Requirements for Jobs, All Employees, Canada, 1983–2004 (%) 80
4.11 Post-secondary Job Entry Requirements, by Employee Class, Canada, 1983–2004 (%) 82

4.12 Comparison of Job Entry and Performance Requirements, by Employee Class, Canada, 1998–2004 (%) *83*
4.13 Post-secondary School Completion and Participation in Further Education, Employed Labour Force, Canada, 1983–2004 (%) *84*
4.14 Level of Schooling by Participation in Further Education, Employed Labour Force, Canada, 1998–2004 (%) *85*
4.15 Most Important Source of Job-Specific Knowledge, Employed Workers, Canada, 1998–2004 (%) *87*
4.16 Topics of Job-Related Informal Learning, Employed Labour Force Participating in Informal Learning, Canada, 1998–2004 (%) *88*
4.17 Employee Class by University Completion, Further Education, and Job-Related Informal Learning, Canada, 1998–2004 (%) *89*
4.18 Relevance of Education to Job, by Employee Class, Canada, 2004 (%) *92*
4.19 Credential Match, by Employee Class, Canada, 1983–2004 (%) *93*
4.20 Performance Match, by Employee Class, Canada, 2004 (%) *95*
4.21 Education Attained/GED Score Match by Employee Class, Canada, 2004 (%) *96*
4.22 Employee Class, by Subjective Qualification-Requirement Match, Canada, 2004 (%) *97*
4.23 Employee Class, by Actual Job Knowledge/Required Knowledge to Perform Job, Ontario, 2004 (%) *98*
4.24 Design Own Work, by Relevance of Education to Job, All Employees, Canada, 2004 (%) *99*
5.1 Employee Class Distribution, Canada and Ontario, 2004 (%) *105*
5.2 Job Demands "Great Deal of Thought and Attention," by Employee Class and Specific Occupational Group, Non-managerial Employees, Ontario, 2004 (%) *107*
5.3 Design Work "All or Most of the Time," by Employment Class and Specific Occupational Group, Non-managerial Employees, Ontario, 2004 (%) *108*
5.4 Job Creativity, by Employee Class and Specific Occupational Group, Non-managerial Employees, Ontario, 2004 (%) *109*
5.5 Participation in Organizational Policy Decision, by Employee Class and Specific Occupational Group, Non-managerial Employees, Ontario, 2004 (%) *110*
5.6 On-the-Job Training Time Required to Perform Job, by Employee Class and Specific Occupational Group, Non-managerial Employees, Ontario, 2004 (%) *111*
5.7 Job Entry Credential Requirements, by Employee Class and Specific Occupational Group, Non-managerial Employees, Ontario, 2004 (%) *112*
5.8 Certification Requirements, by Employee Class and Specific Occupational Group, Non-managerial Employees, Ontario, 2004 (%) *114*
5.9 Job Often Requires Learning New Skills, by Employee Class and Specific Occupational Group, Non-managerial Employees, Ontario, 2004 (%) *115*

5.10 University Completion, Further Education, and Incidence of Job-Related Informal Learning, by Employee Class and Occupational Group, Non-managerial Employees, Ontario, 2004 (%) *116*

5.11A Incidence of Different Job-Related Informal Learning Activities, by Employee Class, Non-managerial Employees, Ontario, 2004 (%) *118*

5.11B Incidence of Different Job-Related Informal Learning Activities, by Specific Occupational Group, Non-managerial Employees, Ontario, 2004 (%) *119*

5.12 Relevance of Education to Job, by Employee Class and Specific Occupational Group, Non-managerial Employees, Ontario, 2004 (%) *120*

5.13 Credential Match, by Employee Class and Occupational Group, Non-managerial Employees, Ontario, 2004 (%) *121*

5.14 Performance Match, by Employee Class and Specific Occupational Group, Non-managerial Employees, Ontario, 2004 (%) *122*

5.15 Subjective Qualification-Requirement Match, by Employee Class and Occupational Group, Non-managerial Employees, Ontario, 2004 (%) *124*

5.16 Employment Experience, by Credential Match and Subjective Match, Non-managerial Labour Force, Ontario, 2004 (%) *126*

5.17 Employee Class and Employment Experience, by Credential Underemployment, Non-managerial Labour Force, Ontario, 2004 (%) *128*

7.1 Relevance, Credential, Performance, and Subjective Gaps among Teachers, Professional Employees, and All Non-managerial Employees, Ontario, 2004 (%) *167*

8.1 Relevance, Credential, Performance, and Subjective Gaps among Programmers, Professional Employees, and All Non-managerial Employees, Ontario, 2004 *190*

9.1 Relevance, Credential, Performance, and Subjective Gaps among Clerical Workers, Service Workers, and All Non-managerial Employees, Ontario, 2004 (%) *230*

10.1 Relevance, Credential, Performance, and Subjective Gaps among Auto Workers, Industrial Workers, and All Non-managerial Employees, Ontario, 2004 (%) *253*

11.1 Relevance, Credential, Performance, and Subjective Gaps among Disabled Workers and All Non-managerial Employees, Ontario, 2004 (%) *273*

Acknowledgements

This book returns to the elusive subject of the relationship between education and employment in analyses that draw upon economics, education, history, industrial relations, philosophy, political science, sociology, statistics, and common sense. The authors together have many years of practical experience of academic research, management, work on the shop floor, teaching, public administration, and policy development. We are also parents, citizens, volunteers, creators and consumers of cultural activities, and hold a range of ideological beliefs. While each of us is responsible for our particular chapters, these diverse perspectives coalesce into a new paradigm that implies a change of focus in policies and practices for learning and work.

Our first thanks are to the people who provided the data for this study. Thousands responded to the telephone surveys. We are especially grateful to the more than one hundred employed workers in the case studies who gave their time and spoke candidly about their jobs, their education, and their learning.

The Education-Job Requirement Matching (EJRM) project was funded by the Social Sciences and Humanities Research Council of Canada (SSHRC), which is gratefully acknowledged. The SSHRC made possible the collection of a large amount of new empirical data by the EJRM Survey as well as the Work and Lifelong Learning (WALL) Survey, both of which were administered in 2004 by the Institute for Social Research at York University. The individual case studies were also funded by the SSHRC.

The EJRM project and the WALL network have been based in the Centre for the Study of Education and Work (CSEW). CSEW is housed in the Department of Sociology and Equity Studies in Education at OISE/UT. The EJRM research is built on foundations laid by the New Approaches to Lifelong Learning (NALL) network, also funded by the SSHRC, between 1998 and 2002. The NALL research developed an expansive framework for (paid and unpaid) work and (formal and informal) learning studies and conducted the first national survey in the world of these forms of learning and work in 1998, as well as a series of over 30 exploratory case studies (all now available through the WALL website: www.wallnetwork.ca).

Many members of the NALL and WALL research teams were helpful in the progress of the project, notably Rosemary Clark, Pierre Doray, Margrit Eichler, John Myles, Peter Sawchuk, Daniel Schugurensky, Harry Smaller, and Alison Taylor. The CSEW staff, D'Arcy Martin and Rhonda Sussman, also offered vital support.

Technical assistance with the statistical and case study interview analyses was provided by Fab Antonelli, Sue Elgie, Doug Hart, Antonie Scholtz, and Susan Stowe. Additional aid in the case study site work came from Malcolm Allen, Roger Garriock, Jean-Yves Leduc, Stephen Perelgut, Peter Scott, and several leaders of the Ontario Secondary School Teachers' Federation and the Toronto and District School Board. The assistance of Donna Dunlop in shaping the final manuscript is gratefully acknowledged. We are very grateful to Anne Brackenbury who shepherded the manuscript from its origins at Broadview Press and to Beate Schwirtlich and editorial staff at University of Toronto Press for their care in the final stages.

Readers who gave valuable feedback on portions of the manuscript include Ivar Berg, Val Burris, Michele Capolieti, Sue Carter, Frederick Glover, Morley Gunderson, Ben Levin, John Myles, Kristine Pearson, Reuben Roth, Peter Sawchuk, Hermann Schmidt, and Wally Seccombe.

Our families deserve grateful thanks for their patient support throughout this research. The book is dedicated to the generations of our children and grandchildren in the hope that their explorations of learning and work will be increasingly fruitful.

D.W. Livingstone
M. Lordan
S. Officer
K.V. Pankhurst
M. Radsma
M. Raykov
J. Weststar
O. Wilson

Key Acronyms

CCS=Canadian Class Structure Survey, 1982–3
EJRM=Education-Job Requirement Matching Project, 2002–7
GED=general educational development index
NALL=New Approaches to Lifelong Learning Project, 1998–2002
SVP=specific vocational preparation time
WALL=Work and Lifelong Learning Project, 2003–7
WCLS=Working Class Learning Strategies Project, 1995–8
WTR=worker trait requirements scale

CASE STUDY ACRONYMS
(T)=Teachers
(CP)=Computer programmers
(CW)=Clerical workers
(Auto QT)=Qualified trades auto workers
(Auto PL)=Assembly line auto workers
(Dis)=Respondents with a disability

Introduction

D.W. Livingstone

This book is about the relationships between the formal education of paid employees, the education required by employers to enter and perform jobs, and the capabilities workers acquire while working. Several dimensions of this relationship have previously been identified and studied in terms of job holders' levels of formal educational attainment and the levels of education required for their jobs. Much recent attention has been devoted to differences between levels attained and required, and especially to an apparent excess of attainments over requirements, which is often referred to as either "underemployment," "overeducation," or "overqualification." The main goal of the various chapters is to explore the relationship between education and jobs in more depth than prior studies.

The paid labour force in the global economy has quadrupled in the past 20 years (International Monetary Fund, 2007: 161–92). This massive growth has occurred in parallel with rapid developments in information technology and with trade agreements that have enabled a geographical diversification of the production of manufactured goods and many services. Political and economic reforms have opened large labour markets in Eastern Europe, China, and India. Participation rates throughout the world have markedly increased as people everywhere, and women with families in particular, are drawn into paid work. The proportion of this labour force with higher education qualifications has grown by 50 per cent over the past 25 years. This is the global context for the detailed studies of employed workers in advanced market economies presented here.

Chronic unemployment rates and the numbers of people in precarious part-time employment have also increased greatly and become recognized as serious global problems (International Labour Organization, 1998; Brown & Pintaldo, 2005). Unemployment and the frustration of not being able to find paid employment of sufficient duration indicate obvious gaps between workers' capabilities and available jobs. But these time-based conditions are beyond the scope of the empirical studies in this book, which are focused on the education-based dimensions of the underemployment of those who do have jobs.

In market economies, where goods and services and labour power are traded competitively, there is incomplete information about workers' abilities and job characteristics. Educational systems have other cultural and social purposes besides vocational preparation, and there is no inherent reason to suppose that workers' capabilities and job requirements will correspond closely. But generations of labour market services, economic theory, and government policy have been devoted to denying their tendency to diverge. Such mismatches have commonly been portrayed as the inadequacies of educational systems to meet economic demand: if there is an economic crisis, blame the schools (e.g., Schrag, 2007).

The expansion of education systems since the end of World War II has been accompanied by expectations that more education would increase national economic growth and improve access to jobs for individuals. Subsequent research has discovered more complex patterns of matching and non-matching between levels of educational attainments and job requirements. *The Education-Jobs Gap* (Livingstone, 1999a, 2004) contributed to this large literature by documenting trends in several dimensions of education-job requirement matching and variations among different occupational groups. Such research, and particularly evidence suggesting surplus educational attainments in relation to job requirements, raises serious questions about the relationship between economic growth and educational investment.

Experience with any type of analytical method inevitably reveals weaknesses that require a refinement of theory and practice, and the time has come to take the analysis of the relationship between education and employment forward. This book is founded on an unprecedented amount of new empirical evidence obtained by linked surveys and case studies.

EJRM RESEARCH DESIGN

The Education-Jobs Requirements Matching (EJRM)[1] project was designed as a sequel to *The Education-Jobs Gap* (EJG). In light of widely differing popular and scholarly views over whether there was an unmet demand for skilled labour, an oversupply of qualified people, or a general balance of labour force qualifications with the needs of the "new economy," the EJRM project was intended to assess the extent of education-job requirement matching more thoroughly than any prior study. The Social Sciences and Humanities Research Council of Canada (SSHRC) funded the project during the period of 2003 to 2007. Subsequent funding by the SSHRC of the Work and Lifelong Learning (WALL) research network for the same period permitted the conduct of a larger national survey.[2]

The EJRM project has two main sources of evidence: large-scale surveys and local case studies. The WALL national survey of the working conditions and learning activities of the employed Canadian labour force was conducted in 2004. The EJRM survey, later in 2004, focused exclusively on Ontario wage and salary employees. The case studies are small, non-random samples of workers interviewed during 2005–6 in several paid work settings, using a semi-structured interview very similar to the survey questionnaires. These in-depth analyses focused on *non-managerial* employees who are without formally delegated authority in these varied work settings. The interview respondents were chosen to represent professional employees, service workers, and industrial workers. The professional employees included teachers working for a public school board in the Greater Toronto Area (GTA) and computer programmers in a large private corporate laboratory in Toronto. The service workers were clerical workers in several different office workplaces in Toronto, and the industrial workers were assembly line and qualified trades workers in an automotive plant in southern Ontario. Workers with disabilities in each of these four types of employment settings were also interviewed. These case studies also involved documentary analysis and participant observation of each work site, as well as interviews with managers.

The specific components of the EJRM project were

- the 2004 Canada-wide WALL Survey of the paid and unpaid work and lifelong learning activities of the entire adult population (N=9063), including all those in the employed labour force (N=5783);
- the subsequent 2004 Ontario EJRM Survey of wage and salary earning employees (N=1709), with particular interest in *non-managerial* employees (N=1301); those with managerial or supervisory occupational titles were excluded from the detailed analysis that focused on professional employees (N=364), service workers (N=555), and industrial workers (N=382);
- specific occupational sub-samples from the non-managerial employee EJRM sample (N=1301), including (1) teachers (N=46), (2) computer programmers (N=60), (3) clerical workers (N=121), (4) auto workers (N=83), and (5) disabled workers in four occupations (N=47);
- the case studies of these specific occupational groups, which included (1) for teachers, two large urban high schools (N=15); (2) for computer programmers, a software research centre of a large private corporation (N=20); (3) for clerical workers, a series of work sites in both public and private organizations (N=23); (4) for auto workers, a large plant (N=20); and (5) for disabled workers, the most comparable sites possible for each of these four occupational groups (N=27).

Social background profiles of the case study respondents are provided in Appendix 1. In addition, interviews were done with managers at most sites to provide a management perspective on working conditions. Each of these sites was chosen by the case study author. Assistance was typically obtained from local managerial authorities and/or employee organization leaders to ensure identification of a cross-section of workers to be asked to participate. No claims are made for the representativeness of the case study participants, but their stories often provide deeper insights into the work and learning relations of these occupational groups than do more statistically representative profiles. The case study authors conducted all the interviews for their respective sites while also completing larger studies that focused on the job requirements and capabilities of workers in the same occupational groups.

The WALL and EJRM Survey questionnaires and the semi-structured case study interviews addressed employment-related learning profiles in terms of formal schooling, further education, informal training, and non-taught intentional learning activities, as well as questions concerning respondents' current job requirements, working conditions, and social background. The EJRM Survey and case study instruments added further attention to job requirements and matching issues. The survey data measures were comparable with earlier surveys. The case studied applied the same concepts of education attained and required, but they provided qualitative evidence that permits more in-depth analysis of the relationships between education and jobs.[3]

CHAPTER OUTLINES

The book is organized in four parts. Part I, Prior Research Perspectives, first provides a critical overview, in Chapter 1, of conceptions of the relationship between workers and jobs, ranging from theories of equilibrium between labour supply and demand to approaches that stress imbalances. Basic dimensions of the matching or gaps between workers' capabilities and their job requirements are identified, and some of the limitations of prior approaches to education-job matching are considered. Then, in Chapter 2, recent empirical research literature on education-job matching is reviewed. Survey-based estimates of job entry and performance criteria, workers' qualifications, and the extent of matching and mismatching between the two are examined; social factors related to education-job mismatches are also considered. Chapter 3 summarizes the contribution of *The Education-Jobs Gap* to this field of study. Livingstone's economic class–based theory of workplace authority and labour utilization is summarized, and a rationale is provided to further examine the relationship between the dimensions of education-job matching by drawing on these class distinctions. General and class-specific tendencies toward increasing levels of *underemployment*[4] are posited.

Parts II and III attempt to advance the analysis and discussion of education and jobs in two stages. First, quantitative data from the recent large-scale Canadian surveys, comparable with previous surveys, are used to address all the previously identified dimensions of underemployment (or overeducation) for employed workers, and primarily for non-managerial employees. These findings yield general matching patterns that are similar to the prior survey research reviewed in Chapter 2, along with new information on trends in matching, new findings for economic class and specific occupational group differences in the education-jobs match, as well as the effects of differences in job control, and other factors such as work experience. Then elements of an integrated theory of work and of learning, and of the nature of problem solving is presented. Particular groups of professional employees, service workers, and industrial workers, are investigated more closely using the new empirical evidence from the case studies about the ways in which workers in specific occupational groups acquire their abilities and perform their jobs.

In Part II, Surveying the Gaps, the statistical findings of the 2004 national WALL and Ontario EJRM Surveys are featured. The survey data include respondents' estimates of the levels of education required for entry into and performance of their jobs, the education they have obtained formally and informally, the control they exercise in their jobs, recent changes in workplace "skill" requirements, and the match between formal job requirements and their actual qualifications. The findings focus on (1) the *relevance* or closeness of the job to field of studies, (2) the match between formal credentials attained and those required for *job entry*, (2) the match between formal education attained and that required to *perform the job*, and (3) *subjective perceptions* of the match between qualifications and job requirements. In Chapter 4, the WALL sample of the employed labour force is used to establish current national profiles of working conditions, learning practices, and education-job matching. Trend estimates are provided based on the 1998 New Approaches to Lifelong Learning (NALL) Survey, as well as the Canadian Class Structure (CCS) Project Survey of 1982 (Clement and Myles, 1992). National comparisons are made among economic classes (employers, self-employed, managers, supervisors, professional employees, service workers, and industrial workers) and demographic groups (by age, sex, ethnicity, and disability status). These survey findings generally confirm predictions of increasing incidence of underemployment, as well as a higher incidence of underemployment among industrial and service workers than among professional employees. In Chapter 5, further analyses of Ontario non-managerial employee classes and specific occupational groups are presented based on the 2004 EJRM Survey.[5] The profiles for Ontario professional employees, service workers, and industrial workers are compared, as well as those for the specific occupational groups to be examined in the case studies: teachers, programmers, clerical workers, and auto workers. These statistical analyses set the context for the analyses presented in Part III.

In Part III, Exploring the Gaps: Case Studies, Chapter 6 outlines an integrated theory of the relationship between work and learning in conditions of uncertainty under an implicit or "open" contract of employment which entails learning by experience. In the following case study chapters, the semi-structured, in-depth interviews provide new and detailed empirical evidence about the capabilities that respondents acquire during paid and unpaid work, and the diverse and evolving nature of the jobs they perform. These findings are at variance with the currently dominant perspectives on the extent to which workers' education and jobs correspond or fail to correspond. The case study analyses locate measured gaps in terms of formal education and explore the extent to which apparently "matched" and "mismatched" workers modify their abilities and the characteristics of their jobs.

Two case studies of professional employees[6] with specialized academic knowledge are presented first; this is followed by two case studies of industrial and service workers whose specialized knowledge is less well recognized. Chapter 7 examines teachers, working in two large suburban high schools in the GTA, who face problems posed by a diverse population of students and by a new government-required curriculum that has standardized testing. The survey data find very little underemployment among teachers. This case study reveals that, in exercising discretion while dealing with multiple practical problems in their classrooms, teachers continually develop their capabilities through on-the-job learning. Chapter 8 looks at the work and learning of computer programmers. While survey measures find higher levels of credential underemployment among computer programmers than among teachers, most of the programmers feel a close match between their formal schooling, their continuing knowledge development, and their daily work requirements: some are looking for more opportunities to apply the abilities they have acquired during work. A fairly flat managerial structure allows a relatively large degree of discretion and initiative in the choosing of work tasks, teams, and methods of work, and programmers are encouraged to engage in further education activities of their choice.

Chapter 9 describes the fragmentation and work polarization of clerical jobs in several workplaces. While clerical workers have the greatest excess of formal educational attainment in relation to their job requirements compared to the other occupational groups, these workers nevertheless continue to enrol in job-related training courses and engage in extensive job-related informal learning. The in-depth interviews illustrate the informal responsibilities these workers assume to keep their organizations functioning, the discretion they exercise in doing so, and the capabilities they acquire through learning by experience. Chapter 10 illustrates through their own accounts how auto workers amass large reserves of abilities. Compared to assembly line workers, qualified trades workers acquire higher levels of specialized knowledge through apprenticeships, tend to have greater workplace autonomy, and report closer education-job matches. However, changes in global competition, machinery, and management models provoke continuing informal learning, which is essential to modify any initial gaps between qualifications and requirements for both types of auto workers.

In Chapter 11, workers with disabilities in all four settings are the focus. Many people with disabilities are excluded from suitable employment in spite of their desire and ability to work. Employed workers with disabilities tend to participate less in further education courses because of accessibility problems, insufficient disability benefits, and negative attitudes of employers and colleagues. To counter these problems, most engage in informal learning to reshape job tasks and augment the competencies they need to fulfill job performance expectations.

In Part IV, Conclusions, the findings are further interpreted. In Chapter 12, the qualitative data from the interviews with individual workers are analyzed using the theoretical framework presented in Chapter 6. Whether workers are formally overqualified, matched, or underqualified for their jobs, the findings suggest that the capabilities of individuals, the requirements of jobs, and the relationships between them cannot be reliably indicated by simple measures of years or levels of educational attainment. These data reveal the importance of informal and implicit learning by workers in performing their jobs, which has the effect of transforming their abilities and modifying their jobs. The survey evidence indicates that professional employees and other workers with specialized knowledge tend to have closer formal attainment-requirement matches. But the qualitative evidence demonstrates how the open contract of employment typically allows workers at all levels of education and organizational authority to exercise discretion in the course of problem solving and decision-making. In so doing, they develop their abilities and reshape some characteristics of their jobs. Workers continually reconstruct extensive and rich reserves of personal abilities of which they are often not fully aware, and subsequently they draw upon these reserves to deal with unanticipated contingencies. Individual abilities and jobs become related in a dynamic process that goes well beyond formal education. Whether measured as underutilized or underqualified, workers are able to adjust both their abilities and their jobs by learning during the experience of work. The prevailing tendency appears to be for workers to modify their jobs, as well as to prepare for a better job. The case study findings demonstrate the extent to which control of their jobs allows workers to apply their abilities, raise questions about the significance of formal educational credentials as job requirement criteria, and suggest the need to make more effective use of workers' capabilities.

Chapter 13 discusses the wider implications of the findings for reformulating policies and practices by employers, workers and their organizations, governments, and education and training institutions, as well as for future studies of learning and work. The time has come to revise the analysis of the relationship between education and jobs that identifies matches and gaps in terms of static measures of formal educational attainment and job requirements. Educational systems will no doubt continue to try to improve the relevance of programs to growing economic and social demands. Formal educational qualifications may continue to be among the criteria for entry into many jobs. However, economic production would be more sustainable if those in jobs with lower formal requirements, particularly service and industrial workers, were more highly valued for their capacity to develop and use their reserves of abilities in their jobs. This need to recognize capabilities applies both to employers and employees themselves. The policy implications of this changed approach are discussed and illustrated first and foremost in terms of employment policy reform and job redesign, but also for formal education practice. Principles are suggested whereby macroeconomic policies and the practices of employing organizations can be reshaped to allow workers to use their capabilities more effectively.

Notes

1. The Education-Job Requirement Matching (EJRM) project was funded by the Social Sciences and Humanities Research Council of Canada (SSHRC) (project # 501-2001-0141) between 2003 and 2007. The SSHRC also funded the collaborative research network on Work and Lifelong Learning (WALL) during this period (project # 512-2002-1011). This combined funding permitted the conduct in 2004 of both the national WALL Survey of work and learning and the subsequent more focused Ontario EJRM Survey.
2. For extensive material from this network, which included national surveys of both the general adult population and public school teachers, as well as a dozen related case studies of relations between paid and unpaid work and various aspects of adult learning, see Livingstone, Mirchandani and Sawchuk (2008), the special issue on work and lifelong learning by the *Canadian Journal for the Study of Adult Education* (December, 2007: 20, 2) as well as the WALL network website: www.wallnetwork.ca.
3. The survey questionnaire, case study interview schedule, and codebook with frequency distributions of all variables for the EJRM project are available at the EJRM project section of the WALL network website.
4. The notion of workers' capabilities exceeding their job requirements has been variously called "underemployment," "underutilization," "overqualification," or "overeducation." The "under" and "over" notions have been associated with largely separate bodies of empirical research (see Chapter 2).
5. It should be noted that the analyses for non-managerial employees were replicated with the Ontario sub-sample of the national WALL Survey (N=1,291) and for the same specific occupational groups in the national survey as in the Ontario EJRM Survey with similar results, but results are not reported in the limited space of this book.
6. We begin with a basic definition of a professional occupation as a calling that requires a specialized body of knowledge acquired through extensive academic preparation. Fully developed professions organize training schools, form associations, and establish regulatory bodies, which enable such professionals to claim overarching authority in their fields of knowledge, make independent judgments about their work, and exclude those without such approved training and certification from legitimate practice in these fields.

Part One
Prior Research Perspectives

Chapter One
Prior Concepts and Theories of the Relationship between Workers and Jobs

D.W. Livingstone and K.V. Pankhurst

This chapter outlines some of the main conceptions of the relationship between jobs and the capabilities that workers bring to them. The chapter provides a background for the review of prior empirical research on education-job matching, the presentation of findings from the recent EJRM survey and case studies, and the formulation of a theory of how work and learning are related. Early normative visions regarded the economy as a self-regulating system that tended toward an overall equilibrium, including a balance between the demand for and the supply of labour, which was treated as homogeneous. Those early perspectives have been replaced by an array of theories that has attempted to take into account the less-than-perfect working of the economy and the labour market, and has placed quite different emphases on the role of labour in productive activity. Human capital theories have suggested that greater investment in education will lead to economic growth, while post-industrial society theories claim that knowledge deficits require a more highly educated labour force. Other approaches, including segmented labour market theories and credentialism, focus on institutional and social factors to account for an apparent surplus of workers in relation to comparable jobs. Many current conceptions of the relationship between education and jobs tend to focus on these apparent surpluses—termed either *underemployment* or *overeducation*—as the most important imbalances, mismatches, or gaps between the levels of education attained and the levels required. In this chapter, several dimensions of the correspondence, or gaps, between workers' capacities and their job requirements are identified. Some limitations of prior approaches to education-job matching are discussed, including a failure to consider the influence of the authority structure of paid workplaces, the neglect of informal learning and unpaid work, and the underestimation of the

THE ROLE OF LABOUR IN ECONOMIC THEORY

In classical economic theory, which described employment before the industrial revolution, work was equated with physical effort, the labour force was seen as homogeneous, and workers were considered to be substitutable. Changes in subsistence wages adjusted labour supply and demand. If population growth raised the supply of labour, a fall in wages to below subsistence level would reduce the population and, therefore, the supply of labour until it was equal to demand. Should labour supply fall, a rise in subsistence wages would induce a population increase until the labour supply was in balance with demand. Neoclassical theories that predominated from the late nineteenth century to the middle of the twentieth century (e.g., Jevons, 1871) conceived a balance between labour demand and supply when wages were equal to the marginal productivity of labour. If the marginal product of labour rose, wages would rise and induce an increase in labour supply, and vice versa. The implicit assumptions remained that wages depended on hard work and that labour was homogeneous and passive in the production process. In both classical and neoclassical theories, the labour market was assumed to be automatically cleared of unemployment or labour scarcities.

The assumption of such a natural equilibrium is contradicted by the historical evidence of prolonged periods of imbalance in the form of unemployment alternating with shorter periods of labour scarcity. The creation in the early twentieth century of public employment services to provide information to help bring workers and jobs together, coupled with unemployment insurance, was a tacit admission that the distribution of the labour force among jobs was not perfect. From the early twentieth century, sociological research has probed the heterogeneity of jobs and the variability of effort among workers. Nevertheless, economic theory has been reluctant to relax the neoclassical assumption of homogeneity.

Perceptions of the role of labour in production and productivity have been slow to change, and the emphasis in economic theory and policy has remained strongly focused on fixed capital investment. In the nineteenth century, when labour was thought to be passive, a focus on fixed and financial capital accumulation seemed a fair description of the driving force in economic development. The presumed central importance of capital investment persisted long into the twentieth century. Keynes (1936) explicitly assumed the homogeneity of labour in order to make fixed capital investment central to his explanation of output determination. Theories of growth, which combined the multiplier[1] and the accelerator[2] (e.g., Harrod, 1973; Domar, 1957), retained the assumption of fixed capital investment as the dominant force that continually generated increased output, and they were silent on the role of labour. Economic productivity estimates, which became fashionable until the 1960s,[3] attempted to assign changes in production between increases in amounts of labour and fixed capital respectively (Cobb & Douglas, 1928). However, investment in fixed assets was still taken to be the key variable in public policy: macroeconomic financial policy could influence investment, but there was little or no direct control over labour productivity.

Education and Economic Growth
The focus on fixed capital investment prevailed until statistical analyses of economic growth in the decades following World War II began to suggest that productivity increases could not be fully explained by additional amounts of fixed investment or labour (e.g., Abramovitz, 1956). The conclusion that there must be another "hidden factor," and that this must be formal education, appeared consistent with the great expansion of school systems after World War II and with rapid economic growth (Denison, 1964). Although estimates of this hidden factor were heavily criticized by some analysts (e.g., Organisation of Economic Co-operation and Development, 1964), formal schooling came to be taken as a measure of the quality of labour. Since economic growth at the time was rapid and labour scarce, political pressure to emphasize the vocational purpose of education was strong. This focus was supported by the perception that an educational credential created individual advantage in competing for a job and enhancing social status. The new assumption that investment in education, rather than in fixed capital investment, governs economic growth proved to be politically convenient, and this idea has persisted despite the converse argument that economic growth also finances the expansion of education (e.g., Schultz, 1960).

In the post–World War II conditions of rapid growth, employers and governments gave high priority to ensuring a continual increase in the supply of more highly educated workers. The extension of the school-leaving age beyond 15 raised the question of what was to be taught in the curriculum, and fears of labour scarcities appeared to confirm that education should be devoted predominantly to occupational preparation. Education and training policies were presented as instruments of equal opportunity, but concern focused on scarcities of labour and fears of continuing labour shortages. Had the labour market been able to reconcile the amounts of labour demanded and supplied by wage adjustments to clear the market of surplus labour (unemployment) or vacant jobs (labour scarcities), there would have been no role for government. However, as labour demand and supply were not automatically reconciled, it was assumed that intervention was needed. Broad educational and employment planning became a task for government, while personnel matching became a responsibility of employers, with the assistance of public employment, counselling, and placement services.

The ethos of centralized state planning carried over into post-war reconstruction.

In several countries, it was reflected in a marked trend in political philosophy toward increased social welfare provision. World War II had been an increasingly scientific exercise during which new equipment and technologies, and advanced methods of logistical planning, were used to combine the armed forces of several countries in air, land, and sea operations and to move personnel and materials around the world. However, in the 1950s, planning the labour supply and matching people's abilities and jobs could no longer be managed by the kind of authority used during the war. Although the wartime vocabulary of manpower[4] [sic] planning, utilization, and efficient deployment were retained, the techniques of planning and personnel selection were adapted to civilian education and employment, which could not be directed with the same instruments of command as were the armed forces. Economic, education, and employment planning seemed necessary and plausible, especially remembering the high unemployment of the 1920s and 1930s. Employers and employees became habituated to wage stability, and there appeared to be little scope for changes in wages to adjust the demand and supply of labour.

The dominant technique of economic forecasting in the 1950s and 1960s was to extrapolate the trends in the main components of the Gross National Product (fixed investment, consumption, government income and expenditure, and external trade).[5] Forecasts of labour requirements calculated the demand for labour in relation to production. The "manpower" demand for education was in turn calculated in relation to the demand for labour.[6] It was possible to make those simple estimates of labour requirements by assuming that the relationship between production and labour could be described by a fixed coefficient, that is, that the elasticity of demand for labour with respect to production was zero, or near zero. Similarly, the simplifying assumption was made that the relationship between new employment and education could be described by a fixed coefficient, that is, a given relationship between education and jobs. Techniques for projecting employment requirements promoted by the Organisation for Economic Co-operation and Development (Parnes, 1962) at first appeared to be a sensible basis for planning labour supply and were widely adopted (Harbison & Myers, 1964; Economic Council of Canada, 1964). Given those assumptions of fixed coefficients and stable wages, it was possible to make projections of the manpower required. The concept of manpower requirements was defined by Parnes (1963: 22) as "more a technological than an economic one".... He argued that if manpower considerations are one of the elements that ought to influence educational decisions, then all such decisions, if they purport to be rational, should involve manpower forecasts. It was claimed that estimates of "performance requirements" would "tell us not only what occupations to train for, but the amount of teaching time and other costs required to train a work force in the new pattern" (Scoville, 1966: 391, quoted by Fine, 1968). But the assumption of mainly fixed coefficients between output and employment took no account of the gestation periods in planning fixed investment and production or in expanding educational facilities;

it also overlooked inter-occupational mobility, technological innovation, and the redesign of production methods and the workplace. Since no mechanism existed to allocate the supply of education by subject field to estimates of occupational requirements, it is not surprising that occupational projections were found empirically wanting (Ahamad & Blaug, 1973).[7]

HUMAN CAPITAL INVESTMENT

In the context of the post–World War II extension of formal schooling and economic growth, there was a new emphasis on the notion that more investment in education and training would lead to even further economic growth. The analysis of the relationship between education and employment proposed by Becker (1964) and developed by Mincer (1970, 1974) was a simple quantitative application of human capital theory.[8] It was a more disciplined and coherent approach than hitherto and was welcomed by economists as a major advance (e.g., Bowman, 1966). Since the method was introduced during the 1960s, when first-generation large computers made it possible to perform very large computations more rapidly, it became possible to replicate the findings many times. Empirical testing has tended to yield consistent findings, with rates of return to formal educational investment estimated between 10 and 15 per cent, and with private rates of return (wages compared with costs of education plus foregone earnings) being somewhat higher than social returns (which also incorporate tax revenues and public expenditure on schooling). The estimates have become progressively more statistically sophisticated and have included some indicators of experience and abilities. These findings have been interpreted as evidence that more education yields higher earnings, and since in neoclassical theory earnings are assumed to measure economic output, it was concluded that more education would yield more output. It is therefore not surprising that calculations of rates of return to schooling should be welcomed by policy makers (Blaug, 1983).

Given the ease with which rate of return to schooling calculations can be made, the concept of human capital became virtually synonymous with quantification, to the neglect of the rich character of a worker's capabilities and of how they contribute to productivity. Several authors have recognized technical and conceptual problems with estimated rates of return (e.g., Weale, 1993). Human capital theory posits a unidirectional causality between economic output and education; however, the relationship between education and economic output is, in principle, reciprocal. The findings are apparently robust but are subject to statistical variation. There are two critical conceptual weaknesses in the attempt to measure human capital: the assumption about the functioning of the economic system and another about the nature of education and learning.

The neoclassical assumption that wages equal marginal productivity and can be taken as indicators of economic output cannot be sustained, however, in conditions of differing degrees of industrial competition, nor in the large public sector that has no identifiable marginal product, nor in the production of non-traded goods. There is a long history of research that explains why the economy cannot reasonably be described by perfectly competitive product and labour markets. Because it is evident that a series of spot market contracts for inputs and outputs would be impossible for private firms to manage, the distinguishing feature of a firm is "the supersession of the price mechanism" (Coase, 1937: 389). That thread was later developed in theories of internal labour markets (Doeringer & Piore, 1971) that describe the firm as acting in the external labour market to recruit labour through ports of entry, and then to exercise authority in the internal labour market (incorrectly described as a market) to allocate, train, and promote its own personnel. Growing dissatisfaction with the limitations of free market assumptions also led to the development of segmented external labour market theories (Piore, 1970, 1983), discussed below.

Equally restrictive is the assumption that measures of formal education—used as the independent variable in rate of return calculations—accurately represent human abilities. The weakness lies in the concept of formal schooling as an institutional process that ignores the inherent nature of learning as the acquisition of cognitive knowledge and abilities by experience. Although attempts have been made to include indicators of experience, learning is a mental process that happens throughout life, including formal education, and its nature cannot be measured in terms of duration. Attempts to include ordinal test scores as indicators of abilities also fail to take into account how abilities are acquired. More important, measurements of the relationship between education and wages implicitly treat the employing organization as a kind of "black box" (Machlup, 1962) in which an unspecified alchemy converts education into output. For a theoretical explanation of the nature of the connection between education and economic output, it is necessary to examine in some detail the nature of the labour process during production. This issue is addressed in Chapter 6 in terms of how a worker both performs a job and learns.

THE DEMAND FOR LABOUR IN POST-INDUSTRIAL SOCIETY

In contrast to approaches that assumed an automatic adjustment of supply and demand and also in contrast to interpretations of human capital theory that assume investment in education will lead to economic growth, more recent theories focus on new demands for labour that are generated by the changing nature of work in modern economies.

The demand for labour is presumed in these theories to derive from new production requirements, most notably the development of an advanced technology including complex problem-solving rules and high-speed computers. Theories of the emergence of a post-industrial society predict that the rise of service sector employment and information-centred production require a rapidly growing array of professional and technical workers and a diminishing number of manual labourers (e.g., Bell, 1973). Similarly, more recent advocates of a "knowledge-based economy" (KBE) assume that the current labour force suffers from deficiencies of knowledge and ability—when compared to the requirement for increasingly complex analytical abilities in modern information-based production systems—and assert that education systems must respond to these deficiencies (Marshall & Tucker, 1994). Conversely, other social theorists see a dominant tendency within production systems toward a greater routinization of the labour process and a heightened surveillance of workers, which leads either to a profound deskilling of job requirements or to widespread automation, with a consequent proliferation of unemployment (Braverman, 1974; Rifkin, 1995).

Both of these "demand-side" arguments imply that school systems and learners will accept these new realities. In both variants, the labour force has been regarded as being reactive to secular trends in production rather than as influencing them through their learning efforts. Whether work can be presumed to tend toward deskilling or upskilling, such approaches have generally paid little attention to the capacities a worker brings to a job.

Knowledge-based economy approaches may use the fact of temporary shortages in certain specialized skilled occupations either to paint scenarios of obstacles to economic sustainability (Murphy, 2000) or to treat demographic projections of an aging current labour force as creating challenges of skill shortage in the future (McMullen & Cooke, 2004). Demand-centred theories cannot explain the nature of education-job relationships, and they fail to account for the surpluses of qualified labour that preoccupy many researchers who focus on the relationship between education and jobs. Nevertheless, similar notions asserting educational deficits in relation to changing labour market demands continue to be prominent in public discourse and must be addressed in further research and policy debate. The discussion now turns to the current theories that try to address persistent mismatches or gaps between workers' capabilities and labour market outcomes.

SEGMENTED LABOUR MARKET THEORIES

Adam Smith (1776), although a strong advocate of a free market, conceded that certain institutional constraints, such as laws and regulations of apprenticeship systems, could create wage differences. When John Stuart Mill later emphasized the value of goods in terms of their differential utility to consumers, he criticized Smith for underplaying the existence of monopolistic industrial groups that placed some workers at a disadvantage. One thread of institutional economics from Veblen (1899) onward has rejected assumptions about market autonomy, seeing markets rather as the result of interactions between individuals and communities of employers and workers, as well as with governments. This approach led to the identification of a variety of labour markets with widely varied degrees of competition and reward for abilities.[9]

Segmented labour market theory was developed in the 1970s to address the persistent poverty and systemic marginalization of people whose unemployment and wage differentials could not be explained by initial skill differentials. An insistence upon the pivotal role of social and institutional influences in constructing and reproducing fragmented labour markets — thereby relegating racial minorities, women, and those from poor economic origins to low-wage, low-skill jobs — was central to this paradigm. As Piore (1983: 252) summarizes,

> At the core of labour market segmentation are social groups and institutions. The processes governing allocation and pricing within internal labour markets are *social*, opposed either to competitive processes or to instrumental calculations. The marginal labour force commitment of the groups, which creates the potential for a viable secondary sector of a dual labour market, is social. The structures that distinguish professional and managerial workers from other members of the labour force and provide their distinctive education and training are also social... as opposed to individual phenomena.

The fact that certain institutional rules and social influences contribute to fragmented labour markets and to wage differentials that are not closely related to initial skill differentials is now widely accepted. However, variants of segmented labour market theory have proliferated, and proponents have not clearly or consistently identified criteria for determining such segments (Leontaridi, 1998). Piore (1983: 252–3) provocatively suggested two alternatives for development of a social framework to build further understanding of labour market segmentation: either Marxist class analysis applied to labour market stratification or the analysis of cognitive processes in different contexts.

CREDENTIALISM

Some approaches to observed mismatches between workers' capabilities and available jobs focus on heightened competition and trends toward higher credential requirements for jobs. Both employers' hiring criteria and also job seekers' specialized knowledge claims are seen as pivotal. Screening theories (Stiglitz, 1975) assume a continuing oversupply of qualified workers; employers use narrow, formal criteria to select the most qualified applicants, and, simultaneously, job seekers use these criteria to compete for jobs, even though there is no necessary relation between the criteria and greater productivity, or attention to workplace relations, or possible labour scarcities. Theories of a credential society (Collins, 1979) assume that groups of workers who obtain certified specialized knowledge will try to set qualifications that restrict subsequent access to such knowledge and that tend to be higher than needed to perform a job. Likewise, employers may inflate entry credential requirements to limit access to jobs, thereby creating systemic gaps between workers' capacities and job performance requirements. Both theories assume that labour surplus stimulates increased labour market competition, as well as individual and collective negotiations between employers and current or prospective employees about entry and certification criteria for employment. From credentialist perspectives, it is likely that some job applicants will become overqualified for available jobs and have to accept jobs for which they are overqualified, whereas some experienced workers will become underqualified in terms of formal credentials for jobs that they are performing quite adequately. Credentialism implicitly acknowledges the partially opposed interests of employers and workers under the open contract of employment, which is discussed in Chapters 3 and 6.

However, while credentialist approaches have sometimes focused analyses on specific powerful occupational groups (e.g., Collins, 1979), they have not examined the underlying authority structure of workplaces in any detail in relation to education-job matching, as discussed later in this chapter.

UNDEREMPLOYMENT OR OVEREDUCATION

Since the 1970s, there has been evidence of continued educational expansion in the context of slower economic growth, apparent surpluses of educated workers for available jobs, and the persistence of high unemployment levels in a more highly educated labour force. Early theories of automatic adjustments of labour supply and demand have been replaced by a variety of approaches. These approaches emphasize institutional and social factors that impede the balancing of supply and demand and contribute to chronic mismatches, or gaps, between job requirements and workers' capabilities. Two largely separate conceptions that have been developed treat this condition as either underemployment or overeducation.

The underemployment concept is most closely associated with segmented labour market theories; it assumes that labour markets and workplaces are to blame for not providing enough decent jobs for the growing number of well-qualified job seekers. On the other hand, the notion of overeducation seems to imply that formal education systems are producing more credentialled workers than the labour market can absorb.

Underemployment and Lack of Adequate Jobs

The rise of student protests and workers' strikes in the 1960s provoked worry that growing numbers of highly schooled youths could not get the sorts of rewarding jobs they expected. Policymakers and researchers became concerned about the problem of youth underemployment (O'Toole, 1977). It was argued that when highly qualified people could only get routine jobs they would become bored and alienated and reject the established social order. Several dimensions of underemployment were identified, including a performance gap between job holders' educational attainments and the actual task requirements of their occupations (Berg, 1970); a credential gap between educational attainments and established job entry requirements (Diamond & Bedrosion, 1970); and subjective underemployment, which involves both a conscious perception that people's jobs do not allow significant use of their qualifications (B. Burris, 1983) and also the incipient development of revolutionary political consciousness as a consequence of objective underemployment (Derber, 1978, 1979; V. Burris, 1983). Early estimates of the extent of these forms of underemployment indicated that as many as 25 to 50 per cent of recent college graduates (Rumberger, 1984) and from 25 per cent (Carnegie Commission, 1973) to as high as 80 per cent of the entire workforce (O'Toole, 1977) could be affected. This body of research focused mostly on highly schooled young people and on those who then held jobs.

Approaches to underemployment overlap with research concerned with *subemployment*. While underemployment concepts are preoccupied with the *inadequacies* of the work for job holders and highly schooled young people, the subemployment approach emphasizes the *absence* of adequate jobs for all those who want to work (National Advisory Commission on Civil Disorders, 1968).[10] Underemployment researchers sometimes refer to unemployment as the most severe form of underemployment for highly qualified people (e.g., Derber, 1978). The subemployment approach has continued to focus on those who have no job at all, but also refers to underemployment in terms of low-income jobs and aggregate-level educational attainment-requirement "mismatches" (Clogg, 1979: 218–23). The two conceptual approaches stress different dimensions of the same general phenomenon: the wasted abilities of the workforce. The generic problem is the extent to which a society's provision of adequate jobs falls short of the supply of qualified workers.

Overeducation and Human Capital Theory

Some attempts have been made to revise interpretations of human capital theory in the light of evident mismatches, either by developing variants of overinvestment in formal education or by arguing that prior investment has been too narrowly focused on formal education.

When marginal rates of return to a university degree declined in the 1970s, this was explained by *overeducation*, that is, overinvestment in formal education, rather than by underemployment of employees' abilities. Freeman (1976) posed the argument that, in the United States, the higher education system had been overdeveloped in relation to economic demand, and he predicted that future periodic surpluses and shortages of educated labour could be expected as graduates adjusted only slowly to changing labour markets. Becker (1992) dismissed Freeman's argument when rates of return to college education again increased in the 1980s. However, as rates of return later declined, and mismatches between attained and required levels of schooling persisted, further explanations of labour mobility were developed. Sicherman (1991) argued not only that some apparent overeducation involved training for future jobs but also that some mismatches were temporary because the more highly educated workers continued to seek jobs for which they were qualified.

Thurow (1975) argued that most workplace skills are acquired through on-the-job training and that individual workers continue to participate in education and training to protect their relative position in the competition for jobs. Both wage levels and relative training costs co-exist as market-clearing mechanisms, but defensive investment in education may lead to overeducation.

Some revisions of arguments about educational investment have suggested that more early childhood education can rejuvenate both human capital creation and economic growth (Heckman & Klenow, 1997). Others now see that the dynamic centre of human capital creation resides either in highly concentrated urban zones where "symbolic analysts" live, work, and continually solve, identify, and broker economic production problems (Reich, 1991; Florida, 2002) or in "learning organizations" that create intellectual capital by facilitating collaborative problem solving within their workforces (Senge, 1990; Nyhan, 1991). The central proposition of human capital theory — that earnings are related to levels of education — is resuscitated by stressing earlier schooling or by emphasizing that effective employees must become continual adult learners in an increasingly worldwide competitive environment (Lucas, 1988; Romer, 1994; OECD, 1996). Few would disagree with the general benefits of early childhood education or lifelong learning. Nevertheless, the broadening of the concept of human capital does not directly address the issue of mismatches between the actual formal education attained by the labour force and the education required for current jobs.

Others have attempted to explain the discrepancies between investment in education and earnings by focusing on the individual's choice of available jobs and sectors as factors that influence the relationship between the individual's characteristics and earnings (Sattinger, 1993). In such assignment models earnings depend on both the individual and the job; therefore, some overeducation is conceded.

GAPS BETWEEN WORKERS' KNOWLEDGE AND JOB REQUIREMENTS

In conceiving the relationship between educational attainments and job requirements, there are two logical possibilities. There could be a match or one could exceed the other. Leaving aside for the moment the empirical question of how much variation constitutes a mismatch, there are two types of mismatch.

On the one hand, educational attainments could exceed job requirements. There is now extensive evidence from different countries and periods of time that an overall skew toward overeducation is typical. When the education system is seen as the source, this mismatch is called "overeducation," whereas when the economy or the job structure is seen as problematic, it is termed "underemployment."

On the other hand, job requirements could exceed educational attainments: a condition called "undereducation" or "underqualification."[11] School dropouts and people with low literacy are frequently described in this way, and advocates of the knowledge-based economy widen this charge to employed workers and to students and school systems. However, this condition has diminishing relevance to researchers who are directly studying education-job requirement relationships and who recognize the role of on-the-job training in permitting formally undereducated job holders to acquire adequate job-performance capacities.

In this book, the *extent* of correspondence or separation between workers' capabilities and job requirements is not presumed. The authors of the 2004 EJRM Survey analyses and case study chapters examine empirical evidence of matching and mismatching. These studies, however, pay particular attention to purported separations or gaps. As the above discussion of underemployment and overeducation perspectives suggests, those whose capabilities are deemed to exceed job requirements have garnered the most attention in recent research, and this will be apparent in the review of recent empirical research presented in Chapter 2.

It should be emphasized that underemployment perspectives have a much wider focus than overeducation ones. From an underemployment perspective, labour market status is becoming increasingly understood as a continuum ranging from long-term full employment to chronic and complete unemployment. Conceptions of the underemployment or underutilization of workers' capabilities now encompass both time-based, complete, or partial exclusion from employment and also skill or education-based underutilization of capabilities in employment (for general reviews, see Livingstone, 2004; Brown & Pintaldi, 2005). Primary *time-based dimensions* are the extent of unemployment (including those actively looking for employment, discouraged workers, and others such as prisoners and retired people who are restricted from the labour market), and the extent of involuntarily reduced employment in temporary, part-time jobs. Beyond official unemployment rates, there is limited definitional agreement or empirical evidence on part-time measures, but it is now widely agreed that time-based forms of underemployment constitute a very significant problem (International Labour Organization, Resolution concerning measurement of underemployment and inadequate employment situations, October 1998). Official unemployment rates fluctuate with business cycles, while long-term structural unemployment and some aspects of contingent part-time unemployment may experience increasing secular trends (see Livingstone, 1999a, for an earlier general review; Jensen & Slack, 2003, for a recent US review of time-based measures). Overeducation perspectives rarely refer to time-based exclusion from employment, except to allude to the greater unemployment levels of those with little formal education and their need to obtain more of it (e.g., Becker, 1992).

Skill or education-based conceptions of underemployment or overeducation refer to the surplus capacities, skills, education, or knowledge that workers bring to the job, in comparison with what is needed for the job. There is much dispute over the notions of skills, relevant education, and knowledge, as will be seen later in this book. Numerous ways of conceiving the gaps between employed workers' capabilities and the requirements of their jobs have been suggested (e.g., Kalleberg, 2008).

Six conceptual dimensions of the relationship between workers' capacities and their job requirements can be identified. These dimensions can be expressed in terms of the potential gaps between the two: *talent use gaps, credential gaps, relevance gaps, performance gaps, general working-knowledge gaps*, and *subjective gaps*. Chapters 4 and 5 are devoted to surveying these purported education-jobs gaps, and in the case study chapters use them as points of departure for fuller explorations.

Talent Use Gaps
The talent use gap refers to educational discrimination against youths from poorer economic class backgrounds as well as those with subordinated race, gender, or other ascriptive characteristics, in terms of their chances to attain qualifications before entering the labour market (Livingstone, 1999a). The currently institutionalized forms of formal schooling may be seen, at least partially, as expressions of unequal power relations between business owners and working-class employees, mediated by middle-class (managerial and professional) employees. Various researchers have documented economic class influences in the historical construction of modern public school systems (Simon, 1974; Katz, 1971). Generations of studies have established that those who are born into affluent economic classes are highly over-represented among those who complete more advanced levels of formal schooling; those from poorer working-class or lower-class families have been largely excluded.

There is considerable evidence that the correlation between fathers' and sons' occupational status and the inter-generational ratio of relative educational attainment between economic classes has remained quite constant, at least in the United States during much of the twentieth century. This has occurred despite the expansion of public education systems (Collins, 1979: 182–3). On the other hand, in periods of major transition in the forms of production, there has been much greater class mobility. For example, during the industrialization of Sweden in the 1880s, there was about 60 per cent mobility out of the class of origin, accompanied by decreasing property inheritance, population growth, and migration and by the increasing importance of formal education (Maas & van Leeuwen, 2002). Canada, as a later "settler economy" with continuing large-scale immigration, has had one of the higher rates of inter-generational economic mobility of all advanced capitalist societies.[12] The apparent growth of middle-class positions dependent on formal educational credentials, the substantial increase in access to post-secondary formal education, and the increasing priority of formal educational credentials over more ascriptive hiring criteria for jobs provide evidence that inter-generational upward and downward class mobility has increased in the past generation, at least in Canada. The talent use gap may therefore have decreased somewhat (see Livingstone & Stowe, 2007).

Prominent, recent explanations for the under-representation of working-class children in higher education have featured affinities between the cultural knowledge or linguistic codes conveyed by affluent parents and those that are dominant in school programs (e.g., Bourdieu & Passeron, 1977; Bernstein, 1996). While such cultural factors discriminate against working-class children, the barriers they face in terms of lack of material resources pose even greater obstacles to their completing of advanced schooling (Curtis, Livingstone, & Smaller, 1982). The expansion of postsecondary education in response to both labour market and popular demand has allowed increasing numbers of children from lower-class origins to complete university and college programs. However, these children remain under-represented by ratios of 3:1 or more, a massive waste of talent in terms of inherent learning capacity, which is most likely to be randomly distributed among children of all classes at birth. This form of discrimination is compounded by the educational exclusion of many non-white racial groups as well as by the continuing lack of representation of women in some fields (Livingstone & Stowe, 2007).

The talent use gap is not examined in detail in this book, given the focus on the relations of learning capacities and job requirements among employed workers. However, it should be stressed that recent research demonstrates that less formally educated youths do not commonly become discouraged learners once they enter the labour force. Rather they, along with other workers, use some of their talents as active learners to gain various competencies, most frequently through informal means (Livingstone, 1999b, 2008). Much of this learning, or "working-class capital," may not be commonly recognized by employers or even by the workers themselves throughout their working lives (see Livingstone & Sawchuk, 2004). As will be seen, workers' informal learning is generally vital in the relationship between education and jobs.

Credential Gaps

In spite of the talent use gap, a growing proportion of each youth cohort is acquiring advanced educational credentials. At the same time, more advanced educational credentials are being used as selection criteria for many jobs, including some which did not previously require them. More formal specialized certification is increasingly being used to determine entry into professional jobs. Increasing numbers of those with general advanced educational credentials may be relegated to lower level industrial and service jobs because of their lack of specialized credentials, while some of those with specialized credentials are relegated to such jobs because of the limited number of professional jobs. Conversely, some of those already doing their jobs become formally underqualified because entry credential requirements increase after they enter a job. Having either higher or lower educational credentials than required for job entry are the two sides of the credential gap.

Relevance Gaps

Once in the job, many employees with advanced educational attainments find that their formal education is not closely related to their jobs because the available jobs use only very general education requirements as screening criteria. Conversely, the relation of professional education to engagement in professional work may become tighter as members of an organized group exercise greater regulatory control over training. The separation between the content of formal educational preparation and the specific job requirements may be termed the relevance gap, or "closeness of field of studies to the job."

Performance Gaps
When people have learned to do a job, the relationship between their formal educational attainment and the actual level of education or knowledge required to perform the job may be quite different than the credential requirements suggest. Once again, both extensive specialized preparatory education and internship programs may facilitate a relatively close correspondence for professional employees. Many workers with less specialized formal education are likely to experience a greater disconnection because the actual performance of their jobs needs less general formal education than is required for job entry. These jobs may require extensive on-the-job training and development of complex competencies, but, with the notable exception of skilled trades, this is often accomplished below the radar of formal job requirements. Conversely, rapidly changing employment conditions may leave some workers scrambling for specific knowledge to continue to perform their job adequately. Changes in both workers' knowledge and the knowledge required to do the job can generate performance gaps.

General Working Knowledge Gaps
In general, all workers tend, through various combinations of informal and formal learning, to gain greater competency in their jobs with experience. One might expect that the greater the work experience, the closer the match should be between the actual job requirements and a worker's knowledge. However, both because of the tendency for supply of formally educated labour to exceed demand in contemporary job markets and, more importantly, because workers inherently tend to continually learn formally and informally to deal with uncertainty and change, a worker's stock of working knowledge may generally exceed job requirements. This relationship can be termed the knowledge gap. This gap is briefly addressed in both the survey and the case study analyses. The empirical evidence of this study and the theoretical perspective developed in Chapters 6 and 12 both suggest that workers' reserves of practical abilities substantially exceed specific job requirements. But those reserves can be neither observed nor measured.

Subjective Gaps
Workers' subjective perceptions of the extent of match between their qualifications and the requirements of their jobs reflect a mix of their formal educational qualifications

and any further education courses with their on-the-job learning, as compared to the formal job requirements and their adaptations of these requirements. The subjective gap summary measure of the education-job match should also decrease with employment experience, as workers apply their natural ingenuity to reshape both the most challenging and the most unchallenging jobs to their actual knowledge levels.

LIMITATIONS OF CURRENT APPROACHES

There are four limitations to the inquiries into relationships between workers and jobs: (1) reluctance to address the potential influence of the authority structure of paid workplaces (i.e., economic class structure) on the definition of job requirements and the recognition of workers' capacities; (2) underestimation of the scope of learning and work, due to neglecting informal learning and unpaid work; (3) failure to recognize learning and work as interactive problem-solving activities in dynamic environments; and (4) failure to recognize the discrepancies between economic and educational systems that have different purposes.

Workplace Authority and Recognition of Workers' Knowledge

Credentialist approaches to explaining education-job relations draw attention to the roles that employers and certain job seekers with specialized knowledge play in shaping access to jobs. However, such approaches take little or no explicit account of the authority structure in work organizations that can constrain claims to knowledge. As noted earlier, classical and neoclassical economic theories treated the labour force as homogeneous and passive. More recent approaches to relations between employment and education have addressed the heterogeneity and more complex division of labour in modern societies in terms of elaborate classifications of occupations. Segmented labour market theories allude to "the structures which distinguish professional and managerial workers from other members of the labour force" (Piore, 1983: 252), and some have argued that owners', managers' and workers' labour markets function differently (Carnoy, 1977). However, research on education-job relations—while sometimes focusing on specific powerful occupational groups (e.g., Collins, 1979)—has typically not examined in any detail the authority structure of paid workplaces, and the underlying economic class structure, in relation to education-job matching. In Livingstone's (1999a) economic class analysis, drawing on Marx and Weber, the capability that workers have to define and design their jobs is conditioned by their location in terms of ownership, managerial authority role, and type of employee occupation. This model is discussed in Chapter 3.

Expanded Conceptions of Learning and Work

An inclusive conception of learning and work should consider informal learning and unpaid work. However, with the development of market economies, work has tended to be identified with paid employment, and learning identified with formal schooling. Increasingly, learning for work became thought of in terms of investment in quantities of formal and further education to attain better paid employment.

Theorizing about learning and work has focused on trying to explain the relationship between paid employment and formal educational attainments, and has largely ignored unpaid work and informal learning. The current research begins with more expansive concepts of both learning and work (see Livingstone, 2006).

Learning involves the gaining of knowledge, skill, or understanding anytime and anywhere. The forms of learning make up a continuum ranging from spontaneous responses to everyday life to highly organized participation in formal education programs. Four overlapping forms have been distinguished in research on adult learning (see Colley, Hodkinson, & Malcolm, 2002). *Formal schooling* is sustained enrolment in age-graded programs from early childhood to tertiary levels, in settings organized by institutional authorities, led by authorized teachers, and leading to diploma and degree certificates. *Further education* includes a diverse array of further education courses and workshops in many institutionally organized settings, from schools to workplaces and community centres. Human beings also continually engage in informal learning activities to acquire knowledge or skill outside of the curricula of institutions that provide educational programs, courses, or workshops. *Informal education or training* occurs when mentors take responsibility for instructing others in more spontaneous situations without sustained reference to a pre-established curriculum, for example, guiding people in learning job skills. All other forms of explicit or tacit learning in which people engage either individually or collectively, without direct reliance on a teacher-mentor or an externally organized curriculum, can be termed *self-directed* or *collective informal learning*. No account of workers' skills and knowledge can be adequate without considering these more informal learning activities. Work-related learning that occurs beyond the direct control of dominant groups in production processes is likely to be less hierarchically ordered in many ways, including the time devoted to it and the competencies attained, than is the case for learning related to formal educational credentials. Job-related informal learning especially may occur anywhere at the discretion of the learner. The survey research attempts to estimate the incidence of workers' *intentional learning* in these terms.

Much of the work that people do is unpaid. In addition to *paid employment* in the production of commodities, most people must also do some *household work* (cooking, cleaning, childcare, and other, often complex, household tasks). Many need to contribute to *voluntary community labours* (such as participating in local associations and helping neighbours) in order to continue to reproduce a society (see Waring, 1988). Recent studies have found that significant job-related learning occurs in unpaid housework and volunteer work (Eichler, 2005; Schugurensky & Mundel, 2005). Even if a researcher's analytic interest remains focused primarily on paid employment, as it does in this book, all forms of labour should be considered in any careful effort to understand the conditions of contemporary work and learning practices.[13]

Learning and Work as Interactive Problem Solving

In prior modelling of relations between workers' learning and their working conditions, learning and working activities are largely treated as mutually exclusive or sequential, and learning is predominantly regarded as a preparation for job performance. Narrow approaches that treat education as external to employment and view training only as the intentional acquisition of knowledge and skills are challenged by traditions of thought that stress the essential value of learning by experience. As numerous theorists of learning (e.g., Vygotsky, 1978; Dewey, 1916; Freire, 1974) have explained, humans learn continually from the cradle until the grave in order to cope with their changing environmental conditions. Adults, in particular, learn continually in order to perform effective work. In addition, a growing body of case study research confirms that most workers' learning arises informally out of the demands and challenges of everyday work experience and interactions with workmates and customers (e.g., Darrah, 1996; Sawchuk, 2007). Workers bring to the job a wide variety of knowledge gained both formally and informally, and they continue to develop this repertoire on the job. There is increasing evidence to demonstrate that informal learning contributes to large reserves of abilities that have a critical role in effective production (Livingstone & Sawchuk, 2004; Pankhurst & Livingstone, 2006). The approach taken to the nature of work and learning in this research recognizes that much of workers' learning arises naturally out of the demands and challenges of everyday experience.

Labour market competition may stimulate intensified learning in some paid workplaces. But the uncertainties of their implicit employment contract, in terms of what workers have to do, makes all work a process of problem solving and allows workers to interpret and reshape their jobs. There are dynamic connections between learning and work, founded on intimate mutual relationships between a worker and a job and between learning and the performance of work. The cognitive processes involved in learning from work experience are outlined in Chapter 6.

The Inevitability of Gaps

In the dominant educational ideology of advanced market economies, two assertions are repeatedly made: the extension of public schooling serves to upgrade the labour force and ensure economic prosperity, and schooling promotes upward social mobility among the disadvantaged. However, in a liberal democratic society, this ideology suffers from a major contradiction. The popular democratic demand for educational equality and wide access to multiple forms of advanced knowledge flies in the face of providing the pattern of occupations demanded by employers (Carnoy & Levin, 1985; Livingstone, 1987). Given the complex, changing nature of demands for labour power in a market economy and the impossibility of meeting them through a universally accessible school system, theories of balancing labour supply and demand as well as theories of the correspondence of education and employment (Parsons, 1959; Bowles & Gintis, 1976) remain a chimera. In this dynamic context, the *formal* correspondences between people's qualifications and the specific knowledge required for employment are prone to chronic separations or gaps. Furthermore, static concepts of job requirements and worker capabilities, which implicitly assume that neither a job nor a worker changes, restrict understanding of how jobs are performed and how workers' learning activities are connected with job performance.

Formal education and employment systems represent different interests, serve different age groups (except further education), have different purposes, are differently organized institutionally, are the subject of different policies, and use different policy instruments. There is no reason to suppose that there should or could be a particular relationship between the two systems, and when one takes such a broad view, it is absurd to expect a balance between them with respect to the labour market. The folly of attempting to narrowly focus vocational education on current labour market needs, for example, is addressed in Chapter 13.

CONCLUDING REMARKS

There has been increasing recognition of the heterogeneity and differentiation of labour in more recent economic theories of supply and demand in labour markets. More sustained attention has been paid to mismatches between current job requirements and workers' capabilities, and there has been some analysis of the contributing social and institutional factors. Current conceptions relating workers' knowledge and jobs tend to emphasize issues of either underemployment or overeducation and also suffer from the above noted limitations.

Some survey researchers (e.g., Felstead, Gallie & Green, 2002) are beginning to register that formal qualifications are only loose indicators of the real skills of the workforce and that many capacities are acquired in the workplace and remain uncertified. Few studies provide comparative assessments of survey findings, with their well-known limitations, as well as provide case studies of particular workplaces. On the one hand, there is a need for multi-dimensional assessments of the relationship between job requirements and worker capacities, using representative survey samples of workers to estimate macro-level patterns and trends. On the other hand, in light of the weaknesses of prior conceptions and quantitative estimates of job requirement-worker capacity matches, closer micro-level studies are needed to refine such macro-level findings.

The statistical analyses in this book attempt to examine the extent of the matching and of the gaps between the varied dimensions of workers' capacities and their job requirements, but we attend most closely to the apparent gaps. In terms of education-job requirement matching, the focus is mostly on employed workers and credential gaps, relevance gaps, performance gaps, and subjective gaps. Chapter 2 reviews recent empirical research on education-job requirement matching, and Chapter 3 outlines the conceptual framework with which the Education-Job Requirement Matching (EJRM) project began. In Chapters 4 and 5, survey evidence is used to make initial estimates of the extent to which gaps exist. In each instance, special attention is paid to the similarities and differences between non-managerial employees in middle-class professional jobs and those in service or industrial working-class jobs. The extent of control that different types of workers have in designing their job tasks and their roles in organizational decision-making are considered in relation to the above matching measures. Then, the case study chapters go beyond static survey measures of matching and begin to examine the dynamic interactions between workers and their jobs. This exploration starts with the integrated theory of work and learning developed in Chapter 6 and continues with the later presentation and comparative analysis of the five case studies.

Notes

1. A measure of how much an increase in fixed investment generates additional income.
2. A measure of how much an increase in income generates additional fixed investment.
3. Such as the Cobb-Douglas production function, $P = K^a + L^b$
4. Employment planning was known during the 1950s and 1960s as manpower planning.
5. Several countries set up what were known generically as *konjonctur instituts* for the purpose.
6. It was recognized that this was only one way of conceiving the need for education (e.g., Parnes, 1963). Other concepts were the social demand for education, or the potential ability of the population to benefit from it.
7. The alternative of cost-benefit methods depended on subjective and therefore contestable judgments of the value of education, and was more readily applicable at the level of projects than of national economies.
8. While broad definitions of human capital may include productive skills and technical knowledge, the most influential analyses have been based on simple quantitative relationships between formal schooling and employment conditions.
9. See (Leontaridi, 1998) for further discussion of the development of, and variation among, segmented labour market theories.
10. The intent of early subemployment research was to develop an index of the discrepancy between the number of capable workers and the number of adequate jobs. Several categories were identified: the officially unemployed, discouraged workers, the involuntary part-time employed, and full-time workers who have low earnings (Sheak, 1994). Using these criteria, US government surveys found that between 25 and 50 per cent of the adult population in the largest urban ghettos were subemployed in 1966 (*Manpower Report of the President*, 1967: 75). Subsequent studies developed a labour utilization framework to deal with the deficiencies of

unemployment measures on a national level (Hauser, 1974; Clogg, 1979). These studies were more inclusive of all capable workers and stressed the lack of adequate jobs for workers at all educational levels.
11. In broader terms of workers' capabilities and job requirements, the logical converse to underemployment is overemployment. There is a sense in which some workers exceed their normal capacities, either by excessive effort, excessive time, or both. These conditions can be stressful, exhausting, and debilitating. But they are beyond the scope of the current study.
12. Measures of inter-generational income variations indicate that only about 20 per cent of the relative income difference between parents is generally being passed on to their children in Canada. This figure is comparable to the figures for Sweden and Finland but much lower than the figures for the United States and the United Kingdom, where between 40 and 60 per cent of the difference is passed on (Corak, 2001: 279–80).
13. For detailed accounts of the findings of 1998 and 2004 Canada-wide surveys and many related case studies on paid and unpaid work, and their relations to formal and informal learning activities, see www.wallnetwork.ca.

Chapter Two
Prior Empirical Research on Education-Job Matching

D.W. Livingstone

INTRODUCTION
This chapter reviews the recent empirical research literature on education-job matching. As job requirements are one of the benchmarks for worker-job matching, the criteria for job entry and performance are first examined. Second, the research that attempts to measure workers' capabilities or qualifications for their jobs is summarized. Then studies are reviewed that combine the requirements of jobs and the qualifications of workers to estimate the extent of matching and mismatching between the two. Last, studies of the factors related to education-job mismatches are considered.

JOB REQUIREMENTS: GRADUAL CHANGE
The bulk of empirical research on job requirements and worker qualifications relies on measures of formal education levels. With the expansion of public education systems over the past century, education credentials have been increasingly used as criteria to get jobs and as measures of the skill needed to perform them. Employers may use interview assessments and other personal criteria for their final selection, but many now rely largely on education credentials as a method to screen out applicants. At the same time, job applicants themselves rely heavily on formal education credentials to compete for jobs. As discussed in other chapters, the assumption of equivalence between workers' abilities and their levels of formal education is problematic.

The specific requirements for many jobs frequently change. Some researchers see automation and routinization of tasks as leading to the deskilling of many jobs. Others see computerization as linked to less manual effort, greater abstract thinking, and skill upgrading. Serious scholarly and political debate over changes in the requirements of paid work is likely to persist (see Handel, 2005). For this chapter, the challenge is to make the best estimates of job requirements in terms of a widely agreed-on standard. For that purpose, the only widely agreed current standard is the level of formal education. The immediate question arises whether an external expert or the worker concerned can more reliably estimate the level required.

Self-Reports and External Ratings of Job Requirements

There are two ways to assess job requirements empirically: by expert ratings based on observed samples of jobs or by workers' self-reports. Expert analyst ratings developed since World War II have equated job requirements with levels of general educational development (GED) and have estimated these levels by years of schooling. Such ratings have several limitations. They tend to confuse the capacities of the workers observed with the general requirements to do the job. Similarly, they fail to distinguish between the education credentials required by employers and the educational levels needed to perform the work, and they assume that this latter criterion is valid across diverse occupational groups. In addition, they are very expensive to develop, become quickly dated in relation to the changing employment pattern of the labour force, and simply equate workers' learning capacities and abilities with numeric years of schooling. Much empirical research continues to rely on expert ratings of occupation-based skill levels, even given these limitations. However, recent studies have increasingly relied on workers' self-reports of job requirements.

Workers' own estimates of the educational requirements of their jobs have the advantage of being relatively inexpensive and up to date. They permit direct comparisons of formal education attainment, credentials required to *get* the job, and the general education level needed to *do* the job. Self-reports treat the workers' information about their jobs as highly pertinent and their perceived job requirements as relevant, whether or not their perceptions may be interpreted as accurate (Maynard, Joseph, & Maynard, 2006). Workers' estimates of the educational requirements of their jobs have their own limitations, the most important of which is that workers do not frequently think of their job-related capacities simply in terms of levels of schooling. In addition, workers may be reluctant to admit that their own capacity levels are below average, and they tend to perceive mismatches as negative reflections of their self-image. However, as sociologists since Cooley (1902) have recognized, people's reflection on their own behaviour is both an effect and a cause of larger societal processes; the reliability and validity of self-reports are arguably greater than those of imposed measures.

The EJRM project largely relies on workers' self-reports of their capacities and job requirements, rather than on skill-level ratings assigned by an expert analyst. But ratings of job requirements by external analysts have been found to be fairly close to workers' own estimates in some studies (see Myles & Fawcett, 1990) and will be considered here as well. The empirical research on job requirements has focused on two distinct dimensions: credential requirements to get the job and performance requirements to do the job.

Credential Requirements

Although there have been only a few empirical studies of the credential employers, over the past century higher formal education credentials ingly been used by employers as criteria for job entry. Collins (1979) the findings of US historical surveys based on employers' reports. Holzer (1996: 56) analyzed 1992–4 surveys of employers in four US cities (Atlanta, Boston, Detroit, and Los Angeles).[1] These studies have shown that by the 1930s, post-secondary credentials had become a common criterion for entry into most professions. With the post–World War II expansion of the public school system, post-secondary credentials also began to be commonly required for managerial posts. A high school diploma had begun to be the criterion for entry to clerical work after World War I; by the 1990s nearly half of all clerical jobs had post-secondary education entry requirements. In the 1930s, hardly any manual labour jobs required a high school diploma. By the 1990s high school graduation had even become a criterion for entry into unskilled manual jobs. There was a substantial basis for the claim that entry credentials were being inflated beyond the education level required to perform some jobs.

Performance Requirements

Once you have a job, what level of skill and knowledge is needed to perform it? This is a much more controversial question than the issue of job entry requirements. The empirical dispute centres both on what technical abilities are needed to actually do a job and also on the most suitable measures to estimate performance abilities.

Two types of measures have been used to estimate the performance skill requirements of jobs: indirect measures using occupational composition and direct measures assessing the skill content of jobs.

As for compositional changes in the distribution of occupations, the proportion of both managers and professional employees appears to have increased, while the proportion of industrial workers has decreased in recent decades in many advanced market economies (e.g., Breen & Luijkx, 2004; Erikson & Goldthorpe, 2002). The typical assumption is that these changes in occupational distribution indicate an overall increase in the skill requirements for job performance. However, there have been few comparative historical studies of actual changes in the performance requirements of different occupations.

In any case, occupational distributions offer limited estimates of skill or educational requirements because of dated expert-rating schemes that may not reflect changes in job contents. In their analysis of the occupational distribution of the Australian labour force from 1986 to 2000, Fleming, Harley, and Sewell (2004) found the familiar pattern of an increase in professional occupations. However, their more detailed assessment of occupational groups showed that most growth of professional employment was in knowledge handling and service provision, with low levels of analytical skills and discretion, rather than in the more autonomous, knowledge-creating jobs. They also found general evidence for an increase in both high-skill and low-skill jobs, or skill polarization (compare Gallie, 1991). While helping to debunk exaggerated claims for the arrival of a knowledge-based economy, Fleming et al. also critiqued the error of imputing a "knowledge-free" or "non-information" character to manual jobs, which may demand substantial technical competence or coordinating ability. They suggest that the notion of "knowledge work" may be used to maintain a managerial division of labour between those who *think* and those who *do*. However, distributional changes should certainly be considered when assessing skill changes of the labour force.

Estimates of technical skill requirements for the United States and Canada have been made primarily by government analysts on samples of jobs and then published in dictionaries of occupational titles (Statistics Canada, 2001). The general educational development (GED) scale is the most commonly used approximation of skill levels in both countries.

The GED scale is intended to embrace those aspects of knowledge that are required of the worker for satisfactory job performance.[2] The scale has three dimensions: reasoning, mathematical, and language development. Originally, seven different levels were distinguished; these ranged from carrying out simple instructions and learning the job from a basic demonstration to applying logical and scientific thinking to a wide range of concrete and abstract problems (US Department of Labor, 1991: 1009–12). Several major attempts were made in the United States to estimate the balance between the performance requirements of jobs and the skills acquired through schooling.[3] Eckhaus (1964: 184, Table 1) used the first GED ratings of occupations by the Bureau of Employment Security in 1956, along with the 1940 and 1950 US census surveys. Berg (1970: 44, 50, Table 3.3) applied the 1956 and 1966 GED occupation ratings to the 1950 and 1960 US census surveys and generated several different estimates of the correspondence between formal education and the education that workers require on the job. Burris (1983: 457) offered estimates based on a 1977–8 US national sample survey and essentially the same mid-1960s GED ratings as Berg had used. As Berg (1970: 51) observed: "Nothing is fixed about the relationship of GED and years of schooling.... Different assumptions can yield extraordinarily diverse findings."

More specifically, a comparison of these three GED dimensions shows the limitations at both ends of the scale. In mathematical abilities, for instance, fractions are a criterion for GED level 3; algebra and geometry are criteria for GED level 4. Across North America, and throughout most of the past century, fractions have been taught well before the end of grade 8, and algebra and geometry before the end of high school. Both Berg's grouped version and Burris's scheme ignore these distinctions among lower GED levels and therefore overestimate the abilities required to do many lower level jobs. Other studies indicate that no more than a grade 8 formal education was required to do the typical factory or office job in advanced market

Table 2.1 On-the-Job Training Time Required to Perform Job (SVP), Employed US Labour Force, 1940–90 (%)

SVP Level	1940 (%)	1950 (%)	1972 (%)	1980 (%)	1990 (%)
1. Short demonstration	1	<1	<1	<1	<1
2. Up to 30 days	17	21	4	3	5
3. Up to 3 months	13	8	22	17	15
4. Up to 6 months	23	24	18	19	19
5. Up to 1 year	4	5	9	10	8
6. Up to 2 years	18	14	16	18	18
7. Up to 4 years	21	24	26	26	25
8. Over 4 years	3	4	6	7	10

Sources: 1940, 1950: Eckhaus (1964, Table 4, 186); 1972, 1980, 1990: David and Smith (1994)

economies.[4] Moreover, there are indications that the rising education level in the population encourages employers to hire more highly educated applicants for jobs that only require lower levels of education or skill to perform (e.g., Mason, 1996).

At the other extreme, these schemes ignore post-graduate education. This is partly a result of an official revision of the original GED scale from seven to six levels (Berg, 1970: 44–5), which had the effect of forcing those with more than 16 years of schooling down to level six in the revised scale of the 1960s. So, at the same time as the later schemes chose to shorten the GED scale at the bottom end, they were forced to blend differences between undergraduate degrees and graduate education at the top end. Such limitations regarding years of schooling add to the problem of equating specific abilities with general educational levels.

Apparently, more straightforward approximations of educational requirements for jobs are provided by the specific vocational preparation (SVP) scale, in which analysts estimate the amount of time needed to learn the techniques, acquire information, and develop facility for an average job performance. This time estimate is intended to include any relevant vocational education, apprenticeship training, further education courses, on-the-job training, and experience gained in other jobs. In Table 2.1, the SVP scale training times for US jobs between 1940 and 1990 are compared. In contrast to the 1940–50 period, there were very few jobs in 1990 in which adequate job performance could be achieved with less than a month of specific vocational training. Both the small proportion of jobs requiring more than four years of training and also the proportion needing more than one year of training had increased somewhat since 1950. A small and gradually increasing majority of the labour force required more than a year of vocational preparation throughout the

1972–90 period. Analysis of the SVP scores of the Canadian labour force, based on census data for the 1961–81 period (Myles, 1988: 340, Table 1), also showed that jobs requiring less than 30 days of training decreased during this period but jobs needing over two years of training increased. In both countries the overall post-1960 pattern of change in required training time was a gradual decline of jobs with very little training time and a gradual increase of jobs with long training time. It is not clear whether this implies that low-skill jobs were gradually declining and high-skill jobs were gradually increasing, or if there has been an inflation of credential requirements.

Expert-based skill ratings of occupational titles have faced strong criticism, including gender bias (see Miller, Treiman, Cain, & Roos, 1980). Most pertinently, occupational groups are more varied than the common titles for classifications might suggest. The US Department of Labor noted the unique nature of each job: "Work is organized in a variety of ways. As a result of technological, economic and sociological influences, nearly every job in the economy is performed slightly differently from any other job" (United States Employment Service, 1977: xv). An example is computer programmers. The Canadian National Occupational Code (NOC) classification system evolved from one code for computer programmers to 13 main occupational codes between the 1980s and 2000 (Statistics Canada, 2001). However, as the later chapter on programmers illustrates, computer programming functions are grouped and categorized in far more diverse ways than these 13 codes represent. A recent report lists 25 information technology occupations, with more than 350 unique job titles, and notes a great discrepancy between the characterization and labelling of jobs by job holders and that done by employers or managers (Gunderson, Jacobs, & Vallaincourt, 2005). There are chronic uncertainties involved in assigning separate and distinct skill levels to standardized sets of occupations and in determining what capacities (or skills) are used in jobs, how frequently each one is used, or how important it is.

While there are continuing attempts to identify occupational groups in terms of particular "worker trait requirements" (WTR)[5] and skill attributes,[6] the estimating of equivalence between required skill capacities and formal education levels of each grouping becomes even more arbitrary. Recently, groupings of education requirements in US and Canadian census ratings have been reduced to four or fewer levels and applied to more varied occupational groups. This trend further emphasizes the conceptual weakness behind such estimates.

Primarily because of a lack of alternate measures for analyses over time, some researchers have persisted in relying on prior expert ratings to assess job skill requirements—even though most rating schemes are decades out of date and subject to the already noted criticism. Recent studies are more likely to use workers' self-reports, either alone or in combination with expert-rated measures. Again, self-reports regarding the education or skills required to get or perform their jobs are subjective, but they do overcome the simplistic assumption of homogeneity within occupations as found in prior expert ratings, and they can more direct changes over time.[7]

Measures based on both experts' estimates and workers' self-reports te. fuse job performance requirements with job entry requirements. Since the 1960s various studies have pointed to differences between these two criteria, most notably the inflation of entry requirements beyond the competence levels needed to do a job (e.g., Berg, 1970; Collins, 1979). Whether because of labour-market frictions, employers' raising of hiring qualifications in response to labour surpluses, or workers' organizations raising qualification barriers to control entry into their professions or trades, the possibility of credential inflation beyond performance needs always exists. Self-report questions should continue to ask whether and how workers distinguish between the formal education level required to get a job and the education level required to do the job.

Berg's (1970: 47–8) comparative analysis of skill content used the US occupational dictionary GED ratings published in 1956 and 1966. He found some substantial changes up and down the scale but small overall skill upgrading. A subsequent assessment, using later editions of these same occupational dictionaries, also found substantial changes in skill content in both directions within existing jobs but small overall effect (Spenner, 1983, 1990). The gradual overall upgrading trend in the technical requirements of jobs, identified by using GED and SVP measures, is corroborated by other large-scale studies that use different data and measures. Cappelli (1995) used a measure of skill developed by Hay Associates, the world's largest compensation consulting firm, a composite measure that includes *know-how* (capabilities, knowledge, and techniques needed to do the job, ranked according to complexity); *problem solving* (how well defined and predictable job tasks are); and *accountability* (autonomy in decision-making). Cappelli analyzed Hay's extensive records for US manufacturing jobs from 1978 to 1986 and clerical work from 1978 to 1988. Taking account of both occupational composition and job content changes, he found a discernible upskilling of production jobs within the declining manufacturing sector and both upskilling and deskilling within the expanding clerical sector. Howell and Wolff (1991) found similar trends for 1960–85 using census-based data and measures. Applying both conventional GED/SVP scores and other measures of cognitive complexity and routine activity to census data, Myles (1988, 342–5) found the reverse pattern for the Canadian labour force between 1961 and 1981; that is, no change in the skill composition of industrial workers' jobs but a substantial upgrading of service workers' jobs. In all of these instances, the overall trend for the entire labour force was a gradual upgrading of skill.

In spite of the limitations of expert analysts' classification schemes, the few available series of surveys based on workers' self-reports have found fairly similar patterns of gradual upgrading. In Sweden between 1974 and 2000, according to one of the longest self-report series of national surveys, the proportion of jobs with no educational requirement fell from half to about a quarter (Tåhlin, 2006). The British Skills Survey time series found that the proportion of jobs requiring a post-secondary qualification rose from 20 per cent in 1986 to 30 per cent in 2006, while the proportion requiring no educational qualifications fell from about 38 per cent to 28 per cent. This British survey also found that jobs requiring training periods of over two years had increased from 22 per cent to 30 per cent, while jobs requiring less than a month's training decreased from 27 per cent to 19 per cent. In addition, using self-reports on literacy, number skills, communication, and problem solving, the British survey identified significant increases in the application of many of these skills between 1997 and 2006 (see Felstead, Gallie, Green, & Zhou, 2007).

One of the most thorough reviews of prior research on skill requirements was done by the US National Research Council in 1999. Drawing on diverse surveys and case studies with varied assumptions, the survey's authors stated: "It does not appear that work is becoming more routine or less skilled than in the past, but we are unwilling to claim that the reverse is true" (National Research Council, 1999: 162–3). They concluded that a skill-upgrading trend was most likely among blue-collar industrial workers, with service workers being more diverse, professionals experiencing little change in skill requirements, and evidence about managerial work being almost nonexistent. A recent overview (Handel, 2003, 2005) concluded that there may have been some gradual increase in educational requirements for jobs but that much better information on the actual skill content of jobs was needed.

Based on all the evidence available, the most sensible conclusion is that, in terms of formal education needed, there has probably been an overall gradual upgrading of both entry credential and performance requirements for jobs in advanced market economies since the 1970s. Yet this information tells us little about the relationship between individual workers' formal education and their jobs, and nothing about their more general knowledge and capacities.

MEASURES OF WORKERS' CAPABILITIES: RAPID GROWTH OF SCHOOLING

Beyond the assessment of specific attributes, the capacity to combine several different attributes into a coherent job performance is more important for understanding a worker's competence. Polanyi's (1958) neglected distinction between skill as a particular attribute and skill as the capability to achieve a coordinated and coherent action (see Chapter 6)[8] is useful for understanding the nature of work. In most of the survey research literature, the term *skill* refers to specific attributes or abilities. However, the primary interest of this study is the capability of workers to combine a number of attributes into a coherent job performance.

Again, estimates of workers' capabilities have increasingly been made in terms of levels of formal education attainment. In contrast to the limited evidence for a gradual, general increase in the skill and educational requirements of jobs, there is overwhelming evidence of the increasing educational attainments of the labour force, both throughout the post–World War II period and since the 1980s. There is a strong long-term rise in school completion everywhere, with the labour force in virtually all advanced industrial countries now averaging nearly 12 years of schooling (Tåhlin, 2006). The supply of workers with advanced education has continued to rise quickly in recent decades in most countries. In Britain in the late 1990s, for example, about a third of each annual youth cohort was completing a higher education; by contrast, 12 per cent of the employed labour force were degree-holders (Green, McIntosh, & Vignoles, 2002). In Canada, which has one of the highest levels of formal education attainment in the world, the proportion of the labour force with post-secondary degrees has increased very rapidly over the past 30 years (see Chapter 4).

Formal education attainments cannot be equated with workers' capabilities. Some recent research demonstrates that formal education attainment and the use of specific abilities are only loosely related (Allen & de Weert, 2007). At least since Thurow (1975) proposed his job competition model to address the shortcomings of human capital theory, the importance of on-the-job training has been fairly widely recognized as central to the development of workers' capabilities to do their jobs. Subsequent efforts to measure job-related further education and informal learning activities have been considerable (see Livingstone, 2002; Wihak & Hall, 2008). However, there has been little effort to theorize workplace learning in relation to job requirements, a gap addressed in Chapter 6. In the case study chapters, evidence is presented of the extensive formal and informal learning in which workers are engaged. Workers' self-reports on their formal education attainments, their participation in further education courses, their variety of intentional job-related informal learning activities, and their extensive learning by experience constitute the evidence. Throughout this book estimates of workers' learning capabilities are distinguished from the formal education required to enter their jobs and perform them.

It is necessary to address two frequently heard claims related to formal schooling: declining educational standards and decreasing literacy among workers. The first point is that, with the massive expansion of public education systems, a much larger proportion of people from all social backgrounds are getting more formal education. Therefore, there is a greater probability that those whose educational opportunities have been limited by their socio-economic backgrounds will be tested at higher levels of schooling. Many claims of declining educational standards focus on limited test scores and generalize from exceptions. In general, achievement test scores for young people today are as high as, or higher than, they were 30 years ago (Handel, 2003). Stories of absolute cognitive skill declines among today's youth have little basis. Similarly, claims that young workers today suffer from low literacy are generally based on a small number of cases and on assumptions that low scores on specific pen-and-paper tests translate into job performance limitations. Literacy surveys show that younger groups have higher literacy ratings than older groups

(Handel, 2003; Statistics Canada & Organization for Economic Co-operation and Development, 2005). Moreover, to infer real-world work capabilities from such tests repeats the errors of the worker traits-requirements approach and ignores the complexity of tasks people, including those in low-skill, low-paying jobs, manage to perform in everyday life (Hoddinott, 2004).

Whatever the limitations of the prior measures of workers' capabilities, it is reasonable to conclude that the formal educational qualifications that workers bring to their jobs are substantially greater than in prior generations.

MEASURES OF EDUCATION-JOBS MATCHING

Studies that have assessed education-based estimates of matching between workers' capabilities and the requirements of their jobs, or skill-based education-jobs matching, necessarily focus on those who have jobs. Most studies have combined job holders' self-reports of their formal education attainments with either job analysts' estimates or worker self-assessments of the education level required for the job to produce education-job matching profiles.[9] The weight of research evidence suggests that the formal education required to do available jobs generally has increased more gradually than the education attainment of the employed labour force during the past 40 years. Hence, the growing attention to overeducation or underemployment as a problem.

Four dimensions of education-job matching have been used in prior empirical studies. These may be termed *entry credential matching, performance matching, field of studies matching,* and *subjective matching*. Entry credential matching refers to the relationship between the education and training credentials that job entrants bring and those required by employers. Performance matching refers to the relationship between the performance capability of the worker and the performance level actually required to do the job. Field of studies matching denotes the extent to which the area or discipline of preparatory education and training is relevant to job performance. Subjective matching is the job holder's personal assessment of the extent to which job requirements generally accord with their capabilities. The findings of surveys completed since 2000 are summarized below.[10]

Much prior empirical research conflates the education needed to *get* a job — which should be used for credential match measures — with the education needed to *do* a job — which should be used for performance match measures. Other studies distinguish entry credential and performance requirement measures but find close correspondence between them (e.g., Green, McIntosh, & Vignoles, 1999). This distinction should be pursued in future empirical research.

Credential Matching

Credential match research can be dated back to the late 1940s when there was the first indication that educational expansion was outstripping workplace demands for qualifications (Harris, 1949). With the rapid increase in post-secondary enrolment, this view became widespread and led to several major studies that analyzed the extent to which the credentials required for job entry were being inflated beyond actual performance requirements (Berg, 1970; Collins, 1979).

Livingstone's (1999a: 75–8) Canadian surveys between 1982 and 1996 used workers' self-reports of their educational credentials and employers' job entry credential requirements; he found that credential overqualification or underemployment remained at around 20 per cent throughout the period. The consistent level of overqualification during this period of very rapid increase in post-secondary completion and the gradual increase in job performance requirements suggests there was some inflation of job entry requirements. Time series surveys of recent Canadian university graduates (Finnie, 2002) have found fairly stable levels of credential overqualification of around 30 per cent in the 1982, 1986, and 1990 cohorts; in each instance the level declined to about 25 per cent after the graduates had been in the labour force for three years. For all Canadian university graduates, Li, Gervais, and Duval (2006) found that overqualification increased marginally from 18 per cent in 1993 to 19 per cent in 2001, but that the total number overqualified increased by about a third because of the increasing number of workers who had obtained university degrees.

In one of the longer time series available on self-reported credential matching, the British Skills Survey found that in 1986 about 30 per cent of the employed labour force were overqualified in terms of the education needed to get their jobs, and, by 2006 this figure increased to 40 per cent. Conversely, the proportion defined as underqualified declined from 18 per cent to 14 per cent during this period (Felstead, Gallie, Green, & Zhou, 2007).

While many of these recent studies indicate an increasing surplus of credential attainments over credential requirements, virtually all studies have found that a majority of the labour force has jobs with credential requirements that match the credentials attained.

Performance Matching
Most prior empirical studies have primarily examined performance matching. An extensive international assessment was done by Groot and van den Brink (2000), who reviewed 25 surveys from an unspecified array of European countries and the United States. Their surveys covered a 20-year period and used either expert analyst ratings, worker self-reports, or the more arbitrary statistical criterion of a standard deviation from average years of schooling. Their conclusion was that the overall incidence of overeducation, or formal education in excess of job performance requirements, was about 26 per cent. However, estimates in these studies varied from 10 per cent to 42 per cent. Undereducation, or less schooling than the job required, was of lower incidence in all studies, but the estimates varied widely from

12 per cent to 33 per cent according to different criteria. The authors also concluded that the incidence of overeducation had not changed significantly over this period.

Hartog (2000) compared the results of over a dozen studies, from five countries (United States, Netherlands, Portugal, Spain, and the United Kingdom) over a similar period using diverse criteria. He concluded that matching occurred about 60 per cent of the time in the European countries with the incidence of overeducation increasing and undereducation decreasing. Matching was somewhat lower in the United States, with overeducation following a more irregular pattern.

Handel (2003, 2005), who has done an extensive review of more recent US studies, found that the rapid growth in the educational attainment of the labour force is slowing down and that job skill requirements may have continued a slower, gradual rise. However, given the varied, insufficient measures of workers' skills and employers' job requirements, there is inadequate research on whether job demands exceed workers' capacities. Handel (2005: 79) concludes that more detailed measures for tracking skill-requirement trends with representative samples of workers are needed to understand how worker-job matching is changing.

Vaisey (2006) provides estimates of a longer trend in overqualification of the US labour force, based on job analyst GED measures. Using data from the annual General Social Survey, he found that overqualification had increased from about 30 per cent in 1972 to 55 per cent in 2002. Increasing overqualification is not limited to the young but appears highest in disadvantaged groups, including women and non-whites.

Verhaest and Omey (2006) conducted a detailed comparative study of several different self-report and expert-based measures of overeducation with the 2001 cohort of Flemish school leavers. Leaving aside measures based on standard deviations from the norm, they found levels of overeducation ranging from 26 per cent to over 50 per cent. Expert-based measures of overeducation were higher than self-reports, and undereducation was smaller on all these measures. They found similar patterns in over a dozen international studies, mostly in the 1990s, which had previously used multiple types of measures with the same data. They noted continuing conceptual confusion among researchers but concluded that most overeducation is built into the system and enduring, while most undereducation is frictional and temporary.

McGuiness (2006) provides the most extensive review to date of both expert-based and self-report measures of overeducation, including over 30 international studies ranging from the 1970s to 2000. He notes that "It is not easy to disentangle the information to derive any discernible patterns." If we eliminate the measures based on standard deviation statistics as being too arbitrary, both the expert-based and self-report measures in this array of studies average around 25 per cent rates of overeducation. McGuiness concludes that the incidence of overeducation has remained stable over time and that it is costly to individuals, firms, and the economy.

Tåhlin (2006) also offers a recent international review of matching studies. He finds that, depending on criteria used, between 20 and 40 per cent o appear to have more education than their jobs require but that trends i tion are very poorly established. He cites long-term Swedish survey da worker self-reports, which found overeducation had increased from 15 per cent of all employees in 1974 to one-third in 2000, with matched workers dropping from 70 to 50 per cent and undereducated workers remaining at about 20 per cent. He goes on to argue that each of the categories of overeducated, well matched, and undereducated are diverse. They include the further distinctions of logically necessary, logically possible but not necessary, and logically impossible combinations of education and job requirements. As many older workers with only compulsory schooling retire from the labour market, the number of undereducated and matched workers will necessarily fall. Considering the assessment of trends in skill demand and job-worker matches at the micro level, Tåhlin (2006: 21) views the state of knowledge as especially weak and suggests that a variety of measures should be used.

Recent studies of other dimensions of matching, namely field of studies matching and subjective matching, remain rare and have little available trend data.

Field of Study Matching

Field of study matching research has rarely been published in scholarly journals (see Wolbers, 2003). This research, largely limited to post-secondary graduates, asks for graduates' self-assessments of the extent to which their programs of study in conventional fields have corresponded with or been relevant to their jobs. The matching found has been closely related to levels and types of formal education. For example, national analyses of Canadian university graduates find that those from more advanced graduate and professional groups, most notably the health sciences, experience better education-job matches, while graduates of programs not linked to development of specific job market skills, such as fine arts, humanities, and biology, have consistently lower scores (Finnie, 2002; Frenette, 2004). Similarly, analyses of field of study match by occupational groups have found that graduates in professional/managerial jobs are twice as likely to have jobs related to their field of study as those in service or blue-collar jobs (Krahn & Bowlby, 1999: 35). To date such studies have provided little original insight into education-job matching relations.

Subjective Matching

Subjective matching research and, particularly, subjective underemployment gained currency in the 1960s, when fears were expressed that growing numbers of university and college graduates who could not find commensurate jobs would become increasingly disenchanted and rebellious. US surveys in 1969 and 1977 found that the number of workers who felt they were not able to fully use their qualifications in the workplace grew from 27 per cent to over 36 per cent during this eight-year period (Staines & Quinn, 1979). Later Canadian studies found that around 40 per cent of workers expressed similar feelings in the mid-1990s (Livingstone, 1999a: 87). In response to a general question about the extent to which people feel qualified for their jobs, about 22 per cent of Canadian workers expressed feelings of overqualification in the mid-1990s, with a slight increase to 25 per cent in 2000 (Crompton, 2002; Livingstone, 1999a). Vaisey's (2006) recent US study, while based on GED measures, found significant links between increasing overqualification and job dissatisfaction, and more critical political attitudes.

All the above dimensions of education-job matching merit considerable further study. They are addressed in detail in the EJRM Survey and case study analyses. It should also be remembered that the massive differences between the number of workers available for employment and the number of jobs available for workers—that is, the workers who are unemployed or discouraged from seeking jobs—are a different issue compared to how well the education attainments of the *employed* labour force correspond to the levels their jobs require. Large numbers of willing workers who are unsuccessfully seeking employment or who are involuntarily employed in temporary or part-time jobs pose a distinctly different problem than the number of employed workers who have formal education qualifications that are greater than their jobs require. It is widely recognized by international agencies that these time-based forms of underemployment present a very serious social problem.[11] However, as this review of recent empirical research confirms, education-based mismatches are also very substantial and persistent. Both time and education-based types of mismatches have widespread negative consequences for individuals, families, and societies (e.g., Kalleberg, 2008).

FACTORS RELATED TO EDUCATION-JOB MISMATCHES

Given the inconsistent measures and findings on education-job matching, there has been little research on social background factors related to matching patterns. There is at least suggestive evidence that each of the following factors has a meaningful association with some measures of overeducation or underemployment: age of worker or employment experience, race and immigration status, gender, geographic location, union or professional association membership, and economic class.

A large number of studies focused on self-reported job requirements have found that overeducated workers tend to be younger and have lower levels of experience and job tenure (McGuiness, 2006). These findings are consistent both with the commonsense notion that people learn from experience and with the increasing recognition of the positive effect of informal on-the-job training. In contrast, a US time series study, based on the GED scale, has detected an apparent shift. Vaisey (2006) found that workers over 55 years of age were only half as likely to be overeducated as workers under 35 in the 1970s, but there was little difference between these older and younger cohorts in the 1990s. Both cohorts of workers appear to have become more overeducated. This finding may be explained by considering the increase in formal credential attainments of older cohorts, as well as the use of outdated GED ratings. Different measures of employment experience are considered in subsequent chapters.

Systemic racial discrimination persists in the employment of non-white minorities in most advanced market economies. Higher underemployment rates on several measures continue for blacks and increase for Hispanics in the United States (Jensen & Slack, 2002). There is considerable evidence from previous generations that immigrants have generally assimilated well enough into the cultures of receiving countries so that the second generation achieved similar employment patterns as other domestic social groups (e.g., Reitz, 1998). However, at least for some non-white immigrant groups, the combination of non-white and recent immigrant status has created a more enduring double disadvantage in education-job mismatches (e.g., De Jong & Madamba, 2001). The effects of race, visible minority, and immigration status are assessed in this study.

Although women have come close to parity in labour force participation, they continue to be overrepresented in low-paid, part-time jobs, to do more unpaid housework, and face gender barriers to promotion (see Livingstone & Pollock, 2004). Some studies of matching have suggested greater overeducation of women because of their greater restriction to local labour markets, but few significant mismatch patterns have been found in such studies to date (e.g., McGuiness, 2006). The EJRM Survey analyzes gender differences, and the case studies examine work settings with quite different gender compositions.

Economic Class

Economic class is one factor that has evaded systematic comparative analysis in relation to education-job matching. The classical social theorists, Marx and Weber, identified three types of economic classes based on ownership of property, specialized forms of labour, and provision of general labour. They each made the case for the intimate relation of these economic classes to various kinds of economic and social inequalities. Given the accumulating research evidence of education-job mismatches, the inattention to a relationship between economic classes and mismatches is somewhat strange. Considerable empirical research has focused on the development of some professional occupations and the efforts within these professions to construct knowledge fields that would ensure the highest possible degree of control over their work (see Collins, 1979; Derber, Schwartz, & Magrass, 1990). However, comparative class analyses of matching are still very rare. Livingstone (1987) published earlier empirical studies in this field, and the contribution of *The Education-Jobs Gap* is summarized in Chapter 3. Here a few other relevant prior empirical studies are noted.

Several studies have compared occupational groups in terms of mismatches. Clogg and Shockey (1984) compared the mismatch (overeducation) of occupational groups in the US labour force from 1969 to 1980. Their calculations were based on the proportion of workers whose years of schooling were more than a standard deviation beyond the average for their occupational group. They found that managers were the most overeducated and that the general labour occupations of clerical sales and other service workers, as well as craft workers, showed marked increases in overeducation during this period. The authors noted that their measure was not applicable to professional occupations. Dolton and Vignoles (1996), using a 1986 UK sample of 1980 post-secondary graduates, found persistent overeducation generally but with significantly stronger effects on the reduced earnings in clerical jobs than in professional occupations.

Elliot (2000) has examined differences in job search processes between managers, professional and technical employees, and general labourers in a US three-city sample in the early 1990s. Employers/owners were not included because they are outside the labour market and not selling their labour power to others. Managers were more likely to get jobs because others with managerial authority reached down to them personally, rather than through their own active searches. Professional and technical employees relied most on open searches based on formal educational qualifications. General labourers were most likely to get their jobs through active searches using personal contacts, such as family and friends. These findings at least suggest that professional and technical employees are likely to have the closest education-job matches, whereas other personal factors are of relatively greater import in job entry for both managers and general labourers, and may be associated with greater education-job mismatches.

A few more recent studies have applied some version of occupational class analysis to the dimensions of matching proposed in *The Education-Jobs Gap*. For example, de Witte and Steijn (2000) found that, for a 1994 Dutch national sample, blue-collar workers had high credential underemployment, while professional workers had low rates. The 2004 EJRM Survey was designed to probe these class-related patterns in much greater depth.

CONCLUDING REMARKS

The recent findings on education-job matching are typically skewed toward an excess of formal education attainment over the level of education required for jobs. It is reasonably clear that underemployment or overeducation — in terms of educational attainments exceeding the credentials required to get jobs — has become a persistent problem in the employed labour force of advanced market economies. In any case, those whose capabilities are deemed to exceed job requirements have garnered the most attention in recent empirical studies of worker education-job requirement relations.

However, it is becoming clear that formal education qualifications are partial and often poor indicators of workers' capabilities (e.g., Green & McIntosh, 2001), and this chapter has examined the limitations of analyses of matching based on measures of formal education. Some researchers of education-economy relations now point to enhanced lifelong learning and informal job-related learning as solutions for education-jobs mismatches and sustainable economic development (e.g., Thurow, 1975). The EJRM Survey (and the NALL and WALL Surveys) are distinctive in their detailed attention to estimating the extent and content of intentional, informal, job-related learning and offering some quantitative benchmarks for deeper exploration of learning and work.

In light of the conceptual limitations of existing surveys based on workers' capabilities, job requirements, and the match between them, it is evident that such measures have to be interpreted with care. Nevertheless, the survey measures used in the EJRM, WALL, NALL, and CCS Surveys can establish some intergenerational trends in the extent of matching, and identify some significant differences in degrees of matching among sub-populations of the Canadian labour force. The main results from these large samples of employed Canadian workers are reported in Chapters 4 and 5. Moreover, the concepts employed in the individual case studies are congruent with the definitions of the EJRM Survey; so there is a strong methodological link between prior statistical research and the deeper qualitative investigation in Chapters 6 to 12 of the nature of the relationship between education and jobs.

Notes

1. These studies are summarized in Livingstone (1999a, pp. 72–8).
2. The GED scale and these prior studies are discussed in more detail in Livingstone (1998, pp. 78–85).
3. Prior to the development of the GED scale, there were other empirical efforts to assess the correspondence between job requirements and educational achievements. These studies, which began in the 1940s and included scholars such as Bell (1940), Harris (1949), and Thomas (1956), are discussed in Berg (1970).
4. See National Center on Education and the Economy (1990). Compare Hall and Carlton (1977), Blackburn and Mann (1979) and the earlier study by Berg (1970).
5. The original WTR schemes consisted of aptitudes, interests, temperaments, work performed, physical capacities, working conditions, training time (levels of general education and of vocational preparation) and industry. WTR schemes were described in later dictionaries of occupational titles as *worker functions*. In the 1971 *Canadian Classification and Dictionary of Occupations (CCDO)*, the term *occupational profiles* was used.
6. Among many other studies of job requirements, too numerous to review here, the Government of Canada has attempted to describe the characteristics of jobs as a list of essential skills that are thought of as the attributes used in a range of different jobs. For a critical review of the concept of essential skills, see Pankhurst (2005).
7. For further discussion of the comparative merits of expert analysts' ratings versus self-reports, see Spenner (1990); Green, McIntosh, and Vignoles (1999); Sloane (2002); Verhaest and Omey (2006); and McGuiness (2006).

8. This capacity for combination criterion was lacking in the WTR schemes and the Canadian list of essential skills, for example.
9. Others have resorted to arbitrary statistical measures of variation that conflate workers and their jobs; over- and undereducation mismatches are identified, symmetrically in either direction, as education levels more than a standard deviation beyond the mean score for a given group of occupations (e.g., Verdugo & Verdugo, 1989). Such measures are of limited use for trend analysis and will not be considered further here.
10. For a general review of education-job matching research findings prior to 2000, see Livingstone (1999a).
11. See International Labour Organization, Resolution concerning measurement of underemployment and inadequate employment situations, October 1998. Livingstone (1999) and Jensen and Slack (2003) provide reviews of time-based measures.

Chapter Three
Starting with *The Education-Jobs Gap*

D.W. Livingstone

This chapter reviews the contribution of Livingstone's (1999a) *The Education-Jobs Gap: Underemployment or Economic Democracy* (later referred to as EJG), to studies of education-job matching. EJG provided one of the starting points for the design of the EJRM project, particularly in terms of identifying conceptual dimensions of education-job matching and developing a theory of the relationship between education-job mismatches and economic class positions.

THE EDUCATION-JOBS GAP

The EJG book focuses on the extent to which the education levels of workers exceed the education requirements of the available jobs. The book documents the general expansion of adult learning activities in the twentieth century, drawing on international evidence on formal schooling and further education, as well as the few available surveys of informal learning. EJG provides a review of the international empirical research on education-job matching until the late 1990s, identifies the main dimensions of a continuum of underemployment, presents the findings of preliminary surveys and case studies of these dimensions, and makes an argument for an economic class analysis of education-job matching.

Underemployment is conceived in terms of both time-based dimensions and education or skill-based dimensions. Time-based dimensions include structural unemployment and involuntary temporary employment. Structural unemployment refers to the officially unemployed, who are currently actively seeking employment; discouraged workers, who want employment but have given up active pursuit of jobs because their search experience told them none were available; and others who want employment but are excluded by mandatory retirement or other restrictive rules. Involuntary temporary employment refers to part-time and contingent workers who want full-time employment.

kill-based dimensions include

- ...p — the inequality in educational opportunity that arises when ...might have benefited from higher education lack the opportunity because of their socio-economic background, thereby denying them job opportunities that match their talents;
- credential gap — formal qualifications exceed declared entry requirements;
- performance gap — actual skill and knowledge exceeds that needed to do job;
- subjective underemployment — when people think that their competencies exceed the requirements of their job.

EJG presents analyses of relevant questions in a time series of Ontario surveys from 1980 to 1996, a follow-up survey with respondents who were identified as mismatched in the 1994 Ontario survey, and in-depth interviews with some people in the Greater Toronto Area who were most likely experiencing extreme underemployment (or underqualification). The most general conclusion, consistent with most other empirical research, is that the overall educational development of the workforce, as measured statistically, exceeded the gradually increasing job requirements, and that a large number of ably qualified people remained excluded from jobs that made suitable use of their abilities. EJG recommends that efforts to address education-jobs imbalances should pay more attention to economic and job reforms rather than insisting on primarily educational solutions to economic problems; this point will be addressed in Chapter 13. EJG has stimulated further research on underemployment (e.g., de Witte & Steijn, 2000; Vaisey, 2006). However, as noted in Chapter 2, the underemployment and overeducation research approaches have continued to proceed in isolation.

EJG critically assesses both human capital theory and the knowledge-based economy approach in relation to this cumulative body of evidence and finds them insufficient to account for the phenomenon of underemployment. To explain the extent of mismatching between education and jobs, the book proposes an emergent alternative explanation, which attempts to take account of different economic class positions in employing organizations in advanced capitalist societies.

Bringing Class Analysis Back into Studies of Paid Workplaces

As noted in Chapter 1, classical and neoclassical economic theories treated the labour force as homogeneous and passive. More recent approaches to the relations between employment and education have addressed the heterogeneity and more complex division of labour in modern societies in terms of more or less elaborate classifications of occupations. However, research on education-job relations — sometimes focusing on specific powerful occupational groups — has typically ignored the underlying economic class structure.

As proposed by Marx (1867), the fundamental economic class division in market economies was between the owners of the major means of production and those who offer their labour to make a living. Marx qualified this division by recognizing the existence of a shifting array of middle classes, including self-employed craftsmen and farmers, and the emergence of foremen and managers as well as those excluded from employment, the *lumpenproletariat*. Since then, scholars have identified the growing complexity of the structure of occupations and focused mostly on the stratification of jobs in terms of market status and income. Later, Weber's (1928) economic class scheme was grounded in a tripartite distinction similar to that of Marx: the distinction between the "market capacities" of those who owned property, those who possessed specialized skills, and those who could claim only their own (implicitly manual) capacity to labour. More recent occupational class models have often been derived from Marx, Weber, or both.

One of the more influential class models has been Goldthorpe's (1980) neo-Weberian grouping of census occupations into a service class, an intermediate stratum, and a working class. This model either ignored owners of capital and employers or folded them in with the service class of employees. This service class position includes those who exercise delegated authority from such owners and others who exercise specialized knowledge at the behest of their employers; however, the property basis of the capitalist class itself is obscured. This model also described a traditional manual–non-manual, or blue-collar/white-collar, distinction that has little relevance to the capabilities (or skill levels) of contemporary workers (see Ainley, 1993: 59).

During the twentieth century, various complex occupational classifications based on task specialization and industrial sector proliferated. The International Standard Classification of Occupations (ISCO) describes the taxonomy of occupations from government and administration to manual work as a "natural order." Some scholars have developed complex maps of economic classes as occupational communities (Weeden & Grusky, 2005). Skeptical scholars have heralded a "classless society" (e.g., Kingston, 2000), to be quickly met by both conceptual and empirical rejoinders (e.g., Kerbo, 2002; Lareau, 2006).

Some of the difficulties in identifying distinctive economic class groups arise because their boundaries are somewhat more permeable than other nominal social distinctions such as age, gender, ethnicity, or disability. Few people are pure representatives of capital or labour alone: many owners perform some labour tasks and many paid workers own some formal shares of financial capital.

In EJG, the distribution of economic power in advanced market economies is analyzed in terms of an underlying economic class structure that, similar to Marx and Weber, identifies positions based on *ownership of property*, other employee positions based on the *provision of paid labour* to produce goods and services, and middle or intermediate employee classes in positions with *delegated managerial authority* or *recognized specialized knowledge*.

Enterprise owners' proprietary rights enable the owners to define the terms of reference of their businesses and the nature of their own involvement. The owners' prerogative to define and assign jobs governs what capabilities their employees are ostensibly enabled to use in their jobs and which of these are recognized and rewarded.

Historically, as private firms grew, owners delegated operational authority to overseers or lead hands to coordinate and control other employees and rewarded them for their effective allegiance. When large corporate business enterprises began to dominate over family businesses in early twentieth-century capitalist economies, managerial personnel assumed operational coordinating control of many production processes in what was heralded as a "managerial revolution" (Berle & Means, 1933).

All large human societies have had a division of labour in which a small number of positions with specialized knowledge, such as priestly classes or members of craft guilds, were deemed important. Professional occupations require a specialized body of knowledge acquired by extensive academic preparation. In modern societies, these occupations involve systematic knowledge of a field or science, usually gained through a university or college and leading to a formal educational qualification. In fully developed professions, full-time practitioners have established training schools, professional associations, and self-governing regulatory bodies, which have powers to set competency tests and licensing criteria for full membership as well as to enforce adherence to an ethical code of practice. These features enable such professionals to claim overarching authority in their fields of knowledge, make independent judgments about their work, and exclude those who do not have the approved training and certification required for legitimate practice in these fields. A number of other occupational groups also have specialized bodies of knowledge acquired through extensive academic preparation, but their professional associations are still in formation and do not yet have the capacity for self-regulation. Some researchers using credential society approaches argue that some professional occupations, most notably physicians and lawyers, indeed exercise great power over the external labour market exchange relations and thereby enable job-shaping possibilities and job-related learning requirements (Collins, 1979). It should be noted here that some professionals such as physicians and lawyers often own their own businesses and collect proprietary fees for their services, and others serve as professional managers. However, most professionals are hired employees who rely more exclusively on specialized technical knowledge to gain compensation for their capabilities from their employers. Whether professionals are regarded as part of an emerging knowledge class (e.g., Burnham, 1941; Bell, 1973) or an array of fragmenting occupational specializations (e.g., Oppenheimer, 1973; Aronowitz, 1973), professional groups attempt to control their fields of specialized knowledge to ensure the highest possible degree of control of their own work (see Derber, Schwartz, & Magrass, 1990).

In contrast to those with ownership rights, delegated managerial authority, or legitimate claims to specialized professional knowledge, employees without these distinctions may find that—however complex the demands of their job and however competent they are—personal capabilities receive little recognition by their employers. Skilled trades workers deserve special mention here as the descendants of the medieval craft guilds. Skilled trades workers and various other technicians today have recognized specialized bodies of knowledge and long periods of practical training and licensing criteria. However, rather than being treated as autonomous professionals, their claims to professional status are usually mitigated by their lack of academic training and a reliance on trade union membership to negotiate terms with employers.

For the most part, studies of class structure have remained separate from studies of internal workplace relations. A fixation on *external* labour market exchange relations has long prevailed in classical economics and other approaches cited in Chapter 1, and little attention has been paid to workplace relations within an organization. Economic stratification has been treated mainly in terms of the distribution of market rewards such as money income. Braverman's (1974) analysis of the degradation of work *inside* the capitalist labour process did stimulate greater research attention both to the production process (e.g., Edwards, 1979; Friedman, 1977) and to the class structure of authority grounded in this process (e.g., Carchedi, 1983; Wright, 1978). During the 1970s the development of economic class analyses with reference to workplace relations generated not only further models of class structure, including "new" corporate elites, working classes, middle classes, and petty bourgeoisies, but also debate about the boundaries between them. However, little attention was given to the dynamics or consequences of relations between these classes (see Myles & Turegun, 1994).[1] Conversely, the growth of interest in the labour process within particular workplaces produced many case studies of the detailed division of labour (see Thompson, 1989; Tinker, 2002). Since the 1980s these two bodies of research have become increasingly disconnected. As Carter (1995: 35) stated: "There is now remarkably little overlap in what are two discrete areas of analysis—class and labour process: class analysis... makes the vaguest of gestures toward the actual day-to-day relations inside the workplace and... labour process perspectives examine what happens inside workplaces without any informed or extended dialogue with class theory." This divide between class analysis and labour process studies persists (Neilson, 2007).

The approach in EJG is to use a model of economic class structure, based on ownership, managerial authority roles, and occupations with recognized specialized knowledge, to identify different class positions in the labour process of advanced market economies and then to assess the extent to which different class positions were associated with differing degrees of matching between educational attainment and job requirement.

In any analysis of paid work, two basic aspects can be distinguished: the *technical division of labour* and the *social/managerial division of labour*. The technical division of labour denotes a structure of designated sets of tasks in the production process carried out by members of a workforce; these are typically allocated according to degrees of imputed substantive complexity and creativity in the level, scope, and integration of mental and manipulative tasks in an occupation or job. The managerial division of labour refers to the extent of authority someone has to direct other workers' and one's own production activities. The management of an organization entails the coordination and control of workers' performance of production tasks, primarily by the delegation of formal and informal degrees of supervisory authority through a workforce.

Theorists and researchers of the division of labour have frequently conflated the technical division of tasks and the division of managerial authority among workers (see Murphy, 1993). There has been a tendency to see the growth of managerial and supervisory positions as essentially determined by technological development. However, in cases of highly automated production, where the detailed division of labour became so segmented and de-motivating for some line workers, technical tasks were recombined in some organizations. This reversal illustrated that technology involves the *interaction* of technical divisions of tasks and managerial divisions of workers, rather than being simply machine-driven imperatives. In the context of the current debate about the changing nature of work in advanced market economies, the relationship between technical task complexity and managerial control over the job needs to be closely examined.

A careful assessment of the contemporary economic class structure of paid work and the macro-trends in job requirements should begin by identifying both the technical division of labour, in terms of formally recognized bodies of specialized knowledge, and also the managerial division of labour, in terms of formal ownership of means of production and formally delegated supervisory authority. Job requirements can then be examined in this context.

The conceptual model of economic class positions used in EJG is grounded in the above distinctions in paid work, namely: ownership, delegated authority, and specialized knowledge.[2] Eight main economic class groups are identified: large employers, small employers, the self-employed, managers, supervisors, professional employees, service workers, and *industrial workers*.[3]

Among owners, *large employers* include owners of substantial capital and also corporate executives who oversee investment in companies and corporations with multimillion-dollar assets and many employees. *Small employers*, typically family firms or partnerships, tend to have exclusive ownership and a small number of employees, and the owners continue to play active coordinating roles in the labour process of their firms. The *self-employed* remain in control of their small commodity enterprises but are reliant on their own labour.

At the other end of the class hierarchy are those workers who lack significant ownership claims, official supervisory authority, and recognized, self-regulating, specialized knowledge. This includes *industrial workers,* who produce, distribute, or

repair material goods. It also includes *service workers,* who provide
of sales, business, social, and other services, and who are similar[ly orga-]
nized supervisory authority or self-regulating task autonomy. (So[me]
service workers, such as skilled trades, are recognized as having s[pecialized knowl-]
edge but not self-regulating autonomy.)

Between the employers and the workers who lack formal authority or recognized specialized knowledge, there are other employees who tend to have mixed functions. *Managers* are delegated by owners to control the overall labour process, at the point of production, to ensure profitability, but they may also contribute their labour to coordinate this process. *Supervisors* are under the authority of managers to control adherence to production standards by industrial or service workers, but they may also collaborate directly with these workers in aspects of this work. *Professional employees* have task autonomy based on their recognized specialized knowledge to design production processes for themselves and others and to execute their own work with a high level of self-regulating discretion, but they remain subordinated to employer directives.

These economic class positions, based on relations of ownership, delegated authority, and recognized specialized knowledge, are distinct from specific occupational classifications, but obviously overlap with them. Those with the occupational designation of carpenter, for example, could be employers, self-employed, supervisors, or industrial workers (see Wright, 1980). Those with professional occupations could be employers, self-employed, managers, or professional employees. Of course, many more specific factors, including personal characteristics (race, gender, age, disability), accumulated knowledge of the job, and other organizational features may mediate relations between workers' capabilities and job requirements, as we assess in later chapters. But if the formal technical *and* managerial divisions of labour are not considered, their effects are likely to confound more specific occupational analyses of education-job relations.

There are few prior theoretical perspectives on education-job relationships that systematically account for the influence of the economic class–based structure of authority and workplace job control on the scope of work or learning. EJG addresses this problem and argues that workers' opportunity to define and design their jobs or the jobs of others are limited by their economic class location. Employees who are subject to the formal authority of owners and managers of paid workplaces have designated job requirements, and these are directly designated by the owners or managers, who exercise managerial prerogative over them. In contrast, owners have the discretion to set their own educational job requirements, subject primarily to entrepreneurial ability and accrued capital assets (Carnoy, 1977). The job requirements of managers may include educational requirements but also involve various other criteria intended to ensure their effective exercise of authority over other workers (see Elliot, 2000). Most prior analyses have ignored these class-based differences in the naracter of job requirements. EJG is the most systematic inquiry into economic class–based education-job matching to date.

Economists have offered alternative general explanations for job search processes in the context of the increasing apparent surplus of qualified labour in relation to job requirements, without addressing economic class distinctions. These include a displacement or bumping hypothesis which posits that those with higher qualifications who cannot immediately find jobs at that level seek jobs requiring a lower level of qualification or remain unemployed and add to the supply of workers competing for lower level jobs (Borghans & de Grip, 2000). Others propose that overeducated workers are younger with less on-the-job training and that experience and upward job mobility will tend to resolve discrepancies between actual and required levels of schooling (Sicherman, 1991). Both of these explanations have grains of truth: job seekers will lower their expectations in poor labour markets, and workers will continue to gain work experience and seek better opportunities. But neither can account for increasing education-jobs gaps per se or the extent of differences in matching found when economic class differences in occupational groups are taken into account.

The EJG economic class perspective on education-job relations posits that the extent to which the relevant knowledge of these different economic classes is recognized is contingent on the differential authority people are able to exert through their class positions in their workplaces. More specifically, class-based managerial authority (i.e., ownership rights, formal managerial authority) and exclusive access to training programs in specialized fields of professional knowledge are predicted to be associated with a closer match between formal attainments and requirements for professional employees and managers. The extent of all employees' job control over designing their job tasks and participation in organizational decision-making is considered very relevant to the closeness of these matching measures.

The preliminary EJG empirical research found that those with the most ownership and managerial power over others, namely large employers, expressed the closest match between their capabilities and their job requirements. They were followed by professional and managerial employees, while industrial and service workers without such formal claims experienced higher levels of underemployment, or underutilization, of their formal educational attainments. These findings were seen as providing a sufficient basis for developing further surveys and more in-depth studies taking these economic class positions into account. If one grants that some such economic class structure underlies the labour process, studies of relations between job requirements and the capabilities workers bring to their jobs cannot afford to ignore this premise.

Continual Change Dynamics of Paid Work and Workers' Learning

EJG assumes the view that the capitalist mode of production constantly turns spheres of activity into goods and services for sale. The most distinctive feature is hired wage labour.[4] In any market-based economy, change is driven by three underlying relationships: (1) inter-firm competition to make and sell more and more goods and services commodities at lower cost and price for greater profits (see Brenner, 2000); (2) negotiations between business owners and paid workers over the conditions of employment and knowledge requirements, including their relative shares of net output (see Burawoy, 1985); and (3) continual modification of the techniques of production to achieve greater efficiency in terms of labour time per commodity, leading to higher profits, better employment conditions or both (see Freeman & Soete, 1994). Inter-firm competition, conflicts between employers and employees over working conditions, and technological innovation all lead to incessant shifts in the number of enterprises, employees, and types of jobs available. Population growth cycles, evolving household needs, and new legislative regulations also frequently serve to alter the supply of labour. At the same time, popular demand for general education and specialized training increases cumulatively as people seek more knowledge, different specific skills, and added credentials, in order to live and qualify for jobs in such a changing society.

In a dynamically changing economy "mismatches" are inevitable between employers' aggregate demand and formal requirements for employees on the one hand, and the aggregate supply and formal qualifications of job seekers on the other. Increasingly efficient production of enterprises, in terms of the relationship between labour input and production, is generated endogenously by workers' learning on the job, as well as by technological innovation. Increasing efficiency leads to either expanded production or unemployment, in either case modifying the overall demand for labour. In societies with liberal democratic state regimes that acclaim the right to equal educational opportunity, and with labour markets in which both employers and job seekers make mainly individual employment choices, the dominant historical tendency—with the notable exception of early post–World War II years—has been for the supply of educationally qualified job seekers to exceed the demand for any given type of job. These same dynamics also generate *formal* underqualification of some workers, particularly older employees who are experienced and competent in their jobs and have had few incentives to upgrade their credentials.

Theoretical approaches that have not attended to the underlying dynamics of advanced market economies, including conflicting aspects of the interest relationship between owners and paid workers, have underestimated the forces underlying change in both work and learning processes. A continual reorganization of the factors of production to increase productivity is the consequence of inter-firm competition as well as the productivity increases generated endogenously by a workforce as it learns to labour and produce more efficiently with given tools and techniques. The forces of production, including tools and techniques and their combination with the capacities of labour, have experienced extraordinary growth throughout the relatively short history of industrial capitalism. Such technological developments, from the water mill to the steam mill to interconnected mechanical and electronic networks, continually serve to expand private commodity production and exchange, while also making relevant knowledge more widely accessible. On the one hand, private ownership of production and the attendant wealth become increasingly concentrated in a smaller number of larger corporations, from the joint stock companies of the 1880s to the massive global corporations of the present. Owners strive to control knowledge of specific commodity production techniques for advantage over competitors (e.g., patents, licences, industrial secrets). On the other hand, workers and the general public gain ever-greater access (via public education systems and such forums as public libraries, public radio and television, and the Internet) to knowledge previously restricted for commodity production by private firms, as well as to diverse sources of knowledge for everyday life. In the context of inter-firm competition and the open labour contract, the expansion of publicly accessible knowledge is greater than any enterprise owner's ability to appropriate such knowledge for private gain.

The microelectronic era and the rise of global financial circuits have almost certainly seen the acceleration of the change dynamics of capitalist economies (Harris, 1999). However, the same basic underlying dynamics persist. Employment demands may intensify, but continual problem solving is still required by virtually all workers, and the matching of qualifications and requirements is still limited by the changing economic class structure.

The increased role of the modern state in managing advanced market economies that have combined public and private activities may moderate the worst effects of this change process on workers through various welfare provisions (see Esping-Anderson, 1990). Conversely, global corporations may take advantage of disasters, instigated by both human and natural causes, to gain immense profits from the most vulnerable populations (see Klein, 2007). Regardless of the specific market conditions, EJG assumes that the opposition between the socializing forces of knowledge production (e.g., widening use of the Internet) and the privatizing relations of commodity production (e.g., commercialization of the Internet and intellectual property claims) is associated with continual change in conditions and requirements of work, and this serves as a further stimulus to workplace learning in advanced capitalist economies.

Related Studies
Two related studies preceded the development of the EJRM project. The first of these was the work of the New Approaches to Lifelong Learning (NALL) research network between 1998 and 2003. NALL produced the first national survey of adult learning, which included substantial questions on intentional informal learning, as well as on formal schooling and further education. The NALL Survey was conducted in 1998, and the basic findings are summarized in the work of Livingstone (1999a, 2002).

These survey results indicated that participation in intentional informal learning is more substantial than in further education, has only weak relations with more formal education, and engages adults of all ages and economic class backgrounds. The NALL network also produced a series of over 30 case studies, in which adults from all walks of life provided insight about a wide diversity of informal learning strategies that people use to cope with paid and unpaid work and their everyday lives (see www.nall.ca).

The second study was the Working Class Learning Strategies (WCLS) project. This study began prior to the completion of EJG, but it drew on the EJG findings and on preliminary results from the national NALL Survey to inform the design of case studies of an array of learning activities of unionized workers in auto assembly, chemical processing, small parts manufacturing, garment industries, and also community college staff. These case studies were conducted with the assistance of the relevant labour unions, which provided unlimited access to their members for representative in-depth interviews and discussions. The research sites varied in union strength, managerial practices, employment stability, and formal training programs. The results confirmed a rich diversity of informal learning practices under quite different employment conditions and also suggested that employment sites in which workers are more highly organized are more likely to obtain more substantial further education programs, as well as relatively more recognition for their informal learning achievements and skills (see Livingstone & Sawchuk, 2004).

Skill and Economic Class

The relationship between economic class position and imputations of skill is especially pertinent to note here. A relationship between occupational class and so-called skill has been assumed in many macro-level studies (e.g., Ainley, 1993; Tåhlin, 2006b). The general ambiguities around notions of skill will be discussed in Chapter 6. Here it is important to note that workers define their capabilities in terms of the elements of knowledge and experience they use in their present and past jobs, as well as elements they have not used but could if required. Employers, on the other hand, tend to define skill and ability more narrowly in terms of their perception of discrete task requirements. As the WCLS project findings suggest and Rigby and Sanchis (2006: 23) also observe, the difference between the effective skills of employees and the skills nominally recognized by employers is likely to be smallest where power relations are most equitable. Some employees also use power gained through organization (e.g., professional association, trade union) to define their work as highly skilled. They may do this in conflict with their employer and sometimes in conflict with other groups of workers. In negotiations between organized workers and employers, the actual skills and abilities required to perform a job can be less important than the power workers have to argue that their work is more skilled and should be compensated as such. While some workers and their jobs may become (over)valued by employers, the work and abilities of others are undervalued, artificially depressed in the dynamic hierarchy of skills. This devaluation and marginalization of some workers and their abilities may occur along the lines of gender and race (Cockburn, 1991; Steinberg, 1990; Jensen & Slack, 2002) as well as different class positions.

One of the clearest illustrations of the effect of differential economic class authority on public recognition of skill is the almost total absence of analytical attention to the assessment of the capability of business owners to perform their jobs.[5] It is widely presumed that owners have the managerial prerogative to impose competency assessments on subordinate employees, without any reciprocal privilege. Beneath the level of ownership, those who have less supervisory authority tend to be prone to the competency assessments of those above them. The assessments owners make of hired managers are rarely known to lower level employees, while the assessments of industrial and service workers are typically available to all management levels. Those who attain specialized knowledge in established fields at least remain likely to have more autonomy over the performance of their designated production tasks.

Estimations of the job requirements of enterprise owners are virtually non-existent publicly. This is a reflection of the ability of those with the most economic power to avoid scrutiny and of the sanctity of private property rights superseding labour capacities in capitalist economies. With the proliferation of formal educational credentials, large employers typically ensure that their own children obtain the most exclusive schooling. However, the celebration of entrepreneurial initiative, notably by employers without advanced formal education (such as Microsoft's Bill Gates), trumps acquired technical skills. The existing estimates of the job requirements of managers or even supervisors may refer to technical task abilities, but these are often conflated with, and superseded by, the formal authority delegated to them from owners. In considering workers' capacities and job requirements in the general context of the economic class structure of paid workplaces, the EJRM study is designed to devote special attention to assessing the capabilities and educational attainments of *non-managerial employees* (i.e., professional employees, service workers, and industrial workers), who do not have ownership rights or formal managerial authority. These capabilities are compared with their job requirements, which are presumed to be reflective of the technical task competencies to do their jobs. These non-managerial employees are the people who are the primary targets of contending theories about changing skill requirements in current paid workplaces.

CONCLUDING REMARKS

The perspective developed in EJG and the subsequent findings of the WCLS and NALL projects guided the initial design of the EJRM project. The following two chapters present findings from the national 1983 CCS and 2004 WALL surveys and the 2004 Ontario EJRM Survey, which estimate recent general trends in education-job matching and provide new findings for economic class and specific occupational group differences in education-jobs matching. In addition, the findings show the effects of differences in job control and other factors such as work experience. The WCLS and NALL case study findings have pointed to the need to go beyond such survey findings, as will be done in later chapters.

Notes

1. For an overview of recent conceptual approaches to class analysis, see Wright (2005).
2. For a comparative analysis of this class model and several other variants of Marxian and Weberian class analyses, see Livingstone and Mangan (1996).
3. Wright's (1978) initial class model was quite comparable to EJG. Empirical estimation relied on survey respondents' self-reports of authority and autonomy to determine class locations. The surveys gathered specific occupational information and then faced conundrums over, for example, how to treat janitors who reported high levels of authority and autonomy within the labour process. The EJG model relies on ownership status and occupational types. In estimating class divisions, ownership positions must first be separated from the rest of the active labour force. While employee positions with official supervisory authority and/or recognized specialized professional knowledge may be continually shifting, the detailed occupational censuses of most advanced industrial countries provide sufficient information to approximate basic ownership, delegated managerial authority, and professional distinctions. But two empirical limitations must be noted immediately. The large employer class is not adequately distinguished in large-scale surveys because of their very small numbers. Also, the much larger underclass of the chronically unemployed and those otherwise excluded from the wage labour force, but dependent on the capitalist mode of production, is also poorly represented in sample surveys and is beyond the scope of such analyses.
4. As Marx and other critics have recognized, labour is not a commodity like the others; rather it is a capacity that cannot be known, with an output that cannot be known in advance.
5. There is now a lot of discussion about the extremely high remuneration of corporate executives in comparison with the much lower workers' wages and in relation to company asset market value, and there is some research on the strategies executives use to increase market share values but little scrutiny of their labour process.

Part Two
Surveying the Gaps

Chapter Four
Education and Jobs Survey Profile I: National Trends in Employment Conditions, Job Requirements, Workers' Learning and Matching, 1983–2004

D.W. Livingstone and Milosh Raykov

This chapter relies primarily on national surveys that were conducted in 1983, 1998, and 2004 to estimate continuity and change in employment conditions, job requirements, workers' learning practices, and the extent of education-job requirement matching. In the current context of extensive organizational restructuring, the chapter first focuses on trends in general economic sectors and the economic class composition of the entire employed labour force. It then examines workers' reported involvement in designing their own work and their participation in organizational policy decisions. Next, evidence is presented of changes in job entry and performance requirements based on required educational levels and training time. Workers' learning activities are then summarized in terms of their formal educational attainments, participation in further education courses, and job-related informal learning. Finally, the extent of matching or correspondence between workers' knowledge and their job requirements is estimated in terms of the relevance of their field of study to the job, the formal educational credential they hold, job performance criteria, their subjective perceptions of the extent of matching, and their accumulated knowledge of the job.

CHANGING EMPLOYMENT CONDITIONS

Some major changes in the world economy, such as increasing international interdependence combined with intensified trade, technological changes—notably in electronic information transfer—and a quadrupling of the global labour pool since the 1980s (IMF, 2007), have generated turbulent employment conditions. Some of the broad changes and continuities in employment will be noted before looking at education-job matching.

In demographic terms, the most substantial change in the labour force during the past century was the entry of women into paid employment. Early in the twentieth century, women were only about 10 per cent of the Canadian paid labour force. They were mainly young, single women who left employment after marriage (Statistics Canada, 2004b). By the turn of the twenty-first century, women made up nearly half of the employed labour force, and over two-thirds of those with children under six years of age were in paid employment (Statistics Canada, 2006b). In 2004 the overall participation rate in paid employment reached the highest level ever recorded, about 68 per cent of the entire working-age population (Statistics Canada, 2004a: 17, 20).[1] The majority of adults capable of paid employment are now either in employment or looking for it. In addition to a rapid decline in the number of full-time women homemakers, others who had earlier been excluded from the workforce (e.g., registered students, retired persons, those with disabilities, and very recent immigrants) are being drawn increasingly into partial forms of employment (Livingstone, 2002). For example, in contrast to the traditional two-stage "school-to-work" model, most young people are now combining school and paid jobs, either because they are staying in school longer and need employment income to afford tuition costs or because they are returning to complete or upgrade educational credentials once they seek full-time jobs.

From the vantage point of workers in the labour markets of advanced market economies such as Canada, the main consequence of a widening global and domestic participation has been the growing uncertainty about job security. As married women entered the labour force after World War II, they took most of the part-time and temporary jobs. These jobs, with their relatively low benefits and economic security, have generally continued to increase, in contrast to the immediate post–World War II standard of a full-time, long-term position with a given employer. In 1976, 12 per cent of the labour force was employed part-time (defined as under 30 hours per week); by 1997 this rate had increased to over 18 per cent and remained there in 2006 (Usalcas, 2008). The rate of *involuntary* part-time employment—for part-time workers who would prefer to have full-time jobs—tripled between 1976 and 1998 to over a third of part-timers (Betcherman, Leckie, & McMullen, 1998: 33) and may have approached one half-by 2004 (Livingstone & Scholtz, 2006). Temporary jobs, including casual, seasonal, and short-term contract jobs, have tended to become a greater proportion of all jobs, increasing to about 14 per cent by

2006 (Galarneau, 2005; Statistics Canada, Labour Force Survey, 2006a). By 2006, only three-quarters of hired employees had full-time permanent jobs and, if the growing numbers in self-employment are included, over 40 per cent of the total employed Canadian labour force were in "precarious employment" involving either part-time, temporary, or uncertain terms (Vosko, 2008). The core labour force employed in permanent, full-time jobs is shrinking; the numbers of non-standard, part-time, temporary jobs are growing; and the destabilizing use of outsourcing and off-shore labour is becoming widespread (Chaykowski, 2005; Kalleberg, 2003).

A trend by more and more businesses to operate 24 hours a day, seven days a week means that a growing number of workers have been compelled to give up regular work schedules. Over a third of employed Canadians now work irregular shifts, split shifts, night shifts, on call, or casually according to market demand (Statistics Canada, 2005; Livingstone & Scholtz, 2006). Since the 1970s, there has been a continuing decline of the standard 40 hours-per-week job with benefits, a growth of contingent part-time and temporary jobs, as well as an increase in those working very long hours (Cranford et al., 2003; Kalleberg, 2003). According to the 1998 NALL and 2004 WALL surveys referenced throughout this book, the average *usual* employment hours for the entire labour force increased from 38 to 40 hours per week during the 1998–2004 period, mainly reflecting an increase in the number of people working over 50 hours a week (Livingstone & Scholtz, 2006). Other, more detailed, longer-term time-use surveys have found increases in average paid work time since the mid-1980s (Statistics Canada, 2005).

Increased global market competition has driven frequent changes in products, labour processes, and organizational structures (Kleinman & Vallas, 2001). The 2004 WALL Survey identified several major trends in the organizational restructuring of paid workplaces between 1998 and 2004. Around 40 per cent of respondents indicated that they had seen each of the following organizational changes in their workplaces: reduction in the number of full-time workers, greater use of part-time or temporary workers, increased reliance on job rotation, and multiskilling (Livingstone & Scholtz, 2006).

In summary, changes in the general condition of employment over the past generation have been disruptive and challenging for the Canadian labour force in terms of demographic recomposition, diminishing job security, and organizational restructuring. A larger labour force is working longer hours, more overtime, and more temporary hours.

Economic Sector Change and Economic Class Recomposition
In all advanced market economies, paid work continues to move away from traditional agrarian and manufacturing activities to jobs in the service sector (OECD, 2000). In Canada, this widespread shift to the service sector is well underway. The majority of workers have been employed in service sector jobs since the 1960s. The

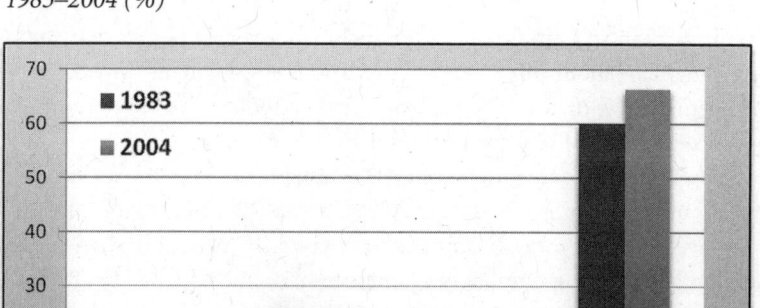

Graph 4.1 *Economic Sector Distribution, Employed Labour Force, Canada, 1983–2004 (%)*

Sector	1983	2004
Extraction	9	6
Processed material goods	23	21
Mixed*	8	7
Services	60	66

Sources: Canadian Class Structure (CCS) Survey, 1983 (N=1758); WALL Survey, 2004 (N=5038)
* Note: "Mixed" includes those workers in the Standard Industrial Categories Transportation and Storage and Communications and Utilities.

trend continued between 1983 and 2004 (Graph 4.1), so that about two-thirds of all employment is now in trade, finance, business, personal, government, health, or other service industries.[2]

A century ago, the majority of the Canadian labour force was employed in agriculture and other extractive industries, including forestry, fishing, and mining (including oil and gas mining). By the early twenty-first century, only about 2 per cent were employed in agriculture and a total of 5 per cent worked in all extractive industries, even though the Canadian economy continued to depend heavily on the export of these staple commodities for foreign trade. Manufacturing employment grew to over 30 per cent during the first half of the last century but is now less than half of that, and while construction industry employment continues to fluctuate with business cycles, the proportion of the labour force involved in producing processed material goods continues to decline to about 20 per cent of the total labour force. In light of the decline of material-goods-producing jobs, it should be noted that manufacturing still matters.[3] Just as less labour-intensive production in agriculture was intimately supportive of the growth of manufacturing, less labour-intensive manufacturing can stimulate development of a variety of service sector jobs. Innovation in the production process has been at the core of international economic advantage in the post–World War II period. Given the extensive foreign control of Canada's manufacturing sector, the need to continue nurturing synergie between less labour-intensive manufacturing and sustainable jobs in the growing service sectors represents a major challenge.

Discussions of recent compositional changes in types of occupations tend to emphasize the growth of professional and managerial jobs, which is consistent with the predictions of post-industrial theorists. Prior empirical studies have documented the substantial, recent growth of these two occupational groups in Canada (Lavoie & Roy, 1998; Baldwin & Beckstead, 2003). Lavoie and Roy's general analysis of census-based occupational distributions over the 1971–96 period in Canada found significant redistribution of jobs from manufacturing to services, data processing, and especially to management and knowledge work. The proportion of people in management occupations nearly quadrupled to 10 per cent of the labour force. People in knowledge-based occupations that mainly involve the generation of ideas or the provision of expert opinion—such as scientists, engineers, and artists—grew from 5 per cent to 8 per cent of the labour force. In spite of these increases, managers and knowledge workers continued to constitute less than 20 per cent of the entire employment picture, while most of the Canadian labour force was engaged in jobs that require fairly routinized transmission of data, processing of goods, or provision of personal services. Lavoie and Roy (1998: 15) concluded: "Based on this one-time snapshot of employment it is rather difficult to make the case that Canada has become a knowledge-based economy."

The changing distribution of economic classes over the past generation in Canada, in terms of the eight employment classes discussed in Chapter 3, is shown in Graph 4.2. Among the owner classes, large and small employers (all those owning companies that have any hired employees) now account for about 7 per cent of the labour force. The self-employed, including consultants, freelancers, and those owning businesses with no employees, are more than twice the size of the two employer categories combined. A comparison of data from the 2004 WALL Survey and the 1983 CCS Survey (Clement & Myles, 1994) indicates that there have been small increases in the self-employed labour force over the past generation.

Intermediate or middle-class positions of managerial and professional employees increased from around 15 per cent to over 25 per cent of the total employed labour force between 1983 and 2004 (Graph 4.2), increases consistent with the previously cited census-based occupational surveys. Conversely, the working class composed of industrial workers and service workers declined significantly from about two-thirds to under half of the employed labour force. The decline of manufacturing workers has been widely documented (Statistics Canada, 2008; Weir, 2007). The apparent decline of non-managerial service workers may be related to the simultaneous rapid rise of automated self-service and quasi-managerial administrative staff functions in an ever-expanding array of service industries (Huws, 2003).

The number of managers and professional employees have been increasing quite

Exploring the Gaps

...onomic Class Distribution, Employed Labour Force, Canada,

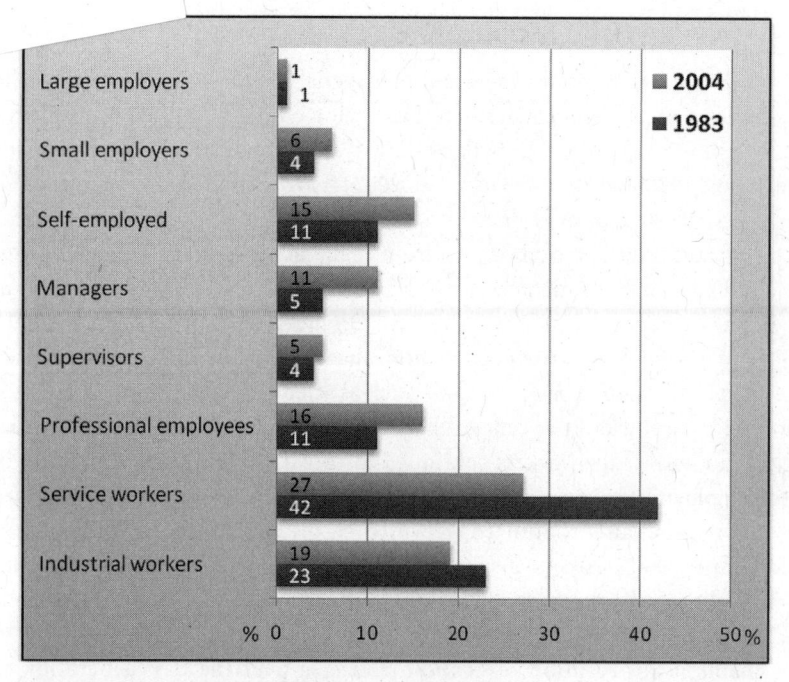

Class	2004	1983
Large employers	1	1
Small employers	6	4
Self-employed	15	11
Managers	11	5
Supervisors	5	4
Professional employees	16	11
Service workers	27	42
Industrial workers	19	23

Sources: CCS Survey, 1983 (N=1785); WALL Survey, 2004 (N=5437)

rapidly in relation to other occupational groups. Some "de-layering" of lower levels of managerial hierarchies has been found in recent international surveys (Littler, Wiesner, & Dunford, 2003). However, the 2004 WALL Survey accounts of recent types of organizational restructuring suggest that a general reduction in the number of employees has been much more common than a reduction in the number of managers. The doubling of the proportion of managers indicated in Graph 4.2 suggests that the general trend in Canadian workplaces has been toward an intensification of managerial authority. The most important point for further analyses in this book is that professional and managerial employee classes have experienced substantial growth over the past generation, while industrial and service workers have witnessed substantial decline in their proportions and numbers in the employed labour force.

It should be noted here that this compositional change of increasing proportions of managers and professional employees does not necessarily translate into increasing discretion and authority *within* these occupational classes. While the proportions of managers and professional employees increase and the proportions of industrial and service workers decrease in the overall occupational class structure, the extent of discretion and authority exercised *within* such positions could exhibit reverse trends, as will be seen in following section.

It should be re-emphasized that most of the analyses that follow in this book focus on *employee* economic classes (i.e., exclude large and small employers and the self-employed). The central concern is with the relationship between job requirements and workers' capabilities. Employers play a pivotal role in determining formal job requirements for their employees. With their proprietorial privilege, the employers' job requirements are more directly determined by such factors as entrepreneurial market circumstances and financial assets than by their occupational skills and knowledge. In particular, the following analysis of worker involvement assumes that the employers and the self-employed retain overarching control of both the technical and managerial divisions of labour within their enterprises, whatever their educational attainments might be.

Worker Involvement: Task Discretion and Policy Decisions

The recent wave of information technologies has made a wider array of work tasks dependent on the engagement of workers' minds. Workers' self-reports about the thought and attention required, and the discretion they can exercise in task performance, confirm this view. About two-thirds of all employees in the 2004 workforce reported that their jobs demand a great deal of thought and attention, compared with less than 40 per cent in 1983 (Graph 4.3). Of course, "thought and attention" could mean different things to those in different economic classes. However, both the service workers, who work directly with customers, and the industrial workers, who process material goods, are increasingly involved in computer-based maintenance and recording functions (e.g., Huws, 2003). Intensification of work tasks could also increase the thought and attention demanded.

In any case, the changes between 1983 and 2004 in terms of the thought and attention demanded appear to have affected mainly service and industrial workers (Graph 4.3). Managers and professional employees gave similar higher responses in 1983 and 2004, but the percentage of service and industrial workers reporting that their jobs require a great deal of thought and attention doubled during this period.

Increases in the amount of discretion explicitly permitted to employees in performing their technical tasks may have been more modest. The proportion of employees who said that they could design their own work all or most of the time increased from 43 per cent to 56 per cent between 1983 and 2004 (Graph 4.4). Once again, service and industrial workers express significant increases in design discretion. Professional and managerial employees report declines in discretionary design control, perhaps indicative of a dilution of managerial and professional functions with the expansion of their numbers during this period. Professional employees and managers are still more likely than service and industrial workers to feel that they have control over the design of their job tasks, but the differences in their perceptions of control are narrowing.

Graph 4.3 *Job Demands "Great Deal" of Thought and Attention, by Employee Class, Canada, 1983–2004 (%)*

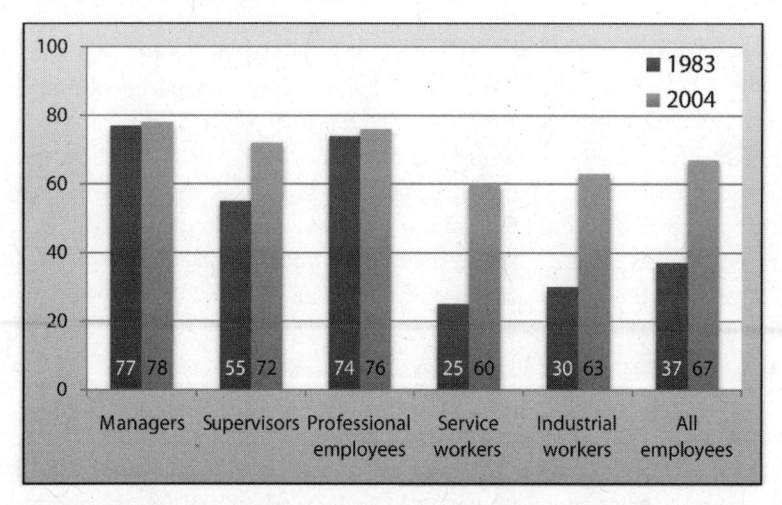

Employee Class	1983	2004
Managers	77	78
Supervisors	55	72
Professional employees	74	76
Service workers	25	60
Industrial workers	30	63
All employees	37	67

Sources: CCS Survey, 1983 (N=1482); WALL Survey, 2004 (N=4249)

Graph 4.4 *Design Work "All or Most of the Time," by Employee Class, Canada 1983–2004 (%)*

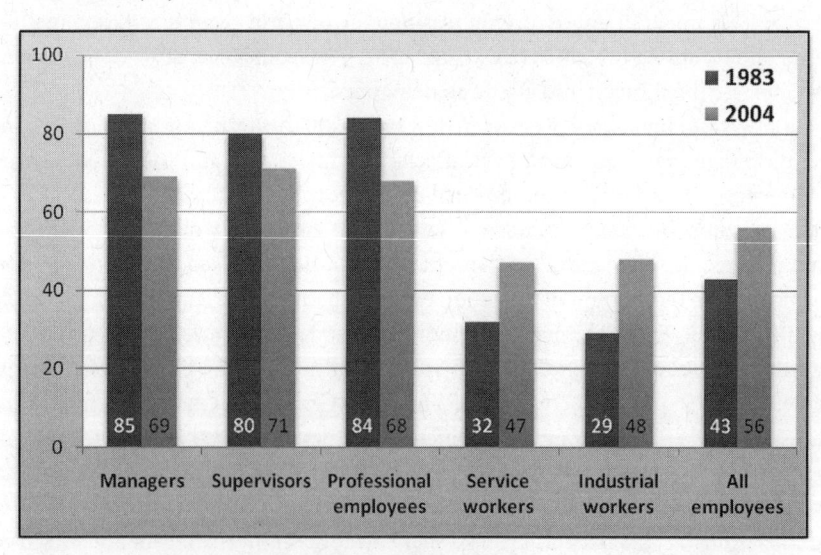

Employee Class	1983	2004
Managers	85	69
Supervisors	80	71
Professional employees	84	68
Service workers	32	47
Industrial workers	29	48
All employees	43	56

Sources: CCS Survey, 1983 (N=1482); WALL Survey, 2004 (N=4246)

Graph 4.5 *Workers Reporting a Supervisory Role in Their Workplace, by Employee Class, Canada, 1983–2004 (%)*

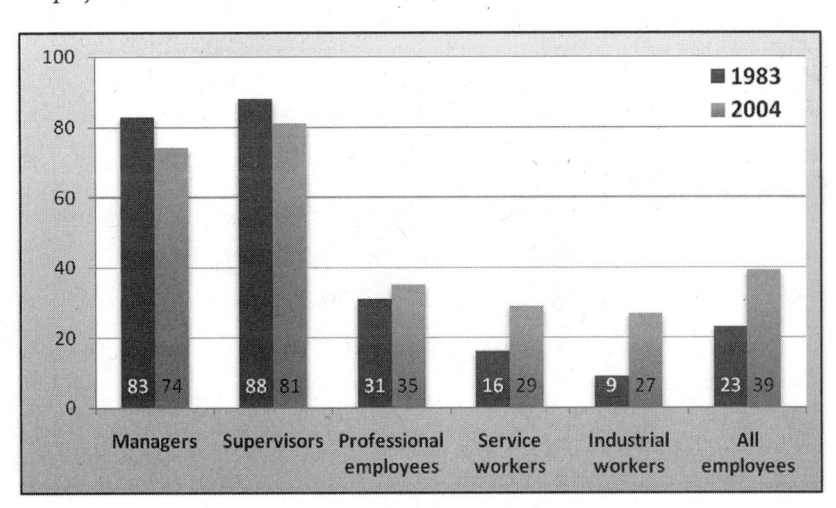

Employee Class	1983	2004
Managers	83	74
Supervisors	88	81
Professional employees	31	35
Service workers	16	29
Industrial workers	9	27
All employees	23	39

Sources: CCS Survey, 1983 (N=1483); WALL Survey, 2004 (N=4250)

Recent empirical research suggests a trend toward wider worker involvement in organization-level decisions (e.g., Giles, Lapointe, Murray, & Belanger, 1999). This trend may include increased delegation of supervisory tasks to non-managerial employees and, conversely, somewhat diminished roles for middle management (Littler, Wiesner, & Dunford, 2003). The extent and permanence of the actual delegation of authority remains in question (e.g., Harley, 1999). However, the 1983 CCS Survey and the 2004 WALL Survey findings support this apparent trend.

Some insight into trends in the delegation of managerial authority in paid workplaces is offered by the proportion of workers who, whatever their official occupation title, report having a managerial or supervisory role in their workplace. Graph 4.5 suggests that there has been a widening delegation of managerial authority from about 25 to 40 per cent of all employees over this period. As the number of employees with formal managerial titles has grown, the proportion with direct line authority may have diminished, while administrative staff functions have grown. However, around three-quarters of those with managerial job titles still exercise direct authority over other employees. The proportion of professional employees with supervisory roles remains about a third. At the same time as the overall number of service and industrial workers has declined, the proportion of service and industrial workers who are delegated some supervisory role over their workmates has grown. More than a quarter of service and industrial workers claimed a supervisory role in 2004, compared to around 10 per cent in 1983.

Graph 4.6 *Employee Input into Organizational Policy Decisions, All Employees, Canada, 1983–2004 (%)*

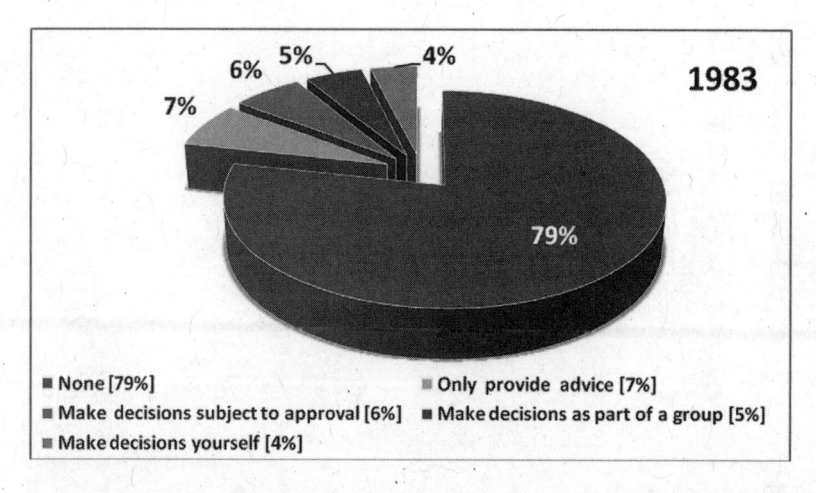

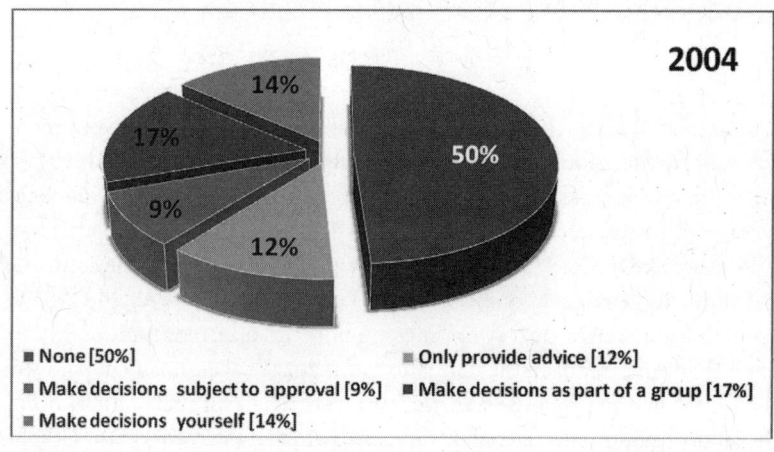

1983
- None [79%]
- Only provide advice [7%]
- Make decisions subject to approval [6%]
- Make decisions as part of a group [5%]
- Make decisions yourself [4%]

2004
- None [50%]
- Only provide advice [12%]
- Make decisions subject to approval [9%]
- Make decisions as part of a group [17%]
- Make decisions yourself [14%]

Sources: CCS Survey, 1983 (N=1485); WALL Survey, 2004 (N=4125).

Respondents in both survey years were also asked whether they participated in organizational policy decisions about the types of products or services delivered, number of persons employed, budgets, and so forth. In general, employees in 2004 viewed themselves as having more decision-making input than those surveyed two decades earlier (Graph 4.6). The percentage of workers who perceive complete exclusion from organizational decision-making has dropped from three-quarters to one-half. There have also been small increases in advisory, conditional, and direct forms of decision-making roles.

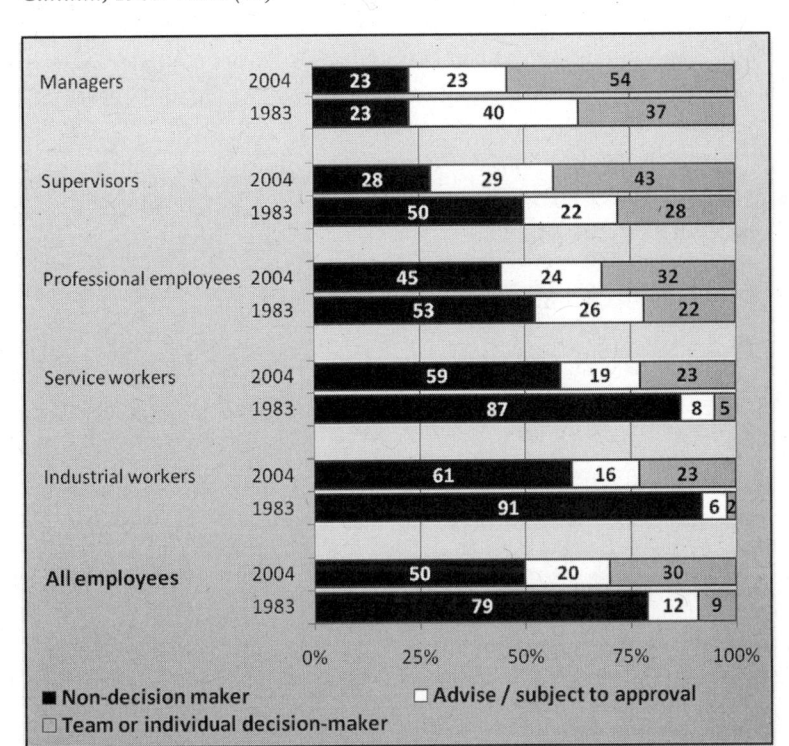

Graph 4.7 Input into Organizational Policy Decisions, by Employee Class, Canada, 1983–2004 (%)

Employee Class	Year	Non-decision maker	Advise / subject to approval	Team or individual decision-maker
Managers	2004	23	23	54
Managers	1983	23	40	37
Supervisors	2004	28	29	43
Supervisors	1983	50	22	28
Professional employees	2004	45	24	32
Professional employees	1983	53	26	22
Service workers	2004	59	19	23
Service workers	1983	87	8	5
Industrial workers	2004	61	16	23
Industrial workers	1983	91	6	2
All employees	2004	50	20	30
All employees	1983	79	12	9

Sources: CCS Survey, 1983; WALL Survey, 2004

Participation in organizational policy decision-making appears to have increased in all employee classes (Graph 4.7). Virtually no industrial or service workers reported participation in 1983, whereas over 20 per cent did so in 2004. Managers, supervisors, and professional employees all reported smaller gains in organizational decision-making. However, policy decision-making remains deeply structured by economic class. Graph 4.7 shows that in 2004 the majority of those in managerial positions, as well as professional employees, had active decision-making roles, while about 60 per cent of service and industrial employees still had no input whatsoever in policy decisions.

Within these shifting patterns of organizational decision-making, the relative exclusion of women and people of colour persists (see Baldoz, Koeber, & Kraft, 2001). Further analysis of the WALL Survey data confirms that white males enjoy much greater access to sole-responsibility decision-making roles, and non-white women have the least (Livingstone & Scholtz, 2006; Livingstone & Pollock, 2005).

In summary, the data on changing employment conditions suggest that job security may have lessened because of extensive organizational restructuring and contingent work conditions. Industrial and service workers perceive some increase in the thought and attention required to perform job tasks and the discretion allowed in their jobs. There has been some increase in participation in organizational decision-making for those in all employee classes. As Livingstone and Scholtz (2006: 77) note, "Workers appear to be becoming more involved in more temporary jobs." With these contextual trends in mind, the evidence on changes in job requirements and workers' capabilities can be assessed.

CHANGING JOB REQUIREMENTS

In this context of extensive organizational restructuring and increasingly contingent employment, it is especially difficult to distinguish between increases in the number of job tasks and the growing complexity of given tasks. As noted above, *multiskilling*—the amalgamation of a wider variety of tasks within a given job—has become quite common. Using more skills in an expanding array of tasks does not necessarily mean using a higher level of skill. Public attitudes on this question are also likely to be influenced by the dominant rhetoric that asserts the need for "skill upgrading" for a knowledge-based economy. In any case, according to the 2004 WALL Survey, over half (55 per cent) of the employed Canadian labour force felt the level of skill required to perform their jobs had increased in the past five years; about 40 per cent thought it had stayed about the same, while only 3 per cent suggested it had decreased (Livingstone & Scholtz, 2006). In surveys over the prior generation, workers expressed very similar points of view about skill increases in their jobs, the extent of skill change, and the impact of technological change on job training requirements (Livingstone, Hart, & Davie, 1987, 1999). Beneath the ideological claims and the possible confusion between the increasing number of tasks and the increasing skill required to do them, these findings at least suggest that the process of *deskilling* predicted by Braverman (1974) has not occurred in a manner that is evident to many workers.

The simplest indicator of changes in job skill level is the time required to learn to perform the job. As reviewed in Chapter 2, prior research, based on either expert ratings of the length of specific vocational preparation (SVP) or workers' self-reports, identified a general trend toward gradual skill upgrading during the post–World War II period. In particular, Leckie's (1996) Canadian studies of census-based occupational SVP scores found gradually declining numbers of workers in the lowest-skilled jobs and comparable increases in the highest-skilled jobs. The result was net skill increases of around 10 per cent over the 1971–91 period.

Graph 4.8 summarizes the findings of the 1983 CCS Survey and the 2004 WALL Survey in terms of self-reported training time required to perform jobs. As in Leckie's study, fewer jobs took less than a month to master and more jobs took more than a year. Jobs requiring only a few days or less of training dropped from 25 per cent

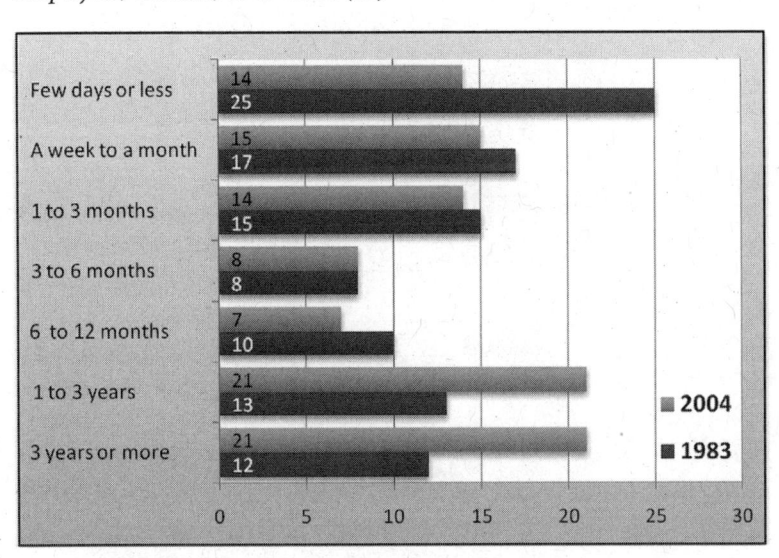

Graph 4.8 *Self-reported On-the-Job Training Time Required to Perform Job, All Employees, Canada, 1983–2004 (%)*

Category	2004	1983
Few days or less	14	25
A week to a month	15	17
1 to 3 months	14	15
3 to 6 months	8	8
6 to 12 months	7	10
1 to 3 years	21	13
3 years or more	21	12

Sources: CCS Survey, 1983 (N=1717); WALL Survey, 2004 (N=4587)

to around 15 per cent, while jobs needing more than one year of training increased from 25 per cent to about 40 per cent. Thus, about a third of the labour force needed longer training time in 2004 than in 1983.

Both expert SVP estimates and workers' self-reports of training time indicate that training time has generally increased over the 1983–2004 period. However, the two measures are not fully comparable. SVP scores for the Canadian labour force in the early 1980s (Leckie, 1996) substantially underestimated the number of jobs needing less than a month's training (15 per cent), compared to CCS self-reports (42 per cent). SVP scores also overestimated the number of jobs needing more than six months training (51 per cent versus 35 per cent). However, *both* the 1971 expert SVP scores and the 2004 self-reports suggest that about half of the labour force needs less than six months to learn how to do their jobs adequately.

Given the previously noted limitations of expert rating schemes, most recent studies rely on self-reports to estimate job requirements. Graph 4.9 summarizes the relationship between self-reported estimates, in 1983 and 2004, of the formal education required to get a job and the training time required to learn the job after being hired. The relationship between these measures may diminish somewhat between 1983 (Spearman r=.349, p>.001) and 2004 (Spearman r=.266, p>.001).[4] In both years, a small majority of jobs requiring more than a year of on-the-job training time also required a post-secondary credential. The main change was that most jobs

Graph 4.9 *Training Time by Credentials Required for Jobs, All Employees, Canada, 1983–2004 (%)*

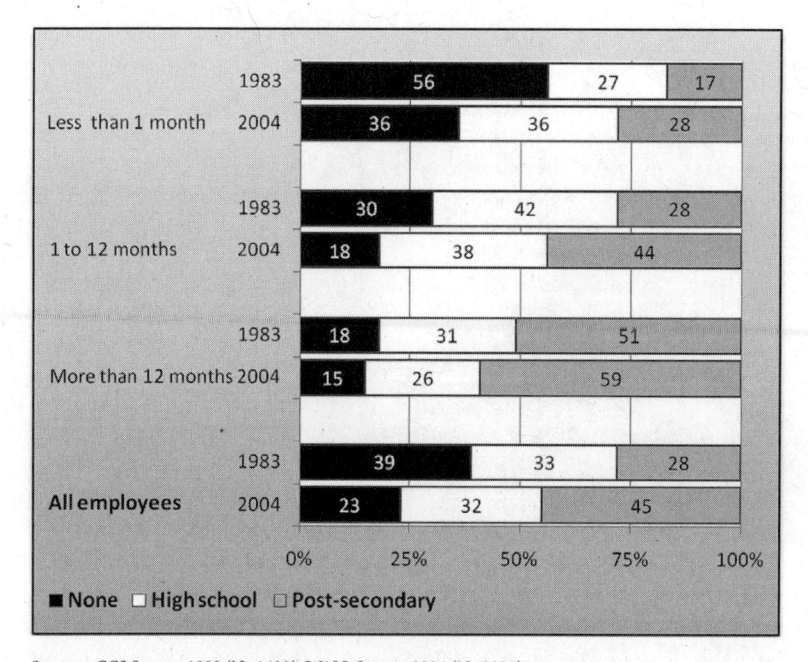

		None	High school	Post-secondary
Less than 1 month	1983	56	27	17
Less than 1 month	2004	36	36	28
1 to 12 months	1983	30	42	28
1 to 12 months	2004	18	38	44
More than 12 months	1983	18	31	51
More than 12 months	2004	15	26	59
All employees	1983	39	33	28
All employees	2004	23	32	45

Sources: CCS Survey, 1983 (N=1439); WALL Survey, 2004 (N=3221)

Graph 4.10 *Educational Entry Credential Requirements for Jobs, All Employees, Canada, 1983–2004 (%)*

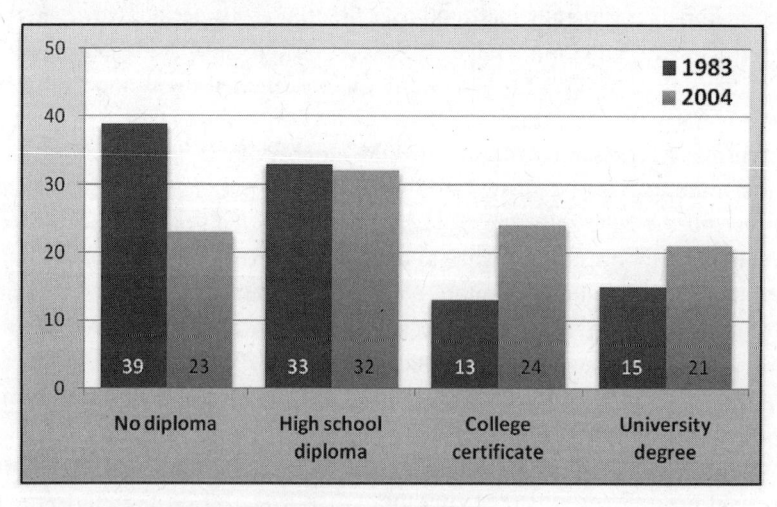

	No diploma	High school diploma	College certificate	University degree
1983	39	33	13	15
2004	23	32	24	21

Sources: CCS Survey, 1983 (N=1484); WALL Survey, 2004 (N=4271)

requiring less than a month of training in 1983 did not require [...] whereas the majority of such jobs in 2004 required a high scho[ol] credential for entry. This shift suggests a certain amount of c[...] relation to capability to do the job.

As Graph 4.9 suggests, a substantial number of jobs requir[e] credentials for entry have little on-the-job training, and other jo[bs with] little formal education have lengthy apprenticeships. Since the primary purpose of this analysis is to compare workers' capabilities with job requirements, initial estimates of their correspondence will rely on formal education attained and formal education required. Self-reported educational levels for job entry and job performance are used as *first approximations* of actual job requirements, and are then compared with workers' actual educational attainments.

In the 1983 CCS and 2004 WALL surveys, a comparison of the self-reported educational entry requirements for jobs indicates an increasing reliance on advanced formal educational credentials. In 1983 about 40 per cent of all wage and salary jobs in Canada had no credential requirement for entry (Graph 4.10). By 2004 this proportion had dropped to less than a quarter. At the same time, the percentage of jobs requiring a post-secondary credential grew from 28 per cent to 45 per cent, an increase of 60 per cent. When these proportions are compared with earlier research on entry credential requirements in North America (e.g., Collins, 1979), it is clear that the job entry requirement of a post-secondary educational credential has continued to increase.

Most of the increase in post-secondary education requirements during this period appears to be in service and industrial workers' jobs. The proportion of such jobs requiring at least a college diploma for entry has doubled since the early 1980s, to a fifth of all industrial worker jobs and a third of all service worker jobs by 2004 (Graph 4.11). On the other hand, while the majority of managerial and professional jobs require post-secondary credentials—and their numbers have grown substantially during this period—the proportion of these jobs requiring post-secondary credentials may have declined, which suggests that much of this growth may have been in lower level, less specialized professional-managerial jobs.

Credential requirements may sometimes be inflated beyond performance requirements in order to control access to desirable jobs (e.g., Collins, 1979). Although this study explores the differences between educational credentials required to *obtain* jobs and the educational requirements needed to actually *perform* jobs, empirical survey research on the distinctions between the two, using self-reports, has had difficulty detecting the differences. This may be in part because of the defensiveness of employers and the rationalizations of credentialled job holders. Both the 1998 NALL and 2004 WALL surveys asked respondents to distinguish the entry requirements from the performance requirements of their jobs.[5] The results for different employee classes

Graph 4.11 Post-secondary Job Entry Requirements, by Employee Class, Canada, 1983–2004 (%)

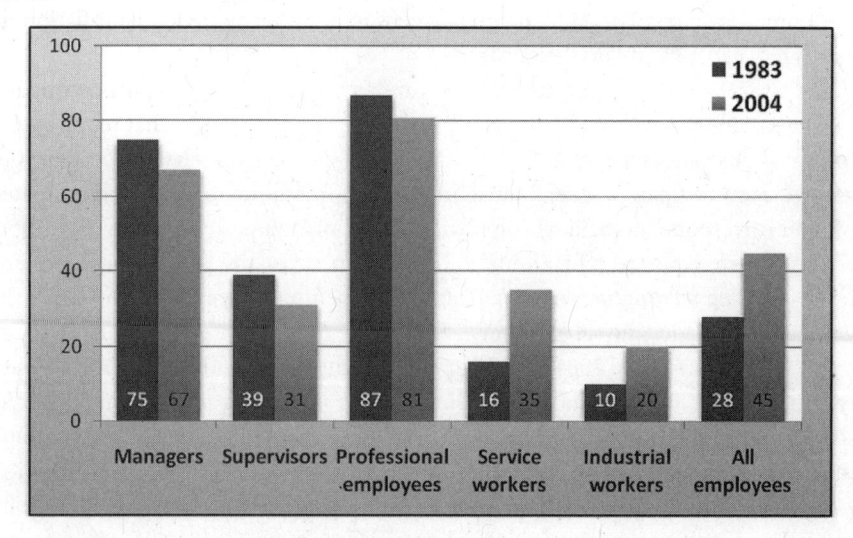

Employee Class	1983	2004
Managers	75	67
Supervisors	39	31
Professional employees	87	81
Service workers	16	35
Industrial workers	10	20
All employees	28	45

Sources: CCS Survey, 1983 (N=1462); WALL Survey, 2004 (N=3877)

are as shown in Graph 4.12. Most employees seem to make very little distinction between entry requirements and performance requirements in terms of the formal education needed. Furthermore, both entry and performance requirements appear to be continuing to increase for industrial and service workers, while remaining fairly stable in recent years for professional and managerial employees.

In sum, estimates using both expert ratings and workers' self-reports indicate significant increases over the past generation in training time and in formal education required to enter and to perform jobs. The question is, what changes have there been in workers' capabilities as indicated by their formal educational attainments and other learning practices?

WORKERS' INTENTIONAL LEARNING PRACTICES

As noted in Chapter 1, four overlapping forms of adult learning can be distinguished: formal schooling, further education, informal education or training, and non-taught informal learning. A central objective of the 1998 NALL and 2004 WALL surveys was to estimate the array of adult intentional learning activities and offer a somewhat more complete picture of Canadian adults' learning than prior surveys (e.g., Statistics Canada, 2001a), which had focused exclusively on formal schooling and further education.[6]

Graph 4.12 *Comparison of Job Entry and Performance Requirements, Employee Class, Canada, 1998–2004 (%)*

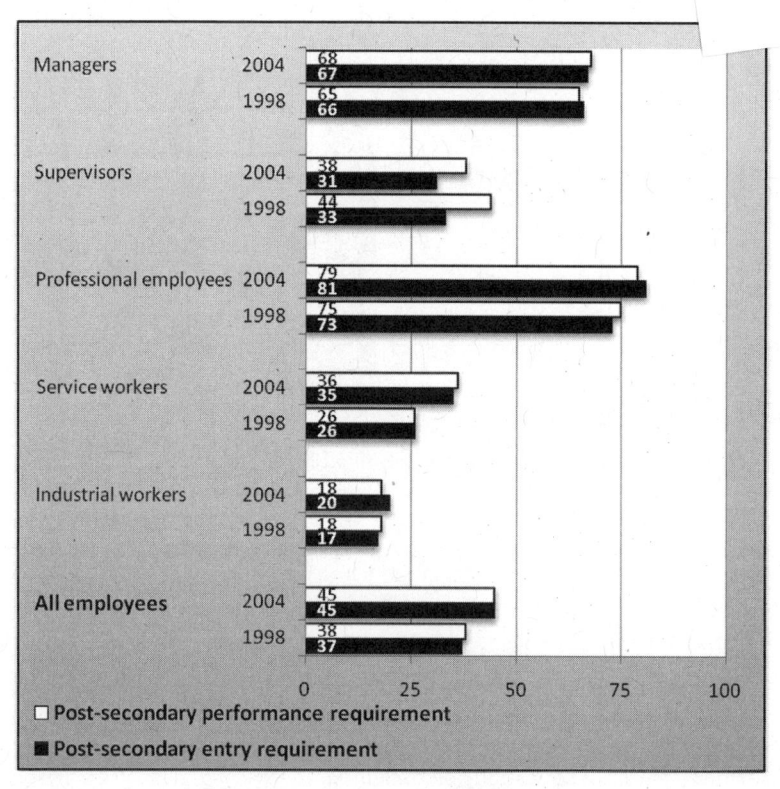

Employee class	Year	Post-secondary performance requirement	Post-secondary entry requirement
Managers	2004	68	67
	1998	65	66
Supervisors	2004	38	31
	1998	44	33
Professional employees	2004	79	81
	1998	75	73
Service workers	2004	36	35
	1998	26	26
Industrial workers	2004	18	20
	1998	18	17
All employees	2004	45	45
	1998	38	37

Sources: NALL Survey, 1998 (N=903); WALL Survey, 2004 (N=4038).

Formal Schooling

Recent comparative surveys confirm that Canada is one of the most highly schooled societies in the world (Statistics Canada & Council of Ministers of Education, 2006: 81–2). A few countries, including the United States, Japan, Sweden, and Finland, have somewhat higher levels of university degree completion. However, Canada has the highest levels of both community college completion and total post-secondary completion among the population aged 25 to 64. About 43 per cent of Canadian adults had post-secondary credentials in 2003, split quite evenly between university degrees and community college diplomas. From small minorities in the 1960s, a growing majority of employed Canadians are now completing post-secondary schooling. The increase in post-secondary completion among the employed labour force since the early 1980s is presented in Graph 4.13. The percentage of the Canadian

Graph 4.13 *Post-secondary School Completion and Participation in Further Education,* Employed Labour Force, Canada, 1983–2004 (%)*

Year	Post-secondary completion	Further education
1983	22	24
1998	49	49
2004	56	55

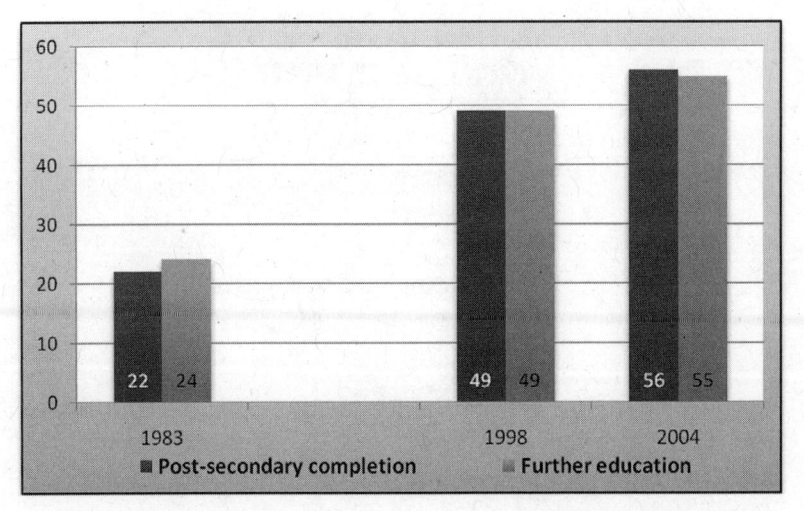

Sources: CCS Survey, 1983 (N=1464); NALL Survey, 1998 (N=769); WALL Survey, 2004 (N=4218)
* Further education in 1983, estimated for employed labour force from the general adult population figure of 20 per cent in Devereaux (1985)

employed labour force completing a post-secondary credential increased from less than a quarter to over a half during this period, a gain of 150 per cent. This very rapid expansion of post-secondary formal education provides an important context for our further analysis of education-job matching.

Further Education

Since the 1960s participation in further education has expanded rapidly in Canada. Less than 5 per cent of adults took a course in 1961, but this increased to 20 per cent in 1981. Other roughly comparable surveys have recorded such continuing increases for the general adult population, from about 36 per cent in 1994 to 49 per cent in 2003 (Statistics Canada & OECD, 2005). Course participation among the employed labour force has been even higher, more than doubling between 1983 and 2004 from about a quarter to a majority of workers (Graph 4.13). Statistics Canada's most recent Adult Education and Training Survey (AETS), conducted in 2003, was limited to participation in job-training courses and programs. The AETS showed that the incidence of such courses for the non-student working age population had increased from 29 per cent to 35 per cent between 1997 and 2003 (Peters, 2004). The available evidence suggests that Canadians' participation in further education has grown over the past two generations more than tenfold. Graph 4.13 suggests that increasing participation in further education since the 1980s has closely paralleled increases in

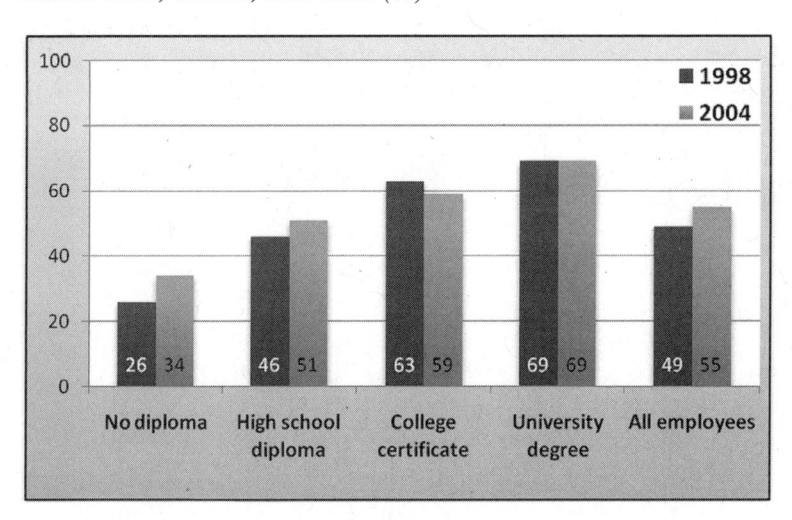

Graph 4.14 *Level of Schooling by Participation in Further Education, Employed Labour Force, Canada, 1998–2004 (%)*

Level	1998	2004
No diploma	26	34
High school diploma	46	51
College certificate	63	59
University degree	69	69
All employees	49	55

Sources: NALL Survey, 1998 (N=633); WALL Survey, 2004 (N=4241)

post-secondary education among the entire employed labour force. However, participation in Canada remains lower than that of Nordic countries, which have more fully developed institutional provisions for further education (Statistics Canada, 2001b; Desjardins, Rubenson, & Milana, 2006).

The most consistent research finding on adult learning has been the strong relationship between formal schooling and participation in further education. These two forms of education continue to be mutually reinforcing (Graph 4.13). However, the participation gap in further education by level of schooling may be narrowing. As Graph 4.14 illustrates, the strength of the association between schooling and further education seems to have weakened somewhat (Spearman $r=.338$, $p>.001$ in 1998; $r=.218$, $p>.001$ in 2004). The huge gains in post-secondary completion have not only led to more post-secondary graduates participating in further education but have also encouraged more of those with lesser credentials to participate in further education to "keep up." Further education, however, still tends to reproduce the prior differences in educational attainment; in 2004 university graduates were about twice as likely to participate as high school dropouts. The Canadian adult education system remains constrained by accessibility barriers, such as inconvenient times and places, as well as the high cost of courses, especially for those with limited formal education (Livingstone, Raykov, & Stowe, 2002; Myers & de Broucker, 2006).

According to recent literacy surveys, over a third of Canadian adults have "low literacy" skills in relation to the imputed demands of a knowledge-based economy (Statistics Canada & OECD, 2005). However, both the NALL and WALL surveys have found that less than a quarter of adults rate their reading skills as only moderate or poor. More significantly, the vast majority of these people rate themselves "at least adequately" qualified for available jobs. Moreover, early school leavers and those with low literacy levels continue to participate highly in further education courses.

Intentional Informal Learning

The 1998 NALL Survey was informed by the research on self-directed informal learning led by Allen Tough (1971) and drew heavily on the interview schedules developed by Tough and his colleagues and used by Penland (1977) in a US national survey. The 1998 NALL Survey was distinctive in probing informal learning related to different forms of work (i.e., paid employment, housework, community volunteer work), as well as general interest–based informal learning.[7] Respondents were asked if they had learned informally over the past year about several topics related to their type of work or general interest. The general interest topics closely paralleled those used by Tough, with the notable addition of computer learning. The work-related learning topics were generated through a review of prior case studies of paid and unpaid work. The 2004 WALL Survey repeated the same basic set of questions. The comparative findings are summarized here for employment-based informal learning. The reader is reminded that the survey addresses intentional informal education and self-directed informal learning; it does not address unintentional and tacit informal learning.

Most job training is done through *informal education*, which includes both learning by experience and mentoring by more experienced co-workers. Relatively little takes place through formal courses (Betcherman, McMullen, & Davidman, 1998; Center for Workforce Development, 1998). The NALL and WALL surveys of employed respondents' views on the most important source of their specific job knowledge appear in Graph 4.15. The results for both 1998 and 2004 confirm that workers regard their informal learning as far more likely than employer-sponsored training programs to be *the* most important source of knowledge to do their jobs. While over 40 per cent of workers most value their own independent efforts, over a quarter recognize informal education by co-workers as their major source of specific job knowledge. Others see co-worker mentoring as the most important, in combination with their own independent learning efforts. Only about 15 per cent regard employer-sponsored training programs as most important. There is now a burgeoning research literature on informal workplace learning, mostly case studies, which may provide useful guides for future large-scale inquiries (e.g., Billett, 2001; Rainbird, Fuller, & Munro, 2004).

Both the 2003 AETS and the 2004 WALL surveys asked employed workers about the frequency of their informal education in terms of mentoring. Both surveys

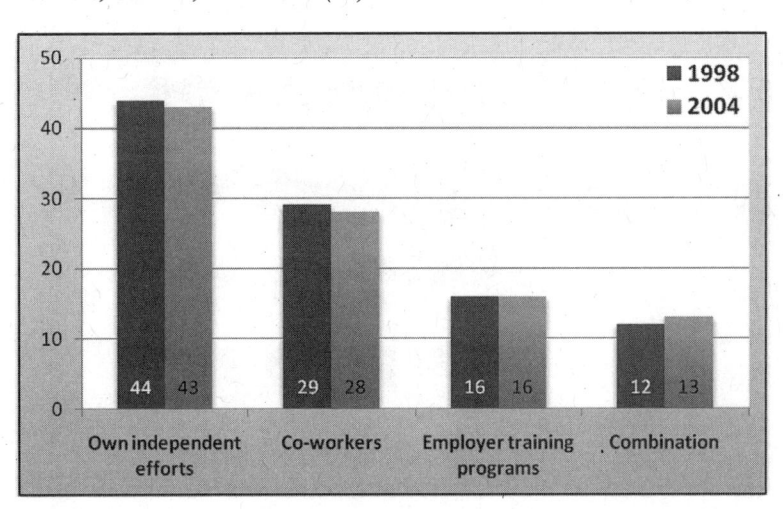

Graph 4.15 *Most Important Source of Job-Specific Knowledge, Employed Workers, Canada, 1998–2004 (%)*

Source	1998	2004
Own independent efforts	44	43
Co-workers	29	28
Employer training programs	16	16
Combination	12	13

Sources: NALL Survey, 1998 (N=864); WALL Survey, 2004 (N=5555)

showed that around a third of all workers had sought advice within the past month from other knowledgeable colleagues to develop their job skills: 32 per cent in AETS and 39 per cent in WALL, using the identical question.[8] These results at least hint at the general importance of mentoring, or informal education, to employment-related learning.

Partly informed by the 1998 NALL Survey, the 2003 AETS Survey was designed with a specific set of yes-no questions about job-related informal learning activities. These questions, however, do not distinguish informal education from self-directed informal learning. The overall finding was that about 80 per cent of all employed workers had engaged in these job-related informal learning activities in the past month (Peters, 2004: 16, 32). The NALL and WALL surveys, using yes-no items and referring to a wider range of learning topics, showed that over 85 per cent of workers had engaged in such informal learning in the past year. The employment-related informal learning topics used in the NALL and WALL surveys are summarized in Graph 4.16.[9] The frequencies of learning the topics listed were very similar in 1998 and 2004. Over half of all workers indicated specific informal learning about new general knowledge, new job tasks, computers, general problem solving, and health and safety. These estimates are admittedly crude. The crucial point is that a very large majority of workers are actively engaged in intentional informal learning related to their paid work.

Graph 4.16 *Topics of Job-Related Informal Learning, Employed Labour Force Participating in Informal Learning, Canada, 1998–2004 (%)*

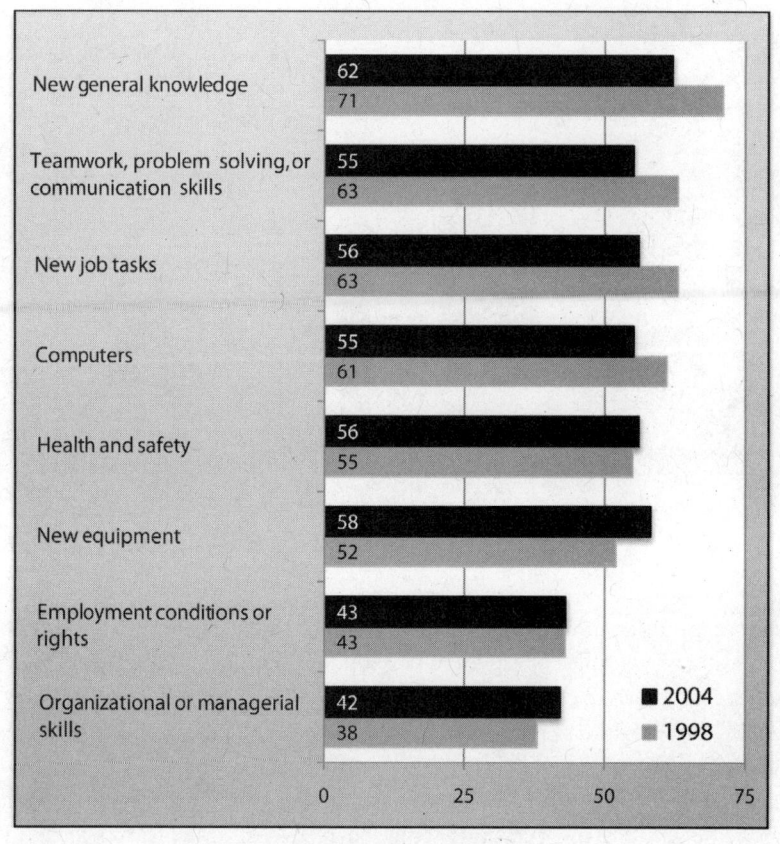

Topic	2004	1998
New general knowledge	62	71
Teamwork, problem solving, or communication skills	55	63
New job tasks	56	63
Computers	55	61
Health and safety	56	55
New equipment	58	52
Employment conditions or rights	43	43
Organizational or managerial skills	42	38

Sources: NALL Survey, 1998 (N=940); WALL Survey, 2004 (N=5428)

Employee Class and Learning Practices

The relations between class and the incidence of different forms of intentional learning are summarized in Graph 4.17 for non-managerial employee classes, and provided in more detail for *all* economic classes in Appendix 2. Large employers, professional employees, and managers clearly have the highest levels of schooling; around three-quarters completed post-secondary education (and a third or more obtained a university degree). At the other extreme, a third of industrial workers have post-secondary credentials (and around 5 per cent has a university degree). Further education participation rates follow somewhat similar patterns, but the extremes are much less: two-thirds of large employers, professional employees, and managers participate annually, compared with around 40 per cent of industrial

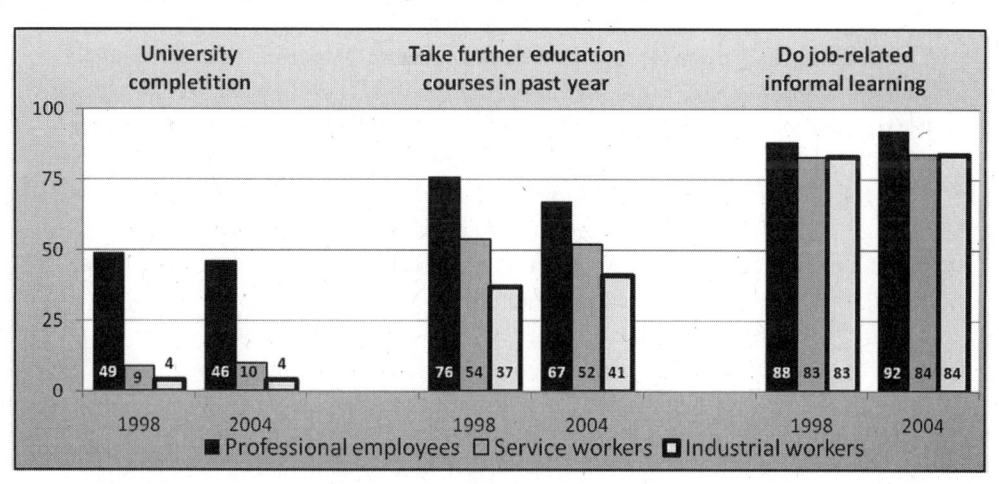

Graph 4.17 *Employee Class by University Completion, Further Education, and Job-Related Informal Learning, Canada, 1998–2004 (%)*

	University completition		Take further education courses in past year		Do job-related informal learning	
	1998	2004	1998	2004	1998	2004
Professional employees	49	46	76	67	88	92
Service workers	9	10	54	52	83	84
Industrial workers	4	4	37	41	83	84

Sources: NALL Survey, 1998 (N=948); WALL Survey, 2004 (N=5436)

workers. It should be noted that employer support for the further education of managerial and professional employees has been consistently much greater than similar support for service and industrial workers (Betcherman, Leckie, & McMullen, 1998; Livingstone & Scholtz, 2006). Patterns of participation in general job-related informal learning are *much less* differentiated. Over 80 per cent of those in all economic classes indicate that they are engaged in intentional job-related informal learning.

According to the recent AETS, the most highly educated workers are more likely than those with the least formal schooling to participate in a few designated job-related informal learning activities over a period of a few weeks (Peters, 2004: 17, 44). However, as Graph 4.17 indicates, differences in participation rates for job-related informal learning in a wider array of informal learning activities over the course of a year are quite small between employee classes with different educational attainment levels. There is also no suggestion in the 1998 NALL and the 2004 WALL data that less formally educated workers are devoting less time to job-related intentional informal learning. Further analysis of these surveys finds that unionized industrial and service workers with relatively low levels of formal education have quite high levels of participation in some types of further education, as well as in some specific aspects of informal learning such as health and safety issues (Livingstone & Raykov, 2008).

In both the 1997 and 2003 AETS analyses, estimates of time devoted to further education courses by participating Canadian workers averaged 150 hours per year, or less than three hours per week (Peters, 2004: 12). Time spent in intentional informal learning activity is much harder to estimate, given the more seamless, less visible character of informal learning. However, the average time estimate for participation in job-related informal learning in 1998 and 2004 was just over five hours per week. The adult participation rate for courses was around 35 per cent for job-related courses, while the NALL and WALL participation rate for job-related informal learning was around 85 per cent. The overall incidence ratio of job-related intentional informal learning to course-based further education was around five to one. The analogy of an iceberg with just its tip showing (Tough, 1978) is quite apt here.

A longitudinal study of a continuously employed sub-sample from the 1998 NALL Survey found that those who did not participate in adult education courses during the 1998–2004 period tended to reduce their participation in job-related informal learning somewhat (Livingstone & Stowe, 2007). However, the great majority of early school leavers stayed actively engaged in intentional informal learning and devoted about the same amount of time to it as those who are more highly schooled. As advanced market economies become increasingly information-centred, lifelong learning in all of its aspects is frequently heralded as very important. The NALL and WALL surveys confirm that a very large part of Canadian workers' learning is done informally and suggest that most of those in all economic classes, regardless of their formal schooling, should be recognized as continuing, actively engaged, informal learners. It is also relevant to note here that the WALL Survey asked all respondents to assess the usefulness of not only further education courses but also informal job-related learning for improving their job performance. Among the 35 per cent who took courses, about half estimated that *both* their further education and their informal learning were very useful. Among the majority who did not take a course, half felt that their informal learning was very useful for improving job performance. The declared importance of informal learning should be kept in mind when considering the following case studies.

EDUCATION-JOB MATCH

The widespread assumption that skill shortages and educational and literacy deficits must be overcome for advanced market economies to be successful in this era of global competition and rapid technological change is largely unexamined. The evidence reviewed in Chapter 2 tends to contradict this assumption. Evidence from the 1983 CCS, 1998 NALL, and 2004 WALL surveys permits fuller assessment of trends in the correspondence or match between the knowledge that workers bring to and the knowledge they need for their jobs, in terms of workers' formal educational attainments and the formal education required for jobs. The extent to which informal learning develops the abilities used to perform a job is examined in Chapter 6 onward.

These survey data provide national-level estimates of the extent of the match for the labour force in general and for different employee classes. The analysis begins by assessing the presumed unmet need for enhanced computer skills. Next, profiles of the general relevance, or closeness, of formal education to job requirements are provided. Then the match between levels of formal educational attainment and job requirement is examined in terms of (1) the match between credentials attained and credentials required for job entry in 1983 and 2004, (2) the match between credentials attained and job performance requirements, and (3) the workers' subjective sense of the match between their formal qualifications and the requirements of their jobs. Finally, the correspondence of workers' general job knowledge and the knowledge required to do their jobs is estimated.

Computer Skill Match
Innovations in computer technology are widely regarded as intimately related to increasing technical skill requirements for the labour force (Autor, Levy, & Murnane, 2003; Machin, 2003). Survey evidence indicates the rapidly growing prevalence of computer use among the Canadian labour force. General Social Surveys (Statistics Canada, 1989, 1994, 2000) have found that computer use by the labour force increased rapidly from under 40 per cent in 1989 to about half in 1994 and to over three-quarters in 2000. The WALL Survey found that by 2004 over 80 per cent of the employed labour force was using a computer. The rapid introduction of computer networks into paid workplaces may be symptomatic of the general pace of workplace change. But we cannot infer from the empirical evidence to date that there has been a similarly rapid increase in workers' required skill level or presume that workers have a skill deficit in this context. In fact, half of all workers in the WALL 2004 Survey reported *higher* computer skills than they needed. Forty per cent reported a match and less than 10 per cent said that their computer-related skills were lower than they needed for their job. This pattern of underutilization of computer-related skills is particularly pronounced among the youngest workers—those born in the computer age—and also the most highly educated. The same pattern persists, however, among middle-aged workers. Even among workers over the age of 55, very few indicate their computer skills are less than required, and over a third indicate higher skills than needed. Computer literacy is increasingly needed, but workers appear to be keeping up with or ahead of these job requirements.

Relevance or Closeness of Field of Study to Job
As noted in Chapter 2, research on field of study matching has found that higher levels of formal education are more closely related to a specific field of studies. Analyses according to occupational groups have shown that those in professional/managerial jobs are twice as likely to have jobs related to their field of study as those in service or industrial jobs (Krahn & Bowlby, 1999: 35). Graph 4.18 summarizes the findings for 2004. The general pattern is quite polarized: Nearly 40 per cent of members of the labour force say their jobs are closely related to their prior formal education, and a similar number state that their jobs are not at all related to their formal education.

Graph 4.18 *Relevance of Education to Job, by Employee Class, Canada, 2004 (%)*

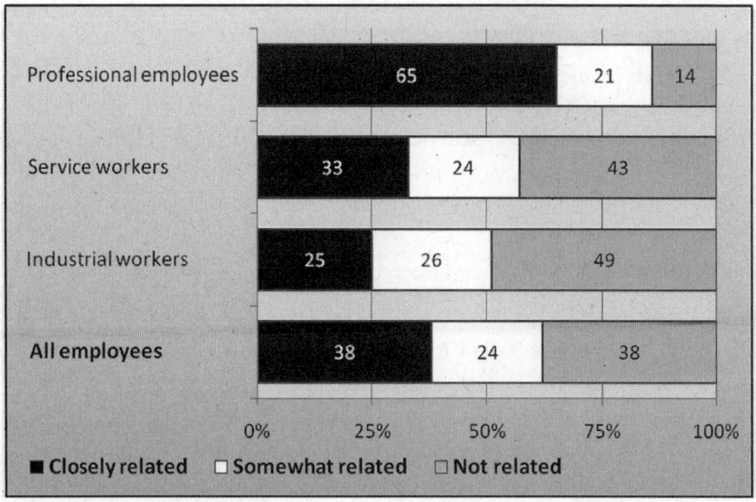

Employee Class	Closely related	Somewhat related	Not related
Professional employees	65	21	14
Service workers	33	24	43
Industrial workers	25	26	49
All employees	38	24	38

Source: WALL Survey, 2004 (N=3354)

The remaining quarter say their jobs are somewhat related to their education. The findings for employee classes are similar to prior research, with two-thirds of professional employees declaring a close relationship between their studies and their jobs, compared to one-third or less of industrial and service workers. At the other extreme, over 40 per cent of industrial and service workers feel their formal education is not at all related to their jobs; in contrast, only a small minority (14 per cent) of professional employees see their formal education as unrelated to their jobs.

Credential Match

There appears to be a growing tendency for educational attainments to exceed job entry credential requirements. As noted above, 28 per cent of employees needed a university degree or a college diploma to get their jobs in 1983. By 2004 this figure had risen to 45 per cent, an increase of 60 per cent. During the same period post-secondary credential attainment more than doubled from 22 per cent to 56 per cent, an increase of over 150 per cent. Clearly, more people completed post-secondary education during this period than needed it to get their jobs. However, it is also clear that these credentials, including a high school diploma, were increasingly required for entry to all manner of jobs. Some who entered employment prior to 1983 with lower formal education may have found that entry requirements increased, but they continued to perform their job without them. Generally, as with computer skills, workers are keeping up with or ahead of required credential levels.

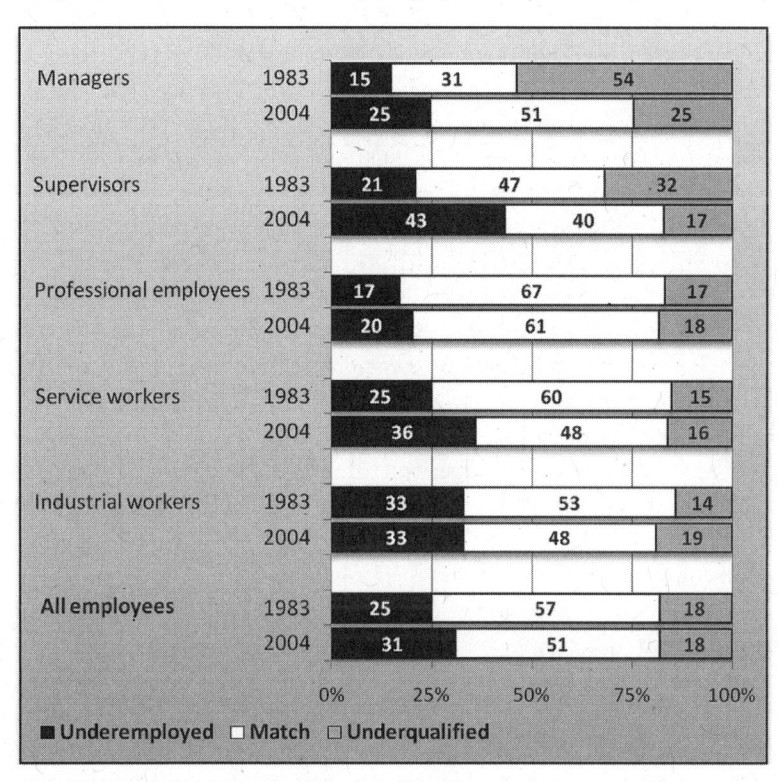

Graph 4.19 *Credential Match, by Employee Class, Canada, 1983–2004 (%)*

Employee Class	Year	Underemployed	Match	Underqualified
Managers	1983	15	31	54
	2004	25	51	25
Supervisors	1983	21	47	32
	2004	43	40	17
Professional employees	1983	17	67	17
	2004	20	61	18
Service workers	1983	25	60	15
	2004	36	48	16
Industrial workers	1983	33	53	14
	2004	33	48	19
All employees	1983	25	57	18
	2004	31	51	18

Sources: CCS Survey, 1983 (N=1461); WALL Survey, 2004 (N=3844)

Graph 4.19 summarizes the extent of education-job match with reference to *all* levels of credential attainment and requirement for all employees. The overall change from 1983 to 2004 was a small increase in credential underemployment and an equivalent decline in matching credentials and attainments of about 6 per cent. The general credential underemployment rate increased from 25 per cent to 31 per cent, while matching dropped from 57 per cent to 51 per cent.

In terms of employee classes, professional employees' credentials have tended to correspond most closely to their job requirements. They consistently exhibit the highest matching and the lowest level of underemployment. In 2004 over 60 per cent had matching required and attained credentials, and their credential underemployment was around 20 per cent. Service workers have experienced higher and increasing levels of credential underemployment, going from 25 per cent in 1983 to 36 per cent in 2004. Industrial workers have consistently high levels of credential underemployment of about one-third in both 1983 and 2004. Managers and supervisors show wide fluctuations during this period, with high levels of underqualification in 1983 and high levels of underemployment, especially for supervisors, in 2004. In light of the relatively stable credential requirements for managers and supervisors noted in Graph 4.11, such fluctuations suggest that other personal network and allegiance factors may be more pertinent than formal credentials for those in positions of formal managerial authority (compare Elliot, 2000).

Since the educational credential attainments of the labour force have increased rapidly and the credential requirements have increased more gradually, overall credential underemployment has also increased. This increasing underemployment has been experienced most by service workers (and more erratically by supervisors). In the context of credential proliferation, professional employees continue to have a closer match between the formal education requirements of their job and their educational attainment than do service workers and industrial workers. As the underemployment of those with credentials grows, non-managerial employees with the least formal education continue to experience the greatest underemployment of the credentials they do have. Taking the underemployed and the underqualified together, nearly half of all employees' educational attainments are now mismatched with the credentials required for entry to their jobs.

Performance Match

As documented in Graph 4.12, workers now tend to make little distinction between the formal education required for job entry and the formal education required to actually perform their jobs. Therefore, the education attainment/requirement measures of performance match generated by the workers' self-reports are quite similar to credential match measures. The findings for 2004 appear in Graph 4.20. Around half of the employed labour force is matched; about 30 per cent is underemployed; and less than 20 per cent is underqualified. About a third of industrial and service workers are underemployed compared to only a fifth of professional employees. All of these patterns are almost identical to those found for the credential match in Graph 4.19.

As noted in the discussion of job requirements, expert ratings have tended to underestimate the proportion of jobs with low training requirements and overestimate those with high training requirements—particularly in comparison with workers' self-reports. Conversely, it may also be the case that increases in their educational credentials have encouraged workers to inflate their own estimates of the formal education required to perform their jobs. Some sociological studies suggest that most jobs only require a very basic formal education for performance (Blackburn & Mann, 1979; Brown, Reich, & Stern, 1990). Given the continuing dispute about performance requirements, it is worthwhile to consider performance match measures based on expert ratings in addition to the workers' own reports. Graph 4.21 summarizes findings for 2004 based on expert ratings of the general educational (GED) levels required to perform jobs in difficult occupational groups in the

Graph 4.20 *Performance Match, by Employee Class, Canada, 2004 (%)*

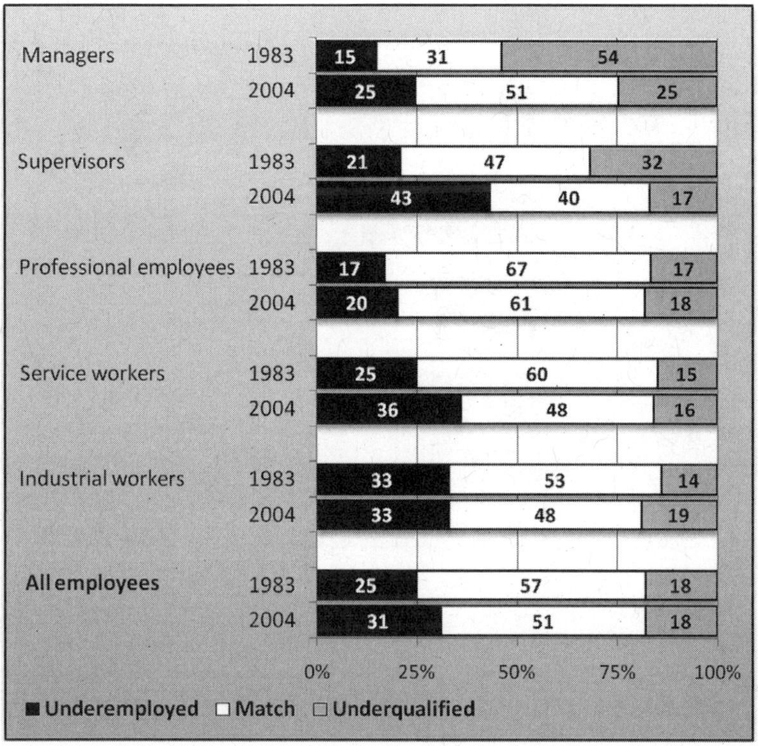

Employee Class	Year	Underemployed	Match	Underqualified
Managers	1983	15	31	54
	2004	25	51	25
Supervisors	1983	21	47	32
	2004	43	40	17
Professional employees	1983	17	67	17
	2004	20	61	18
Service workers	1983	25	60	15
	2004	36	48	16
Industrial workers	1983	33	53	14
	2004	33	48	19
All employees	1983	25	57	18
	2004	31	51	18

Source: WALL Survey, 2004 (N=3181)

Canadian labour force.[10] The finding of greater levels of underqualification in comparison to self-reports, 28 per cent versus 18 per cent, is predictable given the much lower GED estimates of the proportion of occupations that need little training time. General underemployment rates, however, are similar on both measures: 26 per cent for the expert measure versus 30 per cent for the self-report. The expert measure also generates a lower match level, 44 per cent versus 53 per cent for self-reports. The overall pattern is not much different. But the comparison suggests that expert ratings based on general educational development scores may be overestimating the extent of underqualification in job performance.

Expert GED-based performance match ratings also produce somewhat different patterns than self-reports for employee classes. Twice as many professional employees and industrial workers are estimated to be underqualified by GED score than by workers' self-reports, while lower proportions are deemed to be underemployed. In any case, GED-based measures generate similar differences to self-reports in terms of low underemployment rates for professional employees and high ones for industrial

Graph 4.21 *Education Attained/GED Score Match by Employee Class, Canada, 2004 (%)*

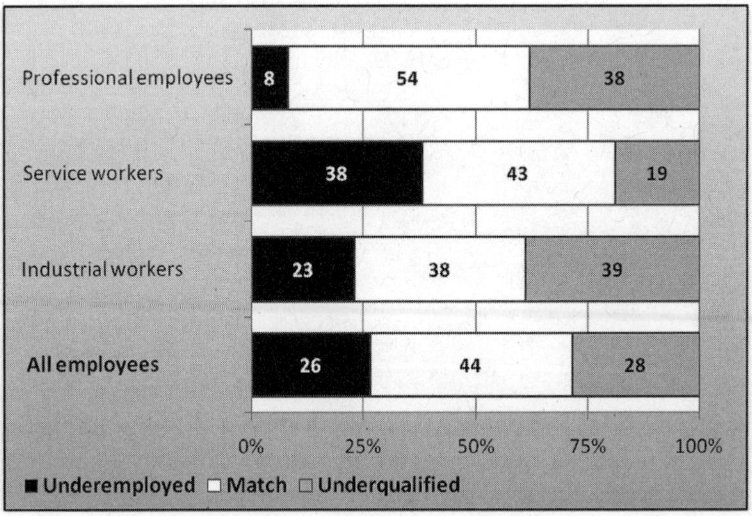

Employee Class	Underemployed	Match	Underqualified
Professional employees	8	54	38
Service workers	38	43	19
Industrial workers	23	38	39
All employees	26	44	28

Source: WALL Survey, 2004 (N=3286)

workers. GED performance match measures also generate the highest rates of underemployment among office workers, comparable to those for the self-reported credential match measures.

Subjective Match
The self-report credential and performance match measures are derived from answers to separate survey questions about attainments and requirements. When workers are asked directly to assess the match between their qualifications and those required for their jobs, the patterns are somewhat different. The findings for the 2004 WALL Survey are outlined in Graph 4.2. About two-thirds of respondents say that their qualifications match the qualifications required by their jobs. Over a quarter say that they are underemployed in terms of their qualifications, while very few (around 5 per cent) feel underqualified. Similar patterns are found for all employee classes. The only notable difference is the familiar tendency for industrial and service workers to perceive higher levels of underemployment than professional employees. The greater subjective correspondence of qualifications and job requirements, in comparison to measures based on formal education, is consistent with the discussion in Chapter 6 of learning by experience. However, this subjective measure finds levels of underemployment and employee class differences in underemployment that are similar to measures based on formal education.

Graph 4.22 *Employee Class, by Subjective Qualification-Re... Canada, 2004 (%)*

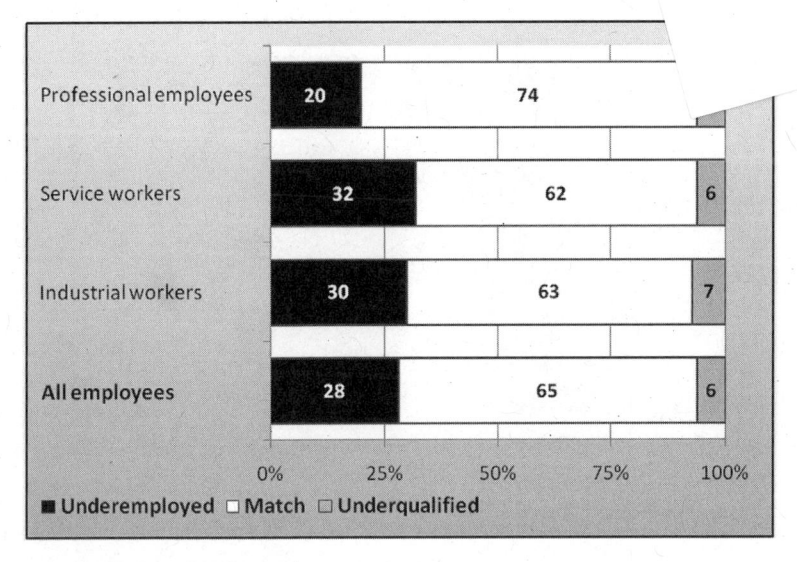

Employee Class	Underemployed	Match	Underqualified
Professional employees	20	74	
Service workers	32	62	6
Industrial workers	30	63	7
All employees	28	65	6

■ Underemployed ☐ Match ☐ Underqualified

Source: WALL Survey, 2004 (N=3309)

Knowledge Match

Prior surveys have not asked workers to assess the more general connection between their job-related knowledge and what they need to do a job. Such a question encourages workers to think beyond specific qualifications and credentials to the types of knowledge and the capabilities they really need to do their jobs. This question was not asked in the 2004 WALL Survey, but it was asked in the subsequent 2004 EJRM Survey of wage and salary earners in Ontario (to be discussed further in Chapter 5). The results, which appear in Graph 4.23, are very different than those for the matching questions asked in prior surveys. Nearly three-quarters of all workers express the view that they have more job-related knowledge than they need to perform their current jobs. Most of the remaining workers say their knowledge matches their job. Hardly any say they have less knowledge than their job requires. This pattern is almost identical for all employee classes.

In summary, these survey findings on matching show a labour force keeping ahead of, or keeping up with, changing formal job requirements. The match between formal education attained and education required is weakening, as credential attainment outpaces formal job requirements and credential underemployment grows. Workers do report a closer subjective match between their qualifications and their jobs than formal education measures of matching generate. The finding that most workers have more job knowledge than required to do their jobs suggests that

Graph 4.23 Employee Class, by Actual Job Knowledge/Required Knowledge to Perform Job, Ontario, 2004 (%)

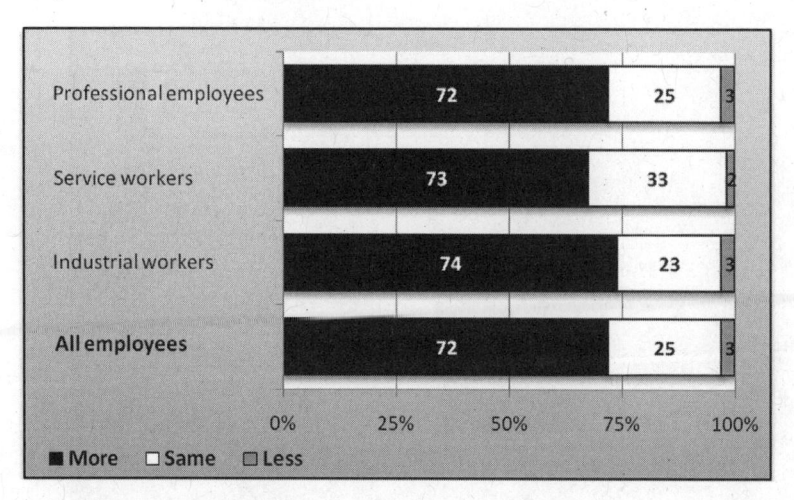

Employee Class	More	Same	Less
Professional employees	72	25	3
Service workers	73	33	2
Industrial workers	74	23	3
All employees	72	25	3

Source: EJRM Survey, 2004 (N=1290)

workers' learning from experience generates reserves of knowledge not used on particular tasks. Most workers surveyed describe a sense of the richness of their job-related knowledge—even if most of it remains in the sea of tacit learning surrounding icebergs of intentional informal learning with tips of further formal education.

JOB CONTROL BY EDUCATION-JOB MATCH

If there is a significant relationship between the exercise of control in one's job and a formal recognition of one's knowledge, it would be likely that those who can exercise more discretion in a paid workplace would have jobs that correspond more closely with their formal education. The WALL Survey data permits several tests of this connection. Graph 4.24 summarizes the findings for the relationship between the extent of discretion workers have to design their own work and the closeness between their formal education and their job. There is a weak positive relationship (Spearman r=.163, p>.001). Nearly half of those who can design their own work all the time have jobs closely related to their formal education. Conversely, over half of those who never design their own work have jobs that are not at all related to their formal education. However, this relationship works mostly at the extremes of control over job design. Nearly half of those in jobs not related to their education feel they can exercise some discretion in their jobs most of the time. Most employees do indicate some degree of design control in their jobs, and Chapter 6 will discuss the fact that employees may underestimate the extent of their discretionary decisions. More per-

Graph 4.24 *Design Own Work, by Relevance of Education to Job, All Employees, Canada, 2004 (%)*

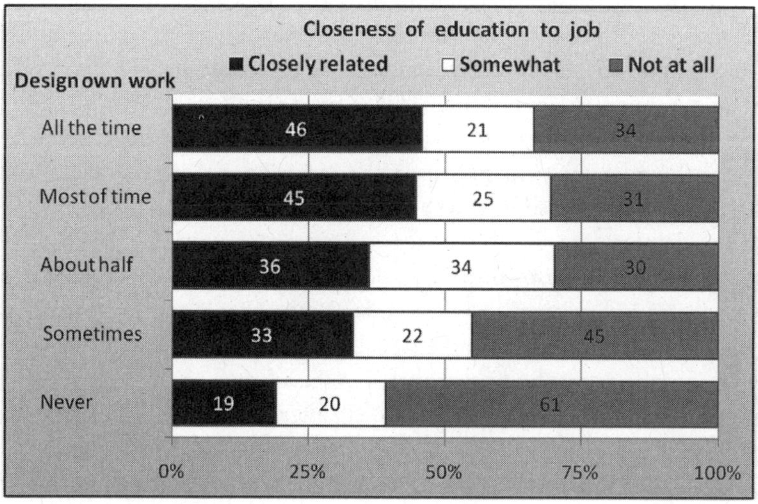

Design own work	Closeness of education to job		
	■ Closely related	□ Somewhat	■ Not at all
All the time	46	21	34
Most of time	45	25	31
About half	36	34	30
Sometimes	33	22	45
Never	19	20	61

Source: WALL Survey, 2004 (N=3333)

tinent to the survey findings, this statistical association masks an overriding relationship between employee class and matching. For example, the relationship between employee class and the closeness of formal education to one's job, as shown in Graph 4.21, is clearly stronger (Spearman r=.306, p>.001) than the association between general sense of task discretion and the closeness of education to jobs. Variations in task discretion *within* the three non-managerial employee class locations appear to be less important than the differences in discretionary control *between* professional employees and either industrial or service workers in relation to education-jobs matching. The same pattern is found in the association between participation in organizational decision-making and education-job matching, with owners having much closer matches than people in industrial and service worker class positions regardless of the extent of participation perceived by those in the latter positions. The effect of job control is an issue that needs further wide comparative class analysis beyond the scope of the EJRM data.

CONCLUDING REMARKS

Paid workplaces have witnessed substantial change over the past generation: growing participation of married women, increases in the part-time and temporary labour force, and organizational restructuring toward smaller organizations with more job rotation. The proportion of professional and managerial employees in the labour force has continued to grow. Some service and industrial workers appear to inally more involved in workplace design and organizational decision-making. In terms of both the length of training time and formal education, job requirements have increased. However, the formal educational attainment and further education participation of the labour force have grown even more rapidly. It follows that the gap between formal educational requirements for jobs and workers' educational attainments is increasing. This is most true for the growing number who can only get industrial or service worker jobs in spite of advanced formal education. Such underemployment is also the case for the growing number of recent immigrants, non-white persons, and those who are disabled, as is documented in the following chapters.

Some mismatches in terms of both underemployment and underqualification are to be expected in a dynamic labour market. Both chronic and more temporary shortages of qualified workers occur, especially in specialized areas such as skilled trades. However, the survey findings reported in this chapter are consistent with the recent survey research literature reviewed in Chapter 2, which finds formal educational attainment increasingly outpacing rising educational requirements.

There are also intimations of a deeper story in the survey findings. Informal job-related learning is much more pervasive than implied by earlier surveys, which were focused on educational attainment and further education, and most workers say they have substantially greater knowledge than their current jobs require. The EJRM Survey data will be used in the following chapter to provide more detail on estimates of education-job matching for employee classes and specific occupational groups in Ontario. The following chapters will examine learning and work relations of particular workers in more depth.

Notes

1. Women continue to hold the primary homemaking responsibilities, and this still seriously constrains their labour force participation and occupational advancement (see Armstrong & Armstrong, 1994; Livingstone & Pollock, 2005).
2. For government survey data confirming these trends, see Lapointe et al. (2006).
3. In contrast to the many heralds of a "post-industrial economy," Cohen and Zysman (1987: 27) have observed that

> The division of labour has become infinitely more elaborate and the production process far more indirect, involving increasingly specialized inputs of services as well as goods and materials located organizationally (and physically) far from the traditional scene of production, the proverbial shop floor. But the key generator of wealth for this vastly expanded and differentiated division of labour remains mastery and control of production. We are shifting not out of industry into services, but from one kind of industrial economy to another.

4. All the survey-based relationships mentioned in the book are significant, at least, at the .05 level of confidence, using a battery of measures of parametric and non-parametric correlation. For the relationships between any two variables reported in this chapter, Spearman correlations are reported in the text with indications of their levels of significance. It should be pointed out that correlation does not prove causation, both because of measurement limitations and because both variables are measured at the same moment.
5. The 1983 CCS Survey does not distinguish job entry requirements from performance requirements.
6. Unfortunately, the 1983 CCS Survey contained no questions on further education. Comparative analyses of further education must depend on government-sponsored national surveys for data prior to 1998.
7. For a fuller account of the findings of the 1998 NALL and 2004 WALL surveys with regard to informal learning, see Livingstone (2007).
8. The AETS figure is computed from the original data file. A higher figure is quoted in Peters (2004: 17) with reference *only* to those who reported participating in specific types of self-directed informal job-related learning.
9. A few topics were added to the 2004 WALL Survey items on job-related informal learning, largely for comparison to similar items in unpaid work-based learning.
10. All occupations in the WALL 2004 Survey were coded by the National Occupational Classification (NOC) scheme and assigned a general educational development (GED) score for their general occupational group. (See Statistics Canada, 2001c; HRSDC, 2006).

Chapter Five
Education and Jobs Survey Profile II: Employment Conditions, Job Requirements, Workers' Learning and Matching, by Employee Class and Specific Occupational Group, 2004

D.W. Livingstone and Milosh Raykov

In this chapter the Education-Job Requirement Matching (EJRM) Survey, which was conducted shortly after the 2004 national WALL Survey, is used to look more closely at the relations between education and jobs in Ontario. The EJRM Survey is similar to the WALL Survey but focuses on *non-managerial employees*. Consequently, both owners and employees who have formal managerial or supervisory titles and authority are excluded from further detailed study. The primary interest of the EJRM Survey and the remainder of this book is employees who are subject to the formal authority of owners and managers of paid workplaces and whose educational job requirements in particular are subject to designation by the owners and/or managers who exercise a managerial prerogative over them. Owners have the discretion to set their own educational job requirements. The job requirements of managers may include educational requirements but also involve various other criteria intended to ensure they can exercise effective authority over other workers (see Elliot, 2000). The intention of this chapter is to focus on non-managerial employees' levels of educational attainment compared with educational levels that employers require of them to enter and perform their jobs. The analysis attempts to avoid confusing an employee's technical competency with any authority that they may have been delegated by an employer. The discussion concentrates on the match between levels of education attained and required for each of the non-managerial employee classes (*professional employees, service workers,* and *industrial workers*), as well as specific representative occupational groups within these class positions.

Professional employees are hired workers who fill positions defined as needing advanced technical knowledge based on specialized formal academic education. Their jobs have features of self-regulation afforded by this specialized academic education (and they may develop professional associations and self-regulatory licensing bodies). In terms of specific occupational groups, *public school teachers* represent professional employees with well-developed academic training programs, nearly universal membership in associations, and licensing bodies that certify entry and regulate conduct. *Computer programmers* represent workers with specialized technical knowledge, typically acquired through post-secondary academic programs, but whose professional status is in a formative stage because they have not yet developed extensive membership associations or regulatory bodies.

Service workers provide a wide range of personal, financial, sales, and recording assistance to other personnel, clients, and customers in all kinds of work organizations. They are represented by *clerical workers* who record and process a diversity of information needed to ensure the continuing production of various goods and services.

Industrial workers are engaged in direct productive work to extract, manufacture, or construct material goods. They are represented by *auto workers*, who are employed in plants that either manufacture automobiles or make their component parts.

This chapter presents summary profiles for Ontario professional employees, service workers, and industrial workers, as well as for specific Ontario occupational groups of teachers, programmers, clerical workers, and auto workers. The chapter includes (1) an examination of employment conditions, with primary attention to the extent of discretion that workers have in performing their job tasks and also their involvement in organizational decision-making; (2) current estimates of job requirements in terms of training time and formal education; (3) a summary of workers' formal education and informal learning activities; (4) an assessment of the extent of matching between formal education and job requirements (on the same dimensions as in Chapter 4); and (5) an analysis of the relative effects on matching of employee class differences and other social factors—such as length of employment experience, immigration status, race, and gender, as well as task discretion and participation in decision-making and union/association membership. It should be reiterated that the findings reported here have been confirmed by comparable analyses of non-managerial employee classes in the Ontario sub-sample of the 2004 WALL Survey (N=1,291) as well as by analyses of these specific occupational groups at the national level; these results are not reported because of space limitations.

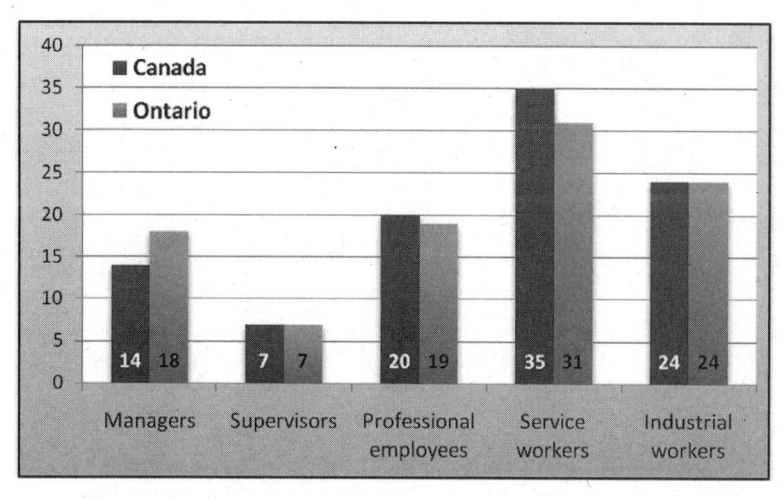

Graph 5.1 *Employee Class Distribution, Canada and Ontario, 2004 (%)*

Class	Canada	Ontario
Managers	14	18
Supervisors	7	7
Professional employees	20	19
Service workers	35	31
Industrial workers	24	24

Sources: Canada: WALL Survey, 2004 (N=4271); Ontario: EJRM Survey, 2004 (N=1641)

EMPLOYEE CLASSES

The analysis of employee classes leaves aside owner classes, including large and small employers—who make up about 5 per cent of Canada's and Ontario's employed labour force—and the self-employed, who, in turn, make up about 15 per cent. The remaining 80 per cent are wage- and salary-earning employees. Graph 5.1 summarizes the distribution of these employees in 2004. Among employee classes, a quarter or less of them are now in managerial or supervisory positions. About 20 per cent are professional employees. One-third are service workers, and a quarter are industrial workers. The latter three class positions—professional employees, service workers, and industrial workers—constitute all the non-managerial employees and are the focus of the remaining analyses in this book.

Both in geographic size and population, Ontario is Canada's largest province. Known as Canada's industrial heartland throughout most of the twentieth century, Ontario continues to be the core location for the manufacture of steel, automobiles, and other large material goods. While the Canadian economy has remained highly dependent on the export of primary products (wheat, lumber, minerals, oil), the employment profiles of Ontario and the rest of Canada are now very similar, both in terms of the economic class structure (as suggested by Graph 5.1) and sectoral distribution of employment. About two-thirds of all employment in Ontario is in service sector industries and a quarter in material-goods-producing industries, with jobs in the service sector growing and in material goods shrinking. Large-scale enterprises in extraction and manufacturing continue to shed jobs, while small-scale service industries grow. The downsizing and closure of large manufacturing plants has been most evident in Ontario in recent years (e.g., High, 2003). However, according to the workers' reports in the national WALL and EJRM surveys, the extent of change, in terms of downsizing, increased use of overtime and part-time workers, and job rotation has been similar to the rest of Canada.

SPECIFIC OCCUPATIONAL GROUPS

The rationale for the selection of specific occupational groups for this study was to ensure the inclusion of professional employees that have jobs with high formal education requirements, as well as other employees that represent service workers and industrial workers who have jobs that are recognized as having low formal education requirements.

Teaching was selected to represent a profession that requires a university degree for entry. In addition to nearly universal membership in professional associations, teachers in Ontario have a regulatory body (Ontario College of Teachers). Public school teachers are almost exclusively hired employees, as distinct from other fully self-regulating professions, such as doctors and lawyers, which contain large numbers of owners and managers.[1]

Computer programmers were chosen as an occupational group because the knowledge required to design and develop computer software is widely recognized as highly specialized, and technical expertise is now provided in academic settings. They might be considered as the prototypical emerging profession of the current era. Programmer jobs now typically require post-secondary formal education. The field is still too new and fluid for associations of computer programmers to have become common or for regulatory bodies to have been established.

Clerical workers are the most ubiquitous service workers; they are needed in all organizations to record and process all manner of information. Their work tends to be regarded as supplementary and subordinate to whatever goods or services the organization produces. Their work generally calls for a lower level of formal education than that required by managerial and professional jobs. The supplementary nature of their work tends to mean that their attributed skill requirements are diminished more than in the case for other service workers who have a closer, more visible association with the direct provision of a distinct and valued product, such as in financial services or auto sales.

Auto workers were selected as classic industrial workers who are typically employed in large manufacturing plants and whose jobs generally require physical dexterity and low formal academic education for entry.

In addition, disabled employees are present in all occupational groups, but there has been little research on their working conditions, learning practices, and education-job match. Since the number of disabled workers in all occupational groups is quite

Graph 5.2 Job Demands "Great Deal of Thought and Attention," by Employee Class and Specific Occupational Group, Non-managerial Employees, Ontario, 2004 (%)

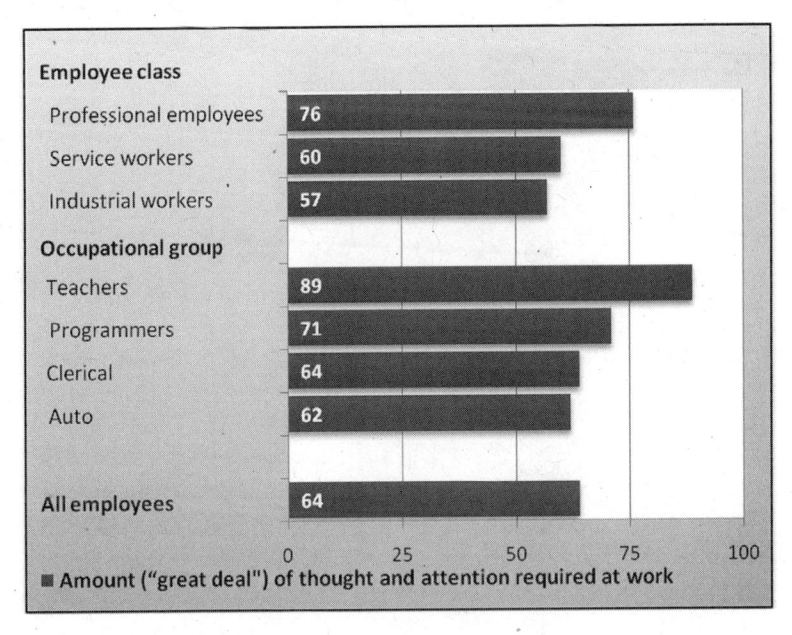

Employee class	%
Professional employees	76
Service workers	60
Industrial workers	57
Occupational group	
Teachers	89
Programmers	71
Clerical	64
Auto	62
All employees	64

■ Amount ("great deal") of thought and attention required at work

Source: WALL Survey, 2004 (N=1240)

small, the relevant survey findings are presented in Chapter 11, which reports on the case studies of disabled workers in the four specific occupational groups.

EMPLOYMENT CONDITIONS: NON-MANAGERIAL EMPLOYEES' TASK DISCRETION AND INVOLVEMENT IN POLICY DECISIONS

The national-level comparisons of 1983 and 2004 presented in Chapter 4 suggest that service and industrial workers are devoting increasing amounts of thought and attention to their jobs and have experienced some increase in the amount of discretion they have to design their own work. On the other hand, professional employees have seen little change in the somewhat higher levels of discretion that their jobs already required. Comparable findings for Ontario non-managerial employee classes and specific occupational groups in 2004 are presented in Graphs 5.2 and 5.3.[2]

As Graph 5.2 summarizes, the majority in all three employee classes and in all four specific occupational groups now believe they have to devote a great deal of thought and attention to their jobs. Professional employees in general, and teachers in particular, are still somewhat more likely to feel that their jobs require a high level of thought

Graph 5.3 Design Work "All or Most of the Time," by Employment Class and Specific Occupational Group, Non-managerial Employees, Ontario, 2004 (%)

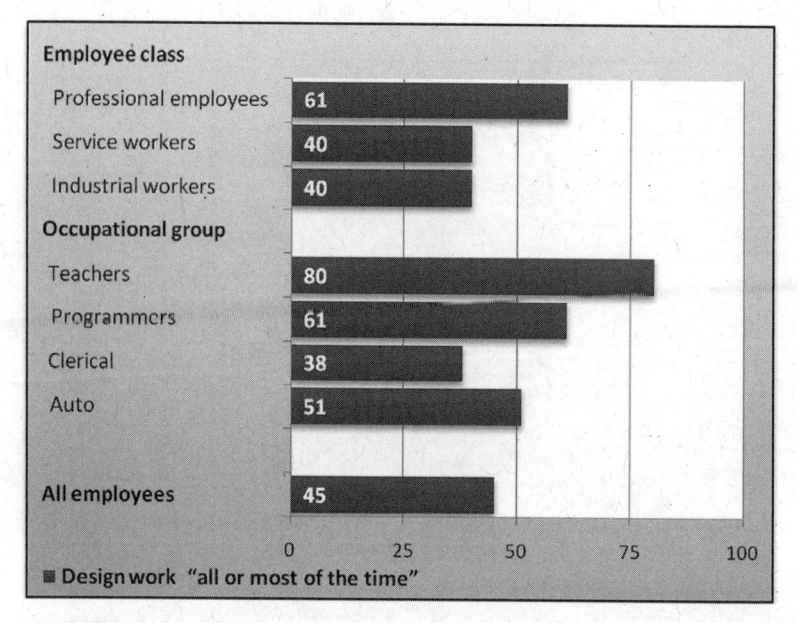

Category	%
Employee class	
Professional employees	61
Service workers	40
Industrial workers	40
Occupational group	
Teachers	80
Programmers	61
Clerical	38
Auto	51
All employees	45

■ Design work "all or most of the time"

Source: WALL Survey, 2004 (N=1232)

and attention. In general, the majority of service and industrial workers—clerical workers and auto workers in particular—now also hold this view; this is in contrast to the minority of service and industrial workers who held this view a generation earlier.

Graph 5.3 illustrates the perspectives of Ontario non-managerial employees on the amount of discretion they have to design their own work. The Ontario findings are similar to the Canada-wide findings in that the majority of professional employees (61 per cent) say they can design their work most of the time, compared to a minority (40 per cent) of service and industrial workers. Specific occupational-group patterns follow the general differences between employee classes: A large majority of teachers (80 per cent) say they can design their work most of the time, followed by a smaller majority of computer programmers. Auto workers are more likely (51 per cent) to feel they have on-the-job task discretion than are clerical workers (38 per cent).

The Ontario EJRM Survey also asked about the amount of creativity involved in performing job tasks. There are sharper differences between professional employees and other workers in terms of the amount of creativity they feel they can exercise in their jobs (Graph 5.4). Nearly half of all professional employees say they have a great deal of creativity in their jobs, compared with less than 20 per cent of either service or industrial workers.

Graph 5.4 *Job Creativity, by Employee Class and Specific Occupational Group, Non-managerial Employees, Ontario, 2004 (%)*

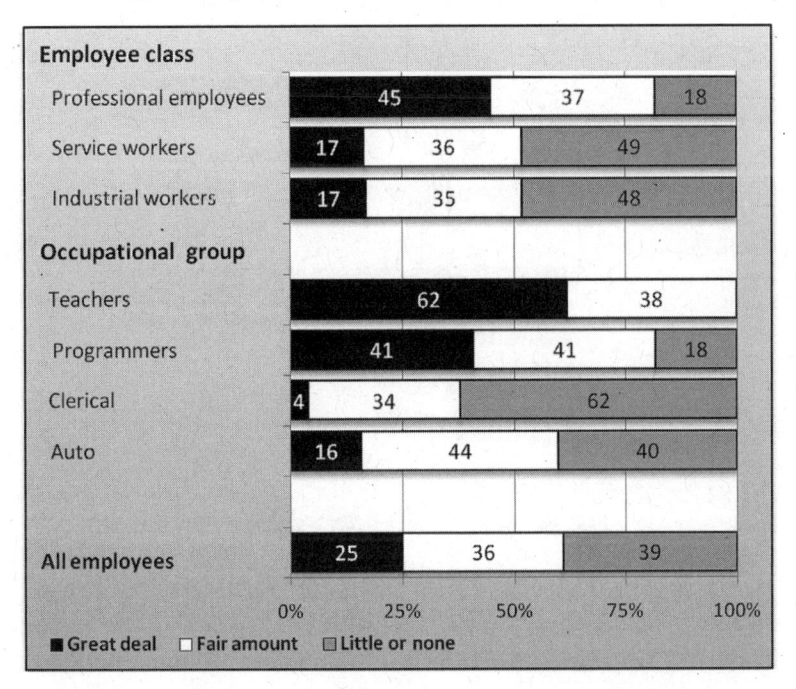

	Great deal	Fair amount	Little or none
Employee class			
Professional employees	45	37	18
Service workers	17	36	49
Industrial workers	17	35	48
Occupational group			
Teachers	62	38	
Programmers	41	41	18
Clerical	4	34	62
Auto	16	44	40
All employees	25	36	39

Source: EJRM Survey, 2004 (N=1295)

Most teachers are likely to think that they have a great deal of creativity in their jobs, perhaps reflecting the wide diversity of student needs to which they respond. Computer programmers' creativity profiles are similar to professional employees in general. Auto workers are similar to industrial workers generally; less than 20 per cent say they have a great deal of creativity in their jobs. Clerical workers are distinctive in that a very small proportion of them say they have a great deal of creativity and a majority feel they have little or no creativity in their jobs. However, it should be noted that a large proportion of service workers generally, as well as a large proportion of industrial workers—auto workers in particular—report the existence of at least a fair amount of room for creative engagement in their jobs. This finding is in contrast to much of the research literature that emphasizes objective routinization of the capitalist labour process. This point is especially relevant for the following case studies.

The majority of employees in all non-managerial classes indicate that they have no informal managerial or supervisory roles. However, consistent with the general trend identified in Chapter 4, a significant proportion say that they participate in

Graph 5.5 *Participation in Organizational Policy Decision, by Employee Class and Specific Occupational Group, Non-managerial Employees, Ontario, 2004 (%)*

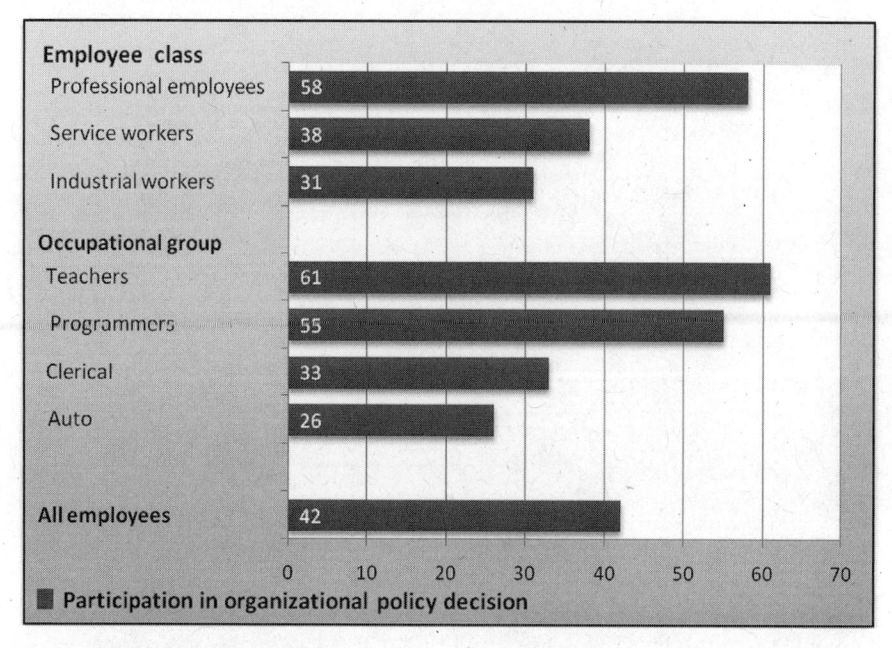

Category	%
Employee class	
Professional employees	58
Service workers	38
Industrial workers	31
Occupational group	
Teachers	61
Programmers	55
Clerical	33
Auto	26
All employees	42

■ Participation in organizational policy decision

Source: EJRM Survey, 2004 (N=1238)

organizational policy decision-making about products, staffing, or financing matters. A majority of Ontario professional employees and around a third of service workers and industrial workers say they participate in such decisions (Graph 5.5). The patterns are similar in the specific occupational groups. The majority of both teachers and computer programmers claim they participate in organizational decisions, but this is the case for only a quarter of clerical workers and auto workers. The amount of influence all such non-managerial employees can exercise is much constrained by employers' and managers' overarching formal authority. The findings suggest, however, that some consultative decision-making takes place in all employee classes and in these four specific occupational groups.

Overall, the findings for Ontario non-managerial employee classes and these specific occupational groups indicate that the majority in all employee classes now feel their jobs require a lot of thought and attention. Smaller proportions feel that they have much discretion or creativity in their job tasks or that they can participate in organizational policy decisions. Professional employees are more likely to say their jobs are creative and that they are involved in organizational decisions.

Graph 5.6 *On-the-Job Training Time Required to Perform Job, by Employee Class and Specific Occupational Group, Non-managerial Employees, Ontario, 2004 (%)*

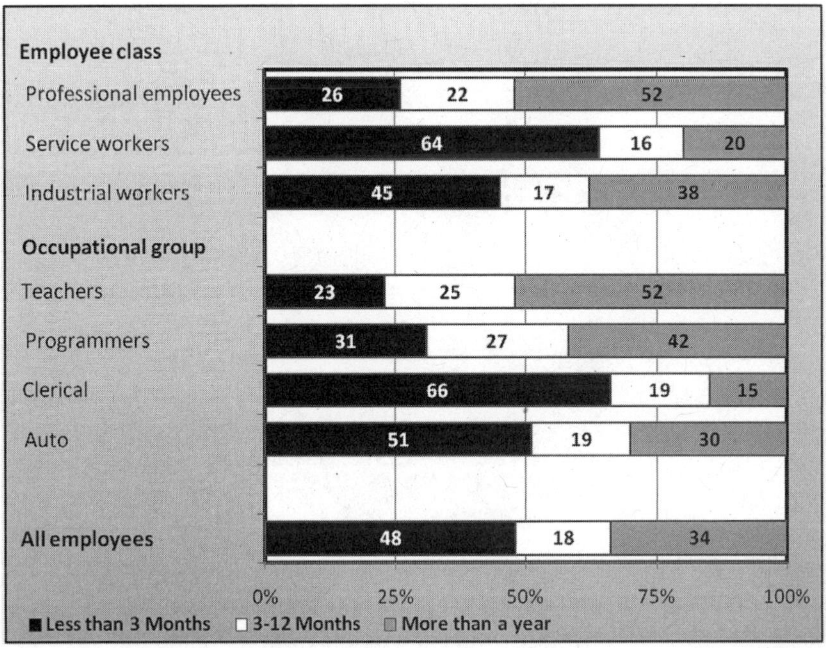

Employee class	Less than 3 Months	3-12 Months	More than a year
Professional employees	26	22	52
Service workers	64	16	20
Industrial workers	45	17	38
Occupational group			
Teachers	23	25	52
Programmers	31	27	42
Clerical	66	19	15
Auto	51	19	30
All employees	48	18	34

Source: EJRM Survey, 2004 (N=1095)

CHANGING JOB REQUIREMENTS

As documented in prior chapters, most available evidence obtained either from expert ratings or from workers' self-reports finds incremental gains in job requirements in recent decades. In this section, we examine workers' self-reports of training time, educational entry, and performance requirements, and also the required licensing certification for Ontario non-managerial employees.

Current differences in training time needed to do a job are displayed in Graph 5.6. The main difference is that a small majority of professional employees take over a year to become proficient, and the majority of service workers (64 per cent) and a plurality of industrial workers (45 per cent) take less than three months. Overall, about half of all non-managerial employees are adequately trained to be able to perform their jobs within the first three months. About a third of workers require over a year to master their jobs.

Comparisons among specific occupational groups reveal differences in required training time that are generally comparable between professionals and other workers.

Education and Jobs: Exploring the Gaps

Graph 5.7 *Job Entry Credential Requirements, by Employee Class and Specific Occupational Group, Non-managerial Employees, Ontario, 2004 (%)*

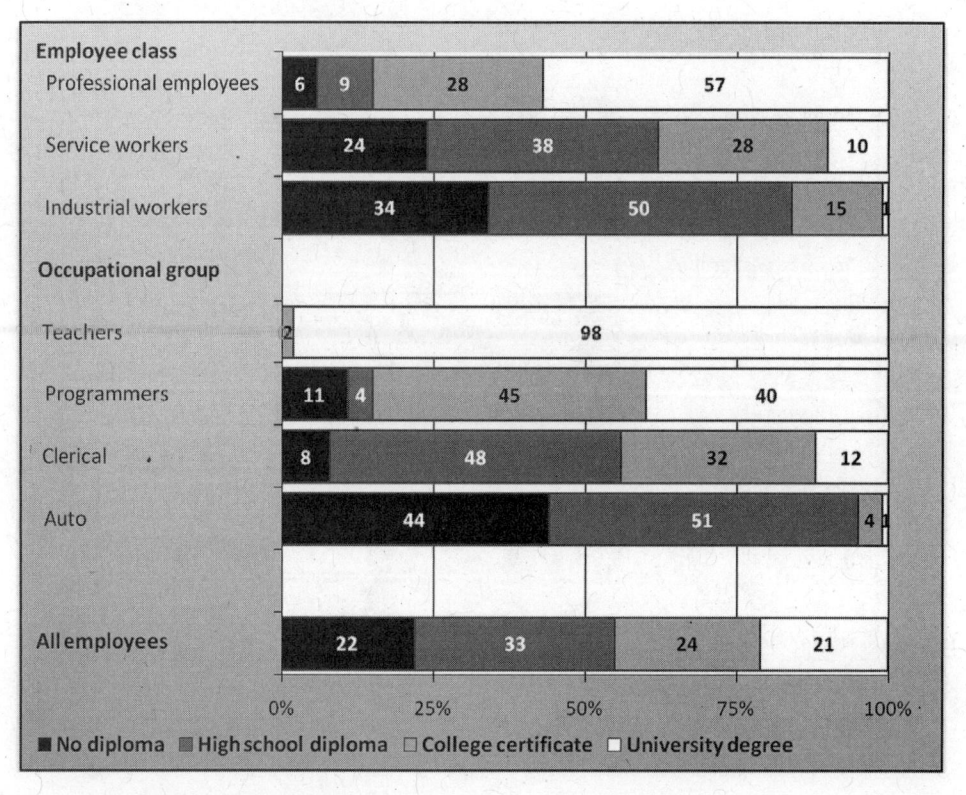

Category	No diploma	High school diploma	College certificate	University degree
Employee class				
Professional employees	6	9	28	57
Service workers	24	38	28	10
Industrial workers	34	50	15	1
Occupational group				
Teachers	2			98
Programmers	11	4	45	40
Clerical	8	48	32	12
Auto	44	51	4	1
All employees	22	33	24	21

Source: EJRM Survey, 2004 (N=1130)

A small majority of teachers estimate that it takes more than a year to become proficient in their jobs after their teacher training programs. Computer programmers are more mixed in their response, but a plurality (42 per cent) take more than a year to perform adequately, and about a third take less than three months. A small majority of auto workers are also trained in less than three months, but significant minorities of auto workers and industrial workers, including trades apprentices and some machine operators, may take several years. Clerical workers, like most other service workers, tend to have the shortest training time, with two-thirds of them needing less than three months.

The formal educational credential requirements for job entry in Ontario are summarized in Graph 5.7. The basic patterns are quite clear. The vast majority of professional employees require a post-secondary credential for job entry, and a large majority of industrial workers and a smaller majority of service workers (62 per cent) require at most a high school diploma. In the specific professional occupational groups, the vast majority of teachers require a bachelor's degree, a professional degree, or a graduate degree. A large majority of computer programmers require either a college certificate or a bachelor's degree. The finding that no credentials are required for 10 per cent of programmer jobs, as well as the small proportions of other professional employees, may indicate that it is possible to enter some emerging professional fields largely on the basis of demonstrated ability. In line with most industrial workers, the vast majority of auto workers require at most a high school diploma. Most clerical workers, like service workers in general, require a high school diploma or less.

In addition to training time and formal education requirements, many jobs now require employees to be formally certified or licensed. Nearly half of the non-managerial employees in Ontario require some form of certification of their training (Graph 5.8). Small majorities of both professional employees and industrial workers (including trades workers and various equipment operators) require certification or licensing to be able to do their jobs; whereas, only a third of service workers have any such requirement.

In terms of the specific professional occupational groups, nearly all teachers require a teaching certificate to enter the profession. In contrast, very few computer programmers (around 10 per cent) require specific occupational certification for their jobs. Again, the newness and fluidity of this information technology field may be a factor that limits the definition of professional requirements.

Like industrial workers generally, a majority (about two-thirds) of auto workers need to obtain either trades certification or some form of operator's licensing to be able to continue in their job. Among service workers, clerical workers have very low certification requirements (around 10 per cent).

The lack of certification requirements in both programming and clerical groups might be related to the absence of well-developed professional associations or trade unions. As previously noted, computer programmers represent a new area of specialized knowledge in which expert practitioners have not had sufficient time to organize widespread associations. Clerical workers tend to be located in relatively small, dispersed workplaces that are harder to organize, compared to settings with larger concentrations of public school teachers or auto workers, for example. In all three employee classes, those who are members of associations or unions are about twice as likely to have a certification requirement as those who are not (Spearman $r=.269$, $p>.001$).

In any case, while training time is generally increasing across the labour force, service jobs, and particularly clerical jobs, now provide the most easily accessible employment opportunities for those with relatively little training time or certification.

One indication of the influence of job requirements on workers' intentional learning activities is offered by the survey participants' responses to the statement that the job often requires learning new skills. The basic pattern is summarized in

Graph 5.8 *Certification Requirements, by Employee Class and Specific Occupational Group, Non-managerial Employees, Ontario, 2004 (%)*

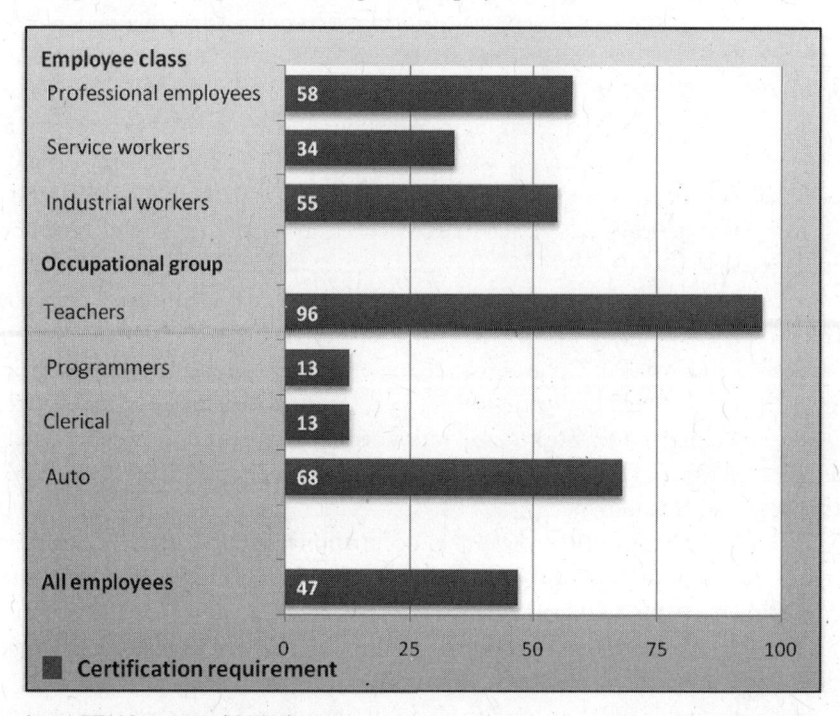

	%
Employee class	
Professional employees	58
Service workers	34
Industrial workers	55
Occupational group	
Teachers	96
Programmers	13
Clerical	13
Auto	68
All employees	47

■ Certification requirement

Source: EJRM Survey, 2004 (N=1293)

Graph 5.9. The majority of professional employees strongly agree with this proposition, and only about a third of service and industrial workers express such strong agreement. Very few professional employees disagree, but about a third of service and industrial workers agree. Teachers and computer programmers agree even more strongly than professional employees generally, compared to a third or less of clerical and auto workers. The most notable finding, however, is that the vast majority of those in *all* employee classes and specific occupational groups agree either strongly or somewhat strongly that their jobs often require learning new skills. Most employees in all three non-managerial classes recognize the need for continual learning about their jobs. We now turn to examining specific intentional learning practices among Ontario non-managerial employees.

WORKERS' INTENTIONAL LEARNING PRACTICES

Chapter 4 and other publications document the rapid increase in formal education attainment and further education course participation of the Canadian labour force

Graph 5.9 *Job Often Requires Learning New Skills, by Employee Class and Specific Occupational Group, Non-managerial Employees, Ontario, 2004 (%)*

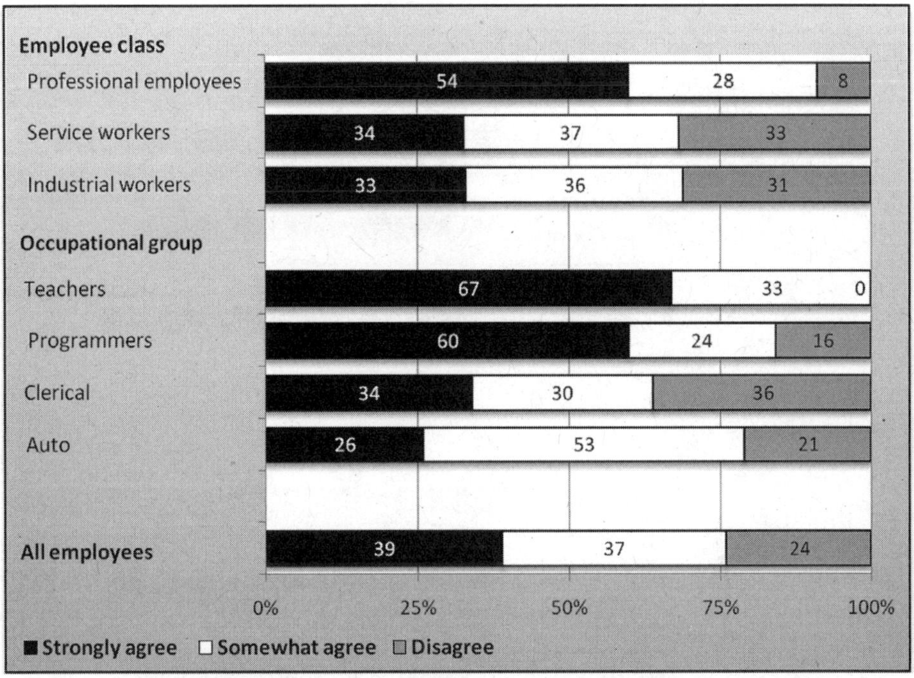

Employee class	Strongly agree	Somewhat agree	Disagree
Professional employees	54	28	8
Service workers	34	37	33
Industrial workers	33	36	31
Occupational group			
Teachers	67	33	0
Programmers	60	24	16
Clerical	34	30	36
Auto	26	53	21
All employees	39	37	24

Source: EJRM Survey, 2004 (N=1288)

over the past generation, as well as their extensive, recent involvement in informal learning (see Livingstone, 1999b, 2007). The patterns of these learning activities in Ontario in 2004 for non-managerial employee classes and specific occupational groups are presented in Graph 5.10 (and in more detail in Table 2 of Appendix 2).

About half of Ontario professional employees have university degrees, and over 80 per cent have completed some post-secondary program. About 15 per cent of service workers have university degrees, and about half have completed post-secondary programs. Only 5 per cent of industrial workers now have university degrees, but over a third have completed post-secondary education. Again, it should be kept in mind that the labour forces of Canada and Ontario are among the most highly formally educated in the world, with over half of all workers completing post-secondary education.

Higher levels of formal schooling are associated with somewhat greater participation in further education, but the differences among employee classes are narrower than their differences in formal education. The majority of all non-managerial

Graph 5.10 *University Completion, Further Education, and Incidence of Job-Related Informal Learning, by Employee Class and Occupational Group, Non-managerial Employees, Ontario, 2004 (%)*

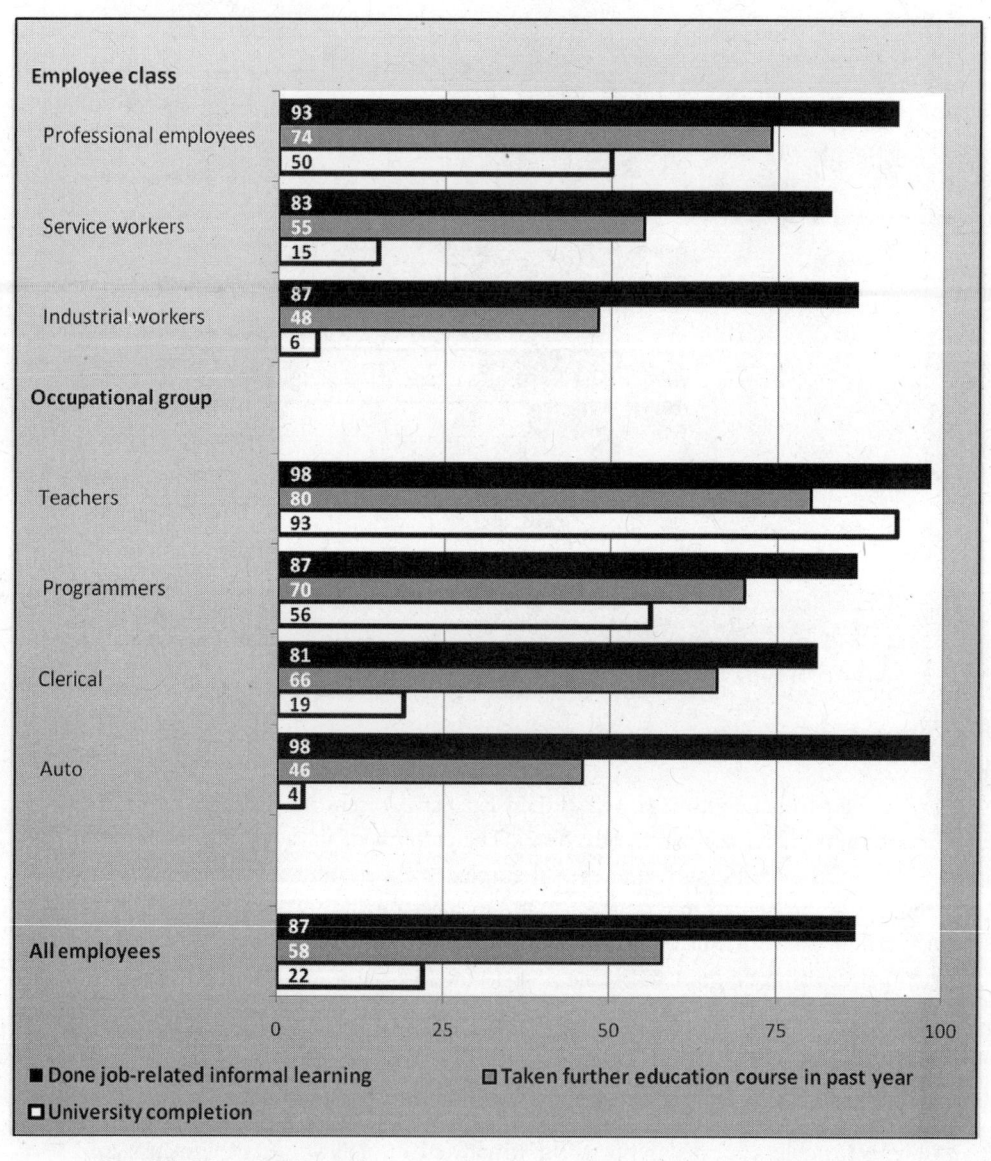

Employee class

	Done job-related informal learning	Taken further education course in past year	University completion
Professional employees	93	74	50
Service workers	83	55	15
Industrial workers	87	48	6

Occupational group

	Done job-related informal learning	Taken further education course in past year	University completion
Teachers	98	80	93
Programmers	87	70	56
Clerical	81	66	19
Auto	98	46	4
All employees	87	58	22

■ Done job-related informal learning   ☐ Taken further education course in past year
☐ University completion

Source: EJRM Survey, 2004 (N=1238)

employees (58 per cent) now take further education courses annually. Three-quarters of professional employees took further education in the past year, compared to over half of service workers and slightly fewer industrial workers. All three employee classes also exhibit a very high rate of engagement in job-related informal learning. All of these patterns replicate those found in the 2004 WALL Survey for the Canadian labour force in general.

With regard to the specific professional occupational groups, nearly all teachers have completed university degrees. Computer programmers have formal attainments similar to professional employees generally; over half have university degrees, and the vast majority have some form of post-secondary education.

The formal educational attainments of clerical workers reflect those of service workers generally. Those of auto workers reflect the attainments of industrial workers in general. Around 20 per cent of clerical workers now have university degrees, and around half of them have completed some form of post-secondary education. About 5 per cent of auto workers now have university degrees, and a quarter of them have completed some form of post-secondary education. The occupational differences are much narrower for further education participation. Eighty per cent of teachers and 70 per cent of computer programmers took a course in the past year, compared to only slightly fewer of the clerical workers and around half of the auto workers. Once more, the hierarchical pattern is broken down entirely with regard to intentional job-related informal learning. The majority of workers in all Ontario employee classes and specific occupational groups engage in such informal learning. Auto workers are just as likely as teachers to do so. These survey findings again suggest the iceberg-like character of adult learning; the largely unseen informal parts are much larger and more widespread than the formal, visible tip.

There are notable differences in the content of job-related intentional informal learning among employee classes and specific occupational groups (Graph 5.11A and Graph 5.11B). Professional employees generally, and teachers and computer programmers in particular, are more likely to devote informal learning time to keeping up with general knowledge in their fields, as well as to learning new job tasks and increasing their computer skills, when compared to industrial and service workers generally, and auto workers and clerical workers in particular. Industrial workers generally, and auto workers especially, are more likely than other employee classes and occupational groups to engage in informal learning about health and safety, which is a pre-eminent concern in many industrial settings. Teachers are far more likely than most other occupational groups to devote informal learning time to language and literacy matters, which are of pre-eminent concern in many classroom settings. Overall, many workers in each of these employee classes and specific occupational groups are involved in intentional informal learning in most of the job-related areas queried. The survey-based profiles begin to hint at a wide and deep array of specific informal workplace learning activities.

Graph 5.11A *Incidence of Different Job-related Informal Learning Activities, by Employee Class, Non-managerial Employees, Ontario, 2004 (%)*

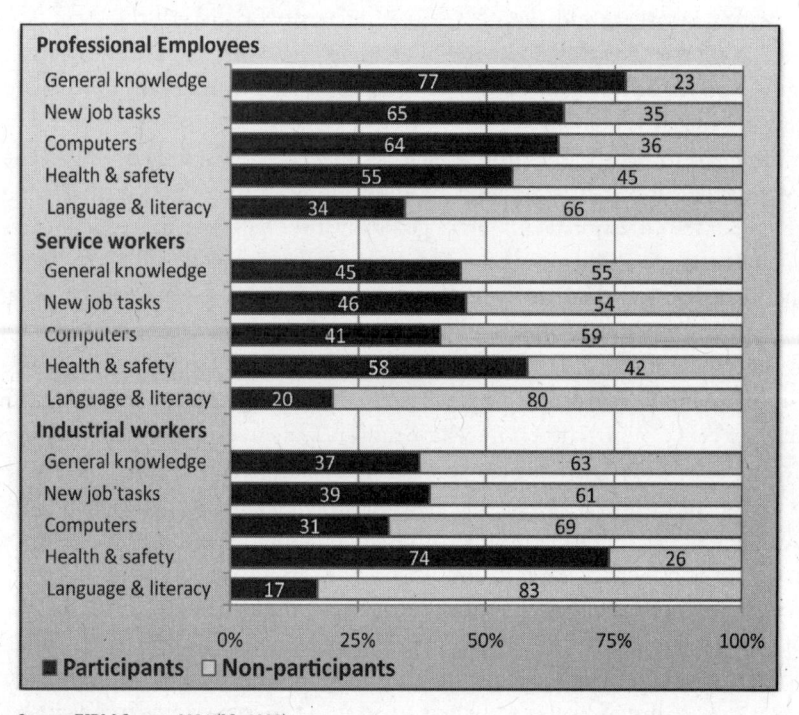

Activity	Participants	Non-participants
Professional Employees		
General knowledge	77	23
New job tasks	65	35
Computers	64	36
Health & safety	55	45
Language & literacy	34	66
Service workers		
General knowledge	45	55
New job tasks	46	54
Computers	41	59
Health & safety	58	42
Language & literacy	20	80
Industrial workers		
General knowledge	37	63
New job tasks	39	61
Computers	31	69
Health & safety	74	26
Language & literacy	17	83

Source: EJRM Survey, 2004 (N=1288)

EDUCATION-JOB MATCH

The national trend analyses in Chapter 4 found that the formal educational attainments of the labour force were increasing faster than the educational requirements for jobs and that underemployment in these terms has increased over the past generation. It was also found that workers were likely to see a closer subjective relationship between their qualifications and their jobs than specific formal measures indicated, and many workers felt they had more job knowledge than they could ever use in their jobs. In this section, the education-job match is examined for Ontario non-managerial employee classes and specific occupational groups. The extent of match is considered in terms of the relevance of workers' fields of study to their jobs, the level of their formal educational attainments compared with the credential and performance levels employers require, as well as workers' subjective sense of the match between their qualifications and their job requirements.

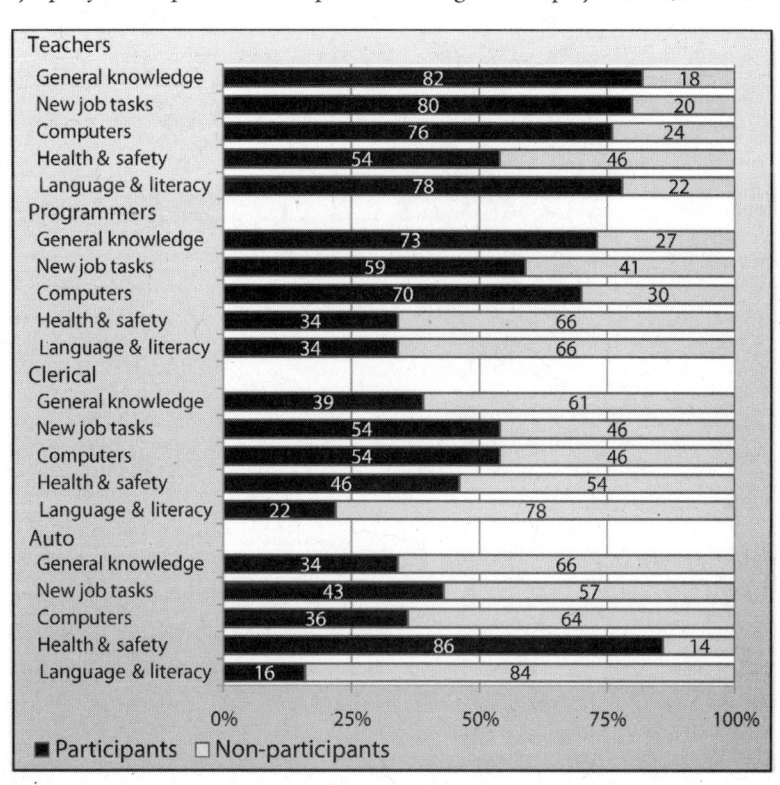

Graph 5.11B *Incidence of Different Job-Related Informal Learning Activities, by Specific Occupational Group, Non-managerial Employees, Ontario, 2004 (%)*

	Participants	Non-participants
Teachers		
General knowledge	82	18
New job tasks	80	20
Computers	76	24
Health & safety	54	46
Language & literacy	78	22
Programmers		
General knowledge	73	27
New job tasks	59	41
Computers	70	30
Health & safety	34	66
Language & literacy	34	66
Clerical		
General knowledge	39	61
New job tasks	54	46
Computers	54	46
Health & safety	46	54
Language & literacy	22	78
Auto		
General knowledge	34	66
New job tasks	43	57
Computers	36	64
Health & safety	86	14
Language & literacy	16	84

Source: EJRM Survey, 2004 (N=1288)

Relevance or Closeness of Field of Study to Job

The general pattern of closeness of match between field of study and job requirement in Ontario is virtually identical to the Canada-wide profile. As Graph 5.12 shows, nearly 40 per cent of all non-managerial employees say that their jobs are closely related to their formal education. An equivalent number say that their jobs are not at all related to their formal education. The remaining quarter indicate that their jobs are somewhat related to their education.

The results for employee classes show strong differences. The majority of professional employees (58 per cent) say that their jobs are closely related to their formal education, whereas only around 30 per cent of service and industrial workers agree. Conversely, the majority of industrial workers (52 per cent) and a large proportion of service

Education and Jobs: Exploring the Gaps

Graph 5.12 *Relevance of Education to Job, by Employee Class and Specific Occupational Group, Non-managerial Employees, Ontario, 2004 (%)*

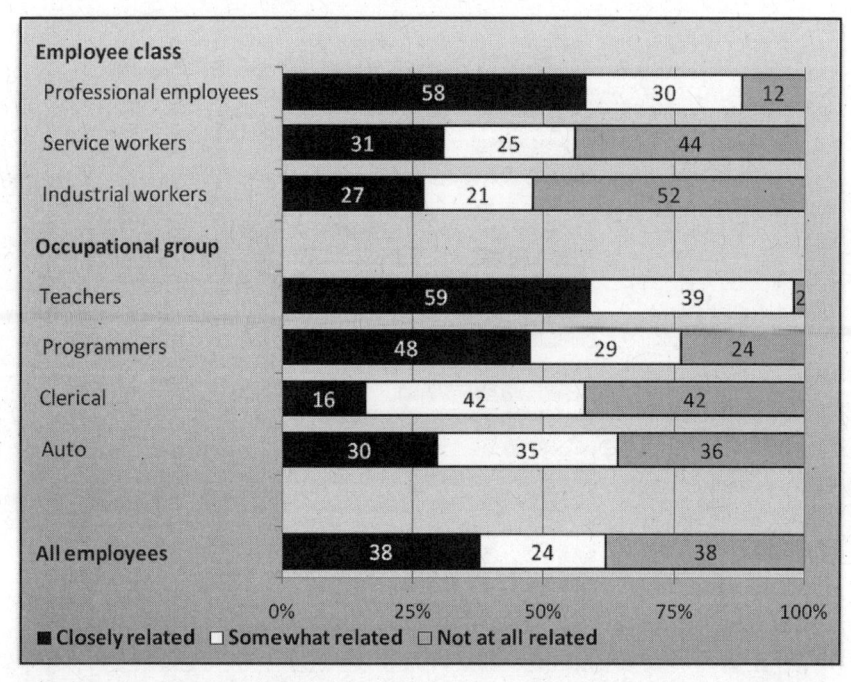

Employee class	Closely related	Somewhat related	Not at all related
Professional employees	58	30	12
Service workers	31	25	44
Industrial workers	27	21	52
Occupational group			
Teachers	59	39	2
Programmers	48	29	24
Clerical	16	42	42
Auto	30	35	36
All employees	38	24	38

■ Closely related □ Somewhat related □ Not at all related

Source: EJRM Survey, 2004 (N=1294)

workers (44 per cent) say that their jobs are not at all related to their formal education.

Among professional occupations, teachers (59 per cent) and computer programmers (48 per cent) are most likely to see their formal education as closely corresponding to their jobs. Among industrial and service workers, only about 30 per cent of auto workers and 15 per cent of office workers do so. Around 40 per cent of both clerical workers and auto workers say that they think their formal education is not at all related to their jobs. For most professional employees, the relevance of their formal education to their jobs seems evident; for most industrial and service workers such direct relevance is more limited or denied.

Credential Match

The extent of the credential-job match for Ontario employees is summarized in Graph 5.13. The general pattern is very similar to that in the WALL Survey and many other recent surveys. The matching of qualifications and attainments remains most common, but underemployment is substantial (around a third of all employees) and greater than the proportion of those who are underqualified (around 15 per cent or

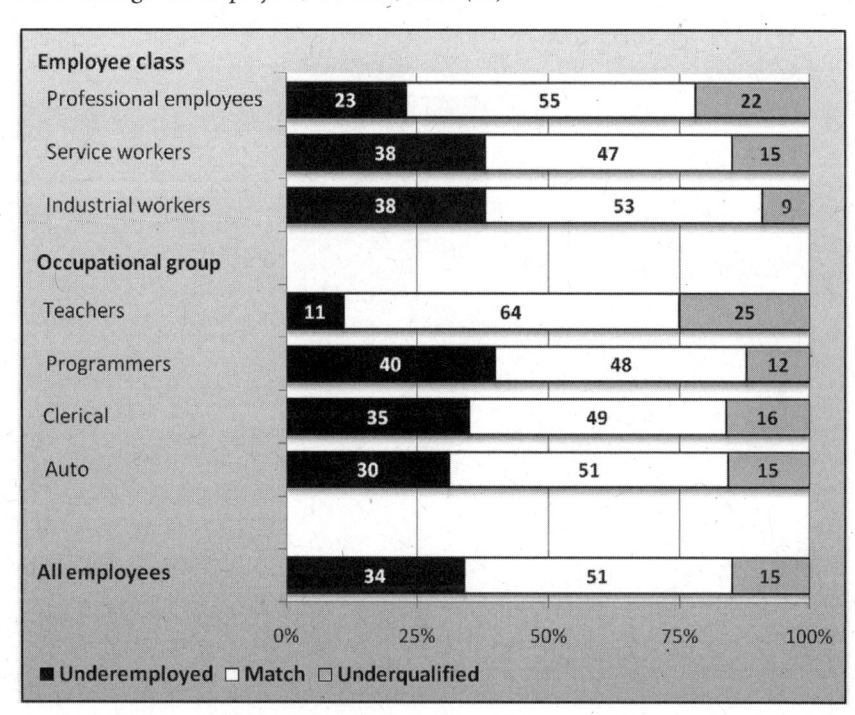

Graph 5.13 *Credential Match, by Employee Class and Occupational Group, Non-managerial Employees, Ontario, 2004 (%)*

Employee class	Underemployed	Match	Underqualified
Professional employees	23	55	22
Service workers	38	47	15
Industrial workers	38	53	9
Occupational group			
Teachers	11	64	25
Programmers	40	48	12
Clerical	35	49	16
Auto	30	51	15
All employees	34	51	15

Source: EJRM Survey, 2004 (N=1118)

less). Professional employees have the lowest underemployment, at around 20 per cent, but similar levels of underqualification. Among service workers and industrial workers, credential underemployment is much higher (38 per cent). Service workers and industrial workers may be less likely to be underqualified than professional employees, given the much lower educational requirements of their jobs.

Among professional occupational groups, teachers have very low levels of credential underemployment, at about 10 per cent. While the credential match is high (about two-thirds), a quarter of teachers indicate they are underqualified. The finding that credential underqualification exceeds underemployment among teachers may be indicative of a continuing tendency for upgrading to be required, that is, credential inflation, in the already highly qualified professional occupations. About half of computer programmers have matching credentials; however, 40 per cent report credential underemployment, which is a very high level for professional employees and indicative of a substantial number of people with advanced post-secondary credentials in jobs that do not have clearly established credential requirements.

Graph 5.14 *Performance Match, by Employee Class and Specific Occupational Group, Non-managerial Employees, Ontario, 2004 (%)*

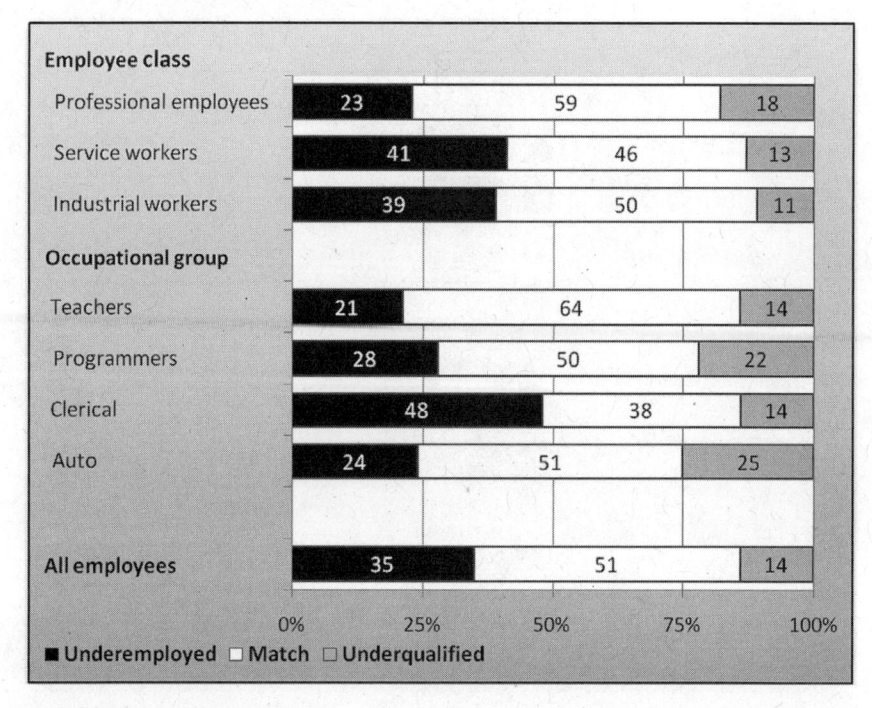

	Underemployed	Match	Underqualified
Employee class			
Professional employees	23	59	18
Service workers	41	46	13
Industrial workers	39	50	11
Occupational group			
Teachers	21	64	14
Programmers	28	50	22
Clerical	48	38	14
Auto	24	51	25
All employees	35	51	14

Source: EJRM Survey, 2004 (N=1146)

The credential match patterns for clerical and auto workers are similar to those for service workers and industrial workers respectively, with around a third underemployed. Like those in most working-class jobs, they are more likely than those in professional jobs to have greater formal education than their jobs require, and they are somewhat less likely to be underqualified.

Performance Match

As in the national comparison of entry and performance requirements in Chapter 4 (shown in Graph 4.12), there is a close correspondence between the self-reported entry credentials required and the education required for job performance among Ontario employees (Spearman $r=.78$, $p<.001$). Therefore, performance match measures, based on comparing educational attainment with performance criteria, will again be similar to the credential match. As Graph 5.14 confirms, the general pattern is very similar, with professional employees' performance underemployment levels being lower than those of service workers and industrial workers.

In terms of performance match for specific occupational groups, it should be noted that computer programmers are less likely to be underemployed on performance criteria (28 per cent) than on credentials (40 per cent), which suggests that credential requirements are still catching up with educational performance requirements in this relatively new field. Conversely, clerical workers are more likely to be underemployed in performance terms (48 per cent) than on credential criteria (35 per cent), which is probably related to the relative ease of entry into these jobs for those with advanced general education. These jobs require relatively little specialized training or certification and are often in fragmented workplaces with low unionization. In general, higher formal education may be more helpful for getting jobs than performing them, but this is particularly true for clerical workers. In addition, auto workers have relatively low rates of underemployment among industrial workers, which is consistent with their very high levels of unionization and relatively strong ability to negotiate job requirements.

Overall, the patterns for credential and performance matching are nearly identical among non-managerial employees in Ontario in 2004. For about half there is matching; a third are underemployed; and about 15 per cent are underqualified.

Subjective Match

Workers' subjective estimates of the correspondence between their qualifications and their job requirements are more inclusive than other measures based on formal educational levels or fields of study. Their estimates may include various forms of learning from experience, for example. Consequently, self-report match measures typically exhibit higher correspondence and less underqualification than estimates based on formal criteria. Over 60 per cent of Ontario employees feel that their qualifications match the qualifications required by their jobs, but very few (5 per cent or less) feel underqualified and about a third feel overqualified (Graph 5.15). Workers are vastly more likely to feel overqualified than to feel underqualified for their jobs. Similar patterns are evident for all employee classes. The only notable difference is a tendency for industrial and service workers to report higher subjective levels of underemployment than professional employees. Programmers express higher subjective levels of underemployment than professional employees generally, which is consistent with their credential underemployment. Clerical workers may express higher subjective levels of underemployment than do service workers generally, consistent with their performance underemployment. The general tendency toward a higher subjective match than found in measures based on formal education requirements should be noted in relation to the following discussion of learning from job experience in Chapter 6 and also the case study findings in Chapters 7 to 12.

As noted in Chapter 4, employees in the Ontario survey were asked how their general job knowledge compared with the knowledge they needed for performance of their jobs. As Graph 4.23 showed, a very strong majority across all employee

Graph 5.15 *Subjective Qualification-Requirement Match, by Employee Class and Occupational Group, Non-managerial Employees, Ontario, 2004 (%)*

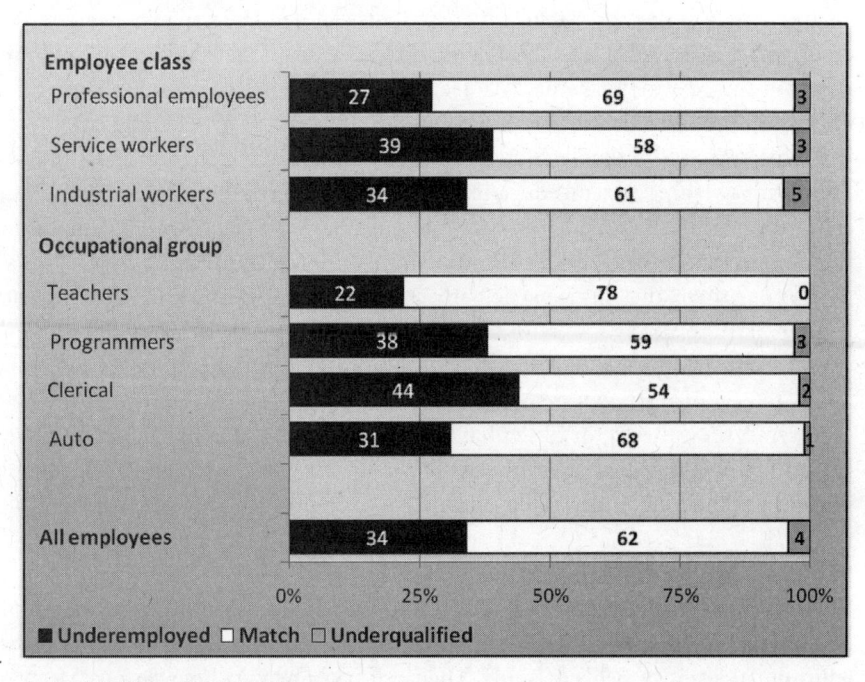

	Underemployed	Match	Underqualified
Employee class			
Professional employees	27	69	3
Service workers	39	58	3
Industrial workers	34	61	5
Occupational group			
Teachers	22	78	0
Programmers	38	59	3
Clerical	44	54	2
Auto	31	68	1
All employees	34	62	4

Source: EJRM Survey, 2004 (N=1275)

classes declare they have more job knowledge than needed to do their jobs, and almost none admit to less knowledge. The same pattern occurs in each of the specific occupational groups. This pattern is in accord with the insights of informed observers: Workers gain reserves of practical wisdom beyond explicit job requirements (Polyani, 1958). The finding is in line with survey respondents' reports of doing a great deal of intentional job-related informal learning, which is generally unrecognized in paid workplaces. Some might also argue that such knowledge reserves are indicative of underemployment, but further discussion of this issue is deferred until the concluding chapters.

In sum, among non-managerial employees, professional employees are much more likely than service and industrial workers to see a fairly close relationship between their jobs and their fields of study. This is also true of teachers and computer programmers in comparison to clerical and auto workers. The most common tendency on more specific measures of qualifications and job requirements is matching. This is true for both measures based on formal educational credentials and workers' subjective estimates. However, by both estimates, around a third of these employees are underemployed; that is, their jobs require a lower qualification than they possess. Underqualification, or having less formal education than the job requires, is less common and—by workers' subjective estimates—very rare. Professional employees, whose jobs usually require post-secondary education, are less likely to be underemployed than service workers and industrial workers, whose jobs usually do not require advanced credentials. Teachers have a closer match between the education attained and required for their jobs than most professional employees. Clerical workers tend to have even greater levels of underemployment than service workers and industrial workers generally. The higher credential and subjective underemployment of computer programmers than professional employees generally is a notable exception; this probably reflects the relative fluidity and credential uncertainties of a professional field in formation. The most important finding concerning matching is that employees usually have either sufficient or greater qualifications than their jobs require, and underqualification is uncommon.

DIFFERENT FACTORS AFFECTING EDUCATION-JOB MATCH

Prior research has suggested that various social background factors affect the extent of correspondence between educational attainment and job requirement. The WALL and EJRM surveys have attempted to test the significance of many of these factors. Those found to be most significant are reported here.

Employment Experience

Learning from experience on the job helps to modify not only the knowledge that workers bring to the job but also the job requirements. Employment experience can be roughly estimated by the years in employment, years in the current work organization, and years in the current job, as well as by the worker's age. Graph 5.16 summarizes the patterns of credential match and subjective match in relation to total years of employment experience. In both instances, the level of underemployment declines significantly from around half of those with less than 10 years of experience to about a quarter of those with over 20 years. At the same time, the proportion of employees with matching qualifications and job requirements increases somewhat. However, the small proportion who are underqualified appears to *increase* with employment experience. This increase is insignificant in subjective terms (from 1 per cent to 4 per cent) but is more substantial in terms of formal credentials (from 5 per cent to 20 per cent). The most plausible explanation for this pattern is the credential inflation of job requirements for experienced workers who have otherwise learned to perform their jobs. The relationship between employment experience and education-job matching is significant for both credential match (Spearman $r=.27$, $p<.001$) and subjective match (Spearman $r=.23$, $p<.001$) measures. These findings support the argument to be presented in Chapter 6.

Education and Jobs: Exploring the Gaps

Graph 5.16 *Employment Experience, by Credential Match and Subjective Match, Non-managerial Labour Force, Ontario, 2004 (%)*

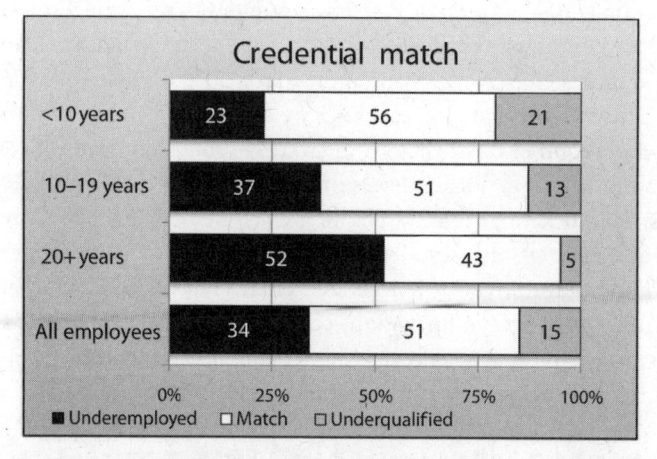

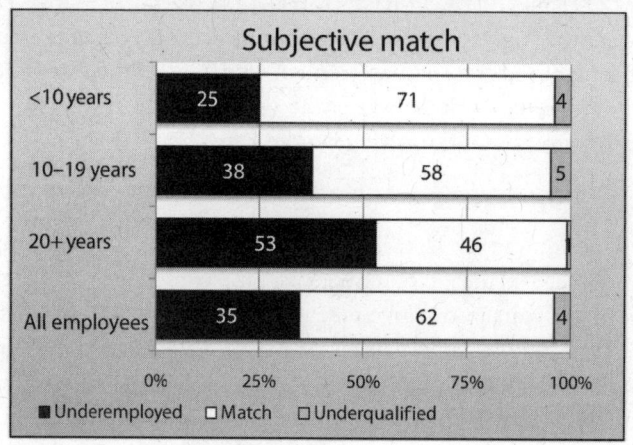

Credential match

	Underemployed	Match	Underqualified
<10 years	23	56	21
10–19 years	37	51	13
20+ years	52	43	5
All employees	34	51	15

Subjective match

	Underemployed	Match	Underqualified
<10 years	25	71	4
10–19 years	38	58	5
20+ years	53	46	
All employees	35	62	4

Source: EJRM Survey, 2004 (Credential Match, N=1091; Self-reported Match, N=1250)

Immigration Status and Race

Recency of arrival is a significant barrier for first-generation immigrants who try to obtain employment in line with the training they had received in their country of origin. There is also considerable evidence from previous generations that immigrants have assimilated well enough into the cultures of receiving countries for the second generation to attain similar employment patterns as those of other domestic social groups (e.g., Reitz, 1998). However, at least in Canada, the situation has become more complicated. Non-white groups have chronically experienced greater systemic difficulty in obtaining commensurate employment than those of white racial background (e.g., Henry & Ginzberg, 1985). In the Ontario EJRM sample, non-whites have higher rates of underemployment both in terms of credential underemployment (46 per cent versus 30 per cent for whites) and subjective underemployment (52 per cent versus 31 per cent for whites). The composition of recent immigrant cohorts has shifted dramatically, from largely white in the pre-1990 period to largely non-white in the post-1990 period (Reitz, 2007). Immigration criteria have also shifted to place much greater emphasis on advanced academic education credentials. People who immigrated after 1990 are now experiencing high rates of credential underemployment (54 per cent), compared with the lower rates of both the Canadian-born population (32 per cent) and immigrants who came to Canada prior to 1990 (31 per cent). Recent immigrants express even higher rates of subjective underemployment (66 per cent versus 33 per cent for Canadian-born and 24 per cent for earlier immigrants). The extent to which recency of arrival, racial discrimination, and raised academic credential requirements contribute to these high underemployment rates for recent immigrants is unclear. However, it is now widely recognized that the underemployment of recent immigrants has become a persistent and serious problem (e.g., Bloom & Grant, 2001). A substantial number of recent immigrants with advanced degrees cannot get jobs in their professional specializations and end up in service and industrial jobs with much lower formal job requirements.

Union or Association Membership

In the Ontario EJRM sample, those employees who are neither union nor association members are more likely to be credentially underemployed than those who are members (40 per cent versus 26 per cent), and the relationship is statistically significant (Spearman $r=.18$, $p<.001$). This evidence might suggest that those with greater negotiating power within organizations are more likely to have their knowledge claims widely recognized.

Immediate Job Control Factors

Employees who have greater control over their jobs are posited to achieve a closer match between their formal education and the requirements of their jobs. In the EJRM sample the most pertinent measures of immediate job control are the extent of creativity that workers exercise in the technical aspects of their jobs and the extent of participation they have in organizational decision-making about working conditions. There is a weak positive relationship between the extent of job creativity and credential match (Spearman $r=.148$, $p<.001$). Involvement in organizational decision-making shows only a very weak association with credential match (Spearman $r=.070$, $p<.023$). As the discussion of job control factors in Chapter 4 suggests, education-job match may be more strongly related to employee class position. The relative effects of class position and of job control *within* class positions are considered in the following section.

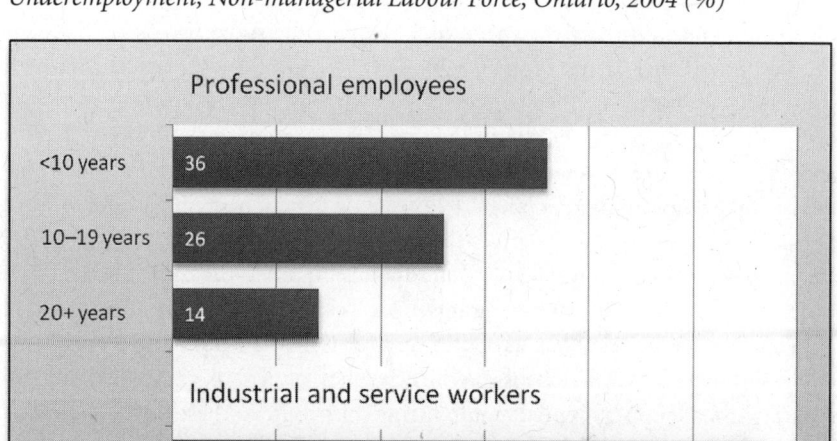

Graph 5.17 *Employee Class and Employment Experience, by Credential Underemployment, Non-managerial Labour Force, Ontario, 2004 (%)*

Professional employees

Experience	% Underemployed
<10 years	36
10–19 years	26
20+ years	14

Industrial and service workers

Experience	% Underemployed
<10 years	57
10–19 years	42
20+ years	27

Source: EJRM Survey, 2004 (Professional employees, N=315; Industrial/Service workers, N=776)

The possible effects of other demographic variables (gender, visible minority status, self-identified disability status, estimated health) and organizational variables (organizational size, private or public sector, shift schedule) were also examined. These have only occasional or negligible effects on most survey measures of the education-jobs match.

The relative effects of the above factors on the degree of job matching are now examined.

RELATIVE EFFECTS ON EDUCATION-JOBS MATCH

Are workers' learning experiences on the job sufficient over time to overcome the effects of different class position on the extent of matching and mismatching? This question is examined first in terms of the effects of employee class position and employment experience on the credential match. The basic findings appear in

Graph 5.17, which compares professional employees with industrial and service workers combined. Credential underemployment decreases with employment experience in all employee classes. However, among employees with over 20 years of experience, credential underemployment among industrial and service workers remains twice as high as among professional employees (27 per cent versus 14 per cent).

Both employee class position and employment experience, when considered together, retain their effects on credential matching. When adjustments are made for age, gender, and immigrant status, further multivariate analyses of the Ontario sample confirm that the effects of employee class and employment experience on the credential match remain significant. Industrial and service workers remain twice as likely to experience credential underemployment (adjusted odds ratio=2.056, $p<.001$; 95% confidence interval [CI] 1.492 to 2.834) as professional employees.[3] Workers with less than 10 years of work experience are approximately four times as likely to experience credential underemployment (adjusted odds ratio=3.969, $p<0.001$; 95% CI 2.316 to 6.801) as workers with more than 20 years of experience.

As noted above, credential underemployment is much higher among recent immigrants than in the Canadian-born population or among earlier immigrants (crude odds ratio=3.661, $p<.001$; CI 2.669 to 5.022). This association does not remain significant in multivariate analysis because recent immigrant status is so closely related to lack of (Canadian) employment experience.

The relative effects of employee class position, employment experience, and immediate job control factors (such as the extent of job creativity and involvement in organizational decision-making) have also been examined in relation to credential matching. When the possible effects of age and gender are also considered, a multivariate analysis shows that the effects of work experience remain very strong (adjusted odds ratio=4.053, $p<.001$; 95% CI 2.472 to 6.643) and effects of class position also remain significant (adjusted odds ratio=1.813, $p<.001$; 95% CI 1.288 to 2.553). Greater job creativity may retain some positive effect (adjusted odds ratio=1.571, $p<0.022$; 95% CI 1.067 to 2.313), but involvement in organizational decision-making has no discernible independent effect on the credential match. That is, the relative effects of these immediate job control variables tend to weaken or become insignificant, while the work experience and class effects remain significant in these comparisons.

In addition, the *negotiated* power that organized workers have gained through their unions and associations appears to be at least as influential in the matching or recognition of their knowledge as the *delegated* authority that non-managerial employees may acquire through participation in organizational decision-making. Unionization retains a positive effect on the provision of further education and enhancement of credential matching, regardless of a worker's role in organizational decision-making (see Livingstone & Raykov, 2008).[4]

The effects of employee class position and work experience both remain significant and of similar magnitude for the subjective match as well in similar multivariate analyses. The effect of class position on the closeness of field of studies to the job is stronger than the effect of employment experience (adjusted odds ratio of 6.272, $p<.001$, 95% CI 4.389 to 8.963 for class position versus adjusted odds ratio of 2.411, $p<.001$, 95% CI 1.443 to 4.026 for work experience).

The jobs of the majority of professional employees are closely related to their fields of study from the outset of their careers (53 per cent compared to 63 per cent for professional employees with over 20 years experience). In contrast, only a minority of the jobs of even the most experienced industrial and service workers are closely related to their formal education (increasing from 19 per cent, for those with less than 10 years, to 35 per cent, for those with over 20 years experience). More experienced industrial and service workers manage to make this relationship somewhat more relevant, but a large number with over 20 years of experience (43 per cent) still see no relationship of their formal education to their jobs, in contrast to less than 10 per cent of the most experienced professional employees.

In sum, the independent effects of both employee class and employment experience on measures of education-job matching remain strong in comparison to most other demographic and organizational factors identified in the empirical research literature to date.

EFFECTS OF MISMATCH

As noted previously, considerable concern has been expressed by many observers over the possible negative consequences of mismatches, particularly the condition of prolonged underemployment (or underutilization). For example, there is growing evidence that underemployment can have significant effects on workers' health (Raykov, 2008). The empirical evidence for the politically radicalizing effects of skill-based underemployment remains limited — although such effects from youth *un*employment may often be dramatic. Berg and Freeman's (1978: 98–100) analysis of the 1969 US Working Conditions Survey found that both underemployment (or underutilization) and low income were associated with less job satisfaction. Replications of their analysis with 2004 WALL and EJRM data confirm these findings. Further analyses find that underemployed workers are not now better paid than matched workers; therefore, the general wage premium that Berg and Freeman posited as compensating for their underutilization status may have disappeared. Those highly underemployed (i.e., holding two credentials more than required) are less satisfied than the highly underqualified (i.e., holding two credentials less) but the majority of employees express at least modest job satisfaction regardless of matching and income levels. This may suggest a pragmatic acceptance of underemployment in the absence of a widespread perception of positive alternatives to current job structures. The available evidence does suggest that increasing proportions of employed workers are underemployed, paid less than their educational qualifications warrant, and experience diminished job satisfaction. The case studies attempt to shed some further light on these effects.

CONCLUDING REMARKS

Detailed analyses of the 2004 EJRM Survey of non-managerial employees in Ontario confirm the basic findings of the 2004 WALL National Survey. Professional employees are generally distinct from service workers and industrial workers in terms of higher post-secondary educational attainments, higher educational job requirements, and higher levels of education-job match. Differences between these employee classes in terms of further education are narrower, and there is little distinction in terms of their involvement in job-related informal learning.

An examination of factors affecting education-job matching confirms that there is a significant association between greater employment experience and narrower formal gaps.[5] Multivariate analyses indicate that both employee class position and employment experience retain more significant effect on education-job matching than most other possible factors. Factors such as recent immigration status, limited Canadian work experience, and non-white racial status are interrelated, which makes it impossible to distinguish the relative effects of each factor using the cross-sectional survey data, but very high underemployment is a serious problem among recent immigrants. Immediate job control variables (task creativity, organizational decision-making role) are found to have little independent effect on education-job matching, in comparison to work experience and employee class position.

Overall, the greatest formal education-job gaps appear to be the underemployment of service workers and industrial workers who have advanced formal education but work in jobs with lower educational requirements. However, the finding that more experienced service and industrial workers exhibit *higher* levels of credential underqualification than less experienced workers suggests that credential requirements are being inflated for many jobs that could be performed adequately by workers who are experienced but less credentialled. If such credential inflation is occurring, the increasing credential underemployment levels suggest that a growing number of workers are getting ahead of the rate of inflation.

In terms of differences between the specific occupational groups of public school teachers, computer programmers, clerical workers, and auto workers, most of the Ontario survey findings are consistent with the general Canadian patterns for professional employees, service workers, and industrial workers. The relatively high level of credential underemployment among computer programmers may be symptomatic of the fluidity of this developing professional field, whereas the relatively high levels of performance underemployment among clerical workers may indicate the ease of entry into these jobs with general educational credentials.

These findings and the questions they continue to raise bring us to the limits of large-scale survey research. The following chapters focus on findings from the semi-structured case study interviews that started with the same questions as the 2004 EJRM Survey and were conducted mainly in the following year. The case studies with small groups of teachers, computer programmers, clerical workers, auto workers, and disabled workers in these four occupational groups were initially intended to explore the apparent gaps identified by the EJRM and prior survey research. The use of qualitative data from these case studies provides new, detailed, empirical evidence about the capabilities that respondents acquire during paid work and the diverse and evolving nature of the jobs they perform. These findings are sometimes at variance with the currently dominant statistical perspective on the extent to which workers' education and jobs correspond, or fail to correspond. The case study analyses start from the apparent gaps indicated by the quantitative measures and then explore if, and how, workers modify their abilities and the characteristics of their jobs. The case studies look closely at workers who report they are underemployed in terms of having qualifications that exceed their formal job requirements. The case studies also look at those who report they are underqualified, as well as those whose formal education appears to match their jobs. Where the case study findings differ from the survey findings, it should be noted that there are levels of discretion both in the labour process and in learning that are beyond the horizon of survey research; these can apply to the most underemployed/overeducated workers as well as to the most ostensibly underqualified. The case studies are intended to provide new insight into how all workers go about performing their jobs and to suggest a need for a new paradigm to represent the complex and dynamic relationship between work and learning.

Notes

1. For analysis of teachers in comparison to doctors/lawyers, engineers, nurses, and computer programmers, see Livingstone and Antonelli (2007).
2. All graphs in this chapter are based on the 2004 EJRM Survey of non-managerial employees (N=1301). The size of employee classes were professional employees, 364; service workers, 555; industrial workers, 382. The size of the specific occupational groups were teachers, 46; computer programmers, 60; clerical workers, 121; auto workers, 83; and disabled workers in all sectors, 47.
3. For the relative significance of (multivariate) relationships of two or more independent variables with the dependent education-job matching variables reported in this chapter, odds ratios are used. An odds ratio indicates the relative probability of an event occurring or not occurring. In the context of the EJRM Survey, a raw odds ratio of 1 represents equal odds of respondents on one independent variable (different employment classes, for example) being or not being underemployed. Coefficients with values below 1 indicate less chance of being underemployed, whereas coefficients greater than 1 represent an increased chance. An adjusted odds ratio takes into account associations between different independent variables and estimates the extent to which the effects of one independent variable (such as employment classes), on the dependent

variable (underemployment), remain significant when the impact of other independent variables (such as work experience, gender, or race) are taken into account. Since odds ratios, like other statistical measures, are probabilities, confidence intervals (CI) are provided to indicate the expected range of the odds ratios at the .05, or 95 per cent, level of confidence. For further explanation and illustrations, see Hosmer and Lemeshow (2000) and Katz (2006). It should be emphasized again that correlation does not prove causation, both because of measurement limitations and because all variables are measured at the same moment in time.

4. It should be noted that computer programmers' low level of professional association membership to date has not enabled their negotiation of greater collective power in most paid workplaces, but the strategic value of their specialized knowledge may have encouraged substantial delegated control from management in many workplaces.

5. Greater prior experience as estimated in the survey data might well be associated with observed narrower gaps in such cross-sectional analysis, but learning by experience may dynamically modify both worker and job, and can even widen the gap between the abilities attained and required over time.

Part Three
Exploring the Gaps: Case Studies

Chapter Six
Elements of an Integrated Theory of Work and Learning

K.V. Pankhurst

The formulation of a relationship between education and jobs either at the level of the economy or at the level of an occupation has proved elusive for the reasons outlined in Chapters 1 and 2. In this chapter the connection between education and employment is restated at the level of a job and a worker and has been reconceived to take into account individual behaviour in work and learning. The nature of paid work is considered, notably the implications of the implicit or "open" contract of employment. The formation of human abilities is then discussed as a generic process of learning by experience that happens in the course of performing any activity, including both paid and unpaid work. As problem solving is an essential characteristic of both work and learning, the relationship between them is symbiotic and dynamic. This theoretical framework is applied to examine the empirical case study data in Chapter 12.

Central issues in understanding jobs are how an employer defines a job and determines hiring criteria and how a worker decides to go about performing a job. When employment was conceived as an exchange of effort for pay, it was assumed by employers that a worker could be controlled and should be compliant. Management styles that rely on extrinsic incentives to work still reflect Taylor's assumption (1911) that workers have a natural instinct for slacking ("soldiering") that becomes systematic in a group. Henry Ford later adopted a similar approach in establishing a required pace of physical effort on an automobile assembly line designed by engineers. In his famous article on economic growth, Alwyn Young assumed that workers were "resistant to change" (1928: 534). It was an error, however, to assume that workers could not or should not be allowed to think for themselves. A few workplace case studies that have demonstrated how workers on assembly lines could exceed the norm and gain time for themselves (e.g., Littler, 1985; Hamper, 1986) indicate that a production system is less definitive and susceptible to control than might at first sight appear. Empirical rate of return studies have been criticized (e.g., Weale, 1993) for relying on highly simplified proxy indicators of workers' abilities and performance. Using grouped data, Berg (1970, 2003), Livingstone (1999a, 2004), Hartog (2000), Borghans and de Grip (2000), and Buchel, de Grip, and Mertens (2004) have documented differences between levels of education and employment—and their mutual connections or disjunctions—using ordinal indicators of educational attainment or duration.[1]

Theoretical and empirical investigations of the nature and content of work and learning remain scarce. Several authors have observed that an appropriate theory for examining the abilities used in work has yet to be formulated (e.g., Bourdieu, 1980; Le Bas & Mercier, 1984; Stroobants, 1993). In economic theory, workers are no longer assumed to be homogeneous and passive agents of production, but the sociology of work (Simpson, 1989; Kalleberg, 1989) has still to examine work in terms of what is done and how. A body of empirical evidence about aspects of work in different occupations is being compiled, including a study of so-called unskilled workers (Kusterer, 1978) and studies of coal mining and hairdressing (Billett, 2001) and collaborative care in hospitals (Engestrom, & Kerosuo 2003). A few rich case studies provide detailed evidence of how a given worker acquires and uses abilities while performing a specific job: for example, the description of jobs in a milk plant to manage stocks of milk and assemble orders for delivery (Scribner, 1986), the autobiographical account of a man who spent a lifetime in different jobs before becoming a sociologist (Schranck, 1978), an account of how a waitress goes about her daily tasks (Rose, 2001), and a description of how fish hatchery workers with low levels of formal education develop expert knowledge through experimentation in apparently routine tasks (Lee & Roth, 2005).

A major practical difficulty in describing a job and the abilities used to perform it has been the absence of a clearly understood and agreed terminology. In popular and even academic discourse about what a job requires and how a worker performs a job, the terms *skill* and *skills* are extensively used but are too vague and undefined (Vallas, 1990; Spenner, 1990) for serious research into the relationship between education and jobs, or to sustain claims of pervasive "deskilling" (e.g., Braverman, 1974) or "upskilling" (Seltzer & Bentley, 1999). The term *skill* is used ambiguously in several ways. First, skills are the personal attributes of the incumbent of a job, but confusion has been introduced by using the word *skill* to refer to job requirements and to distinguish job levels. Second, the term *skill* is sometimes used synonymously with *education* but also to distinguish between those who have an educational credential and those who do not. The term *skilled worker* is commonly used to refer to a qualified person, trained by apprenticeship or in other practical ways to perform apparently manual work, who has not had an academic education. Skill has thus become a socially discriminatory euphemism for lack of formal tertiary education. Third, skill is ambiguous in that it can refer to a particular attribute—such as manual dexterity in a given task—a specific knowledge, or a faculty of the mind. It is also frequently used to refer to abilities required to move to another job. Mobility among tasks and jobs is frequently assumed to require the acquisition of new abilities, often by specific formal instruction, but this neglects the formation of abilities during the experience of work. Skill can also be used to refer to the human ability to combine a variety of specific attributes into coherent action to achieve a purpose; this includes the critically important ability to modify one's own abilities (meta-cognition). However, this concept of skill proposed by Polanyi (1966) has been given too little attention. The common tendency to refer to personal abilities as skill or skills constructs an illusion of shared understanding. However, the abilities workers acquire go far beyond the knowledge they gain during formal education. In the following case studies, the content of a job is referred to as a set of job tasks or responsibilities, and the attributes of a worker are referred to as particular abilities or an overall capability.

THE IMPLICIT CONTRACT OF EMPLOYMENT

In practice, an employer is unable to describe in full detail the content of a job. Since it is impossible to anticipate all the contingencies that could arise within and outside an organization that affect employee performance and output, an employer cannot specify precisely what a worker is to do, and how. According to Durkheim, "the initial act is always contractual, but there are consequences, sometimes immediate, which run over the limits of the contract" (1902: 214). Adam Smith argued that the division of labour was limited by the extent of the market, so as markets develop the content of jobs evolves. Moreover, neither a worker nor an employer has perfect knowledge of the other. Both before entering the contract of employment and afterwards, a worker cannot know all the attributes of an employer or what behaviour to expect. Correspondingly, an employer cannot effectively identify the education needed by a worker to do a job (Rikowski, 2001) or the abilities a worker has acquired by experience in the past, or will acquire while performing a new job. An employer often relies on indirect proxy indicators, particularly of educational attainment or experience. Differences between an employer's and a worker's interpretation of a job are inevitable. An employer recruits a worker according to an approximate idea of a job, and makes a preliminary assessment of that worker's abilities to perform it. However, judgments of that kind are less simple than might appear and have to be confirmed or revised in the light of subsequent assessments of performance after a period of probation. A worker has an initial perception of a job that is modified in the light of subsequent experience. For these reasons, "What a worker exchanges is not directly his work but his capacity for work" (Marx, 1865: 509). "The sole thing provided or bought is a potential, a capacity, of which neither of the parties know all or part of the real conditions under which it will be realised" (Mallet,

1980: 37). Therefore, at the moment a worker is hired, "the two parties do not know what will be the final result of this exchange" (Garnier, 1984: 315) in terms of quantity and quality of output. This concept of an implicit contract of employment that is inherently open or incomplete is quite different from a formal contract, which specifies such matters as wages and conditions of work that are enforceable in law. The capacity for work that a worker acquires and utilizes is a highly complex set of abilities that needs to be investigated in detail.

Continuing uncertainties under an implicit employment contract about the circumstances in which work is carried out, what a worker has to do, and how, make work on all tasks a process of problem solving. A worker provides the ability to work, but not the promise of a specific output, and, in return, receives some continuity of employment and wages and accepts the authority of an employer to make strategic managerial decisions, such as what goods or services are to be produced and the choice of fixed capital equipment, technology, and organization. Neither a worker nor an employer can know in advance what output will result from their respective efforts and collaboration. The two parties to the employment contract have a mutual interest in ensuring that production takes place because they would share the costs of failure in the form of unemployment and lost profits. Nevertheless, as long as the organization remains in existence they can, and often do, differ about how the net output of an organization should be shared between profits and wages.

In the absence of certainty, work under the implicit open employment contract has been conceived as having two components. Although some parts of a job can be prescribed, others have necessarily to be left to the discretion of a worker (e.g, Simon, 1957; 1959; Jaques, 1956; Fox, 1974). Simon (1965: 223) suggested that the balance between prescription and discretion varies among jobs. The degree of discretion was "determined by the number and importance of the premises which are specified, and the number and importance of those which are left unspecified." Simon's implicit assumption that prescription and discretion are discrete and complementary characteristics is questionable, since it is impossible to know whether, or how, a worker will exercise discretion. Furthermore, the use of discretion is largely unobservable to the extent that a worker has developed intuitive thinking and habitual action. As Jaques commented, "the discretionary content of work was often its least evident feature. To the extent that a person was capable of doing his job, and was experienced at it, he tended not to perceive that he was using judgment or exercising discretion" (1956: 34).

If a worker exercises discretion, and is often unaware of doing so, a distinction between managerial decisions and those made by each worker is too simple. Managers cannot be aware of the full extent to which a worker exercises discretion in the minutiae of production. The concept of the implicit open employment contract is at variance with the neoclassical assumptions that workers are passive, homogeneous, and fully controlled by managerial decisions. There is also some empirical evidence that even the lowest-level and lowest-paid workers exercise considerable discretion in their jobs to deal with unanticipated contingencies (e.g., Rose, 2001) or to adapt the operation of machines and govern the speed and quality of output (e.g., Kusterer, 1978). Since, in uncertainty, each worker has some measure of discretion, worker and employer share, albeit unequally, the function of problem solving and decision-making in an organization.

WORK AS PROBLEM SOLVING

These considerations emphasize the psychological nature of work. Whereas work was defined by Jevons (1870: 188) as "any painful effort of mind or body" and by Marshall (1920: 65) as "any exertion of mind or body… other than the pleasure derived directly from the work," Jaques's definition (1976: 108) was solely in psychological terms: "The essence of the effort in work is to be found in the anxiety engendered by the uncertainties which are part and parcel of the exercise of discretion." Dewey introduced problem solving and purposive thinking into the concept of work: "We view work from the outside when we think of it as simply doing things that need to be done. But… from the inside… work signifies activity directed by ends that thought sets before the person as something to be accomplished; it signifies ingenuity and inventiveness in selecting proper means and making plans, and thus, finally, signifies that expectations and ideas are tested by actual results" (1910b: 211).

Work is an iteration of thinking and purposive action, using incomplete information to attain a goal in circumstances that cannot be fully anticipated. The term *problem solving* conveniently describes a sequence of stages that begins with the identification of the problem. "To see a problem is a definite addition to knowledge" (Polanyi, 1958: 100). The sequence continues with reflection on the alternative possible ways of dealing with a problem, arriving at a decision, carrying it out, observing the results, modifying the action, and then repeating the sequence if the results do not accord with the intended purpose. This process occurs in a continuum of thought and action that ranges from a multitude of minute, rapid decisions by each individual worker to large-scale, long-deliberated strategic planning decisions taken by a team. Productive efficiency is governed by how a worker becomes actively engaged in this labour process. Just as many economists have abandoned the neoclassical assumptions of a homogeneous, passive labour force, substitutable workers, perfect rationality, and a determinate equilibrium, cognitive psychologists have correspondingly recognized the restrictive assumption of automatic responses to stimuli in behaviouralist theories. The essence of problem solving is progressive learning by experience, and it is this aspect of work that generates the formation and utilization of a worker's abilities.

EMPIRICAL EVIDENCE OF LEARNING BY EXPERIENCE

Although it is well understood that education is a broad process of acquiring knowledge, abilities, and values, in practice, this traditional description has become occluded by assumptions in policies and practices that treat education as formal institutional learning that is a prerequisite for doing something, especially paid work. It is frequently assumed that to perform a job some prior education and training is needed, and many attempts have been made to specify the components of education for purposes of providing labour market services. Discussions of education tend to concentrate on organized institutional education, which is delivered by accredited teachers according to a set curriculum. However, learning also takes place in the home, at work, and in other social settings; it takes place in the form of further education courses, mentoring, individual study, and in the process of dealing with the problems of daily life. In formally organized educational institutions, a learner is typically introduced to artificially defined problems that usually have a solution, whereas the problems that arise in the course of daily life and work are often ill-defined and may have more than one solution, or even none. A comprehensive account of how workers acquire their knowledge and abilities has to consider the process of everyday learning and the kinds of knowledge and abilities that are acquired that way. Behind all the disparate forms of learning that can be described, there is a single common process of learning by experience, which is discussed below. The presence of learning by experience during production has long been accepted in economic theory (e.g., Rosen, 1972), but the nature of that process, what is learned, where and how, remains to be thoroughly investigated empirically.

There is a large and growing body of empirical studies of cost/output functions, that is, measures of how labour costs are related to production, (e.g., Adler & Clark, 1991; Solow, 1997; OECD/IEA, 2000). The findings of studies during the past 70 years, which cover many countries, periods of time, industries, firms, plants, the construction of fixed capital assets, and the manufacture of consumer goods, indicate that labour costs typically fall as total production cumulates.[2] The rate of decline in costs has been estimated to vary between 5 and 25 per cent with a modal value of about 16 per cent (Dutton & Thomas, 1984). These widespread statistical findings of progressive improvements in productivity are commonly known as "experience curves" and have been interpreted, since Arrow's famous 1962 article, as empirical evidence that learning by experience happens during production. There is, however, an awkward epistemological problem in that it is not clear whether learning by experience is indicated by the measure for production or the one for costs. Attempts to identify the location of learning within an organization, that is, among managers, engineers, or line workers, have been inconclusive, and it is more likely that the entire workforce is engaged in learning. Although these data may be interpreted to indicate that learning happens during production, they provide no account of the process. Arrow (1962) suggested that learning resulted from problem solving, but he made the restrictive assumption that learning took place while capital goods were being constructed, not while they were being used to make goods for consumption. Although Solow (1997) offered simulations that in principle confirm the plausibility of learning by experience, his calculations provided no empirical evidence of how it happens.

The empirical evidence about learning by experience is also inconclusive. If it is endogenous in production, it must also happen during any other activity, notably during consumption (Rosenberg, 1982) and also during unpaid work. There is also extensive statistical evidence that the expenditure on a particular good or service increases at a declining rate, as well as with income and the experience of consuming other goods and services, on the principle of declining marginal utility. That is to say, "the more you have of something, the less you want more of it." The interpretation of these data as evidence of learning by experience is subject to the same epistemological criticism as cost/output functions in that it is not clear where precisely learning resides. Detailed empirical studies provide more convincing evidence of how individuals adapt the algorithms learned during formal education, for example in managing household accounts (Lave, 1988) or while shopping (Capan & Kuhn, 1979), which suggest that a detailed explanation of the mental processes used during work and other activities is needed.

THE FORMATION OF COGNITIVE KNOWLEDGE AND ABILITIES DURING WORK

As the process of problem solving entails the use of abilities, the question is how those abilities are formed and used in work. Adam Smith suggested that the abilities to work are formed while working: "The understandings of the greater part of men are formed by their ordinary employments" (1776: 267), whether they be sharpened or dulled. He provided several subtle illustrations of the kinds of personal attributes that were learned in the performance of various occupations (Smith, 1759, 1776). For example, the agricultural labourer, who has to perform several different tasks using implements drawn by animals that vary in strength and temper, develops a "great variety of knowledge and experience, whereas someone who works in brass or iron uses instruments and materials that are more consistent in quality." Customs officers, whose duty "obliges them to be frequently very troublesome to some of their neighbours, commonly contract a certain hardness of character" (1776: 382). The clergyman becomes grave and severe because of his professional concern with the "awful futurity" of the human race (1759: 294). The soldier is not dissolute by nature, but killing lessens his finer sentiments and he needs to forget the hazards of his profession (1759: 296). The sailor learns to anticipate storms and shipwrecks (1759: 10), and Smith thought a sailor's work improved eyesight. A worker also learns from the employer's example. "The owners of the great mercantile capitals are necessarily the leaders and conductors of the whole industry of every nation, and their example has much influence on the manners of the whole industrious part of it than that of any other order of men. If his employer is attentive and parsimonious, the workman is likely to be so too; but if the master is dissolute and disorderly, the servant who shapes his work according to the pattern which his master prescribes to him, will shape his life too according to the example which he sets him" (1776: 113). Marx's proposition about latent political interests, that during work a worker "develops his slumbering powers" is equally true of learning how to do a job. Durkheim noted that work could diminish cognition, anticipating the deskilling debate, and quoted de Tocqueville by saying that, with the technical division of labour, "art progresses, the artisan retrogresses" (1902: 43). He was also aware of the foundation of mobility, observing that the same personal attributes could be used in different professions: "Courage is as necessary to the miner, the aviator, the doctor, the engineer, as to the soldier. Taste for observation can make a man either a novelist, a dramatist, a chemist, a naturalist, a sociologist" (319).

The Acquisition of Cognitive Knowledge and Abilities

A better understanding of the process of learning has been made possible by the development of cognitive psychology. Whereas behaviouralist theories of psychology since Pavlov (1906) posited discrete automatic responses to stimuli, cognitive psychology is a radically different vision of mental processes. The new perspective was first articulated by Wertheimer (1912), who described it as "bundle hypothesis," and by Koffka (1922), and it came to be known as the *gestalt*. This view of thinking extended the concept of coherence in visual perception to the realm of abstract ideas: Each individual organizes facts and ideas into a coherent, personal understanding that is continuously reformulated. However, although research in cognitive psychology is rapidly advancing the knowledge of how people think, Polanyi's comment that "scientists have run away from the philosophical implications of *gestalt*" (1958: vii) is still true of the philosophy, economics, and sociology of work. Cognitive psychology is the foundation of the concept of individual differences in behaviour based on personal learning by experience, notions of intrinsic motivation and heterogeneous labour, and mutual social relationships.

We are most aware of deliberate, reflective, or propositional thinking, which yields fully explicit knowledge and supports deliberated action. Codified in formal language, and in numerical and algebraic notation, explicit thought permits knowledge to be created, documented, and overtly communicated. Propositional thinking takes its most rigorous form in the scientific method, by systematically relating observations of experience and hypothetical propositions in a cycle that relies critically on doubt (Descartes, 1637). The procedure proposed by Popper (1959) for determining falsification is as rigorous as the rules for formulating a hypothesis and interpreting results. However, Polanyi (1957) argued that scientific thinking is necessarily subjective. Since no hypothesis can ever be absolutely proved, scientific thinking is necessarily imperfect, and there are always unexplained matters that arouse curiosity and further learning. Non-scientists, including the case study respondents in this study, use explicit propositional thinking in less disciplined ways, make unperceived assumptions (Mezirow, 1978), are often biased, and rely on heuristics, that is, "rules of thumb" (Kahneman, Slovic, & Tversky, 1982; Kahneman & Tversky, 1986, 2000). In adults, reflective learning involves a sequential separation of thought and action (Vygotsky, 1978) that can be long enough for complex considerations and the views of others to be taken into account in carefully planned action. This explicit form of thinking, which is only ostensibly the primary medium of formal education, introduces each person to a body of subject-matter knowledge and is indirectly rewarded when employers use formal educational credentials for employee selection and pay.

However, explicit thinking is far from adequate for learning or efficient work. As human abilities are finite, Simon proposed that rationality is bounded: "The capacity of the human mind for formulating and solving complex problems is very small compared with the size of the problems whose solution is required for objectively rational behaviour in the real world—or even for a reasonable approximation to such objective rationality" (1957: 198). Moreover, because explicit thinking is serial mental processing, it is impossible to make all aspects of a problem explicit simultaneously for action within the constraints of time that have to be taken into consideration in productive activity. The practical expedience of modifying a formal algorithm to create a pragmatic rule of thumb, and of progressively monitoring and correcting action, produces less-than-perfect results. Conflicts of opinion among workers with different kinds of expertise require the compromise of a less-than-perfect, or second-best, solution.

In contrast to explicit thinking, there is a type of learning of which people are less than fully aware, and often totally unaware. While consciously learning one thing other things are learned unconsciously, which Dewey (1916) called "collateral learning." Nor are people fully aware of the total stock of personal knowledge and abilities acquired in that way (Polanyi, 1958, 1966). Fully explicit thought does not reveal the hidden mechanisms controlling behaviour (Nisbett & Wilson, 1977). *Intuition*, which preceded explicit reasoning in linguistic evolution, is the immediate apprehension of a concept or a relationship, which makes it possible to grasp several ideas and their multilateral relationships simultaneously. *Intuition* is a convenient term for these less evident cognitive processes, which embrace a continuum of thought and action from individual sensory perception (Lamarck, 1809)—using the five senses[3]—to abstract thinking. Sensorimotor abilities, governed by the nervous system that connects mental intentions and physical movements, enable actions to be performed without explicit thought, but with precision. Perceptions of abstract ideas, constructs of conceptual understanding, and habitual actions happen too rapidly for us to be fully aware of them. The language of communication is often imprecise by purely logical criteria, but we are able instantly to impute meaning to incomplete information, incorrect grammar and syntax, and figures of speech such as metaphors and similes, and also to euphemisms and sarcasm. These verbal devices can often convey an idea more effectively and concisely than a statement in formal language. We grasp a new idea when we can perceive its relevance within an existing context and can extrapolate from an example to the larger concept it illustrates.

Although learning combines these two modes of thinking, intuition and explicit reasoning, it relies on intuition to a far greater extent than on explicit reasoning. The formation of individual cognitive knowledge and abilities proceeds by the subtle modification, often marginally, of an existing representation in the mind. Large amounts of sensory data about phenomena external to the mind are organized into mental representations within the mind. These representations are mental states that combine the particular components of observations. If, at a given moment, newly perceived data are congruent with an existing representation, they are assimilated into it, and if they are incongruent, the representation is modified (Piaget, 1969).

THE ABILITY TO WORK AS AN ECONOMY OF THINKING AND ACTING

Three key qualities combine to create the human capacity to work effectively: the ability to continually change one's own cognition, the perception of principles through learning by the experience of error, and the use of intuition and habit to economize thought and time.

The ability—observed by philosophers since St. Augustine and Descartes—to observe and change one's own cognitive abilities and knowledge is a property of human thought that has extensive implications. Through continual learning a person consolidates and reorganizes concepts and understanding born of prior experience into a complex set of attitudes and practices, which form habits of intention, action, and verification. Intuition is governed by a number of factors: familiarity with information and ideas derived from prior experience; the habitual use of deliberate explicit thinking; and the frequency with which abilities are used, to the point at which they appear to be instinctive. The process is fast and not necessarily explicit. A worker is often only partly aware, and can be entirely unaware, of what he or she is thinking and doing. In practice, someone who is not formally numerate can have a sufficient sense of quantitative relationships to be able to function in life and work, and someone who is not formally literate can be sufficiently articulate to be able to communicate and perform a task. This kind of mental process has low status and is rarely recognized as common to all human beings at all levels of education and work, but it is a central quality of the ability of everyone to think and act in a timely way. Whereas thinking and doing can be separated in time explicit deliberation and planned action, intuition is an economy of time, and habit is an economy of behaviour. Information would be unmanageable and action would be impossible were it not for the ability of the mind to process complex data very fast in the context of prior understanding. Intuition frees the mind to be aware of and attend to new information and unanticipated problems, to perceive incongruities between new observations and existing mental representations, and to resolve them by explicit thought. Intuition makes it possible to think more rapidly and to act in a more coordinated way than if one were to rely on explicit thought alone. It forms a considerable part of the reserve of knowledge and abilities upon which one can subsequently draw for a new type of task. Practical action is inconceivable without intuitive thinking, and could not be taken within the time constraints on action that usually exist, especially in paid work.

To some extent, each person controls his or her own thinking and the use of his or her reserve of mental abilities and capacities for effective action. Everyone can deliberately question assumptions, concepts, theories, and arguments to extend explicit cognitive knowledge and abilities. Everyone can also make explicit thought more intuitive and habitual by deliberately acquiring habits of reflective thinking, while at the same time retaining the power of original explicit thought. Conversely, intuitive thinking habits and psychomotor abilities can be changed by deliberate decision and developed by practice. As competence is acquired, full awareness is partly replaced by intuition (e.g., Shiffrin, 1988). Consequently, people have the ability to alternate, sometimes very quickly, between intuitive and reflective thinking to resolve a problem or to make a decision in the time available. The power to control one's own cognitive knowledge and abilities; combine data, material, and ideas; move selectively among different modes of thinking; and extend knowledge and abilities is a key to understanding personal competence. Substantive knowledge of particular matters, intuition, explicit logic, and physical movement are selectively and flexibly combined into a smooth and apparently effortless performance. Intuitive thinking and its counterpart, habitual action, govern the improvement of competence.

Just as work happens in a state of uncertainty, so, too, does learning. What is learned is provisional and always subject to new data or new conceptual thinking that can invalidate what has been learned so far. The capacity for action is possible because, although the understanding on which it is based is incomplete, it is nevertheless principled. Coherent understanding can be stated summarily either in the form of a formal scientific theory, or as a pragmatic rule of thumb, a loose generalization, a practical guideline, or a line of conduct in ordinary life and work. The organization of data in a way that makes sense to the learner is theoretical thinking. Although a scientific formulation is more rigorous than a practical guideline, the two are identical in principle. Both proceed by the experience of error, which leads to a reconsideration and a reformulation. Both create an understanding that is provisional and open to refinement. Both are theoretical frameworks for action and for monitoring the results of action. This applies to problem solving, whether a large-scale project involving the conjoint effort of a team or the most minute manual action. In either case, prior experience creates an expectation that an action will have a particular result. If it does, a guideline formed by prior experience is confirmed; if the result differs from that expectation, then the guideline is modified. Since each successive experience of new data modifies existing mental representations, cognitive abilities and cognitive knowledge are continually reformulated. Learning is an active process of reorganization, not a passive accumulation of specific subject matter.

The process of learning creates a reserve of personal knowledge and abilities. In 1958 Polanyi drew attention to the vast total stock of personal knowledge that each person possesses. When he worked as a chemical engineer he had observed that so-called ordinary workers often knew more than they realized and were able to do more than they thought possible. He proposed that humanity possesses "an immense mental domain, not only of knowledge, but of manners, of laws, and of the many different arts which man [sic] knows how to use, comply with, enjoy or live by, without specifically knowing their contents. Each single step in acquiring this domain was due to an effort which went beyond... the understanding of its agent and of which he has ever since remained only subsidiarily aware, as part of a complex achievement" (1958: 62). He later concluded, "If... the idea of knowledge based on wholly identifiable grounds collapses... we must conclude that the transmission of knowledge from one generation to another must be predominantly tacit" (1966: 61).

The ability to do something unexpected, and to do it well, is often revealed only while working. Polanyi gave it the term "practical wisdom," which he noted "is more truly embodied in action than expressed in rules of action" (1958: 54). He also described it as *"personal knowledge"* or *"tacit knowledge"* (1958, 1966). However, the term *tacit knowledge* is a misleading simplification. The term *tacit* does not fully capture the nature of unawareness, and *knowledge* can too easily be interpreted as substantive factual knowledge, to the exclusion of abilities. In the field of learning and work, the nature and utilization of abilities is more than a mere application of subject-matter knowledge. Polanyi's work hints at a different approach to those aspects of thought and behaviour of which we are not fully conscious, and which had become described and analyzed as "the unconscious" by Freud, Jung, and Kant. The weakness of these various early theories was in conceiving unconsciousness as a state separate from conscious thought. It is more plausible to conceive degrees of consciousness in a continuum between unconscious and conscious thought and behaviour. Furthermore, the human mind is capable of functioning consciously and unconsciously at the same time, and of shifting among degrees of consciousness. By deliberate intention one can embark on a series of explicit thoughts or actions that can become habitual, but of which one is less than fully aware. The situation is asymmetric: One can be aware of the fact that one is not fully aware of all that goes on in the mind. The general evidence for this proposition is that it is possible for people to discover that they learned something without having been aware they were learning, and also to discover that they were able to do something that they did not know they could do.

The net result of the conjunction of the mental processes of explicit thought and intuition is the construction of a reserve of largely unknown cognitive knowledge and abilities unique to each person, which is continually reformulated by the process of being used. From this reserve, the abilities relevant to the execution of a given task are retrieved selectively, and their coordinated use in action constitutes the experience that shapes further cognitive development. A worker can often perform a new, complex, and difficult task, and yet be unable to describe and explain afterwards the abilities that were used (Polanyi, 1966: 4). The ability to do something, and do it well, is often revealed only in the act, and this can be a source of surprise to a worker (Terkel, 1972; Kusterer, 1978). Polyani observed, "The practice of skills is inventive; by concentrating our purpose on the achievement of success we evoke new capacities in ourselves" (1958: 128). This human quality of practical wisdom "is more truly embodied in action than expressed in rules of action" (54). Polanyi's terms for this phenomenon, personal knowledge, practical knowledge, or tacit knowledge (1958, 1966), have their counterparts in the terms "practical common sense" (Bourdieu, 1980), "know-how" or "folk culture" (Bruner, 1990), "outdoor psychology" (Lave, 1988), and "practical intelligence" (Sternberg, 2000). The variety of terms indicates the difficulty of summarily describing a person's reserve of knowledge and abilities, and creates the unfortunate impression that they describe different phenomena.

The Integration of Learning and Work

Because work, whether paid or unpaid, and learning both entail problem solving in a state of uncertainty, they are united by a symbiosis of thought and action. What is learned during paid work is not always distinguishable from what is learnt during unpaid work activities in the home or in community life, and vice versa. Since problem solving takes place in all domains of human activity, all types of paid and unpaid work are opportunities for learning. As Popper (1972) observed, "All life is problem-solving."

Purposive action unites two essential instincts that define humanity: the motivations to work and to learn. Durkheim commented that "Thought can produce results, for it is equally a utilisation of anterior experience, with a view to facilitating future experience" (1902: 340). The capacity for thinking is reciprocally connected to the action necessary to human existence (Ryle, 1971). Since wants are insatiable, the motivation to work is enduring. Individual self-interest (Smith, 1776) to satisfy primary needs for food, clothing, and shelter (Marx, 1867) evolves into desires for aesthetic satisfactions, and can mature into the enlightened self-interest that drives voluntary activities and moral obligations. Any action embodies a purpose to modify a person's environment (Lorenz, 1970). Each time a worker acts, what is done differs from before: the effects of a previous action are perceived; its effectiveness is judged in relation to the intended purpose, learning by experience takes place; and understanding is reformulated and used to modify subsequent action. Thus, learning is thinking that is generated by and tested against the experience of the consequences of action. "It is essential to action that we should be in principle capable of discovering by observation whether we have in fact achieved that which we intended to achieve" (Hampshire, 1960: 52). The motivation to learn is the inherent human trait of curiosity, evoked continually by the perception of incongruities (Bruner, 1966) between current understanding and new information. Consequently, learning is endogenous in any kind of activity, including paid and unpaid work, leisure, and consumption (Loasby, 2001).

The symbiosis of thought and action is the central principle of a theory of individual learning by experience during work, but differences in terminology occlude the features common to several apparently distinct modes of thinking and action. Dewey (1910, 1916) and Vygotsky (1987, 1997) reached similar conclusions from radically different intellectual and political positions. According to Dewey, "Every experience enacted and undergone modifies the one who acts and undergoes, while this modification affects, whether we wish it or not, the quality of subsequent experiences... for it is a somewhat different person who enters them" (1916: 35). For Vygotsky, the "higher mental functions" are a "complex dialectical relationship" (1978: 73) between "speech" (meaning thought) and action. These mental functions are concurrent in a child and become distributed over time in adult problem solving and work. "This unity of perception, speech and action... constitutes the central subject matter for any analysis of the origin of uniquely human forms of behaviour" (Vygotsky, 1978: 26). A weak statement of these common characteristics is that they are similar and can be considered as variations on a central theme. A strong statement about them is that they are paraphrases of a single proposition, which is that purposive thinking leads to action that constitutes experience and the perception of experience engenders learning.

Although work and learning can be described as separate activities, they are both attributes of human behaviour whose forms have evolved from the instincts to survive and to modify the environment for use and satisfaction. Humans act to adapt all aspects — physical, social, cultural, and intellectual — of their surroundings, and they learn by perceiving the effects of action. The cycle continues because what they learn is used in further action to modify the environment, and they perceive the effects of each stage of action. Learning and work are therefore complementary aspects of the labour process. There is an inherent underlying relationship between learning and work because they are both aspects of problem solving during which a symbiosis between thought and action occurs.

IMPLICATIONS

Adjusting Jobs and the Labour Force
Any description of the milieu of employment as a market, a queue for jobs, a competition for jobs, or a process of sorting workers is too simple; such metaphors cannot

articulate the complexity of matching the unknown attributes of the labour force with an employer's inability to specify the work to be done under an open employment contract. As individual attributes differ, the labour force cannot be homogeneous. As the content of jobs is influenced, even in part by an incumbent worker exercising discretion, a one-to-one match between educational attainment and job requirements cannot be expected. A measure of education and training using a numerical value is too summary to represent the details of cognitive knowledge and abilities, or their variation among individuals, and is too subjective to be reliable (Chapter 2). The use by employers of an educational criterion or a predetermined psychological profile to economize hiring costs is hazardous, and the possibility of error is implicitly admitted by the practice of probation. It cannot be assumed that the costs of hiring, dismissing, and hiring another worker are negligible. The use of a formal credential by a job seeker is a deceptively simple means of competing with other workers for jobs but, once hired, he or she has to continually demonstrate the ability to perform the job. This requires the continuing acquisition, reformulation, and use of a wide set of abilities, including the ability to change one's cognition. Credentials are too static and vague to reveal what happens during the dynamic labour process. The notion of the labour market as an arena in which labour requirements and supplies are matched by changes in wages or the provision of information to the parties fails to recognize the ongoing changing relationship between a worker and a job after a worker has entered into a contract of employment.

Human Capital as an Evolving Reserve of Unknown Abilities

The concept of learning by experience as an iterative process between thought and action that reformulates understanding differs radically from the concepts of education as exogenous formal instruction and of knowledge as accumulation. As mental abilities derive from an interaction between subjective perception and the experience of individual action, each worker's knowledge and behaviour develops idiosyncratically, and the labour force is a heterogeneous collection of actual and latent abilities. This conclusion justifies modern economic theory having abandoned the neoclassical assumption of homogenous labour. The retention by Keynes (1936) of the assumption of labour homogeneity (see Chapter 1) was critical to his proposition that fixed investment was the key determinant of the level of economic activity. Relaxing the homogeneity assumption requires an explanation of performance that embraces the role of workers in making decisions.

Despite serious criticisms of rate-of-return approaches, the concept of human capital has become synonymous with education as a quantity. This is in contrast to the vision of learning and knowledge as an incalculable quality (Polanyi, 1958, 1966). Rather than regarding human capital as a fixed and measurable entity, it can be more usefully seen as a metaphor to convey the idea that each person's abilities are utilized over a working lifetime to yield a flow of benefits. This principle originates with Adam Smith (1776), who postulated that spending on education would provide a future benefit. He illustrated the principle by a calculation to show that a person who spent a certain sum on education would be able to earn a higher income. Numerical illustration is an expository device, and Smith used it effectively to illustrate other points in his argument (such as the advantages of the division of labour and shipping transport). However, its use to frame a quantitative relationship has diverted attention from the essence of the principle. The ready availability of data about formal educational attainment and wages, and the ease with which estimates of return can be replicated, appear to satisfy the criteria of a well-defined experiment, but the meaning of these concepts and the interpretations of the statistical findings have received insufficiently critical examination.

The metaphor of human capital, which includes intuitive as well as explicit thinking, captures the image of a set of personal abilities that enables a worker to create a continuing stream of income and output during working life. This concept is enriched by the notion of diverse individual psychological attributes that are endogenously reformulated by being used. If a worker's personal abilities are not all observable, and are only partly revealed when selectively retrieved to resolve a problem, it follows that this reserve cannot be measured by surrogate quantitative indicators of education, such as the duration of formal schooling or employment experience, or levels of educational attainment or credentials. Similarly, wages are a poor and misleading surrogate for what precisely a worker does in the course of performing a job. Since the publication of the calculations by Becker (1964) and Denison (1964), there has been no lack of critical comment of the measurement of human capital by level of formal educational attainment. Logical criticism is insufficient, however, and the availability of data and computing facilities creates an overwhelming inertia in analytical thinking. Simplistic calculations will no doubt continue to proliferate until empirical case studies of workers' cognitive abilities reach a critical mass large enough to build a detailed view of the qualitative content of human capital.

Human capital is more realistically conceived as a personal reserve of cognitive knowledge and abilities, which necessarily varies among individuals. This qualitative and less than fully observable concept of human capital is incalculable, but can nevertheless be investigated empirically with case study data. It is the germ of an idea which, taken to its logical conclusion, breaches the assumption of labour as homogeneous. The demonstration of the heterogeneity of labour is one of the key findings of this study, the implications of which are discussed in the concluding chapters. Benefits are not limited to economic output, as illustrated by the well-known finding that the education of girls and women can lead to smaller families and higher living standards. The empirical evidence analyzed in Chapters 7 to 12 demonstrates that people make many uses during their unpaid activities of the understanding they have acquired during paid work. Conversely, learning occurs outside paid work and can be used within it. Thus, if the concept of human capital formation is to be retained, it has to be widened to admit the multiple types of opportunity for learning by experience, both within and outside formal schooling. Moreover, the formation of human capital through learning by experience, both during formal instruction and beyond, is a process of ongoing reformulation of cognitive abilities, rather than of accumulation. The most important features of human capital in this sense are the abilities that each individual worker has to reorganize cognitive knowledge and abilities, to combine complex lines of explicit and implicit thinking into coherent and purposeful action, to selectively retrieve knowledge and abilities, and to devise unconsciously the new abilities required to resolve unanticipated problems.

Mobility and Job Modification
The predominant perception of labour mobility is governed by two contrasting and debatable assumptions. From the implicit assumption that learning is the exogenous acquisition of specific subject-matter knowledge, the conclusion is drawn that further formal education and training in substantive technical knowledge is needed to enable a worker to adapt to a given job or to move to another, and can and should be planned (e.g., Pankhurst, 2005). This assumption implies a norm of immobility on the part of a worker and a need to incur the costs of subsequent retraining, possibly more than once. A converse assumption is that labour mobility is possible because members of the labour force possess "generic skills" common to more than one job or occupation (e.g., Sjogren, 1977; Pratzner & Stump, 1978), so that the identifying of those common skills would enable easier transfer among jobs. That once-fashionable concept was not only a misconception of the abilities needed to do a job but also a static view of a worker's possible tracks in the labour market; it also implicitly assumed exogenous learning only.

The roots of a worker's mobility among jobs and of the mutation of jobs are more plausibly found in the symbiosis between individual thinking and action, which is to some extent revealed by the polyvalent abilities a worker develops. The ability to be mobile is acquired during the process of learning by the experience of doing a job. What a worker transfers from one task to another, or from one job to another, is not so much specific cognitive knowledge as the abilities to control cognition, transform knowledge, and reformulate mental attributes. Depending on the scope offered to learn by experience in a job, all workers are, to greater or lesser degree, mobile among tasks. The counterpart of that reformulation of individual abilities is a modification or mutation of the nature and content of jobs.

Competence and Productivity
Trends in productivity are most commonly calculated by comparing changes in labour inputs and production, but such calculations can neither explain how productivity improves, nor reliably guide policy. The continual changes in both a worker's abilities and the job performed can only be observed by empirical case

studies of the details of what a worker thinks and does during work. In the process of perception, the mind organizes observed data simultaneously into many different, overlapping, conceptual categories, each of which consolidates the previous perception of a particular type of experience. Each category is internally coherent and transcends the observed data. An individual's attention can focus selectively on a given concept. Cognitive control also takes thinking further. People can make inferences from perceptual input, manipulate concepts, combine knowledge and abilities in original ways, and form explicit propositions and tacit intentions, which they can embody in intentional action. By recursively combining a finite set of concepts into new conceptual structures that go beyond existing ideas, people can extend their range of action beyond prior experience. Barsalou (1999) proposed the felicitous use of the term *productivity* for the unlimited human cognitive ability to transcend experience. This term captures the human instinct for autonomous cognitive development as the foundation of improvements in personal performance at work and of endogenous economic growth.

Research into Work and Learning

If indirect collateral learning is more important than direct learning, data from surveys of what respondents say they are aware of are likely to be seriously inconclusive, and new qualitative methods are needed to reveal the deeper processes of work and learning. However, the study of the qualitative attributes of work and learning, especially implicit learning, is hampered by being conducted in the formal, explicit language of scientific discourse. Moreover, the process of learning is so rapid that it cannot be observed while it is happening, and the cognitive abilities and knowledge acquired are not only invisible, but can be so complex that it is impossible to describe them. Respondents have difficulty in describing their thinking. Most language in practice employs an extensive array of forms of speech containing statements that are not literally true, and which can create errors of interpretation.

A practical conclusion for research is that empirical evidence about what a worker does during a job, and how, is a source of information about learning that can be more comprehensive or insightful than attempts to observe directly how a worker learns, or what has been learnt. The performance of work is potentially a rich source of empirical data about learning by experience, which are examined in Chapter 12. However, although respondents can sometimes identify matters they have learned explicitly in unpaid work and have been able to use in paid work, or vice versa, much learning remains collateral. Consequently, there is an inherent epistemological problem to be addressed. Since neither a worker nor a researcher can directly observe the learning process or the stock of cognitive abilities that has been acquired, interpretations of the qualitative evidence about the processes of implicit learning and the abilities acquired rely heavily on subjective judgment. The following five case studies will offer some evidence for further exploratory inferences.

Notes

1. For a more complete review, see Chapter 2.
2. The trend in costs, with some slight variation, declines at a declining rate.
3. Sight, hearing, feeling, taste, and smell.

Chapter Seven
Continual Learning, Autonomy, and Competency among High School Teachers

Meredith Lordan

A DAY IN THE LIFE OF A TEACHER

On entering a typical secondary school in culturally diverse Ontario you are surrounded by a throng of students. Looking around at the walls you notice posters, some of which are falling down or slightly torn, announcing upcoming fundraising events, speakers from colleges, apprenticeship programs, meetings of school clubs, and listing universities. In loud, energetic Mandarin, Spanish, Urdu, and English voices, you hear students making plans. Watching your step, you move carefully between students and the piles of their temporarily discarded heavy textbooks, lunches, and clothing in the hallway. As they prepare for their next classes, you hear the latest hit song transformed into a barely audible ring tone coming from an administration-prohibited cell phone, quickly muffled as the locker door closes. While rushing to the next class, a teacher navigates the hall's chaos hoping to finish photocopying, deliver attendance forms, and confer with a colleague about the special education accommodations for a student. With public address system messages urging everyone to get to class, a mere 30 seconds remain before the bell rings.

Just as the next class begins, the teacher sees a large pile of the previous day's attendance forms and a pencil poised atop them on his desk. With numerous details swirling inside his head, including reminders about upcoming major assignments, a staff meeting after school, calls for student volunteers from community agencies, he finishes taking the attendance. Yet even after having the students write their names on cards and place them on their desks for the first two weeks of class, the teacher needs to call out each name. He has not yet committed the names of the changing cast of students to memory. Next, he writes the agenda for the class on the board: a guided visualization about imprisonment, with students sharing their responses to the exercise; a group reading of a pictorial book about the life and struggles of Galileo Galilei; and a class discussion about the nature of truth, censorship, and freedom of expression. For the discussion the class is divided into distinct but complementary learning groups: one group developing a model of the night sky as seen by Galilei, one writing a letter in defence of Galilei, another writing a letter in defence of the papacy, and a final group creating a children's picture book about Galilei's life for a local elementary school.

As the preceding scene attests, teachers assume many roles: curriculum specialists, conflict mediators, school-community liaisons, and lifelong learners. This chapter examines how teachers learn to perform their jobs through an ongoing negotiation between their professional selves and dynamic school environments. What do teachers do while teaching? How do teachers learn to do their jobs? Answers to these questions are derived from the insights offered by public high school teachers in Ontario. Data for this chapter are drawn from teachers in the 2004 EJRM Survey and from a case study of two secondary school sites within the Toronto public school board. For the case study, site observations and 20 semi-structured, in-depth interviews were conducted with 15 secondary school classroom teachers, two school principals, one vice-principal, and two teachers' federation leaders. Their responses provide anecdotal evidence of the challenges facing teachers at a time when political agency and professional autonomy are being actively renegotiated. The central question explored is how teachers' working conditions relate to their learning processes in this changing context.

ORGANIZATIONAL CONTEXT OF TEACHING IN ONTARIO

When considered in view of the National Occupations Codes (NOC), secondary school teachers show job stability and high employability. The profession continues to have a low average unemployment rate (2 per cent) compared to the rate for all occupations (5 per cent) (Job Futures, 2007). The 15 case study teachers have been in the labour force for an average of 22 years. Their average length of employment with the school board was nine years. In addition to all of the respondents holding a Bachelor of Education (BEd) degree, nine respondents had done some graduate work. The case study sample draws from a very experienced group of teachers who have been able to develop their abilities through on-the-job observation, alliance building, and informal mentoring. The portrait of permanently employed teachers in the case study reveals racial homogeneity—predominantly white female teachers, aged 45 to 50 years, with one South Asian–Canadian participant. Among the respondents one had a disability, and all were born in Canada, spoke English as a first language, identified as upper-middle class, and earned a gross annual income of about $70,000. The participants' subject specializations varied widely.

According to the 2004 WALL Survey, teachers possess one of the longest job tenures: 46 per cent have been working in the same type of job for more than 16 years. The survey also revealed a high degree of gender and racial homogeneity. Seventy-five per cent of teacher respondents were female, and 95 per cent were white (Livingstone & Antonelli, 2007). This racial homogeneity raises concerns about the responsiveness of teachers to the ethno-cultural diversity of their students, curricular choices, equitable teaching and learning, and systemic barriers to teacher preparation and employment.

The State of the Teaching Profession 2006 Annual Survey, commissioned by the Ontario College of Teachers, surveyed 1,000 teachers in July 2006. The report identified the following indicators of problems to be solved within the profession: time constraints within which to deliver the new Ontario Secondary School Curriculum (61 per cent of respondents); lack of parental/family support (56 per cent); school politics (46 per cent); teacher performance appraisal system (45 per cent); inability to secure appropriate resources and materials (37 per cent); exams and the Education Quality and Accountability Office's (EQAO)[1] assessment preparations (31 per cent) (Jamieson, 2006: 53). As the following figures also show, teachers' work stress levels remain a central issue and an enduring concern (Smaller, Clark, Hart, Livingstone, & Noormohammed, 2000): stressed all the time (45 per cent) or a few times a week (23 per cent) (Jamieson, 2006: 49–53). Recognizing the importance of stress reduction, one of the teacher federation's district offices has, since 2007, included a session on wellness-based stress reduction as part of the annual board-wide professional development day for teachers (OSSTF, 2007: 1; Kabat-Zinn, 1990).

With less than half of all 2006 high school teacher graduates from Ontario faculties of education securing regular employment by spring 2007, Ontario has recently experienced a market oversupply of teachers. (McIntyre, 2007: 28–29). Four factors contributing to this surplus are declining retirements, increase in admissions to Bachelor of Education programs in Ontario, a vast increase in the recruitment of Ontario students by American teacher education programs, and the arrival of large numbers of foreign-trained teachers (McIntyre, 2007: 29–40). In this situation of excess supply, the following criteria are used to recruit teachers: academic qualifications, Ontario College of Teachers (OCT) certification, the content of the practicum (practice teaching) reports, and specific subject demand. French as a Second Language, computer science, and technology have been subjects with high teacher demand. Conversely, English, drama, history, and the social sciences continue to have lower demand (McIntyre, 2007: 41–2).

The Ontario school system is large, diverse, and multifaceted. The Education Act mandates teachers to perform the following tasks: prepare lesson plans and teach classes; encourage students in their studies and evaluate student work and progress; supervise students' behaviour and maintain classroom discipline; demonstrate good citizenship and respect for all groups of people; and monitor students' school performance and progress toward their career goals. This complexity is not reflected in any official job description. In fact, the Education Act does not detail teachers' daily work and professional activities. One teacher, John, commented:

> Do I have a piece of paper [with a written job description for a teacher]? No, as a job description you have the ministry manuals... you still have to follow certain guidelines. In the classroom you are king... teachers have the latitude to design and do what they do. We have tremendous autonomy.

Abbas, a principal, commented:

> The curriculum is set by the ministry, and it is up to them [the teachers] to deliver it in any way they see fit.... They must deliver the curriculum as set up by the ministry; they must report achievement to parents and the board; and they must be respectful of their clients.

The limits of professional discretion are constantly being negotiated between predefined professional expectations and the political infrastructure within which teachers operate. Professional expectations include the standards of practice and professional membership governed by the OCT. The political infrastructure refers to the increasing politicization of education as a public good within provincial politics. This political focus has personal consequences for teachers and affects their relationships with colleagues, students, families, and communities.

Teachers working for this large urban board must address a wide range of issues, among them the need for representative curriculum and co-curricular programming to address ethno-cultural diversity and varying student learning needs; English as a Second Language programs for children and adults; the need to foster positive school-home ties, especially within families for whom school is not a site for easy dialogue and engagement; and enhanced supports for students living within socio-economic high-need neighbourhoods, including breakfast programs and after-school activities.

The two schools profiled in this case offer a full range of courses to meet the needs of a diverse group of students.[2] Upon completion of 30 applicable credits, students receive the Ontario Secondary School Diploma (OSSD).[3] Optional choices allow students to tailor their education to suit their individual interests as well as to meet workplace, apprenticeship, college, university, and career requirements.[4]

PROFESSIONALISM AND UNION ADVOCACY — THE ONTARIO SECONDARY SCHOOL TEACHERS' FEDERATION (OSSTF)

Ontario public high school teachers work within dual frameworks of unionization and professionalization. Their labour union is the Ontario Secondary School Teachers' Federation (OSSTF), which was founded in 1919. As a professional group, they are represented by the Ontario College of Teachers (OCT). All of the case study participants belong to the OSSTF, the second-largest teachers' federation in Ontario with over 60,000 members. The OSSTF is a member of the Canadian Labour Congress and the Ontario Federation of Labour. Its primary responsibilities are to negotiate and protect collective agreements. Varied professionals, in addition to teachers, are affiliated with it. It represents teachers, some teaching assistants, continuing education teachers and instructors, psychologists, speech language pathologists, secretaries, social workers, some plant support personnel, and attendance counsellors. Negotiated with each board of education, collective agreements are the top priorities of the federation. The most recent four-year agreement, one of many multi-year collective agreements reached between boards of education and teacher federations in Ontario, outlines the key areas of salaries, working rules, employee benefits, and seniority. The federation and the board, at the time of printing, are negotiating. Increasingly, acrimony and the claim of bargaining in bad faith are characterizing this round of negotiations.

The period between 1995 and 2003 in Ontario is known as the "Common Sense Revolution" era. Progressive Conservative government rule centralized decision-making power to itself and created labour turmoil, acrimony, and a common educational curriculum. All of the federations responded to the situation with increased activism. The OSSTF, along with the other Ontario federations, vehemently opposed Bill 160, the *Education Quality Improvement Act* (1996). One of the most contested pieces of legislation from this period, Bill 160, drastically extended the minister of education's power over statutory contracts, class sizes, teaching time, allocation of teaching assistants, changes to pupils' records, the repeal of education taxes, the consolidation of school boards, and teachers' collective bargaining.[5] On October 27, 1997, the start of the 10-day long Teachers' Days of Action, over 125,000 members from all of the teacher union affiliates in Ontario walked off the job to protest Bill 160's proposed erosion of collective bargaining rights and negotiable areas of contracts. Labour discord contributed to a 40 per cent increase in enrolment in private schools between 1995 and 2003 (Ministry of Education [MOE], 2004a: 1); however, in terms of total student enrolment, these schools still educate less than 10 per cent of students in Ontario (MOE, 2004a: 1).

The OSSTF, in representing the interests of its teacher-members, seeks to work with school administrative teams. Unfortunately, the individual approaches of principals and federation representatives can lead to combative relationships. Members have an on-site federation representative, also a teacher, who serves as a liaison, an accountability overseer, and a source of information about federation activities. The political nature of the federation also raises possibilities and challenges for its members:

> I'd love to have a better understanding of teaching as a political act. It's the dog biting its tail. We need to get political as a profession. There should be more input by teachers into policy. I sense the need for more consultation. There's a big gap between that and implementation. I want to see more cooperation. There needs to be more communication. (Salma)

For Salma, the breakdown of communication between the OSSTF and school principals creates a culture of silence. The ability to politicize the profession is evident in Declan's reflections on the state of the profession:

> There needs to be greater politicization of the profession, but in a progressive and invitational way. How can the union use its power to advance public education? There needs to be a savvy media strategy. I think the elementary [teacher] unions have done a better job of it. If 30 per cent of high school students are dropping out, something is really wrong. We, as a profession, and at all levels, need to look at this seriously... go beyond good photo ops.

Declan wants the federation to engage in more public relations as political action to foster greater public awareness of teachers' professionalism and dedication. Declan's comments also imply that the lack of public awareness of teachers' professionalism creates a problem in how they do their jobs. Failure, within the public discourse, to acknowledge teachers' professionalism erodes goodwill toward their work and service, as well as undermining the importance of public education. His observations express the desire to see teaching placed within social discourse as a valued profession. Moving beyond the photo opportunities, as Declan suggests, to a lasting, participatory, and effective political engagement of teachers and the public means raising questions about how teachers exercise their professional discretion.

THE PROFESSIONAL REGULATION OF TEACHING — THE ONTARIO COLLEGE OF TEACHERS (OCT)

Established in 1997, the OCT is the profession's self-governing regulatory body and has 215,000 teacher-members. As a provincially mandated body, it symbolizes the increasing professionalization of teaching in Ontario. The OCT confers professional membership and assesses, evaluates, and disciplines its members. It also conducts research and works with local, national, and international educational stakeholders. The OCT Standards of Practice for the Teaching Profession lists teachers' professional duties as follows:

- Commitment to Students and Student Learning
- Professional Knowledge
- Professional Practice
- Leadership in Learning Communities: Members promote and participate in the creation of collaborative, safe, and supportive learning communities
- Ongoing Professional Learning: Members recognize that a commitment to ongoing professional learning is integral to effective practice and to student learning (OCT, 2006a: 1–12).

Both the OCT Standards of Practice and Ethical Standards for the Teaching Profession state that care, respect, trust, and integrity are central to the teaching profession (OCT, 2006b). Individual teachers are expected to enact the standards using their best professional judgment, but the OCT has the authority to sanction failures or malfeasances.

Teaching is a self-regulating profession that is concerned with standards and accountability. A complex relationship exists between a teacher's professional identity, the high degree of discretion and responsibility he or she is given, and the increased degree of public scrutiny and control over their work. As Connell (1985: 203–4) wrote, "They have a legitimate interest in the *control* of their workplaces, in not being subject to other people's control without their consent, in not being pushed around, and in having the opportunity and resources to make decisions collectively for themselves."

While the OSSTF seeks a middle ground between centralized state authority and the creative autonomy of teachers as professionals, the OCT is an instrument of state authority. OCT membership is mandatory for all teachers in publicly funded Ontario schools. Some case study participants raised concerns about the efficacy of this body. Administrative attempts to standardize and enforce professional regulations through the OCT often interfere with teachers' daily work. Sarah, a first-year teacher, voiced her frustration with perceived bureaucratic inaction and lack of responsiveness to teachers' needs by the OCT:

> The Ontario College of Teachers doesn't do anything for you. You just pay them money to do absolutely nothing. That was a big waste of time and money ... I would rather get $140 off a course every year. They have a network of 200,000 teachers; they can't work some discount with universities for professional development courses?

Responding to a purported need for increased accountability in teaching and, at large, in the public sector and professions, the creation of the OCT was one of the many contentious reforms instituted by the 1995–2003 Conservative provincial government (Ingersoll, 2003; Smulyan, 2003).[6] This period of widespread reform was characterized by sweeping changes that included the implementation of a new and standardized Ontario curriculum from kindergarten to grade 12; standardized testing for students in grade 3 (in reading, writing, and mathematics), grade 6 (in reading, writing, and mathematics), grade 9 (in mathematics), and grade 10 (in literacy) by the Education Quality and Accountability Office (EQAO); the creation of standardized province-wide report cards for elementary and secondary students; the end of the five-year high school program and the Ontario Academic Credits (OACs) typically taken in that year, grade 12 or the former grade 13; and the amalgamation of school boards throughout Ontario.

There is an underlying tension between the skills teachers bring to their roles and the changing nature of their jobs (Ontario Ministry of Education, 2008; OECD, 2004). To what extent are teachers moving, or being compelled to move, away from situational and self-directed learning, notably learning through teaching (Cortese, 2005; Geijsel et al., 2005), to government-mandated professional development? With a possible loss of teachers' professional and autonomous control over curriculum and their daily work (Moore, 2005; Cochran-Smith, 2001, 2003), the increasing focus on education standards raises the possibility of international standards being used to assess teachers' professionalism and aptitudes. From the teachers' perspective, the OSSTF has been their main instrument in this struggle. The public nature of teaching, the view of education as a social good, the increasing regimentation and professionalization of teaching, and investment in public education all place teachers in a challenging position as private citizens with public accountability and professional responsibilities.

FORMAL EDUCATION REQUIREMENTS

OCT membership, evidenced by the OCT Certificate of Qualification, is now a mandatory public school teaching requirement in Ontario. All teacher-members of the OCT fulfill the formal education requirements of the profession. These include successful completion of a recognized undergraduate degree in any discipline and a program of teacher preparation offered by an OCT-certified provider, typically the BEd (Bachelor of Education) degree. Teacher candidates in technological studies, including construction, cosmetology, and hospitality, may present college, apprenticeship, or extensive workplace experience in lieu of a degree for admission to a teacher preparation program. In response to the growing need for these skills in the workplace, expedited diploma programs exist to provide training and professional access to these teacher candidates. Continued professional learning, a core value of the OCT, is shown in case study teachers' formal (graduate degree and additional qualification courses), and informal learning activities such as reading, travel, and community involvement.

The additional qualification courses help teachers to acquire mastery of subject areas, including curriculum familiarity, leadership, and professional networking.

Such courses, offered by all of the faculties of education in Ontario, are approved by the OCT. While not mandated, teachers do avail themselves of these voluntary courses in order to acquire or deepen their subject familiarity. They may also gain insights into leadership within specific subjects through advanced courses. Successful completion of an additional qualification course is noted on the teacher's certificate of qualification, thereby attesting to their ability to teach a specific subject.

Job credentials for teachers now include two elements: a post-secondary university degree (or equivalent work experience for technological studies) and a certificate of qualification from the OCT. Teachers are also among the highest participants in further education, much of it required for credential upgrading. Over half of the case study teachers had a master's degree.

The case study teachers offered mixed reviews of teacher education programs, but they all indicated extensive combinations of continued formal and informal learning activities. They greatly value learning on the job from colleagues and particularly benefit from informal mentoring by colleagues. They also highly rate independent learning in such areas as subject content, assessment and evaluation, and pedagogy. Much learning is collateral, or below the surface and unknown to the learner. Soren, a vice-principal, observed, "With informal learning, you don't even know you're doing it." Most teachers have a sense of the infusion of informal learning in both their teaching and their education courses. As Rajine said, "All of your informal learning informs your practice. I don't think you can separate the two."

Much of teachers' learning originates in unpaid work activities. Julie made a clear connection between her life experiences, her reading, and the developing fabric of the curriculum she teaches. Rather than seeing these as separate activities, she links them seamlessly as a source of both professional growth and, by extension, student learning. Whether watching a news program or a movie, or reading a novel, diverse sources of teachers' informal learning do support the teaching of the official curriculum. As Julie commented, "I think informal learning's important so you're not just teaching out of books, incorporating examples from your life and bringing these into the classroom. My general interest learning, I don't know… I do bring things in from my work with the church group, like team-building." The willingness to participate in ongoing informal learning attests to the respondents' commitment to students and student learning, which is one of the standards of practice. However, pragmatic considerations, including insufficient release time in which to pursue ongoing formal education and lack of funds pose challenges to the balance between learning and teaching.

In spite of the high level of formal match noted in the EJRM Survey findings, the demands of daily teaching practice present challenges for professional growth. Teachers continually respond to the ever-changing demands of their jobs (see Smaller et al., 2000), their added administrative workload, and curriculum expectations. Teaching is a very complex job (Horn, 2005). Teachers' workplace realities have been intensified by several factors: larger classes, expectations for ethno-cultural and learning-need diversity, standardized testing by the province's new Educational Quality and Accountability Office, and teachers' accountability through performance appraisals and the OCT. Despite their intensely demanding work environment, in the EJRM Survey teachers expressed a greater sense of discretionary control over the design of their job tasks (presumably focused in their classrooms) than most other employees. A majority of teachers believe that they participate significantly in organizational policy decisions in their schools. Although teachers may be especially prone to professional "burnout," for those who do not leave the profession, a strong moral calling to teach appears to sustain their commitment (Erickson, Minnes Brandes, Mitchell, and Mitchell, 2005; Ingersoll, 2003).

As case study participants considered the relevance of their formal teacher preparation programs, they often mentioned practical teaching experiences as the most useful means of education. Soren observed, "The BEd prepared me somewhat, providing the basics. It's about interacting with students. That's where I learned." For Signe, a longer professional preparation program would be appropriate: "I think there should be more training required. I wasn't disappointed when they were talking about making teachers' college two years: one in school and one in university... I would find on-the-job training, much more helpful." Salma, while mindful of her formal training, faces ongoing challenges for professional growth: "I did my BEd, but I really learned from doing it. I'm still struggling to get out of rigidity... I'm learning how to relate to the kids better." The unpredictable aspects of working with students have given her opportunities for informal learning that have a positive influence on her teaching.

As outlined by the Ministry of Education and the OCT, performance requirements include membership in the college and teaching practice in accordance with the Education Act, OCT Standards of Practice, and school board policies. In response to growing instability in the profession, a new requirement is participation in the recent New Teacher Induction Program (NTIP). One-third of new teachers leave the profession during their first five years, and with disability-related leaves of absence having doubled since 1991, and reported depression rates one-third higher than in other professions (MOE, 2004b: 2), the NTIP was created to provide a more systematic professional induction. Each school board exercises discretion in implementing the NTIP. This takes many forms, including teacher observations, informal dialogues with colleagues, and professional development seminars. However, outside of the official NTIP initiative, teachers have often formed professional development and induction alliances with colleagues.[7] Almost all teachers in the sample were inducted through informal mentoring.

EDUCATION-JOB MATCH FINDINGS

As Graph 7.1 summarizes, teachers in the EJRM Survey have among the lowest levels of formal underemployment in terms of the match between their credentials and

Graph 7.1 Relevance, Credential, Performance, and Subjective Gaps among Teachers, Professional Employees, and All Non-managerial Employees, Ontario, 2004 (%)

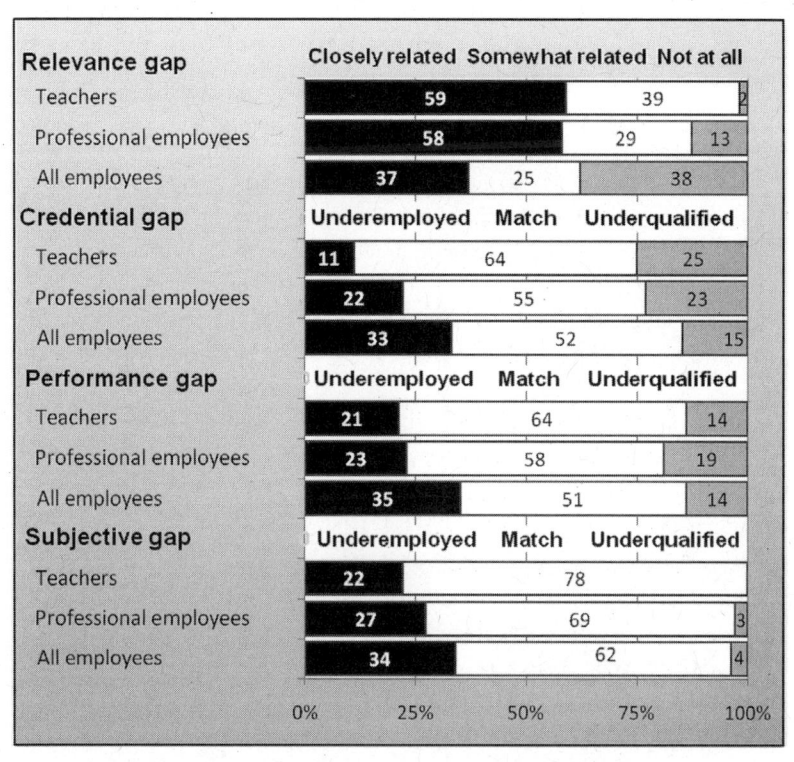

Relevance gap	Closely related	Somewhat related	Not at all
Teachers	59	39	2
Professional employees	58	29	13
All employees	37	25	38

Credential gap	Underemployed	Match	Underqualified
Teachers	11	64	25
Professional employees	22	55	23
All employees	33	52	15

Performance gap	Underemployed	Match	Underqualified
Teachers	21	64	14
Professional employees	23	58	19
All employees	35	51	14

Subjective gap	Underemployed	Match	Underqualified
Teachers	22	78	
Professional employees	27	69	3
All employees	34	62	4

Source: EJRM Survey (All employees, N=1301; Professional employees, N=364; Programmers, N=46)

those required for their jobs, at around 10 per cent. They also have relatively low performance gaps and subjective gaps. That is, only around 20 per cent indicate that they have higher qualifications than needed to actually do their jobs. Finally, along with the majority of professional employees, most teachers say that their field of studies is closely related to their job. In terms of these survey measures, teachers' educational attainments appear to be very closely matched with their job requirements. However, it should be noted that among teachers there is also a somewhat higher level of credential underqualification, around one-quarter. The survey findings in Chapter 5 also show that teachers exhibit very high levels of post-secondary attainment and certification as well as very high continuing learning both formally and informally. This combination of findings suggests a continuing demand for formal upgrading of teachers' credentials. The case study looks at this finding more closely.

WHAT WORK DO TEACHERS DO?

The hierarchical structure of secondary schools, with authority centralized at the level of the principal and divided into discipline-specific departments, inherently limits opportunities for inter-disciplinary and horizontal collaboration and problem solving (Siskin, 1991). John, a science teacher employed for seven years, recounts the various elements of his day:

> Seven a.m. arrive at pool, 8:15 a.m. leave the pool, shower, prepare for first class, teach the class, take attendance, home form duties... noon lunch (I've stopped eating lunch in the staff room in part because the food's bad and because with five preps I don't have the time). Spare, teach, and then marking.[8]

Reeva, a mathematics and science teacher with three years of experience, echoes the range and complexity of her daily work tasks:

> A typical day, huh? It varies, but I check my mailbox, see the announcements the kids have to do. I'm in charge of morning announcements. Then there's period one home form. I open the door, make sure the lab is set up and look for any safety things before the students arrive. I do some liaison with the robotics club, as I'm the staff sponsor. I do some photocopying, lesson layout, and designs. I teach for the rest of the morning, have lunch, and then there's usually a weekly potluck [with staff]. I have my prep period and usually run around doing robotics club items. We're off to a competition soon, so it's a busy time. I teach the rest of the day. I mark after school or at home, staying after class or after school to finish labs and help students.

Julie commented:

> I get to school and do my prep work. I go through the agenda for the class for the day. Once I've answered all of my emails, the prep is over. At lunchtime I'm thinking of the next classes. The last period the students will hang around, other students will come in after school. Most of my marking I do after school and at home.

The range of daily tasks reveals the dynamic nature of a teacher's job. Lessons are planned, and students' work is assessed and evaluated. On another level, some of their activities may imply what they are learning: that is, how to plan lessons by reviewing curriculum expectations; how to address the learning needs of their students by assessing which learning strategies most support their learning and then making adjustments; how to develop interactive lessons with real-world applications; and how best to assess and evaluate students' abilities. Likewise, there is co-curricular involvement with athletic teams, community outreach groups, and volunteer services, as well as communication—including conflict resolution—with colleagues, students, and families. In the process teachers are also strengthening their professional skills by conferring with colleagues about communication methods such as calls to families, in-person meetings, and letters. By serving as staff sponsors or by volunteering for co-curricular events, they further learn how to contribute to the life of the school.

Rajine's recognition and analysis of a student's learning needs reflect her own professionalism and teaching practice:

> In some ways you have a lot of power. And in some ways, it's not at all. I think we do a lot better when I make changes to how my classroom is run. For instance, I have a student who would benefit from a change to a more ESL [English as a Second Language] focused class. It's available in the school, but the principal doesn't want that. The other frustration is kids with high needs. Not being formally identified, it takes a long time to get resources for them. You have a class with thirty-five kids. One of them really needs help, but the parents don't want the testing to be done.

Unable to secure the support of her principal, Rajine exercises her professional discretion to assist student success. In determining that ESL support is needed for a student, she is applying her professional knowledge. The teacher makes this determination by first conferring with a colleague, the leader of the ESL department, to ask whether a particular student has been identified as having ESL needs. In the case of students who are recent immigrants from a non-English speaking country, their first school determines the student's level of English proficiency. The proficiency level of the student is assessed from reading samples, oral interviews, and writing exercises, which are also used to place them appropriately within the five-level ESL stream. Upon completion of ESL programming, the student transfers into mainstream English courses. Progress is tracked by formal marks and informally by anecdotal reports about the most applicable teaching and learning strategies for their success. It is the teacher's learning that has helped her to arrive at the awareness of what will most benefit these students. She will have observed them informally and made a diagnostic assessment of their English fluency, possibly in a class writing or speaking assignment. She will have interpreted the diagnostic assessment results and reviewed her careful notes about each student. She will also have conferred with colleagues, especially those working in ESL, to determine the best supports for each student.

Mary addressed the challenges of navigating the teacher-as-learner role:

> I am even more sympathetic towards the kids and the new teachers, having done this English course this year. It's a transitional course that helps move students

> from applied to academic English. It's a bit of a leap for them, in terms of content, and for me, in terms of teaching this course. My learning process goes like this... I furiously look up the ministry expectations, very bare bones, and then try to piece together this half course. Since it's a half credit, and I'm the only one teaching it, I have freedom. I try to ask around the department. You know, share ideas. I don't like to be a lone wolf. I'm also struggling to pull together enough texts for the kids. I think textbooks, between counting them, signing them in and out, and repairing them, will be the death of me! [Laughter] The course has been good. When I'm not struggling with the whole attendance and administrative parts—fill out a form for the field trip and community service announcements and all that—I can focus on teaching.

The above interview excerpt recounts Mary's learning as part of the course preparation process. In reviewing the official Ministry of Education course expectations, she found she was in accord with ministry and the OCT professional expectations. However, ensuring that her planning accords with expectations does not guarantee that she has the resources and supports needed for effective course delivery. The extraneous details, such as sourcing textbooks and responding to ongoing administrative issues, may distract from course delivery. Mary describes the interplay between her planning and her professional dialogue with colleagues about effective lesson designs, teaching and learning strategies, and course information. By engaging in this dialogue, Mary also communicates her experiences to colleagues, thus supporting a departmental environment that is open to collective learning and the vulnerability of sharing. For Mary, this learning process is even more pertinent. Having taught a course new to her that year, she will be able to draw upon that experience to enhance her future teaching practice.

While individual teachers may suggest school-wide programmatic changes, the authority to make them rests with the principals. Anthony, a principal, commented:

> In fact, the math credit we've actually come up with at different pathways at this school is for the kids who enter in grade 9 and are really struggling. We'll put them down in a grade 9 essentials course and let them get their grade 9 basic credit. Then we put them in a grade 11 workplace course to get their three math credits. If they had to get their grade 9 applied, grade 10 applied, and grade 11 college [math credits] they would never graduate.

This example of responsive math programming demonstrates a professional will to ensure that courses meet the needs of students. At the same time, it evokes a concern about the top-down nature of curriculum reform. While schools may negotiate changes in how a program is delivered through their administration teams, the school is still bound by the Education Act. Programming itself is determined, as

Anthony's comments reveal, by the exercise of a school principal's discretionary power and choice. Further complicating this power dynamic is the management style of an individual principal.

> I think I engage in situational leadership. I change significantly depending upon what the exact situation is. I believe very, very strongly in surrounding myself with good people and letting them do their job. I believe I am a reflective practitioner.... I believe that although there is power in the position [of school principal], if you have to use that power to do your job you're not doing your job properly, you know. I've looked back on what I have done, why it has worked well, why it hasn't worked well. You have to continually reflect on things. (Anthony)

The Education Act sets out a series of required supervisory duties — often presented in terms of what a principal shall and may do — rather than preferred leadership styles. The vision and leadership style of the principal may inform school cultures in positive and negative ways.

> I have worked with some outstanding principals. They understood people, their job. They understood how critical it was to treat people with respect... to see the good in people until they give you a reason to treat them otherwise.... They're good communicators, got back to everyone about everything all the time. (Anthony)

The responsiveness of individual principals to teacher requests and suggestions varies. Guy comments, "It's very consultative. I don't fear bringing forward an idea that needs to be considered. I mention it to the principal. We discuss it at a meeting." For Moishe, this consultative approach invites teacher participation, but only to a point:

> You've got to make it so we're all on the same side. I don't feel principals are trying to do what's best from their perspective. Why not work together? Specifically, with the staffing committee, there's lots of decision-making power, but there's also a lot of decisions that come down from the office.

In pointing out a power dynamics problem, Moishe recognizes that some decisions, notably those mandated by the Ministry of Education, are not open to collaboration. In response to this problem, Moishe distinguishes his desire for input and consultation within the realities of a hierarchical system. A supportive school culture, one where "we're all on the same side," can still exist within such a hierarchy, if the participants distinguish between the areas over which they do or do not have control. Ministry expectations fall within the latter category. School-based meetings, both those with the entire staff and those within subject-based departments, provide a significant forum for teachers to raise concerns. Tellingly, only one of the case study participants mentioned a school-wide meeting structure.

Concerns are being raised about how administrative responsibilities between departments are blurring. The hierarchical structure poses additional challenges for teachers as principals assign an increasing amount of administrative work to them. Citing administrative work as an impediment to teaching, Moishe noted how this work must be done—as a precondition—to address the real issue: teaching.

> We are increasingly asked to do administrative bureaucratic work that is time consuming and ultimately just drains us, and does zero in terms of helping our students in any way. I'm thinking of everything from the amount of photocopying we have to do to the way we input reports of reports cards. Just the volume of email material and hard paper material we get in our mailboxes that have everything.

Moishe provides a detailed account of the administrative aspects of teaching, tasks that are beyond the classroom but necessary for student success. The autonomy of teachers within their respective classrooms and, to some degree, their subject departments, is circumscribed by administrative pressures.

The individual freedom of a teacher is possible within the classroom; however, this freedom is mediated—and negotiated continually—within the authority structure of schools.

> Well, the dilemma is academic freedom—being professionals and having autonomy in the classroom—but what other union worker has that? I look at heads [curriculum leaders] and wonder why they're not making too many decisions. There's a lot of teachers who don't have that sense of empowerment or respect. They want to be more than they are. I can go to other departments; you have to negotiate your territory very carefully. I can do that, but not everyone can. (John)

John captures some of the tensions within the departmental structure. Unlike the clearly defined role of a principal, for instance, individual department heads and teachers define their roles through ongoing negotiation. John, for example, is able to cross departmental boundaries, and have simultaneous departmental affiliations while working effectively with students, colleagues, families, and principals. This flexibility is not available to all teachers, possibly as a result of their approaches to teaching, their years of experience, their personalities, or the interpersonal skills they demonstrated while navigating school cultures. Department heads, also known as curriculum leaders, are teachers-as-leaders. Not possessing the same authority as administrators, they lead, model, and advocate, but cannot enforce or reprimand.

TEACHERS' AUTONOMY

The case study teachers expressed several concerns about their working conditions and the extent of their professional autonomy and control. While the EJRM Survey measures reported in Chapter 5 suggest overall increases in the nature and types of skills and aptitudes required by teachers, the context within which these work changes are occurring is paramount to our understanding of these increases. Changing skills and increasing requirements are evident. The impetus for the changes comes, in large part, from the restructuring and reforms initiated by the Ministry of Education.

> There's no choice. Top-down. Every school now must offer math, science, and English in the essential level. That is brand new. Remediation. In the past you sent them to other schools. It's big, big, big. The Ministry of Education is changing too. (Julian)

Schools are constrained by the imposition of Ministry of Education directives, including a standardized curriculum and report card. The concentration of power, particularly at ministerial and system-wide leadership levels, endures. Teachers must increase their remediation skills, for example, to meet the needs of students who may be struggling academically.

As noted in Chapter 5, a majority of teachers and other professional employees reported participation in organizational policy decision-making. Teacher respondents were particularly likely to indicate a high degree of power and discretion to act on their own.

> In our department we're lucky. In other boards they have to adhere to lesson plans, having no autonomy. I actually like that freedom to design. There we figure out goals and questions. We create an outline for the courses. We design it. That's what I really like. (Julie)

> I'm grateful for my colleagues who provided feedback and resources. The teachers were really good, especially if you don't know what to expect, some of the kids could be difficult. (Soren)

> Well, essentially our curriculum leader, as he is now called, our department heads, will say to us what needs to be covered in the course and offer guidelines generally, but not serious ones. And then it is essentially up to us to deliver the curriculum in a way that we find meaningful. (Mary)

What is noteworthy about these descriptions is the characterization of decision-making power as a collective endeavour within the structure of the subject-based department. In addition to personal autonomy within the teacher's classroom, the department offers a collaborative space for the emergence of professional learning communities.

Declan captures the high degree of freedom expressed by many of the case study participants: "I'm in control of the classes I teach, how I teach, and where I teach." His control occurs within a hierarchical school structure. This freedom is conditional upon adherence to Ministry of Education, the OCT, and board policies. These policies affirm professional autonomy while outlining the expectations of the profession.

> I try to be creative in the classroom. Creativity doesn't mean visually for me, but I tend to perform quite a bit. I get quite intense in my presentations. For some of them, it really gets the students going. I'm quite passionate about politics, about the Canadian political scene. (Moishe)

Focusing his creativity on the classroom, not on school or board politics, Moishe, like many case study teachers, welcomes the opportunity to engage his students with the passion he feels for his subject. He alludes to his own learning as a teacher. Recognizing the need to engage students, moving beyond the literal reiteration of facts, figures, and curriculum expectations, he recognizes the importance of drama. Incorporating information about Canadian politics, knowledge of which he derived from his own informal learning, he learns to literally perform his lesson through dramatic re-enactment. The unseen aspects of teaching—personal reflection about effective teaching practice, observation of colleagues, informal learning about the subject and dramatic pedagogy, in addition to lesson planning and revision and creation of assessments and evaluations—are evident in Moishe's ability to connect student needs, effective pedagogy, and the curriculum. Presumably, Moishe's desire to take a dramatic approach to teaching derives from previous lessons where the students did not "get going" with the content. Additionally, Moishe's use of drama raises the general issue of the relevance of arts-based teaching across the curriculum.

Mary also captures this professional freedom as she describes a unit design:

> So, if I've got, you know, a play, a novel, and a poetry unit, I can essentially sit down and create these things based on my own interests and on what I think the interests of my students would be... there must be one exam, part of a 30 per cent culminating assignment. But generally we even have autonomy in terms of how the exams are designed, and in terms of how the 30 per cent project will be carried out; so we, as a department, discuss how that should be done.

Although bound by Ministry of Education requirements, including the exam and culminating assignment, Mary is able to interpret and deliver the curriculum content in relevant ways for her students. This requires her to elicit student feedback. Whether through dialogue, observation, or responses to surveys, she obtains information about students' interests. This knowledge influences lesson design, as Mary determines the content of assignments and makes pedagogical choices. For instance, students who express an interest in hip-hop might be given the opportunity to create a hip-hop retelling of a Shakespearean play. Like Moishe, Mary incorporates a responsive teaching style and reflection into her own pedagogical choices. The ability to make these choices is cited as a positive aspect of teaching. Julie commented, "I actually like that freedom to design lessons. There we figure out goals and questions. We create an outline for the courses. We design it. That's what I really like." As noted in Graph 6.4, professionals report more opportunities for creativity than other employees, and teachers report more creativity than professional employees generally.

Declan expressed a similar degree of control over what he chooses to respond to independently:

> But all of the [teaching] autonomy needs to be seen within the collective structures of departments and the school itself... while I do not disclose everything to my supervisor, it's largely because I am expected to handle things as these arise. I'm a professional, right?

Noting that he is expected to handle issues as they arise, Declan reveals the essence of teaching—dealing with a vast array of unexpected problems that require open-mindedness, flexibility, stress reduction skills, and course-content familiarity.

Credentialism applies to teachers. The BEd degree allows them to be considered possessors of the knowledge and abilities to do their jobs. Therefore, case study teachers see their formal credential as part of the professional self they express in their teaching practices, one that enables them to make informed, professional choices. The professional designation affords Declan freedom but also implies a lack of disclosure. This type of self-censorship raises the spectre of editing one's concerns within a perceived unsafe workplace.

Work stress is a part of teaching. Examples of stressors include the rigours of teaching course content in a timely and engaging way, demonstrating effective classroom management, responding to students' special needs, and mediating the conflicts and emotional turbulence that characterize the teenage years. Rajine observed, "You deal with stress better when you have a sense of control over it." Technical control is measured by the level of creativity workers have to do their jobs. Autonomy, a related concept, refers to an individual's freedom to make his or her own decisions. Discernment in making autonomous decisions is discretion. Teachers, in their interpretation and methods of teaching the standardized curriculum, exercise professional discretion.

The inability to resolve an issue necessitates the involvement of the curriculum leader of a department or, if it is a federation matter, the federation representative. Either individual would offer professional advice to the teacher, serve as a mediator, or refer the matter to the principal or their designate, usually the vice-principal, or to an executive officer from the local district office. The principal, as the ultimate authority within a school, may make a mediated, negotiated, or unilateral decision. However, students and their families may refer any such decision to a superintendent of education. The superintendent may elect to rule on the matter.

Teachers negotiate their roles within an increasingly complex policy network of regulatory structure and curriculum reforms. The curriculum, with its centrally determined professional expectations, is "the main specification of the labour process of teaching" (Reid, 2003: 567). The curriculum includes course expectations, character and citizenship education, and essential skills training. In their interpretation and delivery of it, teachers assert their professionalism. Critics argue that the "hidden" curriculum reinforces systemic social barriers and oppressions, by virtue of an omitted curriculum, and privileges (white) bodies and curriculum (Dei, Karumanchery, & Karumancher-Luik, 2004; Dei & Kempf, 2006). In making curricular and pedagogical choices, teachers negotiate these curricular spaces.

Functioning within a politically informed—and contested—space, teachers also negotiate their identities as public servants and as members of teacher federations. They do so most directly with their school principals and also with school boards, superintendents, federation representatives, curriculum leaders, instructional leaders (subject specialist teachers who facilitate professional development opportunities), students and their families, and, to a lesser extent, school trustees.

Teachers are granted the professional freedom to teach in ways they find most productive. Signe observed, "For me, a great deal is creative. Teaching's such an expressive art. There's freedom... you have to think on your feet and create analogies to help students understand. Even the organizational structure of a class is for you to do." Rajine saw decision-making as a condition of professional freedom: "I think it's really important to feel you have decision-making in your job." Decision-making must be negotiated within particular school cultures. While some spaces, most notably classrooms, are the domains of individual teachers, effective teaching invites collaboration, sharing of best practices, and opportunities for reflection. As a principal and former teacher, Abbas conveyed the power invested within the teaching role:

> As a teacher, you know, there is a great deal of work. The teacher has total control over their classroom. In fact I tell them that they are and should be dictators in class because they must maintain control. The Ministry of Education sets up the curriculum. It is up to them to deliver it in any way they see fit.

The control of teaching, by schools, boards, the Ministry of Education, and the OCT, conflicts with teachers' needs to feel themselves in control of their daily work. As a consequence of this control, teachers feel that their skills, experiences, and needs for autonomy are not fully respected. And as a potentially top-down, undemocratic bureaucracy, schools may be places where teachers experience depersonalization and deprofessionalization while their autonomy and professional discretion are undermined. (Hatch, Eiler, & Faigenbaum, 2005; Smith & Rowley, 2005).

Referring to the immediate context of her home-subject department, Reeva echoed the need for some discretionary professional autonomy: "We have this power in our department, but not when there's something that affects the entire school. It's very top-down. The administration decides with little input from us [the teachers]." Salma also observed the power and influence of the hierarchy: "It's top-down, with feedback given sometimes but not [always] shared." The absence of candour at the top raises concerns about ongoing feedback. Without giving teachers the opportunity to receive and learn from candid feedback from above, the top-down approach may cause concern about reduced supports for professional growth.

WHAT DO TEACHERS LEARN?

Contemporary teacher education programs provide an intensive eight- to ten-month study of the theory and practice of teaching, subject knowledge, teachable subject courses, and equity and social justice issues in the classroom (ESL and special education programming, addressing bias and harassment, diversifying curriculum and pedagogy, anti-bullying and safe school initiatives, school-community partnerships). Foundation courses in such areas as ethics, professionalism, and field-based teaching practica are included. Evaluations of a teacher candidate's performance during the practicum play a critical role during the hiring process, more so than the grades obtained in the program. Performance criteria do vary from one faculty of education to another, but all require teacher candidates to demonstrate proficiency in the following areas: subject mastery, classroom management, diversity in the classroom, and professionalism. Several participants raised concerns about the relevance of theory compared with the rich learning environment provided by the field-based practicum.

> If you just come out of the Faculty of Education and into the schools, I don't think you can give the same flavour if you don't have some work experience. I have work experience. I've seen how scientists interact. I can bring that into the classroom. It's not that it's not there at all, but you're teaching from a textbook, not real experience. I think you need to bring the real world in. (Soren)

> I didn't like going to class. I went because you had to, but I didn't feel we were learning the things we needed to learn to teach the courses. I felt the practicum [was better].... Thankfully, I had supportive associate teachers who were the ones who really helped me. (Julie)

> I think the university degree gives you, and gives an employer, a sense of organization, the ability to think... to be a team player... you can set goals and accomplish them. But in terms of specific criteria directly applicable to the job, I don't think university does that. (Sarah)

Extending the discussion to include formal schooling beyond teacher education programs, Rajine, like many of her case study colleagues, commented on the applicability of her skill set:

> The BEd degree gave me some basic lab skills, research methods, and protocols. It got me a job in the labs of a local research hospital. So, I suppose, it really helped... it really helps to bring in things from outside. The students see you as a person outside of school.

It is within this professional induction context that teachers acquire their initial training, but they regard it as a starting point for continued professional learning, both formally and informally. Their informal learning consists of leisure activities, including reading, watching or creating media, travel, and community activism, interests that may be translated to support their classroom work. With respect to on-the-job training, all the participants in the case study indicated that it took longer than three months to learn how to perform their job tasks.

> In terms of me doing my job, I mean, you know, I had a mentor last year. This was not the most helpful person around. This was a mentor who kind of had better things to do, if that makes sense. It wasn't quite as I expected. Having said that, there were other people on the job who were not my formal mentors. These were people who, you know, did a significant amount of mentoring of me and helped me in my job. (Goranna)

Goranna, a new teacher, in contrast to the other case study participants who have an average of 20-plus years of experience, cites the importance of mentoring as an example of mandated learning through the New Teacher Induction Program (NTIP). She describes the informal aspects of collegial problem solving, rapport building, and professional confidence development beyond the scope of this program. Her remarks point to an illuminating gap between formal and informal mentoring. Although the official mentor was not a productive match for her, she took the initiative to seek out other colleagues for support. These informal spaces have traditionally afforded opportunities for continued learning and professional growth beyond mandated programs.

There is interplay between formal schooling, continuing education courses, and informal learning for all teachers — new and old. As noted in Chapter 5, teachers register a very high level of participation in further education courses and also typically take over a year to learn to do their jobs adequately.

Since teachers do a very large amount of continuing education course work, as well as job-related informal learning on their own and with colleagues, their formal and informal learning are potentially highly complementary. Greater emphasis is now placed on the formalized professional learning community (PLC) (Richardson, 2004). A PLC is a group of teachers and school principals who work together to develop, share, and refine their best teaching and learning practices. Mary described her PLC experience as connected to her informal learning experience through which she received informal training "just from being in dialogue with my peers." The boundaries between formal and informal PLC structures blur as the teacher contributes to a dialogue about working conditions that include finding a work-life balance, managing stress, organizing course delivery and lesson design, navigating personality conflicts and school politics, and learning by drawing upon one's formal and informal learning to develop lesson plans and teaching and learning strategies. For Rajine, appeals to a PLC model do not address the need for supports in other areas of her teaching practice: "I'd like to see more support for actual team teaching. Rather than just talk about PLCs, you know."

The PLC may open new possibilities for the exploration of autonomy and creativity. This could offer a helpful alternative, given that teachers so frequently experience the tension inherent in the hierarchical school structure. With school community members sharing their best practices, colleagues learn from each other, thus validating their previous learning experiences and avoiding the imposition of professional knowledge by external bodies such as the Ministry of Education. Nevertheless, authority hierarchies do exist and there are limitations. When divorced from the realities of school life, the PLC can be difficult to apply effectively to school practices. Challenges include lack of time for professional development and a reluctance to participate. Recurring themes emerge about the disconnection between teacher preparation programs, previous work experience, idealized PLCs, and the realities of teaching. The theories of teaching and learning set out in teacher preparation programs cannot fully anticipate the responsiveness required to meet the changing needs of students. Teacher preparation courses cannot possibly anticipate the full range of human dynamics that may be active within a teaching context. The PLC may also be seen as an effort to appropriate and control teachers' informal learning. For the teachers in the case study, formal and informal learning are not dichotomous but are intimately related.

CONSIDERING TEACHERS' EXPERIENCES OF WORK AND LEARNING

The desire to learn — formally and informally, from colleagues and one's own reflections, and from the teaching and learning process itself — reflects teachers' overall commitment to relatively high levels of lifelong learning (Smaller et al., 2000). Rajine said, "I pull it [informal and formal learning] into my teaching all the time. Kids love it. I pull this knowledge, my master's in science, into the classroom." She provides important examples of how a teacher works to try to relate the subject being taught to the students' experiences. The students' enthusiasm reveals that both teacher and students are making vibrant connections between her formal and informal knowledge about science and the curriculum. Rajine brings the curriculum to life by linking it to real-world applications, possible areas for post-secondary studies, and career ideas. As a reflective practitioner, Rajine makes important links between her leisure reading, graduate study, and curriculum expectations. In making these connections between her previous studies, she is linking her prior learning to the current needs and expectations of students and their curriculum. Rather than prioritizing one form of knowledge over another, Rajine recognizes that *all* of her learning is relevant and applicable to her being an effective teacher.

Sarah also draws upon various interests and experiences: "I think the more interests you have outside the job make you a more interesting person. The job's all about people. The more interesting you become, the more you are able to make contacts with students and colleagues." In drawing upon her life experiences, interpersonal skills, and genuine interest in students and their success, Sarah is able to connect with her students and colleagues as a complex individual, not just as a distributor of the curriculum. The ability to make these connections is an intangible, but critically important, part of teaching.

The EJRM Survey results in Chapter 5 also show that the vast majority of teachers frequently engage in job-related, informal, general-knowledge learning in their field as well as in new job tasks.

> In terms of job preparation, I think you learn more while employed. I also worked at the Fitness Institute for three and a half years, in the cardiac rehab program, and I learned more there that was directly applicable to teaching there, the hands on, awareness thing, working in the real world. It was like a giant co-op [cooperative education] placement. (Sarah)

CONCLUSIONS ABOUT WORK AND LEARNING

As you take a walk in school hallways after school, you think about the varied job tasks associated with teaching: lesson planning, photocopying handouts, sharing comments about the latest curriculum resource, calling families to discuss students' learning successes and challenges, submitting field trip requests to the principal, writing a reflection about a lesson, completing a student referral form for the guidance department, participating in co-curricular events, or meeting with the administration to secure funding to attend a professional development session. There is a hum, one less animated than that of the students, as teachers negotiate their roles, their previous learning, and their skills and experiences in support of student learning. These tasks reveal the explicit and also subtle realities of teachers' working lives as communicators, problem solvers, learners, and reflective practitioners. Of course, to see the full picture of teaching one would have to follow a teacher home and observe the weekend marking, lesson planning, unit designing, and informal reading that forms their practice. Studies using time diaries (Smaller et al., 2000, 2001) have documented the high degree to which teachers' home and community lives are infused with related learning and lesson preparation activities.

While survey findings exhibit a high degree of matching between their formal education and their job requirements, teachers face continually changing job demands and challenges to their competencies. Some teachers in the case study were acutely aware of not possessing all of the knowledge and abilities they need to perform their jobs. Although some case study teachers were critical of the applicability of their teacher preparation programs, the case study evidence reveals continuing formal and informal learning efforts by teachers to try to ensure connections with their complex and ever-changing jobs. Julie observed, "If you really love learning, you need to keep the lifelong learning going.... What are the students' needs now? How to teach your students better, knowing your subject matter." For Julie, a committed teacher is intrinsically motivated to continue learning in support of student success. The data reveal many teachers are dedicated to meeting evolving classroom needs in such areas as curriculum content, technological integration, professional and ethical standards, ethno-cultural diversity, and the varied learning needs of students.

However, this commitment does not guarantee representative and equitable schools. Sarah commented, "Every school has its culture. Here, it's black, Tamil, very diverse. I don't think the staff reflects that diversity." In making the distinction between the ethno-cultural composition of the students and the implicit curricular, pedagogical, and cross-cultural demands of responding to this diversity and supporting student success, Sarah captured the dissonance between the homogeneity of the teaching faculty and their ethnically diverse students. Teachers' professionalism requires that they be able to access and select relevant lifelong learning opportunities to support their professional growth and student success for all. A summing up of teachers' working conditions, learning practices, and professional development shows a group of professionals who are responsive and in continual movement. Mary commented, "I would say that I still don't know how to do my job adequately! I think that I am always learning how to do it... Really, I don't feel that I am a completely proficient English teacher, and I still think that I have a long way to go in terms of learning."

Mary views her own learning as a necessary and continuing aspect of her professional practice. Experience does not equal teaching mastery. Instead, for this teacher, it offers an opportunity to refine what and how she learns in relation to her professional practice. Although Mary embraces her learning gaps, there are continuing gaps between what a teacher knows and what they are expected to know. This is especially so in response to the emergence of new knowledge within subject disciplines, to varied learning styles and the ethno-cultural diversity of students, and to the multiple professional demands of teaching. These gaps contribute to the complex dynamic of teachers' work. While extensive professional upgrading such as additional qualification courses, workshops, and informal or formal mentoring often closes the gaps, the gaps themselves represent opportunities for self-directed professional learning. Many of the case study participants expressed an awareness of their professional learning gaps. In light of this, it is clear that further refinements of how best to support teachers' learning within teacher preparation, induction, and professional programs are needed.

Teachers' learning and work relations reveal a high level of commitment to ongoing and lifelong professional learning. Survey results find few teachers are underemployed. Teachers demonstrate continual adaptation to changing work and learning conditions. An increasingly wide array of learning needs necessitate this ongoing renegotiation of the teacher's role. Rather than seeing their role as a finite set of job requirements mandated by the Ministry of Education, teachers in the case study demonstrated a nuanced understanding of the complexity of their position as curricular subject specialists, student counsellors, parental advisers, conflict mediators, expert communicators, and lifelong learners.

Two key implications emerge. First, public educational policy should be more supportive and should take into account the wide variety of relevant lifelong learning activities of teachers. Whether it is through the provision of professional development learning sponsored by the board of education, additional qualification courses through a faculty of education, graduate degree courses, or a teacher's informal learning, dedicated learning spaces must be created to support these efforts. Such spaces may include further mentoring programs, summer institutes, year-round professional development days, and release time for training and professional growth. Second, centralized approaches to policy development and implementation, where the Ministry of Education determines the policies to be implemented by individual boards of education, schools, and, ultimately, teachers must include more meaningful opportunities for teachers' insights. As the front-line experts working with students, teachers' voices should inform educational policy in more explicit ways.

Notes

1. EQAO is mandated by the provincial government to gather and report information about student achievement through its use of standardized tests in grades 3, 6, 9, and 10.
2. Rather than labelling a student as academic, applied, or workplace, the Ontario Secondary School program encourages students to explore possible post-secondary destinations through a

selection of courses: academic and university courses, college courses, workplace and applied courses (geared to meet students' experiential as well as college learning needs), essential courses (geared to best serve students with special needs), open courses (available to all students), and technological courses (to provide the theories and practices necessary for school-to-work transitions and experiential learning in such fields as hospitality, integrated and manufacturing technologies, technological design, and computer engineering).

3. This program consists of the following student requirements. Students must earn 18 compulsory credits and a minimum of 12 optional credits, complete 40 hours of community work activity, and pass the Ontario Secondary School Literacy Test or demonstrate equivalency in the form of remedial literacy course work.
4. Thematic clusters often converge around common subject areas.
5. The Days of Action constituted the largest mass teacher work stoppage in North American history.
6. In creating a common renewal date for collective agreements, an amendment to the Education Act (section 277.11) seeks to prevent the acrimony characteristic of the Harris/Eves governments.
7. Prior to NTIP new teachers, defined as those with one to three years of teaching experience, were expected to forge their own informal mentoring relationships. NTIP now provides a formal structure for new teacher mentoring and induction. In 2001 the Ontario Teacher Qualifying Test (OTQT), a multiple-choice test and written case studies, proved another source of contention within the profession (ETS, 2002; Glassford, 2005). Opponents, including all of the Ontario Teacher Federations (Childs, Ross, & Jaciw, 2002; Gidney, 1999; Runte, 1998), successfully lobbied to end the OTQT in spring 2005 in favour of improved teacher induction and mentoring. In response, the Teacher Performance Appraisal System (TPAS), made up of the New Teacher Induction Program and the Teacher Performance Appraisal for Experienced Teachers, emerged. With streams for experienced and new teachers, the Teacher Performance Appraisal System (TPAS) reflects the accountability discourse promoted by the Conservative governments between 1995 and 2003. Teachers with two or more years of experience were evaluated every three years, with two appraisals in their evaluation year. New teachers and those new to a board were evaluated twice in each of their first year of teaching.
8. Preps refer to preparations for separate courses for which a teacher must prepare teaching and learning strategies.

Chapter 8
Staying Current in Computer Programming: The Importance of Informal Learning and Task Discretion in Maintaining Job Competence

Johanna Weststar

Simon focuses on his email and instant messenger. He is coordinating the release of a new product, working with a variety of teams and departments across the organization to time and integrate the production of each component.

Haiyan hovers over a bank of computers. She is checking statistics, running regressions, and slightly altering code to benchmark new features of software programs to the older or alternative versions. She relays her reports to the software developers, who are always building the next upgrade.

Tariq spent his early days on the job writing and debugging assigned chunks of computer code. Now he is in charge of a specific set of product items. He is responsible for the development of those pieces and must address any customer problems with them. He aspires to higher levels of responsibility where he can move away from coding and make strategic decisions about the overall architecture of a large product.

Nisha creates help features and built-in applications, while Abe works on a team that ensures the products are accessible for users worldwide. Chris is responsible for maintaining the computer and information security of the entire workplace.

These vignettes are drawn from work performed in a high-end software development laboratory. They describe specialized aspects of work performed by computer programmers in similar large environments. Computer programmers are defined here as people who write, test, and maintain the instructions, or software, that computers follow to perform their functions and who also conceive, design, and test logical structures for solving problems by computer. As suggested in the Introduction, they may be representative of emerging professions of the current era. Perhaps symptomatic of this formative condition, there is continuing dispute about whether those who also have software engineering skills (i.e., computer engineers, computer scientists), as well as those with related software skills (i.e., graphic designers, computer technicians), should be included under the rubric of "programmers." In any case, the tasks described in these vignettes are common in the core occupations of businesses large and small in the information technology (IT) field. From designing a completely new product line, to finding and deleting a rogue semi-colon in the code, to troubleshooting for clients and customers, workers in these jobs must define problems and find solutions. To this end, programmers and other IT workers employ a combination of thinking outside of the box and doing things by rote or through pre-programmed software. As well as independent computer experience, they need the ability to interact with co-workers, managers, and clients. The terms *programmer* and *IT worker* are used interchangeably in the following account.

The stereotype of a fast-paced environment where new products become obsolete almost before they are off the shelf is the real world of an IT worker. In this world the IT culture is characterized as a meritocracy with a heavy investment in the market-based, individualistic, human-capital notion of skill development (Scott-Dixon, 2004). Such characteristics, plus the natural investigative tendencies of those drawn to the IT field, means that continual learning plays a vital role in any IT job. Due to the rapid pace of technological change and the growing importance of IT across all sectors, computer programmers/IT workers have become a focus in the growing debate about competency gaps in the Canadian labour force.

IT workers can face competency gaps if there are large disconnects between their abilities and the changing requirements of their jobs. Yet because computer programmers are generally very well educated and have high levels of autonomy and control in their jobs, they stand a better chance of being able to integrate their knowledge and abilities with their jobs. To examine the implications of such competency gaps, this research draws on past literature, the EJRM Survey data (see Chapter 5),[1] and a case study of computer programmers at a software development laboratory.

This chapter begins with contextual information about the IT industry and the IBM Canada case study site. Measures of the extent to which education and jobs correspond are presented next in the Education-Job Matching section. Finally, the key aspects of education-job matching in the IT industry are discussed and explained. These discussions include the differential importance of formal and informal learning and the role that job control plays in moderating underemployment.

HISTORICAL AND ORGANIZATIONAL CONTEXT

Profile of the Information Technology Sector

The IT industry is growing and maturing and has generally recovered from the late 2001 economic downturn and the dot-com crashes of the later 1990s. The IT labour force comprised about 630,000 workers in December 2007 (ICTC, 2007). This reflects a growth of about 100,000 workers since March 2000. The industry experienced similar highs, September 2002–3, and low periods, September 2001–2. The EJRM Survey responses reflect these fluctuations. More than two-thirds of programmers in the sample reported that the number of employees at their workplace had been reduced from 1999 to 2004. However, the 6 per cent unemployment rate of September 2001 to June 2002 has dropped steadily and hovered around 2 per cent heading into 2008—one of the lowest rates in the past seven years (ICTC, 2007).

IT workers are younger than the average worker. They are predominately male, and many are recent graduates or immigrants (Gunderson, Jacobs, & Vaillancourt, 2005; City of Toronto, 2003). The sample of programmers used for this study share these demographic characteristics (Appendix 1). IT workers also tend to have high levels of formal schooling. Eighty-five per cent of IT respondents in the EJRM Survey have some form of post-secondary educational certificate. Seventy per cent had engaged in adult education during the year prior to the survey. The case study sample is similar. An overwhelming majority of both samples also reported participation in informal learning related to paid and unpaid activities.

The EJRM Survey sample generally corroborates that the majority of IT workers are in permanent, full-time jobs (ICTC, 2007; Gunderson et al., 2005; Wolfson, 2003). Yet many detailed questions about job permanence and job security reflect instability because the survey overlapped with a rocky period for the IT industry. As of 2004 twice as many computer programmers as the total EJRM Survey sample, or the professional workers sub-sample, were temporary or seasonal workers, the majority being so involuntarily. Half of the programmers said their organization showed increased reliance on temporary or contract workers, job rotation, and multi-skilling over the past five years. Over one-third reported increases in overtime hours. As well, programmers had slightly less confidence in their job security than either the total sample or the professional sub-sample. Almost one-third said they had been unemployed in the last five years.

The IT industry is predominately non-union, with only 18 per cent of the workers covered by collective agreements (ICTC, 2007). Just 17 per cent of the IT survey sample belong to a union, and the case study software lab is not unionized. The low unionization rate in IT relates to the industry profile of IT workers. Five industries account for 80 per cent of IT jobs. Of these, only two, *manufacturing* and *public administration*, have traditionally high unionization rates, and these industries employ only 20 per cent of the total IT workforce. *Professional, scientific,* and *technical service* accounts for almost half of the employment percentage; *information* and *culture* employs 9 per cent; *finance* and *insurance* represents 7 per cent (ICTC, 2007). Ontario accounts for half of the Canadian industry, with 60 per cent of the jobs located in the Toronto region (City of Toronto, 2003).

The mobility of IT professionals is somewhat born out in the survey data. The average length of time a computer programmer remains with an organization is seven years. This is lower than that of other professionals whose average tenure is nine years. The difference between them is statistically significant. Likewise, a programmer spends less time in a particular job within an organization. The average time spent in the same job is 5.7 years for a programmer, as opposed to eight years for a worker in the professional sub-sample. Eighty per cent of the IT sample reported working a regular daytime shift for an average 39-hour workweek. These numbers reflect those for professional workers in general. Most EJRM case study respondents also said that they worked a regular daytime shift at 40 *paid* hours a week. However, throughout the interviews it became clear that considerable work time was not included in these numbers. With technologies that allow access to the job from anywhere, there is a growing tendency to work from home and outside of traditional hours. These hours are often in addition to, rather than as a substitute for, the regular workweek. Gunderson et al. (2005) reported similar trends. On average, IT workers report working 43.2 hours per week: 37.6 are paid, regular hours; 2.4 are paid, overtime hours; and 3.2 are unpaid, overtime hours.

Profile of the IBM Software Lab
The IBM software lab used as a case study for this research has many exceptional features due to its size, international scope, and sophisticated organizational culture. A significant portion of the IT industry consists of small- to medium-sized enterprises that have some different working conditions. Nevertheless, by virtue of its size and scope, the IBM lab employs a range of workers in jobs that can be found across the IT industry. IBM is a major source of information technology hardware, software, and business solution services. The company has more than 580,000 stockholders and employs approximately 380,000 employees in 170 countries (IBM, 2008), though there have been layoffs in recent years (Robinson, 2002; Sayer, 2005). The software lab in Toronto employs approximately 2,500 IT workers.

Organizational Structure
IBM uses a matrix management system that enlists project teams of 10 to 20 programmers with various levels of experience. A team lead and front-line personnel manager or a technical manager oversee the teams and liaise with higher technical employees about the project. The team lead allocates pieces of the project to the individual programmers based on their expertise and experience; however, this is often a collaborative process. EJRM case study respondents said they trade assign-

ments according to ability and preference or assist others as a project progresses. There is considerable interdependence among team members and also among different departments responsible for aspects of development, testing, and release. Projects vary in size, scope, and length. Some of them last more than a year and require a team of 20 or more. Others last a few months and require only one or two workers.

In the core work of development, there are approximately 50 product teams operating in the lab at any time. The rest of the lab employees work individually and in teams in the technical areas of research, customer support, marketing, sales, testing, product release support, and security, or in non-technical administrative or managerial roles.[2] In response to innovations, product completions, and industry demands, lab work is frequently reorganized (Peat Marwick Stevenson & Kellogg, 1992; Interview with IBM manager, 2004). Thus the lab resembles what Burris (1998: 143) calls an "adhocracy": an "organic, integrative, flexible, adaptive, and innovative workplace with a constantly changing internal structure" and, as such, it relies on occupational and task mobility.

IBM supports mobility from within its own ranks. Higher-level programming and lower to middle management positions are typically filled from within. New graduates fill lower-level programming and technician positions. Outside recruitment is more common for senior managerial or technical positions. Employees are encouraged to apply for internal positions and transfer among project teams or product areas to face new challenges and broaden their knowledge (Interview with IBM manager, 2004). In addition to this management philosophy, and reflecting a general trend in the industry, IBM employees are encouraged to move in and out of management positions to develop "soft skills" while maintaining technical expertise.

Training and Education
IBM's commitment to learning and development is a vital part of company culture. The company is a long-time supporter of advanced formal education for its employees. In 2007 they spent an average of $1,700 per employee annually on training and development, a decline from $3,000 in 2000 (Kolbasuk McGee, 2007). To focus on development areas, employees are required to complete Individual Development Plan assessments, and they are given access to a range of company-sponsored learning resources, such as "lunch and learn" speaker sessions, library facilities, and on-line tutorials.

Opportunities for job mobility and reassignment within the company, along with the provision of learning resources, imply a notable trust in a worker's ability to learn through experience. A high degree of task mobility is necessary given industry fluctuations, contract and project-based work, amorphous project teams, lateral movement, technological gadgetry that blurs the lines between work and home life, and the pace of technological change. The cognitive development of each worker is rooted in this mobility and the autonomous, applied, and integrative learning that

Education and Jobs: Exploring the Gaps

Graph 8.1 *Relevance, Credential, Performance, and Subjective Gaps among Programmers, Professional Employees and All Non-managerial Employees, Ontario, 2004 (%)*

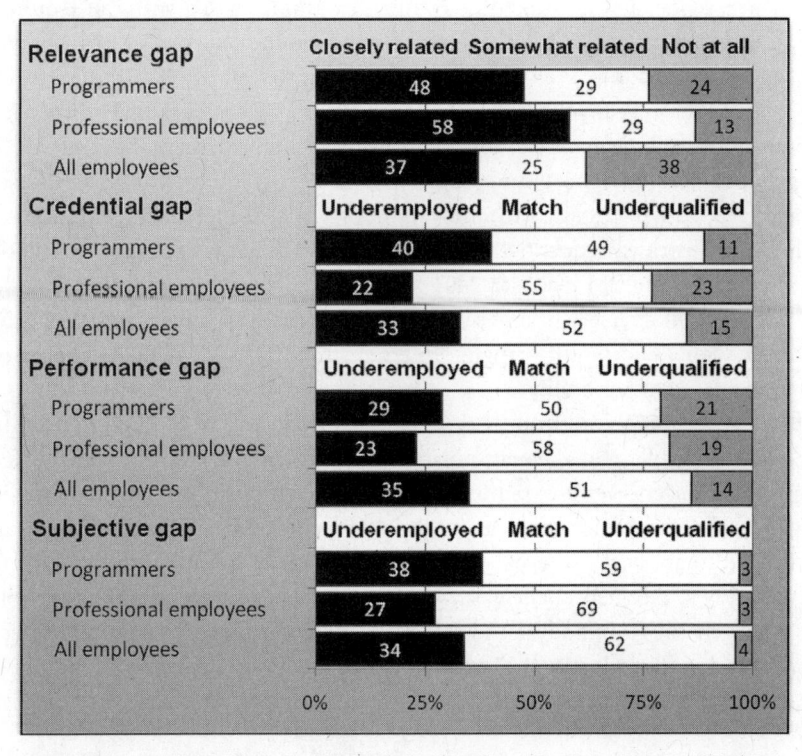

Relevance gap	Closely related	Somewhat related	Not at all
Programmers	48	29	24
Professional employees	58	29	13
All employees	37	25	38

Credential gap	Underemployed	Match	Underqualified
Programmers	40	49	11
Professional employees	22	55	23
All employees	33	52	15

Performance gap	Underemployed	Match	Underqualified
Programmers	29	50	21
Professional employees	23	58	19
All employees	35	51	14

Subjective gap	Underemployed	Match	Underqualified
Programmers	38	59	3
Professional employees	27	69	3
All employees	34	62	4

Source: EJRM Survey (All employees, N=1301; Professional employees, N=364; Programmers, N=60)

occurs within various job scenarios. Thus, the flexible work practices and work organization that characterize IT jobs make it apparent that IT workers are, and must be, able to learn through experience and apply that learning to their work. A more detailed discussion of the correspondences between learning and work follows.

EDUCATION-JOB MATCHING

In Graph 8.1 data for measures of the relevance gap, credential gap, performance gap, and subjective gaps are presented (see Chapter 1 for definitions). The matching between formal education attainments and job requirements for programmers/IT workers is similar to the professional employees sub-sample in most respects. However, some important distinctions are explored on the following page.

Relevance Gap

About half of IT workers feel that their job is closely related to their field of studies. This proportion is somewhat lower than professional employees in general but higher than service and industrial workers (see Chapter 5, Graph 5.12). However, as we will see, the fields of study that have led IT workers into their jobs have been quite diverse to date.

Credential Mismatch in IT

In the aggregate, the educational attainment and entry requirements for computer programmers match. That is, roughly 85 per cent of the respondents report that they have attained a post-secondary certificate, and 85 per cent report that a post-secondary credential is required for entry into their jobs. The data presented in Graph 8.1, however, compare educational attainment and entry requirement measures for each individual worker and reveal high levels of credential underemployment for computer programmers.

These levels contrast with prior research that has shown professional employees generally have the lowest underemployment rates. This difference in credential underemployment rates is partly due to the relative newness of the IT industry compared to the more mature professional occupations. For example, teachers and nurses have standardized educational entry requirements, and it is rare to find workers entering by other means. In contrast, the IT industry is still evolving. People tend to enter the field from diverse career paths, and the jobs are fairly unstructured, with autonomous work and broad job descriptions. IT workers bring diverse experience to their job environments. They draw on past experience and engage in problem solving to isolate, interpret, and complete their specific tasks. Such a dynamic environment presents a wealth of opportunity for new learning experiences, as is suggested by the common mythology of the rogue IT industry bucking the repressive structure of typical bureaucratic workplaces. However, the maturation of the industry seems to be prompting more structured and codified job entry and career progression criteria (Scott-Dixon, 2004). This trend could impair the fluidity and dynamism of the learning environment and restrict the space in which workers can freely apply their cognitive abilities.

The work done at the IBM software lab highlights the diversity of work in IT. Workers in software development spend their days writing code and liaising with other developers who are working on subsets of the same project. Others are part of the testing team who take the product from the developer and apply quality control tests, or work with the usability team who advocate and test for user-friendly design. Some are engaged in technical writing and applications-development and prepare the manuals, help features, and product tutorials, while others prepare the graphics and layout for product packaging. Others work in direct customer support and either field calls and emails or travel to their clients to install specific software to address their needs or problems. A number of workers maintain internal company websites and databases, or the websites and databases of their clients. A growing contingent work in systems security, and others work in hardware and set-up and maintain the servers and computer networks. Some work in research and development, some in marketing and sales, and still others in liaison roles connecting different work groups and departments.

The introduction to this chapter emphasized that most IT jobs share common features. Even so, the diversity of job tasks and their corresponding job titles compounds the credential mismatch in IT. So, too, do the plethora of public and private college and university programs, and the narrow certification programs of professional associations and specific industries or companies. These organizations offer a burgeoning array of IT-related courses and certificates at all levels. For example, the University of British Columbia currently offers IT certifications such as Microsoft Certified System Administrator, Microsoft Certified Systems Engineer, and Cisco Certified Network Associate (see <www.tech.ubc.ca/it/index.html>). To further complicate matters, many IT professionals are largely self-taught. All of these factors make it difficult to assess the knowledge and abilities of IT workers. Add to this industry and employer demand to create a standard measure of IT ability, and the side effect is credential inflation. As noted in Chapter 5, only a small proportion of IT employees require a certification or licence for job entry. Nevertheless, many workers had taken, or were currently enrolled in, certification courses. Employers may not yet have disentangled and specified the credentials that they require. Yet because of credential proliferation, IT workers feel a pressure to acquire the next new certificate to remain on top of the selection pile.

It is difficult to ascertain knowledge and abilities from formal educational credentials alone. It is even harder to translate a fluid list of job tasks and an employer's expectations into a comprehensive job description, and further to deduce from both what a meaningful educational entry requirement would be. The result is that workers and jobs are often incompatible on various levels, particularly in the initial stages. The workers themselves must bring their knowledge and abilities into alignment with the job requirements. This process is discussed in more detail below.

Performance Gap

The continual expansion and redefinition of both IT jobs and the knowledge and abilities required to perform them also confounds attempts to identify long-term performance requirements. The performance gap data in Graph 8.1 suggest that computer programmers are slightly less likely to be matched and slightly more likely to be underemployed than other professionals. Yet compared to the credential gap numbers, fewer respondents register as underemployed and more register as underqualified.

As noted in Chapter 5 (Graph 5.17), and in line with the total sample, a majority of IT survey respondents report that they have more general knowledge than their job requires. At the same time, many programmers feel they can never attain all the knowledge and abilities that their jobs require. Eighty-four per cent of IT survey respondents and 70 per cent of the case study respondents agree or strongly agree that their job requires them to learn new skills. There is wide consensus among most workers on this point (Chapter 5). Comments from the IT case study respondents clarify these findings. Some, like Carolyn, experience learning expectations as job stress: "I often feel like I have not learned how to perform my job adequately. In actual fact I don't believe that that's the case. But there are always three million more things that you could learn to do your job better. And I am often painfully aware of that." Carolyn has a master's degree, yet she strongly agrees that more learning is needed to continually do her job well. Angus, a software developer with considerable seniority at the IBM lab, similarly explained how learning to do your job adequately is a moving wall:

> I got to train one guy who came about a year ago.... After three months, he was able to do his job almost adequately. After six months, he was doing it adequately I think. But that's a lot of on-the-job experience and whenever he hits something hard, he still comes to me—twice in the last week. And I think that's more than adequate. It is not a problem that twice in a week he has questions. There is somebody else... it's four times in the last week he has asked questions and he has been here four years. In this job, nobody knows everything. We cannot.

When asked explicitly about the on-the-job learning time needed to master their jobs, almost one-quarter of the respondents said less than three months, and half felt they could perform adequately after one year. Within three years, 80 per cent said they had learned the job. The remaining respondents said it would take them more than three years and told us how they were continually learning how to do the job.

Technical and Organizational Abilities

The spectre of technical obsolescence threatens all IT professionals and prompts individual and employer-sponsored investment in technical training and upgrading (Bell, Brown, Buddo, Gunderson, Rifkin, Stager, & Vaillancourt, 2002; Rifkin, 2002). Yet even as increased technical knowledge or "technical upkeep" is required, the demand for ability in interpersonal relations, communications, and for business acumen appears to be rising (Chen, Muthitaacharoen, & Frolick, 2003; Fox, Hindi, & Remington, 2001; Medlin, Dave, & Vannoy, 2001; Noll & Wilkins, 2002). Sixty-four per cent of the IT respondents report that the skills needed for them to do their jobs have increased over the past five years. Rather than people who once produced computer products that were "thrown over the fence to customers" (Gallivan, 2004: 34), organizational rhetoric now extols those workers who can become better integrated with the larger picture in which they work as "total consultants... able to deal with business strategy, business processes, and information technology in a coherent way" (Stam & Molleman, 1999: 378). Many employers currently expect IT workers to be simultaneously information providers, problem solvers, coordinators, liaisons, and strategic thinkers (Lee, Koh, Yen, & Tang, 2002; Lee, Trauth, & Farwell, 1995; Verton, 2004).

Clearly, there is mismatch between organizational rhetoric, employee expectations, and the true nature of the job. McLean, Smits, and Tanner (1996) report that IT jobs are less creative and challenging, have less opportunity for promotion to management and other functional areas, have less impact on the overall organization, and require more teamwork than IT graduates desire or expect. They suggest (1996: 24) that IT graduates and new workers base their expectations on the technical aspects of the field, but often have to learn to change from "technical expert to technical *and* people expert" to progress in today's IT careers. What seems generically important is the analytical ability, attention to detail, creativity, and lateral thinking that are required for problem determination and resolution. At the same time, the organization of work around specific teams involves a measure of interpersonal sensitivity in all IT jobs.

Regardless of technological change and written job descriptions, the capacity that workers have to apply and shape their own abilities is fundamental to all IT jobs. Such a capacity is the bedrock underlying the knowledge, abilities, and experiences that each IT professional brings to the job. Thus, by focusing on the IT workers' underlying capacities and the individualized process of job matching that occurs on the job, the discussion of education-job matching is situated firmly in the workplace. A contrasting perspective focuses on formal educational systems and their inability to produce workers who immediately fit with industry jobs. Some argue that IT graduates should be better prepared for the social aspects of IT workplaces (Lee et al., 2002). They criticize computer science and software engineering education programs for being too traditional, for not simulating the more interdependent environment of modern software, and for not differentiating among skill sets for different career paths (Couger, Davis, Dologite, Feinstein, Gorgone, Jenkins, Kasper, Little, Longenecker, & Valacich, 1995; Lee et al., 1995; Shaw, 2000; Noll & Wilkins, 2002). However, these arguments run counter to the rapidly changing environment of IT products and processes and do not recognize the integration that is occurring across the IT sector. These perspectives do not consider the wealth of learning that occurs on the job. Further, they fail to recognize that this experience represents the true nature of learning and that IT professionals place great importance upon it.

Formal Versus Informal Learning
Programmers face an environment in which they must acquire high levels of formal schooling to gain entry into their jobs, but over half of the IT survey respondents

reported that their formal education is "not at all" or only "somewhat related" to their jobs. The IT workers' reports of the irrelevance of formal schooling to their jobs, though seemingly high, is lower than that reported by service workers and industrial workers (Chapter 5). Most programmers interviewed said that their formal schooling provided grounding in the field and gave them a basis on which to develop their abilities to problem solve and handle large workloads, even though the content may have become obsolete.

> I don't remember a whole lot about the specific group theory and other academic subjects. I remember the titles, but I couldn't do the assignments today without getting back into it. But the biggest thing I learned was how to learn and how to problem solve. And that is something I use all the time. (Carlos)

> You learn how to analyze information, and you also learn how to just get work done because you are forced to do a lot of work. I guess also that with actual content of things learned in school... maybe only 10 per cent to 20 per cent of the courses I took would enhance my skills at my job. The other 80 per cent were more broad ways of just becoming better at interpreting. (Zoey)

The distinction between broad, foundational knowledge and abilities versus specific content explains why workers feel that, on one hand, they need a certain degree of formal schooling (i.e., a technical university degree), but when they think about performing their daily job tasks, the formal schooling is less significant. This diffuse relationship between formal schooling and job performance is confirmed through the evenly distributed performance gap data in Graph 8.1 (29 per cent underemployed and 21 per cent underqualified). Due to their volatile work environment, IT workers turn more often to formal and informal learning activities beyond their formal schooling to maintain or acquire needed knowledge and abilities.

Perry, Simpson, NicDomhnaill, and Siegel (2003) assessed the extent of technical upgrading that occurs among older and younger computer programmers. They found no evidence of a technology-related age gap and reported that programmers of all ages share the same degree of specialized computer knowledge. They added that much of this must be an individual effort because many companies do not offer formal programmes that would enable such large-scale refreshing and upgrading. Stam and Molleman (1999: 378) similarly commented that companies do not have sufficient human resource systems to provide the career development and strategic training necessary to develop "total consultants." The survey data and case study interviews support these statements and focus on several problems with formal learning through employer-sponsored courses.

Compared to the total survey sample, programmers were more likely to have participated in formal education or training in the past year and more likely to have a plan to participate in courses over the next few years (see Graph 6.10). However, they were also more likely to have wanted to take courses, but did not. In the case study, 11 out of the 13 respondents said that lack of time was the major hindrance. "No time" was reported by 47 per cent of the IT survey sample. Statements from Simon, a release engineer with six years of experience at the lab, and Carlos, a software developer with 15 years at the lab, elucidate the general experience:

> I got into—I don't want to say rut, but I got into a situation where things were so busy, there was so much to do.... I actually did schedule a course one time, and it came up and I was like I can't go. I've just got too much stuff to do. And I don't want to go to a course and then work 10 hours at night. That is when I said, I'm not signing up for any more courses. (Simon)

> Being able to block off that much time—I get approximately 100 emails a day to read and process. And it's physically impossible to get through that in just a couple of hours. It takes a while to even weed out all of the stuff I really don't need to get into and delete them. At night, you'll see the damage—cry a little bit, buckle down and work till three in the morning and get through most of it. Make sure all of the urgent things were handled and then hope it's not as bad the next day and then it is. (Carlos)

These are important statements that raise questions about organizational investment in formal training programs and opportunities. IBM has a wealth of formal training and upgrading initiatives; however, many workers do not use them to capacity. In fact, many interviewees felt that very few people followed their professional development plan and noticed that those who did not faced no penalty. However, several respondents pointed out that no formal training was available because the software they were working on was too new or too complex to be learned through traditional classroom methods.

Most took formal courses related to specific technical aspects of their work (see also Graph 5.11B). About half also took courses to improve their abilities associated with social authority. These courses included project management, negotiation, management styles, presentations, public speaking, and conversational English. Workers took these formal courses to advance long-term ends such as a promotion, rather than to address specific aspects of their jobs. They were additionally motivated to increase their understanding of the work and workplace overall. Rebecca said she wanted to be able to "have a good conversation about what it is [my colleagues] are doing... have intelligent conversations and know enough that I can point my finger at something and say I don't think that is going to work, but it doesn't mean I can code it!"

Mitesh echoed the desire to take courses and gain more exposure to the larger project, rather than his own small piece:

> They are technical programming courses related to what I am doing and related to what I am not doing so that when I am combining everything, if something goes wrong, I know what [someone else] might have done wrong and what the problem is. So they are not giving you something and you are like, "What is this?"

IT workers assume significant individual responsibility for their own upgrading through learning by experience. For example, studies of young IT professionals indicated that individuals and groups solved the majority of IT problems through daily work experience, and found experienced team members and peers to be the most useful sources of information (Pentland, 1997; Lee, 1999). The EJRM Survey data reinforces this message. More than 80 per cent of computer programmers rated both their own independent efforts and on-the-job training from co-workers as important sources of detailed information to help them do their jobs. Selected less often were employer-sponsored training programs (54 per cent), on-the-job training from supervisors (49 per cent), and pre-employment training programs (13 per cent).

Many IT workers prefer informal learning modes and find the resulting learning experience more relevant to their jobs. Discussing formal learning, Andrew said he is "not oriented that way," and he feels he can "pick up what [he] needs from reading journals and books and the Web." Andrew has worked at the IBM lab for over 10 years in a variety of jobs. Fiona, now a technical lead, described why she hasn't taken formal courses in about five years. "I had a pretty big dry spell for a few years when I first moved over to the technical job because I was doing a lot of on-the-job training with books and that kind of thing." Simon thinks that formal courses had very little impact on his job performance and security, and he is using other means to ascend the learning curve of his new job:

> So I did the first course and I signed up for another and that is the one I didn't go to.... Then I was like I am still doing my job—they aren't going to fire me without it so.... I am [going to take them]. I just have to look at the schedule and find a spot for them. But right now because I just started and I am still ramping up on the learning curve, it is going to be when the job is running more smoothly.

What is particularly interesting in light of the high levels of participation in both formal and informal learning activities is their reported impact on work outcomes. Programmers report that while formal learning helps them increase their income or obtain a promotion, informal learning increases their ability to do their jobs. They rely much more heavily on informal learning to maintain competence in the following areas: job tasks, management of short project timelines, interpersonal relations, organizational and business culture, navigation of larger project domains, and in keeping up with daily changes and challenges.

As Nisha, a young programmer said, "Anything I learn on the job I am learning because I need to know it." High levels of formal schooling or additional formal courses that are separate from the work environment do not account for IT workers' capacity to make the daily adjustments needed to stay current in their jobs. A balance is suggested by the difference in IT survey results for performance gap and subjective gap underqualification. While 21 per cent of the respondents have less *formal* schooling than they claim is needed to do their job, only 3 per cent report that their level of schooling makes them feel underqualified for their job. It is the informal learning and on-the-job training—things that cannot be taught or prepared for in formal settings—that close the performance gap for many workers.

Subjective Underemployment

When asked about their subjective sense of underemployment, IT respondents report the highest degree of matching (60 per cent; Graph 8.1). Only 29 per cent of workers are underemployed on the performance gap measure, yet 38 per cent report subjective underemployment. That is, they are a good fit for their jobs in terms of their educational attainment and the performance requirements of their jobs, yet they still feel a mismatch. As Carolyn and Angus expressed, some programmers feel they never have enough knowledge to stay on top of their jobs.

A comment by Susanna, a programmer with just over two years at the lab, helps to reconcile how workers can simultaneously report more knowledge than is required for their jobs (see above and Graph 4.17) and also describe a need for ongoing learning. With reference to the match between the knowledge and abilities she has and the knowledge and abilities required for her job, Susanna reflected:

> I think they are at par. Because of the nature of my job—especially when I am dealing with customers, there are always so many new things coming in. I'll be dealing with a very specific section of [the product] on a particular [software] platform, and I'll become quite familiar with that. And then the next customer that I get shifts it into a whole new perspective, and so I constantly have to relearn things. So it's never at the point where I feel like I've done this so much and now I'll keep doing the same thing over and over again, and, you know, I know way too much for what I am doing because every other day I have to learn something new.

This quote indicates that within her job Susanna often feels underemployed, matched, and overqualified, depending on the scenario at hand. As Susanna's job continually changes, she picks up new knowledge, new problem-solving approaches, and new perspectives on changing software platforms and products. In doing this she acquires a considerable reservoir of information and experience that may appear obsolete or irrelevant in the face of new problems. This is precisely the process of continual learning and continual job redefinition that Pankhurst and Livingstone (2006) highlight (see also Chapter 12). They argue that all workers will have under-utilized cognitive abilities and reservoirs of knowledge and experience because they will not be applying each of them in every job task. To alleviate Susanna's feelings of both underemployment and underqualification, she must be provided with the opportunity to gain new aptitudes and the opportunities to consciously or unconsciously apply her working knowledge. To present such opportunities means redesigning jobs and workplaces to maximize the connections between learning and working; it also means allowing workers to fully engage their abilities with the problem space. As he learned the requirements of his job, Adnan was aware of the moment when the little pieces of information coalesced into a whole: "Just kind of, you know, experiential learning, as time goes by. You can gain more skills. Sometimes you don't even realize it. You are just telling people, 'No, we have to do it this way,' and everybody is listening to you like you know. And you are like, oh I do? I guess I do."

Adnan's comment is evidence that the process of matching abilities to job requirements for technical workers is in continual flux (Pazy, 1994; Tsai, Compeau, & Haggerty, 2004). As software processes and projects change, "various features of the job may change—for example, the pace of work, the degree of communication and coordination, the role relationships, and power dynamics between employees" (Gallivan, 1995: 107). As the burden is increasingly placed on employees to take the initiative and acquire any new or required ability on their own, and as formal training becomes a decreasing priority in many organizations, Gallivan (1995: 109) surmised that it is not the academic achievement nor the current skill sets of employees that are important, but their capability to acquire new skills, to be "flexible to grow and adapt as the job requirements change." In this fluctuating environment programmers rationalize and justify their current state of match or mismatch. The conclusions drawn from their rationalizations and justifications will then dictate whether resources should be devoted toward learning and upgrading to improve the matching process or whether a mismatch would be acceptable within the current environment.

Living with Mismatch
The above description of learning and job requirement matching in IT harmonizes with many of the interview statements already presented and begins to illuminate how programmers perceive the relationship between their learning activities and their daily jobs. For example, some programmers under-report their underemployment because they justify past experiences and choices to make them fit with their

current circumstances. Chris holds two undergraduate degrees, and he reported being somewhat overqualified for his job. However, when asked how that makes him feel, he said, "I have an overarching philosophy which is that if I had to do it over again I would. Because I am who I am based on the experiences that I have had." Similarly, Adnan compartmentalizes his experiences; he said that his master's degree (in business) is something that he's doing on the side, so it does not impact his feelings of qualification for his current programming job.

For other programmers the norms and expectations of their work environments make them feel that they are always lagging behind in their knowledge. Recall Carolyn's comments from earlier in this chapter: "There's always three million more things that you could learn to do your job better. And I am often painfully aware of that." Computer programmers, particularly those at software development facilities or in similar environments, perpetually feel like they are playing catch-up despite their formal credentials.

There is a more proactive response to mismatch. Rather than merely reframing and justifying educational attainment or normalizing feelings of deficit, many programmers jockey into positions that allow them to use skills that would otherwise be underutilized or they find ways to contribute to their work environment that showcase their particular abilities. This point relates to the hypothesis, outlined in Chapter 3, that workers with more control in their jobs would be better able to use their knowledge and abilities in everyday work.

Easing Underemployment through Managerial Authority and Task Discretion
Zuboff (1988) claimed that the proliferation of computers in the workplace eliminated tedious jobs and paved the way for workers to be more actively engaged in innovative and challenging work. These claims suggest an increase in both managerial authority and task discretion. Others argued strongly against the notion that computers have bridged the gap between Tayloristic divisions of head and hand (Kraft, 1977; Kraft & Dubnoff, 1986) and instead suggested that computerization leads to losses in worker control and scope. Kraft provided a historical snapshot of early computer programmers who were engaged in every aspect of their work from conception to execution. He contrasted this picture with more current realities where tasks have been fragmented and programming work is rearranged into hierarchies of system architects, programmers, and low-level coders (Kraft, 1977; Kraft & Dubnoff, 1986).

Conn also reported this separation of work in a case study of software engineers at an aviation firm (2002: 26). He wrote that "no one person completely understands all of the aircraft's software" and that the segmentation of work is a reality due to the complexity and size of the project. He said the depth, breadth, and inaccessibility of the problem space is one of the greatest adjustments a new hire has to make in the work world of programmers. Conn's report depicted a workplace where small pieces of a whole task are delegated to workers by their superiors and then reassembled at higher levels in the managerial and technical hierarchy. Burris (1998) argued that the increased use of project teams and task forces results in an increase in managerial authority, at least to the point where delegated or advisory decision-making is occurring in those work teams.

Aneesh (2001) introduced a framework that links the level of technical ability needed for a job to the degree of technical discretion a worker holds in the job. He analyzed IT workers and identified two types of work tasks. Tasks that are greatly rationalized and have little room for worker creativity in their execution he labelled *saturated*, whereas those that are less rationalized and allow for high degrees of worker creativity he described as *unsaturated*. An example of an unsaturated task is when workers have an intimate knowledge of the computer's internal makeup and they design and create software and develop new coding procedures often by trial and error. An example of a saturated task is when workers manipulate small pieces of a product with pre-packaged, "canned," programs or operations. In these situations workers require less knowledge of the tools they use and have less leeway in how those tools are applied. In some respects, this parallels Kraft (1977), who described how low-level workers labour in saturated tasks and those higher in the managerial and technical hierarchy engage in unsaturated tasks. This point is emphasized in Tariq's job progression presented at the start of this chapter. Scott-Dixon (2004) also drew attention to IT jobs that bear a greater proportion of the saturated or prescriptive work. She particularly noted women's work, such as office and clerical work, that has become computerized and now has many characteristics in common with IT work, but has not seen corresponding increases in status, wage, opportunities for creativity, or managerial authority (see Chapter 9). Aneesh acknowledged the dual movement of individual jobs toward each pole, but he also pointed out that each IT job can contain both saturated and unsaturated tasks.

The data from the EJRM Survey corroborate various aspects of the above debate. Forty-six per cent of the non-managerial programmers/IT employees reported involvement in organizational and policy decision-making. Based on the case study interviews, these workers are team leads that oversee technical work, senior team members, project coordinators across multiple teams, and supervisors of co-op students. However, managerial authority, which theoretically accompanies these roles, is often delegated or constrained. Only 17 per cent of those who participate in organizational and policy decision-making have independent authority to make decisions. The majority (54 per cent) makes decisions as part of a group or subject to approval. The remaining 29 per cent provide only advice. Three-quarters of IT survey respondents reported that they regularly contribute suggestions during the debriefing phase of completed projects, but this, too, occurs in a team setting. Some workers cynically observed that their input was not often applied and said that subsequent projects were managed with equal inattention to their input. Others felt that such debriefing sessions reflected consequential engagement with their managers and their team members. For example, Simon recalled that his manager vetted deadlines and workload allocations with the team and incorporated their more intimate knowledge of the work into more reasonable expectations.

Compared to the total EJRM Survey sample, and consistent with the above discussion of jobs that contain at least some unsaturated tasks, IT workers described having more job control in the technical sphere. Over 80 per cent said that they had to exercise a great deal of creativity in their jobs as opposed to following set rules or routines. High job creativity was reported by just over 40 per cent of the total EJRM sample. Similar results were reported for the amount of technical task discretion IT workers are allowed (i.e., how much choice a worker has in how the work is carried out).

These data imply that though some literature on the IT industry suggests that teamwork, decentralized structures, adhocracies, and computerization increase worker autonomy and control (Burris, 1988; Zuboff, 1988; Hitt & Brynjolfsson, 1997), the actual effects of these structures are more complex. It is the technical creativity, task discretion, and work management that occurs at the micro-level of jobs — decisions about the distribution of specific pieces of work, task planning, and project debriefing — that is more democratic and informal, in contrast to managerial authority, and people and policy management. Carolyn summed up the degree of task discretion that appears common at the IBM lab:

> We definitely do have input saying how much work to give a project...each project is quite different. For example, right now I am working on a couple of things. One of them is an effort between many teams...so we have somebody coordinating what everybody is doing to make sure we are not duplicating work. But it is a pretty informal structure. And the other major project that I have right now is really small; so I'm really my project and I am responsible for it. But I get feedback from people who will be relying on my piece...if you are very proactive about things, you can often get to work on what you want. People who aren't proactive get assigned to things. There's a mapping between skill sets and projects, and so I try not to ask for projects that I don't have a skill match for.

Many other workers across seniority levels and functional groups reported a similar situation of work distribution, input, and task discretion. At least with respect to technical tasks, the general atmosphere is quite informal and flexible. Workers ask for, or are assigned, components of work based on their abilities and preferences and are then given considerable leeway in how they deliver their portion. This process fits between the extremes of the labour process debate on technical control. In some respects Carolyn's comment echoes Conn (2002) and Kraft (1977), because she is removed from both the holistic conception and also the final execution of the total project. She is assigned, or requests, small and isolated pieces of work that she passes on to other individuals or teams when completed. However, her mention of a smaller project for which she is totally responsible fits more with the findings of Ilavarasan and Sharma (2003) who reported that all computer programmers participate in conception and execution tasks.

Most of the case study programmers reported a middle ground in their daily tasks. Mitesh described saturated or routine tasks such as the daily preparation of computers for developers and testers. At the same time, he engages in unsaturated tasks, such as fixing glitches when the machines break down or procedures do not work. As quoted earlier, Mitesh also engages in learning activities to better understand the larger picture into which his tasks fit. Similarly, Chris said, "I have the corporately mandated side, and then I have my side. And the corporately mandated side anybody could do because it is basically reading off checklists. The other side of it—I purposely challenge myself as much as possible."

Chris defines these challenges as a means to explore his own interests in new technology, and he is able to integrate his new knowledge to improve his job. He said, "I've been pretty free in being able to say, 'Hey, I want to look at this for a while.' I tend to just go off and discover new things and bring them back to my boss and say, 'I think we should be doing this.' And he says, 'Ya, you are right, we should.'" Zoey and Haiyan also noted various levels of control in both saturated and unsaturated tasks, though they are both relatively junior employees at IBM:

> There is some creativity in solving problems and designing models for documentation. The way we decide to build the documentation is not something that is totally prescribed. It is something that you can design and have your input, and my manager encourages all of us to think of new ways to organize our documentation. There is a little bit of creativity, not a whole lot, but it is there. (Zoey)

> What we do takes a lot of problem solving because you are working from a set of symptoms. You know: this is slower, we are seeing this much more disk activity.... You have to take the symptoms and figure out what sort of things you can do to make the symptoms go away or make them more apparent. If things are all hooked up and I just need to push the run button, then I don't have that much input on how it was designed, but if I was putting together a system from scratch, they will just let me do it. And that actually got me into a bit of trouble because I had no idea what I was doing.... My manager got a senior team member to come in and coach me. So he wouldn't do the work for me, but he'd come in every day and go okay, so what data have you collected, what have you done.... So that helped refocus me in terms of what I was doing. (Haiyan)

In this case, Haiyan and her manager benefited from the knowledge reservoir of a more senior team member and the problem-based, situational, teaching style that he used to help Haiyan reorganize and clarify the components of her job. Haiyan and her informal mentor used the control and creativity in their jobs to redefine the task at hand, and they created an opportunity for new learning. This ongoing process of learning and job-shaping is emblematic of how workers engage in their daily tasks. IT workers rely on the job control they have to navigate and renegotiate their largely undefined job descriptions. They draw on many learning resources to match their abilities to the job and complete their work.

Katie, a programmer working in a slightly less technical job at IBM, clearly expressed how her increased control allowed her to apply more of her knowledge and abilities:

> For the question about feeling a little overqualified, it's mainly because I haven't been using my technical skills. To combat that, I reach outside my core job. I work on a... project where I get to write code. Also, my new role [job title omitted] in this area should help with that too, as I plan to have some hands-on activities. My manager has been supportive of all these activities. A plus of this job is that there are many opportunities to do things outside the main scope of the job according to your interests.

Simon also reported that he feels overqualified because his technical skills are being underutilized. His career aspirations are to leave his technical job and enter management. He feels his current position is a frustrating way-station where his technical skills have not yet been traded for managerial authority.

> For my current job I think I am overqualified. I say that because I went to school for six years and I did a degree that gave me the qualifications to design a power plant. And right now I am a liaison between development and project management. I am a project management flunky. I don't feel bad about it because the position I am in now I see as a step to get somewhere else. I consider it to be a lateral move or even a little step backwards from where I was. But for where I want to go... when I get there I will be qualified — I'll be overqualified.

Simon's last comment is interesting because it defines a common problem for technical workers with respect to their education-job match. As they move from technical jobs into management, they are destined to be overqualified for their jobs in some dimension, because they will have more technical knowledge than is really needed to manage even a technical team. However, many technical workers, particularly those with master's or PhD degrees, choose this path because they get frustrated with the lack of authority that their technical positions give them. An interview with Andrew, who has held managerial positions in past jobs, illustrates this point:

> *Andrew:* Given the amount of training I had, I didn't have the level of responsibility.... I used to hire a lot of PhDs, and one after the other they left. There are only a couple of us that stayed.
> *Interviewer:* They were frustrated with not being able to have as much influence?
> *Andrew:* That's right.
> *Interviewer:* So, you stayed. What did you do to deal with that frustration?
> *Andrew:* To some extent I was more successful than some, for reasons... I would have to think about it... I went into management, which of course gives you more influence. I also worked a lot at the corporate level, more input that way.
> *Interviewer:* You put yourself out there more and got yourself into positions where you could exert the influence?
> *Andrew:* Exactly. I didn't know until we had this discussion, by the way—that's very nice. I didn't realize I had done that, but that is what I had done.

Throughout the interviews many other workers spoke of experiences similar to those of Katie, Simon, and Andrew (and Carolyn earlier) where they either (1) use their technical creativity and task discretion to expand and shape their job and more fully use their technical knowledge and abilities or (2) move into positions or take on projects that better reflect the authority they feel is appropriate for their level of knowledge and ability. As a result of their own actions, these workers feel a decreased sense of underemployment. Their observations are consistent with the theory of work and learning outlined in Chapter 6. Professional workers can, in general, enjoy higher degrees of education-job matching than service and industrial workers, in part because of their greater task autonomy. The relationship between authority role and education-job match is weaker for professional workers in the survey data than it is for some of the IBM workers. IBM workers in particular may have greater delegated authority through their flat organizational structure and team format. As well, all workers can likely manipulate the content of their jobs more easily than the managerial hierarchy in which they work.

Populations at Higher Risk

Contrary to the above discussion, some workers experience situations of mismatch that they cannot directly eliminate. Particularly in danger of underemployment are recent immigrants to Canada (see Chapter 6; Scott-Dixon, 2004; Weststar, 2009). It is increasingly recognized that the foreign qualifications and experience of immigrants are discounted in favour of local education and experience (Green & Worswick, 2002; Frenette & Morissette, 2003; Aydemir & Skuterud, 2005). Since immigrants make up a relatively large proportion of the IT workforce, this issue is an important one. A respondent at IBM exemplifies the problem and provides a candid assessment of her situation. Mayko obtained a bachelor's degree in electrical engineering in China and worked in the IT field for several years before immigrating to Canada. Once here, she obtained a second bachelor's degree, in computer science, because her electrical engineering degree was not deemed a sufficient prerequisite for a computer science graduate program. "I spent three years in China to develop my career, and now I am starting at the beginning. The position that I am in now is kind of junior; I did this already years ago, and there is a part of me that is really upset with myself."

Mayko explained that she has been working with her manager to find more challenging projects and to have more interaction with people, as opposed to doing coding and book work. She feels that she is beginning to progress, but she also feels that gaining formal recognition will be more of a challenge for her and for other immigrants (particularly from Southeast Asia) because of her accent and her cultural background:

> It's not how hard you work. It also depends in part on communication, how you make yourself visible to your department. It's also a different cultural thing. Even if you do something, you are not supposed to show it to other people. Other people will know. They will find it out. Here if you do something, right away you write email to the whole team—it seems showoff. In the Asian culture, people won't like that, but here it's a totally different story.

Mayko's personal solution to her underemployment is to work harder at her language skills and to assimilate into the North American business culture to gain more visibility. She will continue to request interesting projects and assignments. Though this strategy may ultimately earn her more satisfying positions that she can better rationalize in terms of her competency match, she will likely never achieve wage and status equality with her native-born counterparts.

Rebecca also consciously tries to maintain her visibility at the lab, but she does so to deflect attention from her formal qualifications. She has a high school diploma and has taken some college- and university-level courses in areas relevant to her work but does not hold a degree. While she does not think that her formal schooling is insufficient for adequate performance of her job and she does not directly report subjective feelings of underqualification, she is conscious of her credential gap. She says that this is one reason why she is so active in the lab community:

> I've got this complex since my manager reminded me that I don't have a computer science degree. I feel that if I go into these communities, that's going to give me the edge over these other people they are comparing me to because I don't have that degree. In my opinion, it does not mean anything because I have the years of experience, but the management, for some reason, it bothers them.

Rebecca's case is not that common, and it is likely that only workers with considerable seniority will have credential gaps as the entry requirements for IT jobs increase. Regardless, this case is noteworthy because it demonstrates how pervasive the valuation of credentials has become. Though Rebecca has years of experience, possesses many college- and university-level certifications, and is an active contributor to her workplace, she feels that she is more vulnerable in her position than if she had a degree. Her case also emphasizes the rarity of the actual job performance gaps. Even with a credential gap, Rebecca does not feel that she is underqualified for her job. Indeed, despite academic and industry reports that call for more technical and social skill upgrading, and more alignment of industry and academia, very few workers are not meeting the challenges of their jobs.

CONCLUSION AND RECOMMENDATIONS

This chapter has presented a considerable amount of new data about the working and learning environments of computer programmers/IT workers. With respect to the education-job matching thesis, the central point is that IT workers are not reporting competency gaps in great numbers. They are not overcome by job demands in the areas of technical change and interpersonal relations. The large majority feels a close match between their formal schooling, their continuing knowledge and skill development, and their daily tasks. One-quarter to one-third are looking for more challenge and more opportunity to apply their abilities.

This could be achieved if workers were given more room in their jobs for increased creativity and task discretion, the authority to participate in project and policy decisions and evaluations, and access to more information about the larger project domain. Case study respondents noted several areas where their input would create better jobs and better products: realistic project deadlines that allow for adequate troubleshooting before a project release, rather than ad hoc fixes and last-minute marathons; greater integration and equal authority across departments to build features such as usability and testing into the initial development design; higher priority for project debriefing sessions; real time for individual development, courses, and interaction with colleagues; and a more well-rounded view of what makes a good employee. With added managerial authority and technical creativity, IT workers could add significant value to the production process and better balance the demands of their jobs through more complete utilization of their evolving competencies.

A second important conclusion stems from recent reports warning that the sustainability of Canada's Information and Communications Technology (ICT) workforce is in jeopardy due to the substantial decline in undergraduate enrolments in computer science over the past six years (Slonim, Scully, & McAllister, 2008). Though the conclusions of this and similar reports are somewhat contentious,[3] the response to potential IT labour shortages (i.e., increase enrolment in computer science degree programs) remains steeped in the traditional school-to-work models of aptitude development. The problem arises from the shift toward standardized credentials. As noted above, university degrees from technical programs, such as computer science, are increasingly becoming the required entry point to technical jobs in IT. Standardized industry credentials are now heavily marketed and actively sought by workers wishing to successfully compete in the IT job market. As well, IT industry giants are engaged in marketing their software and hardware to educational institutions. This thereby dictates the content and processes that will be used and taught. An example is the hiring practice of IBM, which gives preferential status to those applicants who have gained experience with IBM products through their formal schooling.

These industry trends carry several implications for the IT industry. First, the industry could lose much of the capacity for innovation gained from the melding of multiple perspectives and experiential backgrounds. Increased tightening of entry requirements and greater saturation of job tasks will result in a growth in "knowing that" and a decline in "knowing how" (Scott-Dixon, 2004: 83). That is, educational institutions and workplaces will increasingly promote and encourage the processing and retrieval of information rather than foster an understanding of larger processes and their application to new situations. In her interview Rebecca explained the nuance and intricacy of testing and the "out of the box" thinking required of testers, who must essentially try to break a machine or program rather than use it. In her opinion, computer programmer graduates with computer science degrees are entirely unsuitable for a job in testing. They have been conditioned to a system of rote learning and linear thinking that is unique to the programming of code and specific interpretations of how computers and technology should work.

Second, standardized entry requirements constrain and negate learning experiences that could contribute to a successful IT career. They close the alternative pipelines from where the dynamism and innovation of the industry emerged. Constrained entry requirements also translate into inaccurate and inadequate job performance criteria, on the one hand, and rigid and micro-managed jobs, on the other. Both of these situations negatively impact workers' capacity to apply their cognitive abilities or expand learning. Standardization also perpetuates education for screening purposes, as opposed to the actual relation of education to job demands. High-end technological training, either through universities or vendor-specific certifications, is very expensive, yet increased technical credentials often do not carry corresponding increases in control, authority, or compensation. As well, this credential inflation may not reflect the current skills or the job experience needed for particular jobs (Scott-Dixon, 2004). Therefore, industry standards contribute little to the field and create unnecessary barriers for entry, particularly for women and immigrants who seek access to the IT field (Scott-Dixon, 2004). Based on these negatives and in light of the learning behaviour documented in this chapter, human resource departments and employers of computer programmers and other IT workers would do well to consider a reassessment of the entry requirements needed for a job in IT.

Notes

1. The specific occupational composition of both the EJRM and WALL survey programmer samples is a majority with computer programmer or computer systems analyst titles. These samples include about 25 per cent identifying as computer engineers, 10 per cent as electrical engineers, and a smaller number of graphic designers.
2. All of the interviewees for this research are in technical roles. Half are engaged in core development work. Of the remaining half, one-third are in testing or user-centred applications, one-third are in product release roles (i.e., writing accompanying manuals, creating help applications, coordinating product integration), and the remaining third are in research and security functions.
3. Some argue that these numbers do not predict an ongoing downward trend. Rather they reflect an enrolment period during a time in which IT was in decline and so naturally show a dip as informed students considered more stable or fruitful career options. Others believe that there are political and business motives behind the perpetuation of a skills shortage "myth" to support universities' heavy investment in science and technology infrastructure and faculty and to justify the movement toward offshore IT outsourcing (Chickowski, 2008).

Chapter Nine
Clerical Workers: Work and Learning in Fragmenting Workplaces

Marion Radsma

Aubrey[1] works in a multinational retail organization as a research coordinator. He coordinates marketing research projects, helps managers and colleagues create presentations, catalogues/monitors department library materials, and provides general administrative assistance.

In some ways, Aubrey is a typical clerical worker, but in others he is not. Aubrey is male, a minority in this field. His work is more wide-ranging than that of many of his clerical counterparts. This may be partly attributed to his gender and white background. Research (Abercrombie & Urry, 1983; Lowe, 1987; Wilson, 1996; Henson & Rogers, 2001) has shown that white males in the field are likely to be awarded more senior roles—with greater career opportunities—than female or minority workers.

Jennifer is executive secretary to a vice-president at another large retailer. She manages her boss's calendar, screens callers, builds his presentations, and generally runs interference for him. He considers her his partner in managing his work and time. Although most clerical workers are women, Jennifer cannot be said to represent them—her senior position holds considerable trust and independence. On the other hand, her close alignment with her boss's interests is typical of clerical workers in support roles.

Isolde is an administrative assistant for a government ministry. She fields email queries, types letters, answers phone calls from the public and other departments, and tabulates spreadsheet information.

Isolde's work falls into the general office work category. Her job description, written more than 10 years ago, does not reflect her current duties. This kind of mismatch is a common complaint from clerical workers. An immigrant with many years of Canadian experience, she has a steady job but frets that she cannot get ahead. Isolde is starting to lose interest in her job and turning her mind toward retirement. Isolde is unionized. She and her fellow union members worry about their union's ability to protect their wages and jobs throughout the successive waves of organizational downsizing.

Shelley, a temporary worker, arrived less than a year ago to a job that had no description. Over her tenure the role has expanded, and her duties have become more complex. Her contract will expire soon, but no one has approached her about renewing it, despite her repeated reminders. Shelley is exasperated with her employer's casual insensitivity. Without giving further notice, she will leave after her final contracted day. On her first day away she expects an agitated phone call from her supervisor to ask why she's not at the office.

Shelley is part of the temporary workforce, a growing contingent in today's clerical work environment. She feels (with reason) that her employer exploits her need for the job by overloading her with work and neglecting her learning and personal needs. Shelley, with a background in early childhood education and a diploma in graphic design, is leaving clerical work to start a childcare business, with a sideline in graphics work. Shelley's option of an alternative career is atypical. Employers are usually correct in assuming that workers need the marginalized jobs they hold. Most temporary clerical workers scrabble out poorly paid livelihoods in precarious jobs.

These vignettes show that clerical occupations form a cluster of divergent work situations. However, there are some general characteristics that apply to clerical workers, as a number of researchers have pointed out (e.g., Lowe, 1987; White, 1993):

- They are mostly women.
- They work across all industries and sectors. Unlike teachers, computer programmers, or auto workers, no specific industry or sector claims their loyalty or safeguards their work opportunities—their own efforts at professionalization are scattered and ineffective.
- They inhabit a contradictory class situation, often identifying with management classes while accepting more typically proletarian working conditions such as low pay and status relative to their educational level.
- They often labour in relative isolation, making it difficult for them to empower themselves in solidarity with similarly situated workers. Except in the public sector, attempts to unionize Ontario clerical workers have largely failed.

Workers continue to be attracted to this group of occupations for reasons that include parental influence, unrealistic media portrayals of secretarial work, and the direction of school guidance counsellors.

This chapter looks at some of the background to the growth of clerical occupations, their gradual transformation into what some have called a "pink ghetto," and the implications of this transformation for the learning and work of clerical workers.

The Early Years: The Arrival of Women in Clerical Roles

During most of the nineteenth century, clerks[2] showed a much more homogeneous face to the business world. They were typically white, male, and middle class. Because these clerks were most often drawn from middle- and upper-class families — these being the ones with easiest access to education — and because they aspired to managerial roles, they quite naturally felt a kinship with the ownership classes.

This situation started to change as industrialization and its aftermath increased owners' desire to cheapen product costs by lessening labour costs. The Industrial Revolution transformed the employment environment by providing technology that supported the growth of mass production. In combination, these two conditions led to the growth of hierarchical organizations that effectively limited the scope and variation of jobs.

Bureaucracies with voracious appetites for clerical support mushroomed. The invention of new office equipment, notably the typewriter (Lowe, 1987; Keep, 1997; Wershler-Henry, 2005) circa 1880, was perceived to simplify clerical work, precipitating further change in the organization and role of clerical work. Women started to enter the public sphere of paid clerical work. Previously, their paid work had been limited to private-sphere jobs, such as domestic and farm work. When World War I drew large numbers of men out of the labour force to fight abroad and the amount of work at home continued to expand, the trickle of female clerical workers grew into a broad stream.

The inclusion of women in the office benefited both employee and employer. For the first time, paid work became accessible to middle-class women who could simultaneously maintain middle-class mores and achieve a level of independence previously unobtainable; their industrialist employers appreciated the quality of the work and comparatively low-salary expectations of their new employees.

Women thus became part of the office landscape but under severely curtailed conditions, usually limited to low-level roles with minimal access to career growth opportunities. However, they were seldom successful in trying to unionize for greater control over their working conditions, for some of the following reasons:

- Clerical workers aligned themselves with their managers, partly because management support was included in their general job description and partly because they were drawn from or aspired to the same social class as their supervisors;
- Women worked transiently, making it hard to sustain union drives (White, 1993), and union organizers constantly had new job entrants to educate;
- Unions were hostile to the participation of women because they believed women undercut male wage expectations (White, 1993) and they endorsed women's homemaker role;
- Women clerks worked alone or in very small groups, making it difficult for them to see unionization as possible and making collaboration complicated.

As the bureaucracy grew, so did women's participation in the labour force and their presence in clerical jobs. In 1891 only 2 per cent of women participated in the labour force and only 2 per cent of jobs were clerical. By 1921, 20 per cent of women in Canada were in the labour force, and clerical work absorbed almost 7 per cent of those workers. Between 1891 and 1921 the proportion of women in the clerical workforce jumped from 14 to 42 per cent (White, 1993: 47; Lowe, 1987: 49).[3] To quote Lowe (1987: 47):

> When the depression hit in 1930, clerks were the fastest growing occupational group in the booming white-collar setting. The typical nineteenth-century clerk, a skilled male bookkeeper hunched over his ledger in a small counting house, had been eclipsed by an army of female clerks.

The Middle Years: Feminization and the Proletarianization of Clerical Work

During the 1960s second-wave feminists, such as Betty Friedan (1963) and Germaine Greer (1970), heightened women's awareness of inequities. At the same time access to better birth control gave women more freedom in life and career choices. It had become easier for women to choose to work outside the home after marrying. Simultaneously, as labour conditions improved, unions experienced membership declines. Clerical workers became the focus of the union movement during this time. Although unions were not generally successful in their private sector drives, they did obtain significant support in the public sector. That situation still holds: Private sector clerical workers are almost entirely non-unionized, while the majority of permanent public sector clerical employees belong to unions. Statistics Canada data (2003) has shown that while 73 per cent of all public service workers (including clerical workers) were unionized, only 28 per cent of all clerical workers were unionized (Akyeampong, 2003).

Clerical Work at the Dawn of the New Millennium

Women's roles as clerical workers have never had much formal authority, but the need of organizations for large contingents of clerical workers provided some level of job protection in the past. More recently, that need has been eroded by the development of new office technologies. Office technology improvements have resulted in the loss of many clerical jobs: approximately 92,000 in the Metropolitan Toronto area alone between 1985 and 1995 (de Wolff & Bird, 1997; Eyerman, 2000).

While some clerical occupations have declined, sometimes to the point of extinction, others have risen rapidly. Using Canadian census data[4] to tabulate changes between 1991 and 2001, de Wolff (2005) reported that many significant changes to clerical occupations were not adequately represented in the 2001 NOC codebook or its 2003 revisions.

Table 9.1 Changes in Clerical Occupations, Canada, 1991–2001

NOC	Title	1991	1996	2001	% Change, 1991–2001
	All Occupations	14,220,230	14,317,545	15,576,585	9.5
	All Clerical Workers	1,608,840	1,548,600	1,450,695	-9.8
1231	Bookkeepers	100,810	103,400	108,625	.6
1241	Secretaries	418,405	317,275	271,110	-35.2
1411	General Office Workers	250,055	224,630	267,465	6.9
1413	Records and File Clerks	31,220	24,965	27,035	-13.8
1414	Receptionists and Switchboard Operators	131,015	124,965	123,315	-5.9
1423	Typesetters and Related Occupations	8,635	7,725	5,725	-33.7
1431	Accounting and Related Clerks	257,610	264,910	178,200	-30.8
1432	Data Entry Clerks	85,950	89,325	55,965	-34.9
1433	CSR—Financial Services	101,915	98,935	92,100	-9.6
1434	Banking, Insurance and Finance Clerks	60,715	56,350	38,425	-36.7
1435	Collectors	15,990	17,415	16,650	4.1
1441	Administrative Clerks	52,555	67,975	69,065	31.4
1452	Correspondence, Publication and Related	7,680	7,340	7,005	-8.8
1453	Customer Service, Information and Related	63,305	114,955	164,775	160.3
1454	Survey Interviewers and Statistical Clerks	22,960	28,535	27,035	17.7
	% of workforce	11.3%	10.8%	9.3%	

Source: Alice de Wolff, 2005; from Statistics Canada, 1991, 1996, 2001 Census

Table 9.1 shows how the unevenly escalating capabilities of information technology have caused declines in some types of clerical work and generated new ones. The category of telephone switchboard operator, for example, lists four occupations, although the occupation itself is virtually extinct. Traditional clerical roles, such as secretary, also show serious decline. Meanwhile, office and communications technologies have generated entirely new categories of clerical work, such as call centre telephone clerks and agents.

Although new technological capabilities have eliminated some clerical tasks and simplified others, many workers find that clerical work itself has intensified, demanding not only increased skills, but also different skills—personal, interpersonal, and technical. Not only typing skills are required today: Even junior clerical workers are expected to be able to create and maintain computer databases. Eyerman (2000: 72) cites a poll conducted by the International Association of Administrative Professionals (IAAP), which found

95 per cent of the respondents reported that their responsibilities increased in several areas including accounting, supervising and more administrative work. This additional work would have meant that these women had to learn to be more flexible not only in their skills, but also in how they planned their days.

Economic conditions have made it possible for employers to demand high levels of education (Livingstone, 1999a) without offering an increase in either salary or status. The competition for diminishing numbers of clerical positions is tight. More and more people are being laid off from what were once stable jobs. Between technology-driven reductions in jobs and organizational initiatives to "outsource" tasks that support the main business (Drucker, 1995; Massachusetts Report on Temporary Work, 1998; Huws, 2003), temporary labour has involuntarily become an inescapable work condition for many clerical workers. The director of a clerical workers retraining centre in Toronto remarked that her agency was assisting workers who had been laid off after decades of service.

Despite the limited jobs outlook, clerical workers are expected to have relatively high levels of education. Furthermore, ongoing technological advances require clerical workers to continually revise and renew their skills. De Wolff and Bird (1997) noted that employers look for clerical workers with skills in current technologies, knowledge of the employer's industry, and, often, good language skills so they can interact with customers. Continual, self-directed, work-related learning is imperative for clerical workers to retain job currency and maintain "employable" status.

Contingent workers find themselves in especially vulnerable positions. The jobs they fill are short-term and fragile, providing uncertain incomes. Their pay is usually lower than what their full-time counterparts earn, and benefits are often non-existent. To be hireable, they must have comprehensive and current computer skills, which they must develop and maintain on their own time and dime.

Even permanently employed workers, however, are expected to take responsibility for their careers. Employers may provide some training opportunities, but clerical workers are expected to take the initiative to enrol in them — and only if their workload and supervisor permit. In some cases, employers provide little training, and the clerical workers themselves must identify their learning needs and how to meet them. According to the WALL Survey (Livingstone & Scholtz, 2006), only 16 per cent of service workers are offered opportunities for ongoing training. Finiola, a vice-president of human resources at a multinational financial institution, explained:

> Clerical and support staff have to really go out there and seek [the business skills] themselves. If you understand what you are good at, you should take the initiative and grow on that. Once you are in those types of positions, it's difficult to get a career path... people tend to put you in that box.

Composition of Clerical Workforce in Ontario

Ninety per cent of clerical workers in the 2004 EJRM Survey were women, a proportion consistent with the findings of other recent studies. With waves of downsizing continuing to devastate the private sector and civil service, the percentage of unionized clerical workers continued to decline to less than a quarter by 2004 (Livingstone & Scholtz, 2006).

The age profile for clerical workers is similar to that for all service workers (EJRM Survey, 2004). Reflecting the general aging of the Canadian workforce, almost a third (32 per cent) of clerical workers are at least 45 years old. However, people continue to enter clerical work despite the typically low wages and poor job outlook—42 per cent of clerical workers are under 35.[5]

Clerical workers' salaries start and finish lower than those of industrial or service workers in general. Approximately 58 per cent of clerical workers polled in the EJRM Survey earned less than $30,000 annually. Only 1 per cent earned more than $50,000, compared to the 36 per cent of industrial and 17 per cent of service workers who did so. According to a government-sponsored website (<www.jobfutures.ca>), clerical workers can anticipate earning 20 to 25 per cent less than equivalently educated workers in other occupations, and they will likely experience unemployment rates about 2 per cent higher than the average for other types of work.

Nonetheless, when case study clerical workers spoke about their wages, they expressed their dissatisfaction primarily by way of internal comparison. George said, "The person who was [reviewing salaries] did an evaluation of my job, and apparently I'm being paid $10,000 less than I should be." Paulina noted, "There are people that do less than we do two corridors away and they are level 7 and we are level 4. It makes me crazy when I think about it." Only one of the clerical workers made a categorical comment about the insufficiency of clerical pay. Danielle, who had lately been bargaining on behalf of the union, commented, "In the clerical area in the... government, clerical workers are living in poverty if they are living in the city of Toronto. It's amazing out there, how many women I am finding that [do] full-time work during the day and part-time in the evenings or weekends to cover their lives and the majority are working families."

These workers' willingness to accept low wages may reflect their fear of job loss. The number of clerical workers—26 per cent—who thought they were somewhat or very likely to lose their jobs over the next year was almost double that of those in other fields of work.

Their managers affirm the legitimacy of these fears. One manager in the public service explained that her clerical support had been reduced from 11 people to 1 over the previous few years. A financial institution vice-president noted that it had been years since she had a personal assistant.[6] The director of a clerical workers' retraining centre said she increasingly encountered workers who had two, even three, decades of single-employer experience and now were faced with the uncertainties of self-employment.

Public Service Clerical Workers

According to the Ontario Public Service Employees Union (OPSEU Table Talk, 2004), the Office Administration Category (OAD) — clerical services, court reporters, data processing technicians, office administration staff, and equivalent positions — forms 37.8 per cent of the collective membership. Women comprise 85.3 per cent of the bargaining unit, the largest unit in the union.

Of these employees, 28.3 per cent are unclassified, a civil service euphemism for temporary contract people.[7] The erosion of stable situations for clerical workers is apparent in the dramatic increase in the ratio of unclassified to classified workers. Within the union as a whole, unclassified work assignments increased from 15 per cent to 25 per cent between 1993 and 2003.[8] Over a similar period (1995–2003), the number of employees in the union dropped by 40 per cent. We can predict that a majority of the cuts were directed at low-status work such as clerical jobs, for which skills are deemed readily interchangeable and technological advances are perceived to easily compensate for the loss of workers.

Case Study Site Profile

It was difficult to find an appropriate research site. The original plan called for research at one public service site. However, the repeated downsizing of clerical jobs made this impossible. The first public service union we contacted was unable to participate because of ongoing turmoil within the union itself and with its civil service employer. After several months of negotiation, we approached another union, the Ontario Public Service Employees Union (OPSEU).

Although OPSEU immediately endorsed the project, obtaining access to the 20 people needed for interviews proved challenging — no single ministry or department had a large enough cadre of clerical workers to accommodate our request. The invitation that OPSEU's communication department emailed to its complement of approximately 40,000[9] members in the Greater Toronto Area (GTA) generated only a few responses, three of which resulted in interviews. Other individuals gave various reasons for declining the request, after having initially expressed interest, but a sense of personal vulnerability permeated most refusals: One worker, an immigrant male, reneged on his initial willingness for fear his manager would find out and disapprove; one worker's job was downsized and he became unavailable; one worker claimed to be too busy; several workers indicated interest, then ignored all follow-up emails and telephone calls.

In addition, one active union member agreed to participate but balked at signing a release form, and she refused to be recorded, claiming this would be disloyal to her employer. Given her willingness to comment off the record, we inferred that she felt fear of reprisal rather than compromised loyalty.

Later, in a summer meeting we explained the project to a group of GTA union executives, and this generated strong signals of interest. Several said they would promote the project among their local membership. By means of an electronic newsletter promoting this project, one of the OPSEU contacts produced two new interview subjects. The number of interviews at OPSEU remained at five.

We made one more attempt to find interview subjects within the union, and we met with a senior executive and the education liaison. They culled 20 potential candidates from their membership lists. A few more referrals were contributed by the interviewed clerical workers, and this generated another five interview subjects.

We decided to extend the search to include non-unionized private sector and temporary clerical workers, which turned out to be a slow and laborious process. We relied on various sources, including personal contacts and word-of-mouth requests from one interviewed clerical worker to her network of colleagues. Sandria Officer (Chapter 11) located two more candidates on behalf of the case study. The participation of three of the temporary workers was due entirely to the assistance of the Office Workers' Career Support Centre in Toronto. Ultimately, a non-random sample of 23 clerical workers — 21 women and 2 men — discussed their work, learning, and lives during in-depth interviews lasting from one and a half to three hours.

In this chapter, the case study participants' stories are explored against a backdrop of information that was provided by the 550 service workers and 120 clerical workers who were surveyed as part of the EJRM Survey. The results summarized in Chapter 5 will be revisited to the extent that they have specific application to the discussion in this chapter.

However difficult they were to obtain, the stories of the individual clerical workers are most interesting and valuable. They helped with the interpretation and understanding of the statistics that describe the current relationship between work and learning for clerical workers in the GTA.

The Job Duties of Clerical Workers

The 2001 National Occupational Codes (NOC)[10] identified more than 135 separate clerical roles and categorized them into approximately 20 categories. However, the duties ascribed to particular clerical occupations show a tremendous amount of task overlap among these job categories. For example, the NOC codebook notes that both secretaries and general office clerks are responsible for typing reports, preparing presentation materials, answering the telephone, processing mail, and ordering office supplies.

Despite the overlap in officially documented duties, de Wolff (2005: 5) found polarization of clerical workers' job tasks; this condition is corroborated by our case study sample, which included clerical workers at both ends of the complexity spectrum. Within the customer service category, for example, Paulina dealt with the complexities of securities exchange in her role as call centre specialist, but her day was structured around call answering quotas. She needed to achieve 98.7 per cent compliance in order to meet call centre standards. Even Paulina's washroom breaks were monitored. Corrie's day was much more flexible and provided personal connection with the clients she served. An outreach customer service clerk, she visited hospitals, shelters, and community centres to register births and deaths and issue documentation such as health cards. Every day her duties varied, as did her emotional response to her work. Paulina and Corrie exercised very different levels of control over their workdays and experienced widely disparate opportunities for the expression of personality and creativity, even though they both had important specialized skills.

Some workers were able to adapt their work until it corresponded with their abilities and interests: "I've made my job what I want it to be," Renata said. In similar cases, such as Laura's, the employer added responsibilities — without adding salary — with the expectation that a clerical worker could (and would) shoulder the additional burden. Laura, an office legal administrator in a small law firm, said, "I have had to take on new things, so I have had to learn to cope and to find out what to do." Laura, as did many colleagues, considered the new responsibilities to be task dumping rather than skills development opportunities, even though she welcomed the learning they engendered.[11]

Only half of the interviewed workers[12] said they had job descriptions. Of those who had one, several noted the descriptions were old and irrelevant. Isolde, for example, commented: "It's maybe 10 years old or more...I do a lot more than what is put in the paper, put in my job description."

Clerical duties have changed a lot in the past quarter-century. Executive secretaries such as Jennifer and Ophelia agreed they still retained responsibilities for maintaining their boss's schedules, but the differences in their work lives illustrate some of the unevenness of work changes. Jennifer's role was largely traditional; she worked exclusively for a vice-president, screening his contacts, scheduling his time, preparing his presentations, and so forth. Her boss considered her his partner: "He tells them that he and I are a partnership and that he tells me everything.... If he is not around, they can come to me.... He feels if they criticize me then they are criticizing him. So they better be very sure of what they are saying and very clear."

Ophelia described a more mixed work experience:

> I am responsible for my boss's schedule. That involves setting up meetings and making hotel arrangements and such and talking to different people who are involved in that. As well, I report to one person directly, well, actually two people, the president and the financial director, but he is not there all the time.... As well, I work for any of the other people if they need assistance preparing documents and things like that.... If I only had that to do, it would be a full-time job, but I do much more than that...such as preparing reports and looking after arrangements for various meetings, assisting the HR when they have special events and things like that; so I am basically the help centre....
> If a meeting is coming up, I will make all the arrangements for it and chase

everyone down. I get all the reports in. If it's the end of the month then I gather everything up for the expense reports; if it's the end of the quarter, I'll get everything ready for that and different things like that.

In Eyerman's (2000) words, Ophelia effectively acted as the "glue" that held the office processes together. She spent up to 13 hours a day at her job; her workload had increased substantially since she accepted this position more than 15 years ago. She felt, however, that her inability to cope was because of her ineffectiveness,[13] not work volume, and believed someone else would cope better.

Work was even more varied among those not in secretarial roles. Typical tasks cited by case study workers included answering the telephone, managing filing systems, interacting with internal and external clients, handling mail, administering invoice systems, and acquiring supplies.

Although some duties seem similar to those traditionally done by clerical workers, they are performed differently now. Even those who are directly responsible for interacting with clients may never see them. As the following interview excerpts illustrate, the computer and other electronic media define work:

> I check my emails... I log in data forms, I do some transcribing of booklets; they are surveys and questionnaires... I do the tracking and logging of what forms we have received already. I do mid-month data collection and queries. I have to get these reports and send out reminders to our centres about any data we are missing. I do queries, I send back any data that has queries... dealing with the data we receive from our centres, entering it, tracking it, transcribing it, logging it, checking it, etc. That would be the bulk of my work. (Maggie)

> My routine? I come in, and I log into the computer and go to my req pool that is all the requisitions from all the ministries, and I have to begin distributing them... and then I do my reporting every morning; I do my reporting on workflow... what was done, how many are finished. It's not a database; I do the report in Excel and send it out to the managers. (Franca)

> I would get the physical records of a patient's chart... it could be two inches thick or five volumes long, depending on whether or not they had surgery and things... those doctors and what their specialties are and to be able to identify their signatures... so it's basically double checking for legal purposes... interaction, even with the doctors, the communication is on the computer system. (Beatrice)

> One of our main responsibilities is to answer that phone all the time... you're front line; you're the voice of the office to the public. You're the first point of

contact. Whether it is internal or external, all calls are zeroed out. So we are required to answer all incoming calls. (Danielle)

One type of clerical role deserves special mention. Call centre work, the fastest-growing clerical occupation (as de Wolff, 2005, stated), is characterized by rigid structure and low task discretion.[14] Danielle, quoted above, worked in an informally structured call centre. Paulina's job as a call centre specialist was more typical. When she reported for work, she logged into her computer system, set a toggle showing she was ready to accept calls, and spent the rest of her day responding to customers. She was expected to meet a pre-set number of calls per hour, all of them under electronic surveillance. As she said, "There is no social life now. It's all call numbers and volumes."

WORKING CONDITIONS

Job Changes
Technological innovation and evolving management philosophies continue to generate change, which eliminates some jobs, modifies others, gives rise to entirely new clerical occupations. Sixty-six per cent of surveyed clerical workers in the ERJM Survey, corresponding to 58 per cent of industrial workers and 62 per cent of service workers, said they were experiencing great or moderate change in their job techniques and equipment.

Clerical workers who reported change pointed to computer and computer software upgrades. For example, George said, "Our computers have been upgraded—a great deal of change." Those who saw little change pointed to the same upgrades but agreed with Shelley, who said, "They just come out with new versions and stuff like that, but I would say they are basically the same."

Some workers felt equipment changes required no additional skill. Fifty-one per cent saw no change in the skill level they needed. However, most who reported change (45 per cent) thought skill requirements had risen. Some of the perceived increase may reflect work intensification more than equipment change. Both Aubrey and Laura, for example, said their job responsibilities had risen and they had taken on more complex tasks. Renata reflected that she had the skills, but her company wanted "more." She was regularly required to be recertified on an internal suite of organizational programs and policies.

Organizational Decision-making
Few clerical workers find themselves in roles of authority within the organization. This may seem unworthy of comment as most organizations, like chess games, require more pawns than queens. However, clerical workers have less authority than most. As Finiola, a vice-president, recognized, "They have lots of accountability; they have to do this and get that, and they have to meet that deadline, but they have little author-

ity in getting other people to help them, so it's a lot of responsibility on their head."

Clerical workers are almost all at the low end of the influence scale. About two-thirds of clerical workers in the EJRM Survey sample did not participate at all in decision-making at their organizations. Only about 10 per cent said they could make decisions subject to approval or as part of a group (none could decide alone), compared to a third of industrial workers and service workers in general who could make decisions subject to approval, as part of a group or alone.

When clerical workers were probed for more detail, their decision-making often seemed limited to peripheral issues. Isolde, for instance, said she could design her own report layouts and had made many decisions during her department's United Way charitable drive. Danielle noted, "Not that I wouldn't want to — I'd probably have some valuable information, and I think I'd be a huge contribution to the employer."

Moreover, even when their feedback was solicited, their supervisors did not necessarily use it. Some case study workers, such as Ophelia, expressed clear reservations: "There is no problem discussing how things went, but...I'm not sure if...the person would listen or not." Or, as Shelley succinctly stated, "They welcome the input, but they don't do anything with it."

Input was often very basic. When George's organization participated in professional conferences with online information, handouts, etc., he would contribute by saying, "Oh, we forgot to do this or we forgot to do that"; his aim was to have the organization's presence at the conference be more effective in the future. For others, input was explanatory and, sometimes, exculpatory. For example, Beatrice commented, "They will want to know why it is taking so long, and we have input there."

Paulina cited the annual employee survey as her opportunity to provide feedback that she felt her employer took seriously. However, the actual influence of her opinion, when diluted by the input of large numbers of her colleagues, is quite limited.[15]

In sum, although clerical workers may perceive that they have some control over their work environment, their actual input tends to be highly constrained.

Job Creativity

Although two-thirds of clerical workers said they had a "fair amount" or "great deal" of task performance discretion, just over one-third said their jobs allowed them to be creative. About 38 per cent of this group reported exercising a "fair amount" or a "great deal" of creativity in doing their jobs. Another 40 per cent of these workers reported they could exercise little creativity; more than a fifth said they just followed orders.

People in more senior clerical roles had more freedom to define their job boundaries. Corrie, who visited clients to register them for public records, said, "We have managers, but sometimes we don't even see them. They are there doing their own thing, but we work on our own." Jennifer, an executive secretary, saw her role as collaborative, but "it's up to me to get it done."

Creativity meant different things to the different workers interviewed. Helena, who regularly exercised her own initiative in dealing with people confronting property appropriation, thought she had only a moderate amount; Isolde, who designed and formatted Excel spreadsheets, felt she had a great deal. Aubrey, despite an "open mandate" to change his job, said he had a moderate amount of leeway for creativity, and said, "Even being creative becomes routine after a while."

CLERICAL WORKERS' KNOWLEDGE

To summarize the discussion up to this point, clerical workers earn less than other workers who have comparable education. Their skills and knowledge are, in general, not highly valued. Nonetheless, clerical workers must be literate, have numeracy skills, and desktop software expertise. As well, they need specialized knowledge of the areas related to their specific industries and work roles.

To maintain and improve their workplace status (Burris, 1983), clerical workers often supplement employer-supported learning by taking courses during evenings and weekends at personal expense; however, as subsequent discussion will show, most are already well qualified or overqualified for their work.

In their jobs, clerical workers draw on three forms of learning: (1) the formal academic attainment with which they enter their careers; (2) job entry and ongoing training offered by employers (to the extent that these are available); and (3) informal learning on and off the job.

The knowledge and skills clerical workers bring to their workplaces are sometimes, but not always, aligned with the educational requirements demanded by their employers.

Formal Education Required

Clerical workers need a relatively high education. Of the clerical workers surveyed, 44 per cent—compared to 16 per cent of industrial and 34 per cent of service workers—said they needed a college diploma or university degree to qualify for their jobs.

By contrast, the case study clerical workers said their employers did not necessarily require post-secondary qualifications. Helena commented, "It's really skills and knowledge...because having a degree doesn't guarantee that you're going to be able to sit in front of a homeowner and tell them what's happening and still maintain control of the situation." Paulina observed, "They want someone that will take the job seriously," and Renata said, "You don't need college or anything like that."

However, while these clerical workers may have *said* employers require only high school completion, they recognized this might be insufficient to actually land a job. Emily explained, "Most people that apply for this position will have a bachelor's degree." Corrie emphatically denied that a college degree was necessary: "As long as you do well at the interview and have computer background," but then she added, "Most people are from college...if I wasn't in the government years ago, for me now to get there, it would be a slim chance because you couldn't beat the college students."

In George's case, entry requirements had rocketed. Despite his lack of a college or university degree, he was the department's go-to person, but a new candidate would need at least a master's degree. Aubrey also needed a university degree. Unlike George, however, Aubrey considered this appropriate: "You have to be able to comprehend certain things here that you might not somewhere else."

Even though managers disavowed the need for post-secondary qualifications, they often made hiring decisions based on them. Glynnis, who worked with displaced clerical workers, observed that she had seen an executive assistant posting requiring an MA. Finiola, the vice-president, said, "If you have people who are overqualified for a role, you probably have a bad fit," but her three most recent receptionists had been university graduates.

Formal Education Attained

Clerical workers are under-represented at both the highest and lowest extremes of education, compared to people in other occupations. Clerical work requires at least some degree of literacy, which eliminates illiterate workers from clerical occupations. Workers also may realize that employers use credentials as a screening tool to identify preferred candidates (Stiglitz, 1975). However, clerical work offers neither the status nor the pay that would justify investment in advanced educational credentials. At the middle levels of education, clerical workers achieve the level they need to compete effectively for their desired jobs.

In the EJRM Survey of clerical workers, 88 per cent had completed at least high school (compared to 68 per cent of industrial and 80 per cent of service workers in general); 54 per cent had earned a college diploma or university degree, which is similar to service workers (49 per cent) but higher than industrial workers (37 per cent).

Learning the Job

Approximately two-thirds of clerical workers needed less than three months of training to become competent in their jobs (see Chapter 5). Nineteen per cent needed three months to a year, and the remaining 15 per cent needed longer than a year to achieve competency. These numbers are not statistically different from those for service workers in general.

However, clerical roles are more complex than the above paragraph implies. Several workers based the length of time for learning on their prior experience. Emily said a new person would need previous experience plus at least a year to become fully competent in her job. According to Kara, to fill her role someone would have to have several years in the field. Even temporary workers cited the importance of previously learned skills. Vanessa remarked that it would take her "a week to a month [to become fully trained].... I'm going on 30 years of experience too." Shelley used the skills she had developed in senior full-time roles to reduce the job-learning time for her replacement worker to less than a month: "I've organized it all so it would be easier for someone else coming in." A month is a substantial amount of learning time for someone in a temporary role.

Several workers indicated that new incumbents would need significant time on the job to become fully conversant with its requirements. Beatrice said her role needed six to eight weeks of orientation training plus a full year of work. Danielle said that someone would need more than six months to master her job because, "There's so much for you to learn. It's not just about the clerical work that you're doing; it's about the role you play in the ministry. It's the mandate, the knowledge about the actual office."

Not many clerical workers received formal job entry training. A few were able to learn informally from a colleague. Helena, for example, shadowed a more experienced worker, and George was teamed with a colleague to learn correct procedures. More commonly, the workers learned on their own. Aubrey commented, "You kind of get thrown into it... you're always loop-de-loop until you get some kind of framework." Jennifer was the first in her role and learned by "perseverance." Renata said, "You just do it," an attitude echoed by Emily, Franca, Gabrielle, and others.

Continuing Learning

Clerical workers learn continually, both formally and informally. Corrie was unique in saying that she learned every hour she was on the job, but most workers ascribed several hours a week to their learning activities, although sometimes these were for household and general interest rather than job-related learning.

Continual job-related learning is required, partly because of changes in the tools, content, and organization of clerical work. However, although clerical workers regularly confront new software and software releases, they do not always perceive these as significantly different from previous versions. Laura, who frequently accepted new responsibilities, commented, "Nothing much has changed." This attitude, although not held by all of them, was expressed by several clerical workers.

For Laura, significant change was embedded in her job content. When she started, she "did their correspondence, their invoices, their accounts payable and receivables." At the time of the interview, she had added motion records and federal court research, typically the province of trained law clerks, to those earlier responsibilities.

Shelley, despite her tenuous job, said her role had changed greatly during her tenure:

> I do a lot of tracking of information and recording of certain pieces of information like contracts, getting things signed. I do follow-ups on that, I prepare contracts. I take problem calls... people that I work with they often encounter problems, and they come to me because I have acquired all this knowledge.

Braverman (1974: 199) and his adherents suggested that modern technologies were deskilling work, but the clerical workers in our case study did not agree with him. George, for example, said he was always learning in his job. Shelley, who said the degree of skill required had somewhat diminished, immediately countered her own comment by adding, "Somebody had to have advanced computer skills, Excel primarily, and with the new [simplified] software they've launched, they've added different types of work, so...now I'm all over the map."

Ongoing Training and Further Education
About half of the clerical workers, compared to service (42 per cent) and industrial (47 per cent) workers, said they had taken formal training in the previous year. Future training was planned by 44 per cent, while 43 per cent said they had not taken at least one course they wanted.

Over a quarter of clerical workers, quadruple the number in service and industrial jobs in general, said they participated in job upgrading and computer courses. Pending further investigation to clarify the disparity, two possibilities seem to account for the difference. Perhaps clerical workers have greater exposure to technological change than workers in most service and industrial roles encounter—expensive and unwieldy industrial equipment, for example, is much less likely to be replaced as often as obsolete computers. In addition, perhaps a greater proportion of people in clerical roles regularly encounter office technology changes than do workers in the other groups, who may have more members working in low technology areas (e.g., retail clerks and restaurant waiters).

For full-time employees, access to training is usually controlled by the worker's supervisor. For most, access is highly constrained. Danielle, a public service worker, commented, "You may have an individual that's very interested in developing further but, however, that just doesn't seem to happen."

Clerical workers in the private sector experience the same restrictions as public service workers. Although large organizations may have training budgets, clerical workers do not generally have access to a broad range of courses. In smaller organizations, training budgets may not exist at all. Laura had to learn things on the fly because no training was available to her: "When they ask me to do something, either I know how to do it or I learn how to do it," often by trial and error. Renata's employer was unusual in requiring all employees to maintain internally defined certifications.[16] Access to formal training was probably best described by Finiola, the vice-president, whose company spent $50 million to 60 million a year on training: "If you were to go back to the clerical population, I would think that we probably don't invest a lot into that population...they wouldn't be seen as a priority population."

For temp agencies, clerical workers are the "product," as manager Margriet pointed out, saying her agency provided free training online. Talma's agency offered training as needed to her registered clerical workers: "[If] they need some instruction on how to manipulate Excel, for example.... I would do that, no problem." These agencies appear to be atypical. The displaced clerical workers interviewed for this case study uniformly found it was difficult to obtain access to training, although all but Shelley (who was leaving the occupation) were registered with multiple agencies.

Informal Learning

Although 81 per cent of surveyed clerical workers said they participated in job-related informal learning, this statistic may understate their true involvement. Interviewees did not recognize the extent of their efforts until specifically asked about activities such as reading, web-surfing, and dialogue. Naomi said about her informal learning, "Since I have been here with you and answering these questions, you realize how much time you spend ... if you stop and think, it's amazing the things you have been able to accomplish without realizing it."

Half or more of the survey respondents declared they spent time learning about new job tasks, new equipment, teamwork and communication, health and safety, and general knowledge. Between 30 and 50 per cent learned about computers, organizational management skills, workers' rights, and workplace politics. Less than a quarter of clerical workers participated in informal literacy and financial learning activities.

Case study participants also found it important to enhance their knowledge and skills informally. All but one case study interviewee reported spending time to increase their general knowledge. Aubrey, with a corporate library at his disposal, said, "All these magazines here that I've dabbled in whenever they come in ... I like to keep my head around what's going on." Isolde commented, "We have a lot that we could go in and learn about the ministry, about new programs, new projects, so I go into those websites ... and get familiar knowledge about projects. I also go on other websites that I feel are of interest." Temp worker Theresa added, "I was browsing on the Internet a lot; also I was going in the library checking some financial statements from different companies, how're they're doing at the end of the year. Checking to find my way in."

Computers were a focus of learning for 44 per cent of the survey sample. Naomi commented, "We had this new program that was offered internally to us by leaders that we could learn, and I went in and I did it." George noted, "If I'm going to learn something, I have to play with it. I can read ... but it's not until you actually get the hands on, that you get a better understanding. I think you actually learn more that way." Uma, too, worked on her computer skills, especially accounting applications: "I did ACCPAC and Simply Accounting ... I kind of just went in there and learned what I needed."

Traditionally, informal learning is a communal activity. Clerical workers, too, learn from others and each other. George commented, "Maybe they'll say something that may tweak something that's in my life ... maybe I should try that approach." When Aubrey started, one of his co-workers helped him: "I was a little apprehensive about it at first. I don't think I liked the idea of having someone coach me. We have a symbiotic relationship now. We all learn from each other."

However, as Isolde's experience shows, collaborative learning is sometimes difficult to access:

> There was one girl who came to work in my department...the kind of work that she was doing, even if it was contract, was better work, like more interesting type of work. So I said to her, "I would really like to learn more financial stuff." She said, "No problem, Isolde, would you like me to show you?"...So I sent an email to my manager...and I said, "How about job sharing, because she's willing to do the job sharing," and they said no.

A few clerical workers interact with peers in professional associations. For Jennifer and Ophelia, the IAAP[17] was a helpful source of personal and professional development. Other interviewees appeared unaware of this organization or others like it.

Clerical workers in small offices usually learn in isolation. Laura is typical: "I just read. I type it up on the Internet and see how other people are coping, or you just read instructions and their manuals and stuff like that."

Ophelia aptly summed up workers' informal learning experiences, "These days you need to have quite a lot more of an entrepreneurial approach to your job."

EDUCATION-JOB MATCH

Relevance of Clerical Workers' Formal Education to Their Work

As Graph 9.1 shows, 42 per cent of clerical workers said their work and education were unrelated. They cited various reasons.

Some workers did not really think about what they needed for job entry. Instead they focused on their school experience. Aubrey said he never connected work and school: "School was learning and the job market was doing."

Some defaulted into clerical work when their original career choices were unsuitable or disagreeable. Paulina had wanted to be a teacher all her life: "In my first year of university, I did a co-op and I hated it. The children weren't listening, and I hated it...so I had to start all over again." Jennifer had studied to be a dietician: "I took a co-op program at a hospital, and I hated that...at the time the only thing I could think of to fall back on was I could type."

For others, changes in work methods over the past decades affected the relevance of school to work. Helen, for example, reflected: "I remember sitting in class taking shorthand...good thing I quit, because it went out the window shortly after that."

Still others wanted to attend university but lacked funds or encountered circumstances (notably romantic liaisons or pregnancy) that forced them into the labour force prematurely.

Graph 9.1 Relevance, Credential, Performance, and Subjective Gaps among Clerical Workers, Service Workers, and All Non-managerial Employees, Ontario, 2004 (%)

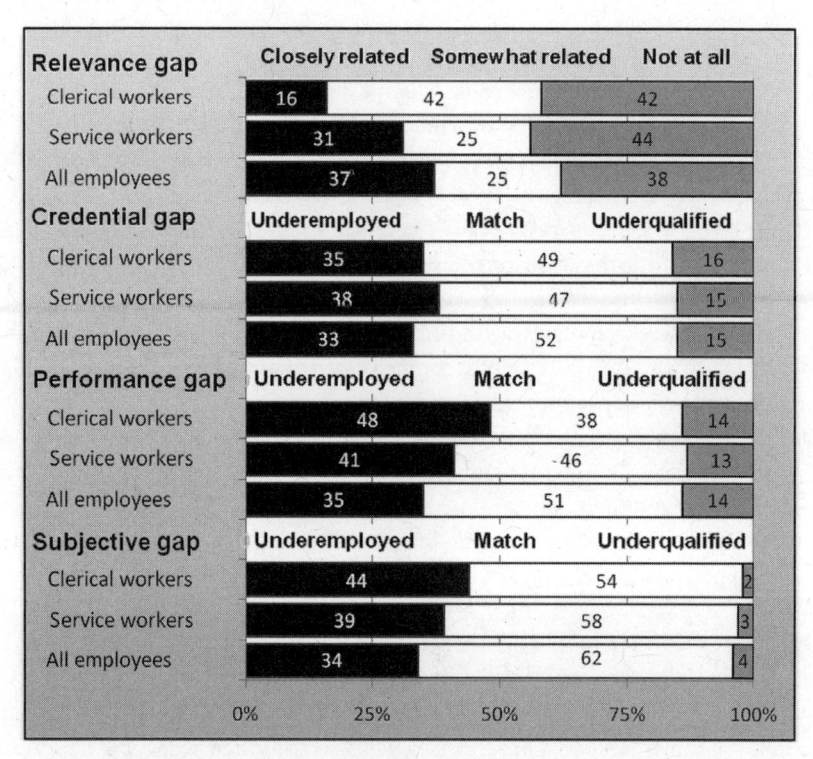

Relevance gap	Closely related	Somewhat related	Not at all
Clerical workers	16	42	42
Service workers	31	25	44
All employees	37	25	38
Credential gap	Underemployed	Match	Underqualified
Clerical workers	35	49	16
Service workers	38	47	15
All employees	33	52	15
Performance gap	Underemployed	Match	Underqualified
Clerical workers	48	38	14
Service workers	41	46	13
All employees	35	51	14
Subjective gap	Underemployed	Match	Underqualified
Clerical workers	44	54	2
Service workers	39	58	3
All employees	34	62	4

Source: EJRM Survey (All employees, N=1301; Service workers, N=555; Clerical workers, N=121)

Occasionally, lack of career focus was culturally structured. Franca said, "The lifestyle down there, you didn't really think of those things, especially being a girl." Gabrielle reported a similar situation, adding that she had not really started preparing for a job until she immigrated to Canada.

More recent job entrants, even those with specialized education, found that tight job markets reduced their ability to find work within their areas of interest. Shelley took a temporary job, until she could find work that made use of her graphic arts training, and stayed in it to provide for her young son. Paulina had completed studies in an alternative psychotherapy, but, after her marriage dissolved, her practice generated insufficient income. The two and a half years she subsequently spent studying financial planning[18] led only to her current call centre position.

Only 16 per cent of clerical workers, compared with 31 per cent of service workers generally in the EJRM Survey, felt their education was closely related to their choice of occupation. Of the clerical workers interviewed, only a few said their education was highly relevant to their clerical roles. Beatrice found her program at Ryerson College[19] was well designed and the practical approach very helpful. Two workers from other countries commented with pride that at school they had learned professionalism in dress and attitude, qualities that they found were very helpful during their careers.

Credential and Performance Match
The formal education attainment of clerical workers and the qualifications that employers require can be used to approximate how well these workers are matched to their jobs on three dimensions: (1) credential, that is, the level clerical workers have attained compared to the level demanded for job entry; (2) performance, the educational attainment relative to the attainment needed to perform job duties; and (3) subjective, the extent to which clerical workers *feel* they are underemployed in their jobs.

Graph 9.1 shows that just over a third of clerical workers, like their counterparts in the comparison groups of industrial workers and service workers generally, are credentially underemployed. About half appear to be appropriately matched. Only 16 per cent of clerical workers appear to be credentially underqualified for their work.

Employers seem to require more education for job entry on the part of their clerical staff than is actually required to perform their jobs. Only clerical workers with high school or less, a subset of just 29 per cent, seem to have less knowledge and skill than their positions require. Interestingly, some post-secondary education is necessary for the closest match between job needs and worker capabilities. Most interviewed clerical workers thought high credentials were unnecessary. Maggie noted:

> The one job that was available was spotting errors and such for questionnaires, so you would need more of a clinical background, but it's something that can easily be learned. I mean somebody with a master's degree, how would they have a clinical background? And I have been working on the study and would know it better.

The performance match is calculated by subtracting the education that workers need to perform the work from the education they have attained. As Graph 9.1 shows, almost half the clerical worker sample said they were underemployed, indicating that an extremely large number of workers believe their job inadequately engages their capabilities. Only 15 per cent thought they were undereducated for the jobs they hold, while the rest considered their education well matched to their duties.

Few case study respondents felt university degrees were necessary, and some disputed the need for a college diploma. George, whose employer requires applicants to have a master's degree, thought courses in records management were sufficient. Laura said, "You just have to be willing and eager to learn. The Internet has everything you need. And common sense is good." Emily remarked, "I don't know why they put that level because all you really need is a high school diploma."

Some felt they needed specific skills in their area of specialization. George, for example, needed to learn about managing information files, which he accomplished by taking an archiving course. Helena's work required detailed skills and knowledge in legislative rules and practices, which she learned by studying the legislation: "mainly it was the Appropriations Act...you have to know it but I didn't, but I said I did when I applied for the job...I bought the Act and I studied it and by the time I had my interview, I knew it." Corrie needed strong specialized skills to cope with diverse people and register their life events appropriately. All these workers had senior administrative support roles, but they agreed that university was not where or how they learned what they needed.

Aubrey was the rare exception who thought his university background was necessary, less because of the content of the degree program than because "it takes a certain amount of being able to learn...you have to be able to comprehend certain things." However, he, too, commented on the difference between having "a degree in anything" and the need for formal training to do his job.

In short, most interviewees felt that the literacy, interpersonal, computer, and specialized skills their jobs demanded were best learned outside the setting of a degree-granting institution, but they were very aware that post-secondary credentials were preconditions for job eligibility.

Graph 9.1 shows that clerical workers *felt* underemployed slightly more often (44 per cent) than service workers or industrial workers in general. But only 38 per cent of clerical workers, compared with 58 per cent of service workers and 61 per cent of industrial workers, felt well matched subjectively.

Interviewed workers who felt underemployed attributed this to either an inability to use their complete range of skills or a sense of being underpaid. Emily felt she could do more; Uma stated that she had skills she was not using. George and Paulina both said they earned less than others filling similar roles. Corrie, too, felt she should be at a higher level but thought she wasn't because her department's headquarters was located in another city.

As Graph 9.1 illustrates, few clerical workers felt subjectively underqualified.

FURTHER COMMENTS AND CONCLUSION

Despite the declining availability of jobs and the vulnerability of the remaining permanent positions, clerical work continues to attract people, particularly women. Sometimes parents and schools encourage this career direction; sometimes other options fail; sometimes clerical roles accord with the worker's own aspiring self-image as a professional in a romanticized white-collar setting.

Consequently, clerical workers inhabit a tightly contested occupational locale. Nor are unionized workers at decreased risk. At the time of the interviews, OPSEU was bracing for yet another downsizing initiative that would cut large swaths of clerical jobs.

If full-time workers feel vulnerable to job loss, contingent workers are situated even more precariously, reliant as they are on the vagaries of intermittent and usually lower paid, temporary or part-time assignments. Most temporary workers today feel forced into such roles and would work more hours at permanent jobs if they could.

It is fiction that clerical workers are free agents in control of their work destinies. Employers hold the controls. One result of this one-sided relationship is creeping credentialism, as previously discussed by Livingstone (1999a), among others. Though jobs may not require formal credentials, employers use credentials to arbitrarily eliminate some applicants. To make themselves eligible for this very competitive labour market, clerical workers must formally educate themselves well beyond the level necessary to do the jobs that they want to do.

However, the situation is more nuanced than such a simple equation suggests. Infinitely variable human beings are involved in negotiations for a type of work that supports personal lifestyle needs and interests, accords with self-image, and matches dreams of a desired future. Clerical workers undertake learning not just to obtain or retain their current jobs but also to create new futures for themselves. Their goal may be higher status — to become managers themselves, as several respondents wanted. They may want to transfer their energies and intelligence to new occupations. Unfortunately, for many older workers, resignation has replaced vision, and hopes are concentrated on retirement. Isolde expressed this intention:

> My future plans are to retire... with age and service because I won't be 55 yet... I really don't know what to do at this point. I don't know if I should continue on another five years and then quit, because if I retire next year, my pension is not that big and I cannot survive on that pension.

Clerical workers in general have the misfortune of being seen as office overhead rather than as contributors. Some exceptions, such as Jennifer, see themselves, and are seen by their bosses, as key partners, but many clerical workers feel undervalued.

Many clerical roles incorporate a strong need for the type of skills that organize and facilitate the work of the workplace — the "relational practice" (Fletcher, 1999) that functions as organizational glue (Eyerman, 2000). There is little room in business language to value most relational activity; organizational discourse tends to focus on the functional tasks listed in workers' job descriptions. When support tasks embedded in clerical work do become visible, they tend to be ascribed little value, and they are seen as personal virtues, attributes of femininity or, equally likely, a weakness instead of the deliberately executed activities and behaviours that promote cohesion and productivity.

Educational programs do not usually incorporate formal training in human relations skills, and clerical workers do not necessarily recognize that the collaborative support behaviours that they practice are skills. Therefore, their self-assessed value tends to echo that of their employers. Interviewed workers acknowledged the importance of a human relations capability in their work, but none were able to articulate this as a skill.

As other workers, clerical workers come to the job with a deep toolkit of capacities, many of which, including human relations abilities, are learned informally. In general, employers demand higher credentials than the work requires, but they simultaneously ignore the multi-dimensional relational practices of clerical workers and informal learning that clerical workers do both on and off the job. As Maggie said:

> You go and you learn because you want to know it, not because you are working toward a degree or because you need it for your job. You're doing it on your own, so it's your 100 per cent.... It helps when, anytime there is a problem at work and you need to find solutions for things, I think it helps in that aspect. I think it helps you to work better... I know people that have the formal education, and they can't really do their jobs. I don't think that formal education necessarily shows that someone can do his or her job, or not. It just shows that they went to school and got the grades they needed. I think someone who, whether or not they had formal training, if they had informal training they might be able to do their job better.

Development of a discourse that exposes the multifaceted characteristics of clerical work and also recognizes worker development through ongoing informal learning efforts is an important starting point from which to generate a reassessment of the value of clerical workers and their work.

Notes

1. All respondent names have been changed and specific work environments masked to ensure confidentiality.
2. Exclusively western European and North American work cultures are written about here.
3. By 1951 clerical work comprised 11 per cent of all Canadian jobs, with women holding 57 per cent of clerical positions (Lowe, 1987: 49).
4. In 1997 de Wolff noted a loss of about 35 per cent of clerical jobs between 1989 and 1997 in Toronto. In 2005 she quoted a clerical job loss of about 10 per cent for Canada between 1991 and 2001. The apparent discrepancy is because the majority of the job losses occurred in the five years between 1989 and 1994, so the job number at the starting point of 2001 is lower than it was in the previous analysis. The broader range of occupational categories she used in 2005, compared to 1997, may also have contributed. Finally, Toronto is an urban market with scope for much greater rationalization of workforces than smaller centres and more rural areas; rural-urban workforce differences may also have factored into the differences reported.

5. A number of reasons may explain the ongoing interest of this occupation for young women, including romanticized media portrayals of clerical work; streaming of female students into feminized roles by school counsellors; family pressure on daughters to take on traditional "feminine" work; default job entry when other options fail or are unavailable due to financial, or personal, constraints.
6. The department receptionist doubled as her secretary when she needed meetings organized, a presentation prepared, or word processing support.
7. This percentage is exceeded only by the percentage in health care services, another area with notoriously low pay and high female participation.
8. The statistics for reclassifying jobs from permanent to temporary are not broken down by occupation, but since outsourcing most often targets the more "expendable" junior positions, we can speculate that the bulk of this increase lies in the clerical and health work/maintenance areas.
9. The number dates from December 2003; according to the union, the number of employees is at its lowest during this period and may increase by up to 10,000 during the summer months.
10. 2003 NOC revisions had little effect on the overall categorization of clerical occupations.
11. Since the interview, Laura's employers started funding a certification program in law clerking. This is to their benefit as well as hers as she is already their de facto law clerk. Her employer's support is limited to the cost of books and examinations. Laura must learn the program material on her own. She has found this difficult for areas of law not handled at her office.
12. Of the 17 respondents who answered this question, eight had a job description, eight did not, and one did not know.
13. Although she commented that her predecessor had left because she could not cope with new job stresses, Ophelia did not acknowledge how her own situation mirrored that earlier one.
14. In typical call centres, the calls of customer service representatives (CSRs) are recorded for possible later audit. Supervisors supplement the automated surveillance by listening in on occasional calls. CSRs never know when they are being monitored and have little freedom to diverge from response norms.
15. The aggregation of employee opinions in such environmental scans usually mutes individual voices and reduces employee feedback to generic statements.
16. Only 13 per cent of clerical workers are required to have certification (see Chapter 5, Graph 5.8).
17. International Association of Administrative Professionals
18. Ontario's stringent requirements (minimally) include, for mutual fund traders, a mutual fund course and, for securities traders, the Canadian Securities Course (CSC®).
19. At the time of Beatrice's enrolment, Ryerson was a college of applied arts and technology; it has since attained university status.

Chapter Ten
Auto Workers' Learning in Lean Production

D.W. Livingstone and Olivia Wilson

Jeff is a machine operator on a General Motors assembly line. His talk about his job focused on the intensification of his physical effort:

> I basically lift a 20-pound part every 9 seconds all day. It comes to me on a conveyer belt, I twist it up out of the pallet, flip it 180 degrees—the laser operation is so fast, it is incredible.... There are not that many jobs now that you actually have to use your hands, everything is "upstairs." The repetition does get to you.... When I started in the early 80s, we used to work to a quota, say 1,600 to 1,700 parts a day. When you got that count, sometimes you were done early, right. Well, now we work buzzer to buzzer. I used to have 11 seconds to do my job and now I have 8.33 seconds a pallet. Once I pick up the part, it used to release in 6 seconds, now it releases in 2, but more and more.... We used to be 30 minutes on, 30 minutes off for recovery time. Now we work 45 minutes on, 15 minutes off, so obviously we are working more and we are lifting more... more lifting, more speed up, longer hours, less people, more profitability.

Martin is a certified electrician who has also been working at this General Motors plant since the mid-1980s. He services and maintains machines like Jeff's and various others. He completed an apprenticeship under a qualified tradesman. In his account of his job he emphasized what is "upstairs":

> You come in the morning, grab a cup of coffee. I try to get there early to find out what happened on the earlier shift. It's better to hear about these problems from the horse's mouth because if not, by the time it gets to you, it's nowhere close. Then we wait for the supervisor to give us any instructions that are pertinent for the immediate day as focuses change from day to day. That sort of sets

the tone of the day, as sometimes there are problem areas and things you need to put extra emphasis on. Then you wait for your first troubleshooting assignment.... You get a call on a particular machine, go up and talk to the operator, see if you can work these things out. It could be a number of really simple things or something extremely complicated that could take days to figure out with engineering support. The first thing that you do is find out what they think the problem is. I take that with a grain of salt, do my own little thing to try to figure it out and then think of solutions, if I need to go get parts, try this, try that. If it works, we're off. Then it's the next job, then that repeats all the way down the day. Sometimes you need other tradesmen involved to help you, or engineering support, whatever, and then you work at it together.... Not everything's exciting. Some of it's plain dirty and ugly... you know, you have to pull a cable through slop and junk and it's not fun. But getting to that point, analyzing, troubleshooting, it gives me a real rush.

As Jeff says, not many heavy manual labour jobs are left in auto assembly plants. Most workers are operating increasingly automated machines, cleaning or resetting the specific tools on these machines or, like Martin, troubleshooting to ensure their continuous operation. Division of labour between production workers and tradespeople persists. However, the most distinctive features of the labour process — whether termed "Toyotism," "lean production," or "neo-Taylorism" — are the declining division of labour and the intensification of work (see Pruijt, 2003). Production workers are increasingly involved in a widening array of tasks, with job amalgamation or job rotation, while tradespeople move toward multi-crafting.

Auto assembly work is often seen as a leading example of deskilling in modern automated industries. This chapter first sets the context of this EJRM case study and then examines the working conditions of auto workers in terms of recent skill changes and job control. Then it follows a review of the education and training required to get and perform these jobs and a consideration of auto workers' actual learning activities. Next, the different dimensions of the formal match between job requirements and workers' capabilities are looked at more closely. Finally, the relationship between the extent of auto workers' job control and their education-jobs match is briefly assessed. Throughout the chapter, similarities between production workers and tradespeople are presented. Deskilling of auto workers is not the whole story.

THE AUTO SECTOR

Canada's automotive industry represents a significant segment of the global automotive industry and is Canada's largest manufacturing sector, accounting for over 12 per cent of gross domestic product in manufacturing in 2006. At that time, nearly 160,000 people were employed in automotive assembly and auto parts manufacturing and about twice that many in distribution and aftermarket service. More than three-quarters of automotive assembly and component manufacturers were employed by General Motors (GM), Ford, and Chrysler. About 40 per cent of those working in the major auto assembly plants worked for GM (Industry Canada, 2007). The industry has been heavily unionized, with almost all union members belonging to the Canadian Automotive Workers (CAW), which was formed in 1985 when it separated from its US parent, the United Automotive Workers (Gindin, 1995).

Since the mid-1980s, auto production has become an increasingly integrated global industry, with the growth of a small number of giant firms and widespread outsourcing of component parts. Even with global parts interdependencies, growing pressures for companies to build where they sell have encouraged these firms to place final assembly in more countries (Sturgeon, Biesebroeck, & Gereffi, 2008). GM has been surpassed by Toyota as the largest automaker and is compelled to move more of its final assembly work offshore, at the same time as it faces greater competition for market share in North America. In the past decade Canada's previously strong domestic automotive industry, nurtured by the 1965 Canada-US Autopact, has experienced a serious downturn in the wake of "transplanted" Asian auto assembly plants, the development of Mexican auto assembly plants following the North American Free Trade Agreement, and the abolition of the Autopact in 2001. GM layoffs and plant closures have been occurring in Canada since the early 1990s.

GM, Ford, and Chrysler have responded to their decline in market share, sales, and profits by increasing investment in automation and by restructuring their production and management systems with the goal of greater efficiency. This model is most commonly known as *lean production*, a concept developed by Toyota's Taiichi Ohno following World War II (Womack, Jones, & Roos, 1990). The "Japanese model" became the standard against which other automakers measured their performance. Lean production is distinguished by

> its minimalist approach to factory management. Inventories in a "lean" plant are taken on a just-in-time basis to minimize handling and expose defective parts before they accumulate in the warehouse; stockpiles of in-process work are also sharply reduced so that defects are immediately exposed at their source, before they fill the plant's repair bays with defective products; "indirect" labor (supervision, inspection, maintenance) is pared and specialized job classifications are reduced or eliminated, replaced by teams of cross-trained production workers who rotate jobs and take on responsibilities for quality control, repair, housekeeping, and preventative maintenance (Babson, 1995: 6).

Lean production was heralded as having the potential to increase job satisfaction by increasing workers' responsibility and productivity (Womack et al., 1990: 14). More recent surveys suggest that lean production does not empower workers but intensifies workplace demands (Landsbergis, Cahill, & Schnall, 1999). Lean production may result in greater standardization of work and erosion of workers' sense of autonomy by diminishing their control over the pace of work. GM workers have been more inclined to report lower levels of autonomy and control as well as a faster pace of work and increasing workload than workers at other Canadian auto companies to (Lewchuk, Roberts, & MacDonald, 1996). Lean production techniques also appear to be related to an upsurge in repetitive strain injuries (Leslie & Butz, 1998). The CAW has come to the conclusion that lean production goes against the fundamental union goals of a more democratic workplace with more worker control and improved working conditions (Kumar & Holmes, 1997; CAW, 1993). It appears that the implementation of lean production has been less successful in North America than Japan due to both the lack of institutional mechanisms incorporating workers' shop floor concerns in the production process and union resistance to the team concept (Fairris & Tohyama, 2002).

A Southern Ontario Auto Assembly Plant

At the beginning of the twentieth century new mass production industries, such as automotive, rubber, petrochemical and electronics, developed in southern Ontario. This industrial development thrived on access to a growing steel industry and other raw materials, large labour and consumer markets, dependency on nearby US parent firms, and protective national policies. By the 1930s Depression the automotive industry had become North America's major manufacturing sector, and GM was the largest manufacturer in the world (Gindin, 1995). The GM site at which this EJRM case study was done started production in the Depression era. It expanded its number of linked plants and jobs into the post–World War II period, reaching a total of over 9,000 employees in the 1980s. In the early 1990s layoffs and plant closings began. By the time of this case study in 2005, employment had dropped to less than a third of the late 1980s. Numbers continued to decline through retirements because no new employees had been hired since the early 1990s. Virtually all workers with less than about 18 years of seniority are now gone.

The remaining labour force in such older auto plants continues to age. According to the EJRM Survey, the average age of all auto workers in Ontario, including those at the more recent transplanted Asian companies with younger workforces, was around 45 years; these had an average of about 12 years of job experience in their current plant. In this case study, the average age of workers in the plant was early 50s, and the average seniority was over 25 years. The youngest worker in this plant was in his early 40s. As in auto plants generally, workers are overwhelming male, that is, around 90 per cent of both production and trades workers. In the 1980s under affirmative action initiatives, more women were hired. However, as the last hired, they were also the first fired in the 1990s. Similarly, while ethnic minorities are well represented in newer plants, this older plant, with no new hiring, remains almost exclusively white. It should also be noted that the auto industry generally has a high proportion of workers who have become disabled. Jeff, for example, was on temporary disability for repetitive strain injury when we spoke to him.

According to the EJRM Survey, around a quarter of the remaining auto workers in Ontario assembly plants were in the trades, most commonly millwrights/machinists, tool and die makers, electricians, and welders. The main production jobs were machine operators and material handlers.

All non-managerial workers in the case study auto plant are members of the CAW Union. Respondents in the EJRM case study were randomly selected from the membership list provided by the union local. Twenty workers were interviewed: eight trades workers and 12 production workers. Sixteen workers responded to an information sheet, and eight of these were tradespeople. About a third of the workers in this plant are trades workers; so the trades were overrepresented in the initial sample. Four additional production workers were found through snowball sampling. The under-representation of production workers in the initial sample may be related to their more tiring working conditions. All respondents worked at least 40 hours a week and most had occupied the same job for more than 15 years.

THE CHANGING NATURE OF AUTO WORK

With increasing automation, manual production jobs are disappearing in auto plants. Those, like Jeff's, that remain have increasingly short cycle tasks with little apparent autonomy (Schumann, 1998). Most remaining production jobs require increased multitasking, as well as increasing conversance with computerized machinery. Tara, a metal-working machine operator, described an average day:

> I go in, start my machine. I shut it down after the first cycle and pull out a part. I check the part for height, face size, bore size, and for runoff. I start it up again. I start up another machine and do the same thing, making sure that it will be on size and that it will run at the same time as the other machine. And then I turn on my shavers and I pull two parts out of there and check those for size as well. Parts from the hob [a cutting tool] and parts from the shavers go to the gear lab. I put out two parts from each of these three machines. The gear lab comes and takes them and checks them to make sure everything is good. I check parts from all of the machines every half hour to make sure they are on size. If there is a problem, I then go into the computer and make the adjustments or do repair. Then the parts go on a conveyor to be washed and taken to a heat treat area. Then I have to fill up and replace these baskets and bring them back to my area. That is what I do everyday.... Some days, if I am having a problem with my tools, I might not get the numbers but we generally run between 1,800 to 1,900 pieces per shift.... They want to declassify jobs.... Now we take away our own chips, we fill up our own oil, and we clean our own areas, so they have declassified all those janitorial and oiler jobs.

Tradespeople experience some multi-crafting, but they generally perform a wider array of more complex discretionary tasks. The account of Ethan, a certified tool setter, is fairly typical:

> Every day is different.... The whole plant is my work area and I will do anything from installing dies, working on dies...and then I could be doing tool maintenance for the older tooling. I could be doing troubleshooting with electricians and machinists; I could be working with other tool and die makers on a project. Sometimes the [machine] operators just write down whatever needs to be done, whether the drill needs to be changed on the machine, the die changed, or cutters reset. Sometimes they will just say that the machine is not running, we will go, and we will diagnosis the machine, and we will contact electricians, maintenance, whoever needs to be contacted.

The intensification of production places an increasing premium on the trades to ensure continuous equipment operation. As Doug, a service electrician assigned to an assembly line, stated:

> If a machine doesn't work, the people working the machine put a call out, and I try to determine why it isn't working and if it is my job as an electrician to fix it, or if I need perhaps a machine-repair or tool-maker or a pipe-fitter. What that entails is getting your laptop computer out and getting the right software program and backtracking. Sometimes it's a big pain and sometimes it's easy.... They don't want the line to go down ever — even for a few minutes. That's a critical situation.... You go from job to job, trying to keep things running.

Many tradespeople in such older auto plants are now primarily involved in rebuilding these plants, and most of them have experienced work intensification as well. Michael, a millwright, described the uncertainty and intensification of current working conditions:

> Production has undergone a major reconstruction over the last 10 years. Part of the plant is gone. The other part has been almost completely retooled with new equipment in the last several years.... So it has been a major upheaval for the last 10 years. We have bounced between being a tear-up crew, to a construction crew, to surveys, to everything in between.... In a union shop in the automotive industry, there is always a big conflict between cost cutting and getting things done in a timely manner. GM would like to make cars with no people. They just want to push a button somewhere and have every kind of vehicle come out of there perfect without any breakdowns.... We say we need more people

> because our safety procedure says so, and they say "No, no, we need less people because that machine will make 97 parts an hour forever." Well, it's going to break, you know, and when it breaks, if you are going to send me to fix it by myself when I am supposed to have someone else there, now we have a conflict. So I wish there was more communication between the "bean counters" and the floor where you actually do the work, because they want to do things with nobody.... How can you do maintenance on a machine when bean counters schedule it to run continuously 24/7?

In the EJRM Survey about half of Ontario auto workers reported that the work techniques and equipment they use regularly at the workplace had changed either a great deal or moderately over the past five years. Most production workers reported the intensification of work techniques, while most tradespeople reported frequent involvement with getting new equipment up and running. Katharine, a machine operator on an assembly line, expressed a concern common among line workers about the health consequences of this work intensification in an aging workforce.

> Now they've got us working faster and putting up more parts. We've been there for 20 years already, so our bodies are half broken down anyways, and now they want you to move faster. You are getting people put out the door on medical leave once they've suffered repetitive strain from doing a certain motion and can't do that motion again.... Some people don't want to report it, so they just keep working until they get to the point that they can't use that hand because they don't want to say anything because they can't collect compensation for long. It's a major, major battle.

As Michael, the millwright, added to his earlier account of changing production techniques, "Retooling is ongoing all the time. Every new piece of equipment presents a new set of problems. The mechanics of the job remains pretty consistent from one thing to the next... but you never stop learning."

The most distinctive features of lean production — intensification and declining division of labour — are quite evident in the accounts of working conditions in this plant. While profound differences remain in the complexity and diversity of production and trades jobs, increasing computerization and an ever-closer determination of the pace of work on assembly lines are diminishing these differences.

Job Control

As noted in Chapter 4, according to the attitude surveys, industrial workers appear to have gained more say in organizational decision-making, as well as somewhat greater task autonomy, over the past generation. With regard to organizational decisions, team consultations have become widespread, and some older production workers especially find these consultations a significant improvement. Carlotta, an assembler, expressed a fairly common sentiment:

> At the start of the day, we have a team meeting. So everybody meets, and if there were any issues from the day before, then the supervisor will voice those. And if we have any concerns, we voice ours. And they're hashed out somewhat. And then, you know, we start work at a certain time. Say there was a big concern, you would call a union rep, and they would come down, and you'd be taken off the line, and you would have your chance to have a union rep with you and discuss the whole thing with the supervisor until it was reasonably worked out.... It used to be "OK, you got to do this." But they don't really talk that way anymore. Plus there is a softening of the union; they work things out too with the supervisor. So it's not a yelling and screaming match, where years ago it was — everybody trying to prove how tough they are. We've come a long way. And so have management — there are certain human rights boundaries and that sort of thing that they can't cross.

But the distance between consultation on the shop floor and the actual decision-making to change management practices remains substantial. Tradespeople who have tried to alter management practices are particularly skeptical. As Martin, the electrician, said:

> There's been some new ways of doing business that don't seem to be working.... The management techniques are not really that new, they come in cycles.... I think it all boils down to the fact that there could be better communication across the board. Sometimes middle management doesn't talk to the people on the floor; there isn't a good exchange of ideas there, and that leads to bad decisions being made. In my immediate area right now, there's things that we told them won't work, right from the get-go and they're not working... It is unfortunate because at the end of the day, the product has to get out the door.... The profit margin has become more important than ever and there's pressure on. But they're abandoning spending money up front to keep the equipment running so they can put it out... so it's unrealistic. Some of the [middle management] positions haven't had the floor experience and won't listen to guys who have had the experience.

Overall, three-quarters of Ontario auto workers still feel that they do not participate in organizational decisions about products, personnel, or budgets. This sentiment is shared by over 80 per cent of production workers and over 60 per cent of tradespeople. Beyond everyday shop floor details, team decision-making appears to be a lean production indeed.

In terms of the discretion or autonomy workers have in performing their jobs, all auto workers have assigned tasks, ranging from highly repetitive assembly line routines to tradespeople troubleshooting throughout the plant. Workers generally seek whatever discretion they can within these assigned tasks to make their work more interesting or bearable.

For assembly line workers, this discretion often involves trying to find more recuperative time from the rigours of repetitive motion. Hamper (1991) and others have illustrated the tactics auto workers use to accomplish this. Kusterer (1978) has provided profiles of how workers in other apparently highly routinized jobs use their own judgment and initiative to solve problems and avoid disruptions. Katharine, the machine operator, described the approach she uses to cope with line work:

> I work steady midnights, but that's by choice because my theory was that a steady shift was better than three shifts. A lot of people hate midnights, I don't have a problem sleeping and, as a single parent, I'm basically available for my kids' waking hours.... From the time you get in there we have a few breaks, and midnights you could probably take a 30-minute lunch. On the other shift, you get only 20 minutes. On midnights there's not a lot of supervision around, and you have a lot of leeway.... The job itself is very repetitive machining. But if some of [the product] turns out defective, you have to turn off the machine and get new rolls and put it on and feed it through... happens about once a shift. But there are about a dozen rolls involved, so in one shift, you could end up replacing half of them. You feel lucky if you only have to change it a couple times a shift. Then you have to take the [products] out and put them through another machine... and you take it off and you put it in another machine... then you remove it from there and you hang it on the line. So you're actually moving that one [product] one, two, three, four times. It's repetitive. On that particular job, they have two people. So what we do right now is work a half an hour on and then we're off for a half and hour. Just because there is a lot of work involved.... What I like about the work is the time off, it's quieter, and there's not as much pressure, probably because there isn't as much supervision. On day shifts, they're everywhere.

Although few production workers relish midnight shifts, many will try to move away from the most repetitive and heavily supervised line tasks. Tara, the machine operator, is representative:

> I started on the assembly line. Now I am in machine and tool setup. When you are in assembly you are stuck on the line, you cannot walk away; you have to put your arm up to go to the washroom, that type of thing. You are there whistle-to-whistle, break-to-break. Where I am now, I have more freedom. I can go to

the washroom; I can go get myself a cup of tea; I can sit down while the machines are running. So there is a big difference.... The work in itself is not that heavy. I only change small, very minute tooling.... It is not a fast and furious job.... Once you get into this department, very rarely does anybody leave.

Even the most apparently routinized, or unskilled, assembly line work involves numerous decisions about how to perform specific tasks most consistently, efficiently, and safely. This may take a lot of trial and error to figure out. As Tara observed:

If I had a real problem, I call over the tool setter and watch him fix it. But it was mostly through trial and error. I mean we were taught the basics... now you are on your own basically. If something came up on the screen and said what was wrong, it was like, hmm, this is troubling, how can you get out of this? I do not call [the key tool setter] unless I have tried every avenue [that time permits]. You might have to show me once.

Production workers who are able to move further off the line may express more negative views about assembly work and greater relative discretion. Greg, a truck driver, recalled:

When I started I was on the assembly line, my brain went to mush. It was a different world.... It's a big adjustment to start there. I mean you're a kid, and you have to sit in front of an assembly line that goes by. You are doing tasks that a monkey could do, that's a big adjustment. It took several months. The mental aspect of it... Now [off line], I get a chance to use some skills. You're driving, you have to make decisions, you have to apply yourself and use your time wisely. It's not like sitting on an assembly line; there's not that repetitiveness.... But in the GM context, there's little choice in how you perform the job. I don't have to be told what to do, I know what to do. But it's all there, you just do what you have to do.... As an old-school guy, management will sometimes come and ask me what I think. But as far as the job design and operation, minimal. I have some say in what goes on at the local union, but not at GM.

Trades workers have more complex tasks and move about more diverse settings through the plant. Some tradespeople celebrate the amount of discretion they can apply on the job as compared to line workers. Charles, a toolmaker, declared:

I think the trades are kings. You pretty much have all the freedom in the world to do your job the way you see fit. There is not too much interference.... Now, there are certain jobs like the production jobs, they are given job instructions and they have to follow those, but for trades, it will be wide open. You are really at things that you do regularly that might have some formal procedures written out, but there is very little.

Other trades workers have more sober views that focus on management constraints on the freedom to design their own work. As Martin, the electrician, observed:

> We have some choice in the way we perform our jobs, but we are limited by... the priorities management set. Sometimes the way I'd like to do a job, I'm not allowed to because they put time constraints on me, or whatever. Like they'll say, we have to get this running in an hour—don't fix it—just get it going. So I can't get too creative about that. In the ideal world, I would have absolute control, but I only really have partial. There are excellent people on the floor in production and skilled trades that are willing to put in a good day's work to put out a good product, but they're not allowed to. If our input was valued, if we were treated with respect and our opinions mattered... if I came to you and said why don't we try this—and you had the respect to say to me, "we'll think about it" and get back to me... I'll have learned something, you'll have learned something. And I'm going to be willing to share my next idea. But they don't want that. It's too much trouble or it takes away from their authority. It's disappointing, but at this stage in my career, I'm not going to change jobs at this age just because of that.

In terms of general attitudes about control of their own jobs, about half of Ontario auto workers in *both* trades and production jobs say that they can design their own work most of the time. When asked about the amount of creativity in their jobs, a third of trades workers said they exercise a great deal of creativity, compared with only 5 per cent of production workers. But trades workers are divided. They are also at least as likely as production workers to say they have little or no creativity in their jobs. The meaning of *design* and *creativity* may vary substantially between the different contexts of trades and production jobs, and both types of workers try to shape their jobs in tolerable ways. It may be that in this old plant, older trades workers are particularly sensitive to the constraints of lean production on their traditional discretion. Also, the extensive working knowledge of the veteran production workers, coupled with some more consultative management practices, may be aiding them to reshape details of their jobs. In any case, a pragmatic acceptance of their changing working conditions and a sense of limited capacity to change organizational features beyond their immediate work sites is fairly pervasive. As Doug, the electrician, put it: "I knew that years ago when I started [at GM], that it wouldn't really be interesting. But you try to make the best of it, right? I mean it pays well."

FORMAL JOB REQUIREMENTS

The formal educational requirements for entry into auto work jobs have been relatively low. According to the EJRM Survey, over 40 per cent of these jobs did not require a high school diploma, and very few required more than a diploma. The majority of trades workers did require a high school diploma to enter their apprenticeship training, but a majority of production workers did not require a diploma to get their jobs in the plant. In terms of the formal education needed to perform the job, workers' self-reports again indicate that most trades jobs require at least a high school diploma, while most production jobs need no diploma. It should also be noted that certification or licensing is widespread in the auto industry, with around two-thirds of both trades and production workers requiring certification. In addition to licensing of the trades, machine operators require certification, and health and safety certification is also common. It should be added that much of this certification, especially for production workers, is employer based and not very portable between employers.

The most striking difference is in training time. Less than 20 per cent of production workers report a need for more than a year to do their jobs adequately, whereas virtually all trades involve both a longer period of apprenticeship (under a qualified or licensed tradesman) and attendance at an accredited trade school. Typically, it takes about five years to gain both the practical and theoretical knowledge to become a qualified tradesperson.

Some of the older tradesmen in the EJRM Survey did not require a high school diploma, but it has become mandatory for entry to trade school. Many older production workers in the case study required no formal education at the time of hiring, but some younger workers indicated that college completion was required to get their jobs.

Machine operator Mimi's view of formal requirements is typical of older production workers: "Way back then? They asked me if I'd be willing to work shift work and I said yes. I think when I was hired you didn't even have to have grade 12. No certification. Grade 10, maybe. It took about a week to learn the job." In contrast, Greg, a truck driver, observed that

> Grade 12 was required.... We had some guys in there with grade 8. It's changed a lot now because of the computer skills you need now. I'm not sure what GM requires now; it's been so long since I was hired here. I'd think they'd be looking for college people now.

Trades workers invariably stress the discipline of their apprenticeship program. As Stephen, an electrician, expressed it:

> We're talking years, five or six years, even seven. When I started my apprenticeship, it was in construction, very little preventative maintenance, very little. So

it took me a few years in control work to get a handle on it. To become a good electrician takes years.

Like most workers, the vast majority of both trades and production workers indicate that their jobs require them to learn new skills. For trades workers who are directly involved with computerized processing operations this often means taking related further education courses. As Doug, the electrician, said:

> All these machines have their own software packages that are unique to the company that built the machine. It's a whole electrical/computer language for all these different boxes that do these different things.... So they'll send me off on a week of training on the new package.

Ethan, the tool setter, added:

> I have done a number of courses to upgrade to do CNC [Computerized Numerical Control] machining. We were sent to a training company for a couple of weeks at a time to learn these new CNC machines.... It was pretty extensive and it was pretty mind wracking, because you have to know your math to keep it together.... One previous to that they sent somebody into the plant, and we had, like, a week long seminar.

In contrast, the production workers in the case study rarely indicated that they received any further education courses related to the new equipment they operate. However, the formal requirements for diplomas, certification, and further education courses tell only a small part of the story of both trades and production workers' learning and knowledge in auto plants.

WORKERS' LEARNING AND KNOWLEDGE

Since auto plant jobs historically required little formal education, it is not surprising that, according to the EJRM Survey, just under half of all auto workers have not completed high school, including similar proportions of both trades and production workers. About a quarter of all auto workers have completed post-secondary education. These are mostly younger workers with college diplomas. About half of all auto workers took some type of further education course in the past year, including 60 per cent in the trades and about 40 per cent of production workers. Since the inception of the CAW Union in 1985, extensive training provisions have been negotiated, including courses on health and safety, ergonomics, union awareness and workers' rights, sexual harassment, as well as tuition support for degree programs. However, even with these extensive formal provisions for further education, most auto workers' learning remains informal, done on their own or with workmates (see Roth, 2004).

Virtually all auto workers indicate that they have participated in job-related informal learning activities in the past year, and there is no difference between trades workers and production workers in the general incidence of these activities. There are some differences between these workers in terms of the topical focus of their intentional informal learning. Trades workers are more likely to do informal learning to keep up with general knowledge in their field and to learn more about computers than most production workers. Production workers are more likely to devote time to learning about the operation of new equipment. However, both trades and production workers devote considerable time to learning about workers' rights and, above all, health and safety. In auto plants, danger to health is a constant focus for both further formal instruction and workers' informal learning. As Michael, the millwright, said:

> We depend on each other for our own safety.... Through our union we get regular updates to safety concerns. There are monthly meetings you can attend. Any issues that arise, you are immediately informed of them through the union and/or the company jointly. So, learning's pretty well ongoing all the time.... We are always being told what we can and can't touch...health and safety is always at us for that kind of stuff. It's the nature of the beast.... They are always reminding you...and you have to have had the training, the proper equipment to use. It's a constant horizon there all the time.

All case study participants gave numerous indications of their job-related informal learning. The trades workers learn their jobs through semi-structured informal learning in their apprenticeships, and all noted that continual informal learning was a necessary part of their work. In most cases, they did not receive formal training on the machines or programs that they work with and often taught themselves by drawing on prior experience and instruction manuals. Stephen, the electrician, recalled that

> sometimes you just have to pull out the manual. One day, we had a problem and we didn't know what to do with it. I took the manual up to the roof, spent hours there just thinking about the problem and referring to the manual. Finally figured it out.

Intentional informal learning has been a dominant strategy for trades workers from their apprenticeships onward. As Robert, a tool and die maker, summarized:

> A lot of informal learning, that's basically how I learned almost everything. The best way to survive is to do this type of learning. There's so much variation in the field, and you learn by the seat of your pants right there on the job, because if you don't, you're not useful.

For production workers, accounts of working knowledge are more likely to refer to the tacit learning of processing techniques and decision rules that can be of vital importance to both health and productivity. Such informal learning takes much longer than the short time that many production workers say is required to perform their jobs adequately, and it often involves ongoing fine-tuning (see Kusterer, 1978). For example, machine operators develop expertise in diagnosing operating problems by subtle sounds. As Tara, the machine operator, said:

> Just the experience of working it, knowing the sounds. I can tell by a sound whether there is something wrong with my machines.... There are certain things as noises that you pick up. I am always in tune to all my machines. There are things that you pick up after you know the job for years.... I can go to another machine and I am just as lost as you would be listening for those sounds because they are run differently. They are all the same machinery, but they all have their own little quirks, their own little behaviour problems I call them.

For most workers in the plant, however quickly they become comfortable in their jobs, detailed problem solving continues. Katharine, the machine operator with a college degree, put it this way:

> I can do it comfortably now. It probably took a month. The job itself isn't complicated; it's the little problems that come up.... You have to make sure that that part is good. If you don't know what to look for, you can miss it. And if you do, then hopefully someone else will catch it before it goes out the door.

In addition to workplace learning, many workers, who reflected on their learning beyond the plant, recognized the relevance of their hobbies, such as motorcycle maintenance and woodworking, in providing them with knowledge that contributed greatly to their paid work (see Roth, 2004). Stephen, the electrician, reflected:

> Sure, hobbies give you the ability to look at things in different ways. Because you've experienced different things, you can look at things from a different point of view. It gives you a more objective outlook. Like when I was in high school, I worked with ships, learned about their motors, took that and used it later with the machinery I deal with.

Katharine, the machine operator, saw her knowledge developing in the plant, at home, and between the two domains: "I apply the same principles to both things. I use stuff I learn at work, at home. Construction, stuff that I picked up along the way at work. I take the same principles of learning at home and at work and apply them to both."

More generally, when case study participants were given the opportunity to talk about the relevance of the knowledge they had gained both formally and informally throughout their lives, the depth of their implicit knowledge somewhat surprised them. As Martin, the electrician, reflected:

> From time to time, I need to draw on every bit of knowledge that I've got to fix a problem on a machine. And I thought to myself, never in my wildest dreams, did I think that what I learned 20 years ago...totally unrelated to what I'm doing now, that little snippet of information would be useful. And I can say that it is amazing. But it goes to show you that what's in here [head] is important, and from time to time that resource will be called on and if you're lucky enough, you can remember [laughter]. It is amazing.

Ethan, the certified tool setter, expressed similar surprise at the extent and interrelatedness of his working knowledge:

> Basically, you realize all your information every time you step up to a new job. You have to keep a lot in your head. It is amazing how much you can catch and keep there, and keep it all together without losing it.... I do all my own home maintenance. You learn it as a matter of necessity...just by doing it, basically self-taught, most of it. Some friends will come over and give me hand... it was fun, I learned a lot. I love working with my hands... I am always into the computer and over the Internet checking out things, learning things. And work, it is like half an hour on day-to-day things. It is ongoing. It just does not stop.

Older auto plants rely extensively on the working knowledge and continual, largely informal, and often implicit learning of their very experienced workforces. The reliance must be even greater in conditions of lean production. In the words of Jane, the machine operator:

> When a person came in to operate a machine, they used to spend at least two weeks with the trained operator. Now you might be lucky if you get about three hours training, and then you are thrown on a machine by yourself. It is not very good.... It is key to [be] motivated. You're not going to get enough training there, so you have [to] learn it on your own. You have to be gung-ho about learning.

EDUCATION-JOB MATCHING

The EJRM Survey measures provide estimates of the extent of matching of educational qualifications and job requirements for auto workers compared with other non-managerial employees. Graph 10.1 summarizes the most pertinent dimensions. Like most workers, the majority of auto workers have formally matching attainments

Graph 10.1 *Relevance, Credential, Performance, and Subjective Gaps among Auto Workers, Industrial Workers, and All Non-managerial Employees, Ontario, 2004 (%)*

Relevance gap	Closely related	Somewhat related	Not at all
Auto workers	30	35	36
Industrial workers	27	21	52
All employees	37	25	38

Credential gap	Underemployed	Match	Underqualified
Auto workers	30	55	15
Industrial workers	38	53	9
All employees	33	52	15

Performance gap	Underemployed	Match	Underqualified
Auto workers	24	51	25
Industrial workers	39	50	11
All employees	35	51	14

Subjective gap	Underemployed	Match	Underqualified
Auto workers	31	68	1
Industrial workers	34	61	5
All employees	34	62	4

Source: EJRM Survey (All employees, N=1301; Industrial workers, N=382; Auto workers, N=83)

and requirements on entry credentials, performance criteria, and their subjective views. However, like industrial workers generally, and in contrast to professional employees, a relatively high proportion of about a third of auto workers are underemployed in terms of their educational credentials and their subjective views. The performance gap may be somewhat smaller for auto workers than for some industrial workers, with about one-quarter underemployed. Auto workers are very unlikely to report subjective underqualification and are also unlikely to be underqualified in terms of entry credentials. They do have relatively high levels of underqualification on the performance measure. This is probably a reflection of the somewhat older average age of auto workers and their own increasing estimates of the general educational level now required by employers to get the same jobs. The relevance gap is also similar to that of other industrial workers, with more auto workers indicating that their job is unrelated to their formal education than those who feel it is closely related.

Among auto workers, the credential and subjective match measures are similar for both trades and production workers, with about a third underemployed on each measure. However, the performance gap is smaller for trades workers; around 10 per cent are underemployed, compared to about a third of production workers. Trades workers (40 per cent) are also more likely than production workers (20 per cent) to say that their jobs are closely related to their formal education. The smaller gaps for trades workers on performance and relevance measures are consistent with their more extensive apprenticeship training and consequent specialized knowledge. The larger credential and subjective gaps suggest that for both trades and production workers there are similar tendencies for general educational attainment and overall qualifications to exceed job requirements. It should be noted that, while the performance gaps of trades workers in the auto industry are as low as those of teachers, the larger credential and subjective gaps of trades workers are likely indicative of less self-regulation and the lower academic status of their particular bodies of specialized knowledge. It should also be noted that, along with most other workers, over two-thirds of both trades and production workers feel that their knowledge about their jobs exceeds what is required to perform them.

The previous comments of the case study participants provide somewhat deeper insight into the relationship of workers' capabilities—developed through their formal training and informal workplace learning—and their official job requirements. Trades workers often commented on the relevance of their apprenticeship training but less commonly remarked on the usefulness of their more general formal education. Michael, the millwright, said, "I use it [my formal education], yes. You need to know the fundamentals of mathematics, definitely." Production workers rarely indicated that their formal education contributed to their job performance. Sam, a driver, stated, "Well, it doesn't take too much formal education, I would say you would need high school education, but that's not even true. They want you to have that, but you don't really use it at all."

JOB CONTROL AND EDUCATION-JOB MATCH

Trades workers, with their more specialized technical knowledge compared to production workers, tend to have a closer match between the relevance of their studies and performance capabilities and their job requirements. Production workers tend to have a general formal education that is not perceived as directly relevant to, or required for, their jobs. Both the survey findings and the case study comments suggest that trades workers generally perceive greater creative control of their jobs than production workers do. Further analysis of the EJRM Survey data shows that, whatever the extent of creativity trades workers perceive in their jobs, their performance gap remains low. In contrast, there are wide variations among production workers: Those who are able to exercise a fair amount of creativity have low performance gaps, while most of those with little creativity are underemployed on performance criteria. Overall, these findings suggest that trades workers tend to have greater discretionary control than production workers in auto plants, and they are also more closely matched with their jobs on relevance and performance criteria. Production workers who think they have greater discretionary control also tend to have smaller performance gaps than other production workers.

However, as the case study analysis also suggests, most auto workers perceive heavy constraints on their ability to play substantial roles in the design of their jobs or in organizational decision-making. The variations in their perceived creativity have little relation to their profiles of credential and subjective matching. The extent of participation in organizational decision-making appears to have no significant relationship to the extent of correspondence on any of the basic dimensions of education-job matching. These findings may suggest that the more participatory team model introduced with lean production has had little effect to date in ensuring more effective use of workers' knowledge in the production process of auto plants (see Pruijt, 2003).

CONCLUDING REMARKS

In recent years there have been drastic changes in working conditions in the auto industry. Mass layoffs combined with increasingly computerized control of production processes have led to intensification of work for remaining workers. Both the EJRM Survey data and the case study analysis indicate that these workers generally are responding to these conditions by engaging in continual learning—partly through further education courses but mostly from experience—in order to perform and reshape the detailed forms of their changing jobs while keeping the plant running. The veteran workforce in this case study has vast work experience from decades in this auto plant and deep tacit knowledge of the basic aspects of their jobs. Much of their work-related learning in response to either production disruptions, or the introduction of new equipment, or management models occurs seamlessly and is integrated with their job performance. They have been largely teaching themselves how to fine-tune the complex machinery that dominates this auto plant.

The data suggest that auto workers often act on their own initiative to gain the abilities that enable them to do their jobs more effectively. These auto workers have developed abilities that are used in their work but that often go unrecognized in the plant. Formal job entry requirements do not accurately describe the vast stock of abilities that workers acquire informally and that the company relies on. When focused on formal education, measures of matching between workers' capabilities and job requirements miss this informal learning and barely begin to estimate the actual relations between the expanding capabilities of workers and the changing job conditions. In terms of formal education, trades workers reported a closer formal match with job requirements than did production workers. However, in this veteran workforce virtually everyone professed competence at their job and described continuing efforts to learn more about the nature of their job and how they try to adapt it. Whatever their formal qualifications, most have reserves of abilities that could be more effectively used if workers and managers were more aware of them.

Many of the auto workers in the case study expressed frustration with management's lack of interest in their production ideas. Production workers may be more inclined to want further training on new equipment and have suggestions for reducing repetitive strain activities, but trades workers described their lack of influence on more general job design issues. Most of the workers in this plant appear increasingly concerned that the lean production model, with "management by stress," ultimately means producing a poorer product. Martin, the electrician, expressed it this way:

> It doesn't matter if you're skilled trades or production — we all have skill, we all have knowledge, and by and large you have dedicated people willing to do a good day's work and produce a good product. Some of these management decisions are making it difficult for us to do that.... It's a constant battle for time and money — it all boils down to money.... When some of us make suggestions to make improvement, you almost get the impression "don't confuse me with the facts, my mind's made up".... You walk out of there after eight hours... it is frustrating.

These veteran auto workers are continually learning to try to perform their jobs better, but they are also learning how to sustain themselves in their relations with a management that is primarily concerned with intensified production.

In the context of an aging workforce, continuing plant closures, downsizing in the auto industry, and the lack of hiring for almost a generation, a labour force renewal strategy that combines new hiring with phased retirements is sorely needed. Otherwise, the vast reserves of working knowledge of this veteran workforce will soon be gone, and plant closure will be the last testament of this experiment in lean production.

Chapter Eleven
Struggling to Remain Employed: Learning Strategies of Workers with Disabilities and the Education-Job Match

Sandria Officer

> I adjusted my schedule because of my carpel tunnel. I used to take one day and do all my repairs. If I had 20 of them, I would untorque and torque them all and go through a checklist to make sure that they met criteria—but obviously I injured myself doing that. There were just too many. So I told my boss not to expect me to do that anymore. I'll do one or two a day. I don't care if it goes on for weeks and they pile up. That's the only way I'm doing it now because my health comes first. I'm already injured, and I don't want my condition to get worse. (Maria, auto worker with pain, repetitive strain injury, and cancer)

> The union has to become much more proactive and advocate for people with disabilities. I think if you present them with an issue they are forced to react; although in my case it didn't amount to much. The union has to realize that we are aging, and there will be more of us. (Toula, teacher with polio)

There is an increase in the number of Canadians reporting a disability. A nationwide survey from Statistics Canada in 2006 indicated that the disability rate for the population aged 15 and older increased from roughly 12 per cent in 2001 to about 14 per cent in 2006 (HRSDC, 2006). Researchers attributed the growth in disability rates to population aging and to changes made in the way disability was profiled and reported. The unemployment rate for people with disabilities decreased from about 13 per cent in 2001 to roughly 10 per cent in 2006 (HRSDC, 2006). But these figures were still significantly higher than the 7 per cent estimated for people without disabilities during the same five-year time period (HRSDC, 2006). They reflect the high degree of exclusion of disabled workers from the labour force. Most working-age people with disabilities experience countless difficulties in their attempts to find and retain employment (HRDC, 2004). Employers have demonstrated stereotypical thinking about disabled workers' abilities and job performance levels. Their negative attitudes and the additional concern about the cost of accommodating disabled workers have been identified as the principal causes of high unemployment and underemployment for these workers (Stein, 2000; Campolieti, 2004). Much of the research on disability and employment is anecdotal, impairment-specific, deficient in empirical analysis, policy-led, and concerned primarily with labour supply. Little is known about the work and learning activities of workers with disabilities in the workplace.

The purpose of this case study is to examine disabled workers' job requirements and compare them with the education and knowledge they have gained from formal education and informal learning. This study is based on the disability employment literature, data from the 2004 EJRM Survey, and semi-structured interviews with disabled workers from each of the occupational groups represented in the prior four case studies. The focus is restricted to disabled workers in non-managerial positions. The disabilities of all the case study respondents are identified in Appendix 1.

This chapter is in three parts, the first of which presents general profiles of the employment conditions of disabled workers, in addition to formal and informal learning practices. The middle section looks at job requirements. The last part of the chapter explores the education-jobs match, workplace culture, and job control needed to circumvent unemployment and underemployment.

HISTORY AND ORGANIZATIONAL CONTEXT

Employment Trends

Globalization, rising health care costs, and human rights issues have directed international attention to the employability and job retention abilities of workers who are chronically impaired or who become injured. Since the 1960s, legislation has been enacted in an attempt to improve disabled workers' participation in the labour market (HRDC, 2004). In spite of such policy initiatives, organizations are confronted by fiscal demands to stay globally competitive, frequent technical changes, and pressures to downsize. All of these factors put the employment of vulnerable disabled workers at risk (Roulstone, 2002).

In 2003, the federal and provincial governments endorsed the Multilateral

Framework for Labour Market Agreements for Persons with Disabilities (LMAPD), which replaced the Employability Assistance for People with Disabilities initiative (HRDC, 2004). The LMAPD's goal to improve the employability and job prospects of Canadians with disabilities officially took effect among the provinces through bilateral labour market agreements in 2004 (HRDC, 2004). However, as Canada's labour market tightens, the preference for flexible employment rarely includes long-term commitment to the development of a worker's capacities (Shields, 1996). Employers increasingly hire more non-standard workers and reduce core, permanent full-time staff to save costs. This polarity in labour market trends poses a serious threat to disabled workers who want standard employment. They may face more competition for jobs and find it more difficult to obtain and retain good employment. Furthermore, changes based on general population standards and ideas of individualism include built-in constraints and performance expectations that fail to recognize their unique abilities. The entry of disabled workers into jobs could become even more restricted by matters unrelated to competence and, therefore, job-related learning opportunities may not be available, let alone equitable.

While the majority of disabled workers in full-time employment usually work a regular day shift of 30 hours or more per week (HRDC, 2004), they are overrepresented in service sector jobs that have low pay, little security, and lack opportunity for advancement (Briscout & Bentley, 2000). However, demographic patterns indicate that younger workers with mild impairments and a post-secondary education have better prospects for employment (HRDC, 2004). In addition, the employment rate and income level of Caucasian disabled men is consistently higher than disabled people of colour and disabled women. This inequity is compounded for recent immigrants who are disabled and face obstacles to integration. These obstacles include finding a job, locating accommodation, learning a new language, and adapting to a completely different society and way of life, while at the same time being without equal access to health care and housing (Rajan & Penafiel, 2002: 1). Clearly, disabled people confront complex barriers on the path to employment.

DISABILITY WORKPLACE MANAGEMENT

Canadian employers have a legal duty to provide qualified disabled workers with workplace accommodation in a manner that respects their dignity and allows them to perform their jobs, unless the accommodations would cause undue hardship for the organizations (Canadian Human Rights Act, section 15.2, 1985). Workplace accommodations include modified or alternate tasks, workstation redesign, activity restrictions, or reduced hours (Campolieti, 2004). Workplace accommodation law requires employers to demonstrate that they have made every effort to fulfill their duty. Employers must determine if an employee can perform his or her existing job; If the employee cannot, then the employer needs to assess if the job can be performed in a modified form. If not, the employer must determine if the employee can do another job in its existing form. If the employee cannot, then the employer needs to consider whether the employee can perform another job in a modified form. Workplace accommodations have been shown to prevent protracted work absences and the added costs associated with replacement workers (Lynk, 1999).

Despite these initiatives, several factors impede workplace accommodation efforts. There are organizational barriers for small employers with limited resources who cannot relocate workers or modify job tasks. Job sectors with very physical job demands (e.g., construction) are unable to reduce workloads to levels that provide adequate accommodation. Further organizational barriers to workplace accommodation result from labour union agreements, wage scale requirements, and public safety concerns that limit job modifications (Shaw & Feuerstein, 2004: 208). Yet the most significant barrier to workplace accommodation efforts remains the procedures that employers use to assess the functional abilities of disabled workers in relation to the job requirements. Employers use the impairment-job match tenet of accommodation to assess physical function and workplace exposure solely to prevent or reduce new injuries or illnesses, rather than to modify jobs for workers with distinct functional limitations. Conversely, rehabilitation service providers create functional limitation assessments mainly to chart patient progress in terms of their daily activities and paid work, and to make judgments concerning their legal disability status. Clearly, the measures of functional limitation and workplace exposure were not principally developed for workplace accommodation (Shaw & Feuerstein, 2004: 208–9).

WORKING CONDITIONS

The continual restructuring in organizations to lower costs, by forcing greater productivity and flexibility from workers, characterizes today's economy. This poses a threat to disabled workers who find that constant changes in job demands are difficult. About three-quarters of the EJRM total sample reported that their jobs did require new skills in the last five years, and a similar proportion of disabled workers agree. Additionally, disabled workers have experienced similar rates of technical change in their work. Even though they are overrepresented in low-status jobs where less recognized skills are required, around 40 per cent of disabled workers have increased their skills in the past five years. Of those in the case studies three-quarters reported the sense of skill increase.

Some disabled respondents have found that technical changes in their workplace have exacerbated the impairment-related health problems that they already experience on the job. Toula, an elementary teacher who has decades of seniority, remarked:

> I've had up to 32 students. Last year and the year before that I taught a split 7 and 8, which just about did me in. The split occurred because the new curriculum prevents you from combining courses...so I basically did two math, two

religion, two family life, two sciences... you have to be really experienced and well organized and have the kids well trained.... I didn't have time to sit back and have the kids come to me. I was constantly teaching.... I found it very taxing physically even though I had materials to rely on and knew my curriculum.

Disabled workers generally take the same time to learn how to perform their job tasks as other workers. Disabled case study respondents also indicated that they required similar time to become adept at their jobs. The apparent difference is that some disabled workers are inclined to take longer than the standard time to *complete* some job tasks. As Barbara, a teacher with vision problems, explained:

I have difficulties in specific areas and take longer to read, write, organize, and follow through with deadlines.... I would like to see when the [board] makes a change that I am able to learn it before the next change. Or when they give me paper work, they give me the time to fill it in. Everything that has to be done now ends up being done on my time.

The Canadian National Institute of Disability Management and Research (NIDMAR, 2000) published occupational standards and the first code of practice for disability management in 2000. Vocational rehabilitation experts who assist insurance agencies and employers to match disabled workers' abilities and interests with job requirements now use the established terms from NIDMAR, although this matching normally happens after workers have been injured or problems with their pre-existing impairments have occurred on the job. The employers and insurance agencies focus most of their attention on the cure and prevention of impairment, rather than on addressing the needs of disabled workers at job entry and beyond.

JOB REQUIREMENTS OF DISABLED WORKERS

The National Occupational Classification (NOC) resource provides standardized occupational information on educational and technical requirements in Canada (HRSD, 2006). However, because employers differ in their interpretation of what they consider essential and reasonable job requirements, the standard NOC information may disproportionately disadvantage workers with disabilities. For example, an employer at one organization may consider disabled workers competent, while another employer may have expectations of job competencies that do not include the disabled workers' distinct areas of strength. While anti-discrimination laws serve to encourage employers' consistency in this regard, the processes that disabled workers go through to obtain employment and the technical requirements expected of them in their paid work remain unaddressed. Demitri, a government computer program analyst, pointed out:

> When I was young, they had a program for people with disabilities who had an aptitude for education to get their school tuition paid. That is really important because a lot of the time people with disabilities don't get summer jobs. They can't work at McDonald's. They can't do construction. You know it's very difficult to get those jobs.

There is evidence that the characteristics and symptoms of certain impairments affect employment opportunities for disabled persons (Gates, 2000: 86). These characteristics can include "a lack of vocational experience, low self-esteem, fluctuating gaps in functional capacity, interpersonal skill deficits, inadequate social supports, [and] medication side effects" (Gates, 2000: 86).

A growing body of empirical research shows that private sector organizations require both formal education and technical competence from workers with disabilities, in addition to a social aptitude for teamwork, customer relations know-how, and leadership ability (Gates, 2000; Gates, Akabas, & Oran-Sabia, 1998). The subjective performance appraisals of these workers increasingly include basic social competency criteria, which can influence employers' decisions about promotions, training opportunities, and task assignments (Colella & Varma, 1999). Many employers now expect new workers with disabilities to "self-socialize"; they are expected to use tactics learned through job training, job coaches, or appointed work partners to familiarize themselves with organizational standards and thereby improve their job entry and advancement prospects (Ashford & Black, 1993). Kamene, a program analyst, said:

> It doesn't matter how you do the job — the main thing is your cooperation with others. When my manager hired me, she told me that she wasn't hiring me because I was really smart and had the qualifications. I had just finished college, and the foremost issue on her mind was that I fit in with the department.

Tom is a senior systems analyst with a speech impediment. He joined Toastmasters International to learn public speaking and leadership skills as a way to counteract the negative reactions he received from colleagues:

> My interactions with colleagues were not good. It was hard for me to communicate with people. I would go to someone's door and then get a pretty serious block. I could see my colleagues looking at their watches. This used to make me even more anxious. There were a few who went to management and complained.

Many disabled workers would benefit from formal disability-based competency training in the workplace to advance in their careers but few receive it (Jones, 1997; Payne, 1995). Disability management studies have shown that organizational support is vital to a disabled worker's successful job maintenance (Westmorland, Williams, Amick, Shannon, & Rasheed, 2005). In Akabas, Gates, and Kantrowitz's (1996) US study of a comprehensive disability management program, they discovered that most supervisors were not trained to provide accommodations or disability-specific information to disabled workers in need.

Some researchers who subscribe to human capital theory contend that disabled workers have fewer employment opportunities than able-bodied workers of a similar age because they have less education and employment *capital*, which, in turn, reduces their job offers and career opportunities for learning and acquiring knowledge (Briscout, 2003, 2000; Roulstone, 2004). However, several studies on workplace discrimination have found that even with high education levels disabled workers still had problems in terms of lower income and reduced opportunities for upward mobility. These difficulties were compounded for women, ethnic minorities, older persons, and people with severe or very severe types of impairment (Braddock & Bachelder, 1994; Morley, 2001).

On the other hand, some studies have shown that the job performance of disabled workers has improved in progressive organizational cultures that reflect values of inclusion, cooperation, mutual respect, and support (Briscout, 2003; Spataro, 2005). Other studies have found that some of the workers benefited from new technologies, but mostly they were young, less impaired, highly educated, and already employed with greater earnings (Roulstone, 1998). Research by the Canadian Council on Social Development (2004) found that disabled workers who were union members experienced reduced barriers to job entry and were more likely to have better wages and increased training opportunities.

FURTHER EDUCATION AND FORMAL TRAINING ACTIVITIES

Workers with disabilities strive to attain higher educational levels and continually engage in formal job-related training to increase their chances of employment, job retention, and promotion. Roughly 50 per cent of the EJRM disability respondents had completed some type of post-secondary education, and 53 per cent reported that they had been certified for their jobs; this finding mirrors general labour force trends. When asked, however, what formal educational qualifications were required for job entry, 13 per cent of the EJRM Survey respondents with a disability said they needed at least university—even though 40 per cent said they really needed only high school or less to perform their jobs. The correspondence between formal education, job entry credential requirements, and self-reported job entry requirements appears higher in this case study. The main point is that most disabled workers have kept up with the changes in job requirements.

A majority of the sample of disabled workers actively engage in further education to keep up with job demands, and this is similar to the pattern for workers in general (see Graph 5.10). Most of the disabled workers in this case study took courses to cope with persistent job changes, even though they were not formally required to do so. Those in the teaching and programming professions often participated in technical training, specifically in response to rapid changes in computer-based job technology, as did disabled clerical and auto workers when new technologies were introduced. As noted in Chapter 7, teachers are required to take workshops in classroom management, curriculum development, and new technologies that standardize tasks and help to grade and monitor student achievement. Disabled teacher respondents, at the start of their careers, frequently chose to take summer courses to move up the pay scale and advance in their professions, whereas those further on in their careers often took only the required courses. Deteriorating health compelled some older, disabled teachers to conserve their energy and choose early retirement. This pattern is contrary to the general findings of Smaller, Clark, Hart, Livingstone, and Noormohamed's (2000) study of teachers' learning activities, which showed that over 80 per cent of them, regardless of age, and with over 20 years experience, continued to engage in formal courses and workshops for their own sake.

The disabled computer programmers interviewed in the case study regularly took employer-sponsored technical courses in new technologies, such as JAVA and Oracle, to remain current and positioned for promotion. Some took courses in business communication, problem solving, and proposal writing to enhance their social abilities, while others obtained credentials outside their disciplines, primarily out of personal interest but also to earn extra income. Demitri, a program analyst, remarked, "I've completed a paralegal program and I am completing my certification as a financial planner.... I like the financial industry.... I will be able to earn extra money on the side." Tom, a senior systems analyst with a doctorate, is working on another graduate degree to assume an additional career in university teaching. He said, "I don't think I'll teach full-time. I'll probably do that in the evening.... I have a financial adviser who has advised me for years to do something else with my education." These workers keep their day jobs and offset their performance mismatch by directing their unused knowledge and abilities to other paid work. They can presumably use their extra income to reduce the cost of living with impairments.

Disabled clerical workers engage primarily in employer-sponsored software program training in Excel, Windows, Microsoft Word, and Outlook Express. Few of these clerical workers advance their technical, administrative abilities in other areas through formal training. Some take employer-sponsored courses intended to improve their social abilities, but these are primarily one-day in-house workshops in self-defence, entrepreneurship, train the trainer, and personality temperament analysis. All auto workers attend mandated occupational health and environmental protection workshops. Production workers with disabilities obtain training when new technology is introduced, but report no other formal learning activity. Those responsible for the supply and maintenance of automotive parts stay informed of procedures by regularly taking employer-sponsored quality assurance and safety workshops. To move up the career ladder, some auto workers with disabilities also take college courses in problem solving and programs in management development, and they acquire college certification for the production parts approval process.

In all of the employment groups there is an absence of mandatory courses on disability awareness and sensitivity training. Most of the disabled workers interviewed said they wanted training in social competency to manage the discrimination they face on the job, but there was no such training. As Toula, a teacher said, "It would be very good if there were programs in place on disability issues, but there aren't any. I learned my strategies by luck and by trial and error. A lot was luck because my colleagues and superintendent were very good, but a lot of it you learn because you need to cope and survive."

While the majority of disabled respondents engage in formal and informal workplace-based training to deal with changes in their job task requirements, this learning seldom results in their gaining technical abilities of a higher, more complex sort. In addition, a hierarchy exists among disabled workers who participate in formal education and work-related training activities. Those in professional-level occupations attain more job-related training and are more engaged in job-related learning than those in lower job ranks who take workplace-based training but do so to learn standard job tasks.

JOB-RELATED INFORMAL LEARNING

Like other workers, the disabled respondents indicated high levels of participation (over 80 per cent) in job-related informal learning activities (see Graph 5.10). Disabled workers emphasized the benefits of informal learning for job performance and job retention. They appear to rely on their credentials and formal learning activities to improve prospects for job entry and advancement, but they depend on their informal learning to address immediate changes in job tasks.

Some disabled workers rely heavily on informal learning to counteract the physical and social barriers in their environments that thwart formal learning activities. They use employment manuals, books, magazines, and the Internet to augment their technical job-related abilities. They seem to prefer the opportunity to select the mode of learning that fits their individual needs, as Kalam, a receptionist, commented:

> I didn't know how to make computer attachments.... I would always ask a colleague to do it for me, but now I do it for myself. I learned on-line through my club for visually impaired people. So if I have a problem now, I post it on-line and someone responds with an answer.

Others, like Claire, an administrative assistant with minimal dexterity, use their other abilities to manage job tasks:

> I have a good memory... if you can't write things down, other skills become sharper to you. I type a bit but, I mean, if you have to be sharp on your feet with different job tasks then I rely on my memory and my understanding of things.

Mike, a teacher, meets his learning needs while incorporating disability-related issues into his teaching:

> I read from the textbook and do a whole bunch of other things... scrapbooks, bringing in the Internet, television, bringing in stories from the past that I know are not in the textbooks.... You are supposed to, in my opinion, because you can't talk about an issue without providing the visual.... In my curriculum, there is a section on human rights and there is a section on disability. My class asked me if I was willing to put the book down... and talk to them instead about my own experiences... but colleagues disagreed. They thought it was inappropriate because it was outside of the curriculum.... I said to them that I am the curriculum. If it is asking about impairment then I qualify. And who better else can know what is written in the books than the people who actually have to live with it.... I also bring in the newspaper and tell [my students] to read it for the first 15 minutes of class. Then I ask them to describe what they've read. This is about literacy as well. They have to read the paper... they are going to be adults one day.

Until they are proven wrong, supervisors' and co-workers' opinions about disabled workers are influenced by stereotypical thinking and narrow categorization. They often assume that these workers will be unproductive (Braddock & Bachelder, 1994). Such biased thinking stands in the way of disabled workers gaining access to the valuable learning that is the result of having role models, mentors, and formal work group activities (Jones, 1997). And since a relatively small number of them are employed full-time, they have fewer disabled colleagues available to assist them with job-related concerns. Consequently, several participants said they relied on initial instruction, additional courses, and their own efforts to manage job challenges. Mike, the teacher, explained, "You learn from the mistakes that your teachers made with you and how not to repeat it.... I would have to say I've picked up a lot of skills from dealing with complications right on the spot." Maria, an auto worker, described the instruction she received on her first day of work: "The guy that brought me to this plant... didn't even show me where the parts were. He didn't show me anything. I had to learn everything on my own." Another auto assembly line worker, Juan, talks with colleagues daily to learn and develop job tasks, obtain social support, and resolve job conflicts:

> I get together with a group of guys in my section to talk about stuff related to work like the new equipment we get or any concerns or complaints we might

have.... A while ago some workers started smoking in areas that they weren't supposed to, and it really affected [my ability to breathe]. I made a formal complaint to the union and refused to enter those areas. But it got very stressful because they continued to smoke, so I decided to stop the complaints.

From the respondents' feedback, we saw that many who lack job-related formal competencies appear to gain them informally through their practical experiences with disability. Claire, the administrative assistant, grew up in a tightly structured children's facility, attended segregated schools, navigated her way through an inaccessible college, and now lives in a tenant-care building. She said:

When you live in a tenant-care environment it's like you're not living alone. You're not really working with a team, but you've got to negotiate and ask to change times with your provider.... If you want to switch off and not be accessible, you have to negotiate that as well. Basically, it's all about problem solving because what if Wheel-trans is coming at a time when you don't have prearranged assistance... you've also got to see whether or not you can book prearranged space; it might not be available when you call. We have an office in this building, and I've learned to contact them for help. Also, you have to actually talk to other people, your peers that live in different apartments that are receiving services but are living independently. You have to negotiate with them. If they say no to something, then you have to solve another problem.

Some disabled workers experience problems with colleagues and, without their employers being aware of it, intuitively manage them. Claire's subsequent statement is representative:

I sometimes ignore it and then, at other times, I address the comments if they are directed at me.... I remember this one co-worker saying that they're never going to touch me because I'm disabled. They might get rid of her before they get rid of me. I confronted her and told her that it's based on decisions made by the positions that we hold, not based on who's in the position. So I've learned to respond in a business-like manner. It's not personal.

Most disabled workers depend on informal collective environments to meet technical job demands and gain disability support. Cynthia, a teacher who recently completed her master's in education, formed a group of other teachers, who have similar impairments as her own, said:

Since I did my research, I keep in contact with participants through a more informal network. We've gotten together for coffee and lunch, and keep informed about other teachers who are going through similar things in this board. I know there's a secondary school teacher right now who's off, and she has, with the help of a health and safety representative, requested a tally of the number of people working for the board who have environmental illnesses... but I informed her that there is no such documentation.... She can start at meetings and inform others what's going on.

Through these networks, many disabled workers acquire a valuable understanding of their disabilities and employment rights. Their collaborations also enhance their social abilities. Mercedes, an administrative assistant, talked freely about the friendships she's formed with tenants in her condominium. From these gatherings she acquires knowledge and abilities that she can apply in her job: "My evening get-together with friends from my building is my wind down time. We talk about current topics that are in the news and, since my mother works in the human resources field, we talk a lot about employment standards and labour force issues." After work, Kalam, the receptionist, teams up with others at sports clubs and a disability volunteer organization and unconsciously acquires a broad array of social techniques that improve her job performance:

> I am pretty busy in my spare time. I am training for a marathon, so I go for a run on Saturdays and Tuesdays. I also joined the trailblazer group, which is purely for recreation. There is also a tandem bike club for people with disabilities that I've joined. I am also a board member at a non-profit organization for the blind.

Kamene, a program analyst, is a relatively recent immigrant from East Africa. Through her volunteer activities she acquires the social acumen and the physical and psychological agility she needs to keep her job:

> I've learned a lot volunteering at my disability association. There is a lot of mental strain being disabled. But my polio association taught me how to listen to my body. After 20 years with polio, your body deteriorates and you can get more paralyzed. But if you know how to manage your impairment and rest you can avoid it. Thanks to them, I've learned to do that.

Chandra, a teacher, attends special needs workshops. She appears to gain theoretical knowledge from her courses and practical comprehension from her informal conversations with others:

> I always get together with other teachers [at these workshops] in the same situation as myself and we discuss what we're doing. We learn from each other and

are motivated to try something new to help the students. Things that work you share, and things that don't work you discard.

These disabled workers use a wide range of work-related informal learning to keep their jobs by staying technically up to date. Most might benefit from more formal training to improve their job performance and promotion rates, but they appear to acquire enough experience informally to manage individual situations. The next section looks at disabled workers' job control.

JOB CONTROL

Organizational Decision-Making

Few disabled workers are involved in policy decisions that affect their workplace experience (Westmorland & Williams, 2002). Less than 10 per cent of disabled workers in the EJRM Survey said they had a high level of involvement in organizational decision-making, which is lower than the general labour force. Many disabled respondents attributed their lack of involvement in the decision-making process to social discrimination in the workplace. Toula, the high school teacher, who has 32 years of job seniority, talked candidly about her lack of decision-making power and the unfair treatment she experienced at work:

> We do make decisions about things here. It is a collaborative environment. However, because of my disability, it would make sense if schools had elevators, even just a service elevator. I believe new schools do.... We have children with disabilities here and they dictate where classes are held. Teachers have been moving classes because a disabled child can't get upstairs.... It took me falling in the parking lot three times before I got accommodation for a parking spot closer to the entrance. Also, the first time we had a fire drill, I fell and created a backlog. The kids were in a panic and didn't know what to do. My colleagues and I had to come up with a plan after that.... You know, if I had an impairment where I couldn't get up the stairs at all, I suppose if the Board wanted me in the school badly enough they would change my classroom to the main floor. But would they change the whole intermediate division? Or would they force me to take a grade I didn't want?

To improve organizational commitment and output, some employers routinely consult with workers about workplace concerns, even though they seldom involve them at the decision-making stage (Livingstone, 1999a). As Tom, a senior systems analyst, said, "I don't directly make decisions. We have staff meetings and we'll discuss our budgets and new equipment, but my job does not involve active participation in budget decisions."

JOB TASK CREATIVITY

Workers, in general, have more chance of being creative in their jobs than in taking part in decision-making. A higher proportion of disabled workers than workers in general (40 per cent versus 25 per cent), said that they exercise a great deal of creativity in their jobs. Perhaps the social discrimination they experience compels them to further develop their technical abilities. As Kalam, the receptionist, remarked, "Basically I am on my own. My supervisor trusts me to make sure that everything is in order. She doesn't nag me — she lets me create my own projects." Other disabled respondents modify their pace at work to keep up with changing demands. Claire, the administrative assistant, said, "I've learned to complete job tasks the same day. When I first started here I would drag things out, but you learn that you have to speed up the process to get tasks accomplished. When no one directs you, you have to be productive or you may lose your job."

The following comment from Lina, an accessibility information technology officer, is typical: "I always have a choice in how I perform my job — as long as it gets done; although I don't have as much flexibility when it comes to the formation of projects and plans."

Nonetheless, constant and competition-driven organizational restructuring, along with new technologies and a general lack of economic resources, can have adverse consequences for disabled workers with certain impairments. Some of them develop compensation strategies to manage job responsibilities. They will forego requests for workplace accommodations out of fear of being refused or of being seen as inept, or to avoid dismissal (see Harlan & Roberts, 1998; Church, Frazee, Panitch, & Luciani, 2006). Bethamie, an elementary school teacher, arranges class times informally with colleagues to accommodate her impairments. She explained, "I've been going to the doctor once a week; so I leave work early.... I pre-arrange times with other teachers...to cover my classes...or the next morning I'll give my students 20 minutes extra, or I'll do a favour for my colleague."

To remain fit to handle increased workloads, some disabled workers adopt preemptive health practices, but this often intrudes on their personal time. Toula, the teacher, described her double day of domestic and paid labour:

> I do a lot of resting, which is basically all you can do with polio — you are tired all the time. One of the symptoms is fatigue; so you rest. I limit my resting to after work. The family has to kick in there too. I do as minimal as possible during the week...a little cooking, no laundry...I'll do the groceries but right after school.

Fatigue is a common aspect of impairment. A few participants in the case study said they find it difficult to manage the intensification of work demands and often use official channels, such as sick days, to control the pace of work. Barbara, a teacher, explained:

> I take a lot of time off because I just reach the point where I'm too tired to keep going. So, I'm not sick, I just need to have a day. Mental health breaks. I take a lot.... I get 20 sick days; so I try to take one mental sick day a month. I used to get more last year and I'm missing it. I'm really feeling it.

Other disabled respondents use vacation days to avoid inclement weather and risks to health. Kalam, the receptionist, said, "In the wintertime it's really hard to get around.... If there's a bad snowstorm or something, I'm prepared because I always save a couple of vacation days ... then I just take a leave."

Some disabled workers are challenged by the changing demands of their work but choose to manage their disabilities unaided, rather than ask that their jobs be modified. Their health, however, can deteriorate if they conform to work practices based on general population standards (see Harlan & Robert, 1998). Such self-limiting behaviours may also leave some disabled workers with less time and energy to pursue career advancement opportunities, which adds to their underemployment ratings.

Disabled workers often exhibit high levels of technical creativity in job tasks. Kalam, the visually impaired receptionist with 13 years of job seniority at a non-profit agency, is in charge of over 300 telephone calls daily, along with other administrative duties. She, like many respondents in our study, creates techniques to complete job duties:

> What I do is put all telephone numbers into my computerized phone list so that I just have to do a quick search and the numbers appear in the dialer. All the serial numbers of my Xerox machines and fax machines are in order; I input them into my computer ... and JAWS reads them out for me.... I am not exaggerating but I am faster than the other receptionist here because she has to look up all the numbers and I memorize them all. If someone calls and says they need a number in Ottawa, I have them memorized — whereas, my colleague has to look it up.... I really rely on my memory, and when something is happening like our board meeting in a month or two ... I send myself a voice message a week before so I can order the food.

Another administrative assistant, Mercedes, described how she modifies work practices:

> I have a talking calculator, a closed circuit television and JAWS speech software on my computer at work. I change the colours on my computer screen to white text on black background ... to read email.... Sometimes staff forget that I am visually impaired; so I have to remind them. At times I'll get handwritten notes from them, but I can't read handwriting.... I'll ask them to read them to me.... And when I write at work, I use a black marker because I can't read anything else.

Even though disabled workers in the case study exercise high levels of technical discretion and creativity in their work roles, they experience considerable underemployment. Workplace restructuring has made it necessary for them to assume more responsibility and engage in continual job training, but the prevailing outcome is that many disabled workers now have more knowledge and abilities than their jobs demand. Maria, a customer quality liaison auto worker, described the situation:

> My job went from just checking parts, to repairing, to going into finding problems for repair. It's evolved into stuff I think my boss should be doing. [Management] has given us more to do. I think they want to put more [responsibility] on each worker to get more out of us so that they don't have to hire another person. Get one worker to do two jobs.... There's also extra paperwork.... You have to be more accountable.

Temma, a file clerk with limited dexterity, angrily described the gradual increase in the number of her menial jobs, in spite of the job-related training she has taken but rarely uses:

> Right now, I'm having a heck of a time getting people to help me bring down the water cooler bottles. Everybody drinks water, but they're too lazy to replace the empty containers with new ones. I also now have to go downstairs and get my department's supply of photocopy paper. These duties are not in my job description, but I've added them to my evaluation report.... Also, I use the Excel program to monitor the time I take off from work. But that's all I use it for. I take these courses and end up not using them.

EDUCATION-JOBS MATCH

Graph 11.1 summarizes the education-jobs match on four basic measures (relevance of studies to job, credential match, performance match, and subjective match) for the EJRM sample in general and for disabled workers. The patterns for both groups are similar. The disabled workers' responses are examined further below.

Relevance of Field of Study to Job

As workers generally devote a great deal of time to learning activities, their formal educational attainments have sustained the continual inflation of job entry credential requirements (Livingstone, 1999a). About one-third of the EJRM disabled respondents felt there was a close relationship between their formal education and their jobs, a proportion similar to that of the general labour force. Claire, the administrative assistant with college certification, observed:

Graph 11.1 *Relevance, Credential, Performance, and Subjective Gaps among Disabled Workers and All Non-managerial Employees, Ontario, 2004 (%)*

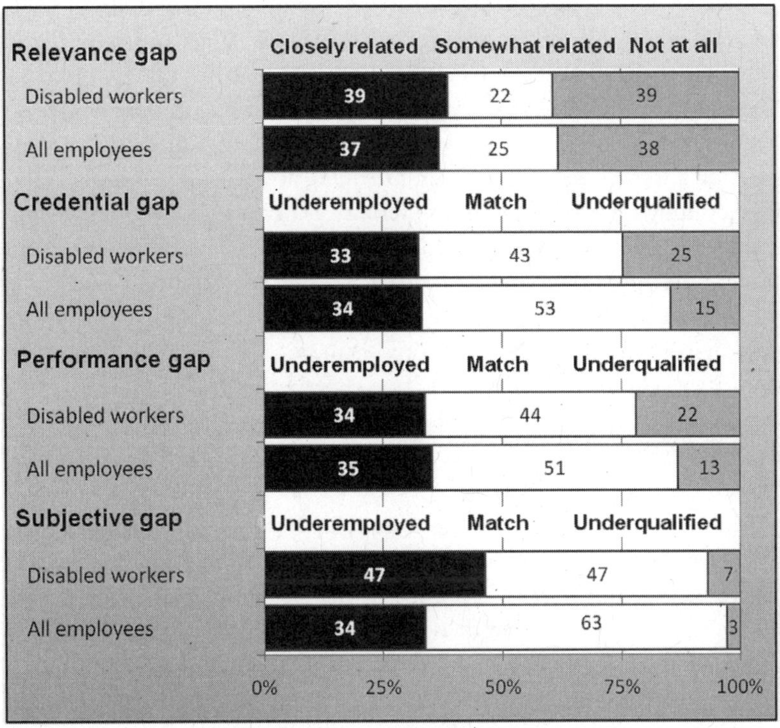

Relevance gap	Closely related	Somewhat related	Not at all
Disabled workers	39	22	39
All employees	37	25	38
Credential gap	Underemployed	Match	Underqualified
Disabled workers	33	43	25
All employees	34	53	15
Performance gap	Underemployed	Match	Underqualified
Disabled workers	34	44	22
All employees	35	51	13
Subjective gap	Underemployed	Match	Underqualified
Disabled workers	47	47	7
All employees	34	63	3

Source: EJRM Survey (All employees, N=1301; Disabled workers, N=47)

> I think I have the qualifications for what's required in my job. I'm continuing to learn as things change in my job. I'm building on my experiences and background knowledge. I'm basically learning how to problem solve and bring in my past experiences and knowledge to solve job problems with new approaches.

A few disabled respondents have formal qualifications that differ from the educational entry requirements of their jobs, but they have engaged in extensive on-the-job learning and feel adequately qualified. As Juan, the automotive assembly line worker with some high school education, said:

> You have guys who have gone to university who are on the line. You have teachers and lawyers on the line too. My formal education does not relate to my job requirements, but I'm adequately qualified... because I've learned many things. I've been here for a long while.

Credential Match for Disabled Workers

Graph 11.1 illustrates that about one-third of the total EJRM sample and one-third of the disabled workers are credentially underemployed. Other evidence suggests that even more disabled workers experience a credential gap related to the discrimination they face before they are hired. When positions are being filled, employers are often biased against disabled workers. They express their bias in different ways and at different stages: giving "job-irrelevant reasons" for failing to hire a disabled applicant, offering lower (initial) salaries, not providing access to higher-skill-level jobs, and not recruiting for certain positions (Terborg & Ilgen, 1975). Too often employers' negative expectations are conveyed in how they treat disabled workers in the workplace. Their prejudice manifests itself in "slower promotion rates, assignment[s] to less desirable or challenging tasks, lower or fewer raises and fewer training opportunities" (Perry, Hendricks, & Broadbent, 2000: 925; see also Colella, 1994). The majority of disabled respondents have experienced such problems at work, which suggests that they are not given opportunities to fully develop and use their abilities. Tom, a senior systems analyst with a doctorate, remarked:

> There are people here who don't have a university degree, but years and years of experience. A degree helps, but it isn't absolutely necessary.... I think my speech impediment has affected my chances at promotion because I think academically I'm quite strong, my skills are quite strong, although I think people's perceptions of me are that I am not capable of doing certain jobs.... My concern is always that my speech challenge does not affect me in job interviews. I know that some of the time it projects a negative image of me. In my work I have noticed that [my impediment] causes me many problems.

Conditions of credential entry mismatch are common among some disabled workers who try to counterbalance their impairments with advanced formal education. Barbara, a teacher with a master's in education, commented:

> To have the master's is great; I can say I am learning disabled but have a master's. I am trying to counter the stigma of not being smart because of my disability. I spoke to someone once who worked with disabled people. They said that one of the problems we have is that we don't have a yardstick to know when we have done enough. I was called lazy throughout my elementary and high school years because I wasn't successful. I could talk the talk incredibly well, but I just couldn't put it down on paper; so everyone assumed I was lazy. My mother, who is also dyslexic, didn't find out until I was tested; so we share the same characteristics. She was once told by a co-worker that she was a workaholic. She had the same feeling as me that if they ever found out how

little we did, they would be so angry at us; so we must always do more. So you don't have that natural yardstick to tell you when you've done enough.

The credential mismatch of disabled workers also stems from employers' hiring decisions that place them in jobs below their formal qualifications. Mike, the teacher with university certification, described his first year of teaching:

> I was formally recruited for my job and placed in a pool that the principals have to pull from, and knowing that I have an impairment, I went through every single principal of that school board.... I needed to introduce myself and show them that I have an [impairment]. To show them who I am in my opinion. So they offered me a chance — all of them told me special education. Some of them had other comments to make as well. That is why I got hired on August 31 because no one wanted me. I was hired to teach parenting.
>
> Interviewer: Why parenting?
>
> Because my principal was [dishonest]. She hired me and told me that I was teaching world religions, when she had every intention of having me teach parenting because she needed someone to baby-sit the students. My hire on August 31 was the last ditch effort. Let's put someone in there, and there was no real textbook, no materials, and no support. It was just baby-sit [the students]. Make sure they don't kill each other.

Even if people with disabilities have credentials that match job requirements, they will face transportation and physical accessibility issues, health and safety standards, and prejudicial attitudes that will make employment harder for them to obtain and retain (Hurst, 1999; Barnes, Mercer, & Shakespeare, 2000).

Performance Gap

Workers with disabilities generally have longer job searches and more employer-initiated job changes than workers without disabilities (Baldwin & Schumacher, 2002). Once these workers find an adequate job match, they may more likely choose to remain in that job. This choice may be a contributing factor to their high underemployment estimates. Disabled workers are likely to remain with their current organizations longer than workers generally (an average of 12 years compared with nine years), but they are less likely to receive promotions than other workers (12 per cent compared with 31 per cent). Overall, these findings suggest that disabled workers are more likely to remain in their jobs, but if they do change jobs, it is within their organizations and at a horizontal level. Mercedes, the administrative assistant with a college diploma, explained:

> I started at my agency for the blind as a client first. I also volunteered in one of their programs until I was offered a secretarial position in 1999 with their Ontario disability support program. In 2000 I was offered an administrative support position in group programs. The job was created for me; so I am basically setting standards. [However], I could have done this job while I was still in high school... when I was there I took business courses and received a business certificate before I entered my college program.

Some disabled workers feel fortunate to find and retain employment and are reluctant to change positions, even when their knowledge and abilities exceed performance requirements. The following comment by Kalam, the receptionist with high school education, is fairly typical:

> I have been here 13 years and I think I'm overqualified. When I go on vacation, I'm replaced with a temp and when I return my clients tell me that they were not as good as me or as friendly.... I know my organization so well and I [pay attention] to everything that is happening. I know more than people who are a level above me.... I don't feel that I am doing more [job tasks than required] even though I might be doing more stuff because I do not want to get bored. [I do] ask other [workers] if they have a task that they need help with, such as calling clients or stuffing envelopes.... I am shy and not a risk taker because I don't take advantage of internal job competitions. But now I'm thinking that maybe I will this summer. The phones are normally quiet.... I spend my time reading my Braille because I cannot leave my desk. I am limited. I can't mingle with people. I can only really get up when it's my break.

Several studies have found negative bias in employers' performance evaluations of disabled workers. This bias contributes to the mismatch between formal education attainments and job performance requirements (Colella & Varma, 1999). According to Colella (1996), biased performance appraisals may psychologically influence these workers to "live up to" negative expectations by mistrusting their organizations and employers and never becoming fully integrated at work. Empirical studies comparing performance assessments of workers with and without disabilities have found no bias when performance standards were present. Noticeable exceptions occurred when impairment-job match (i.e., the fit between functional limitations and job requirements) was poor (Colella, DeNisi, Varma, & Lund, 1994), when strained relations between supervisor and worker existed (Varma, Colella, & DeNisi, 1996; Varma, 1996), and when performance standards were vague (Czajka & DeNisi, 1988). The following observation was made by Kamene, the college-educated program analyst with almost eight years of job seniority:

I think the only thing I was a little disappointed about was when I returned [from sick leave after a year] my employment monitor said that I had to prove myself again. That pissed me off for a long time, and I complained to her about it. Also, when I came back I applied for a senior position, but my employer said no. I think that was because I had cancer. It is a big thing, and I already have an impairment. Those two things combined just don't give my employers confidence in me anymore. So no promotion. But I complained to human resources about that. They gave me a small objective to meet and said they would review it in three months. Somebody like you who got cancer and returned to work versus someone like me with cancer and an impairment is a totally different situation.... Also, in terms of getting a conference, I'm sure they don't consider me for conferences because they would have to find an accessible hotel. These things are limiting me professionally.

Some disabled workers interviewed fulfill job demands through their formal education and job training but still feel underqualified in terms of their job performance because they lack workplace support. Petra, a government office clerk with a high school diploma and fifteen years of job seniority, said, "I'm not given much to do at work. This job requires no special educational requirement. However, I feel somewhat underqualified because my co-workers make me feel this way. They don't communicate with me."

Studies have found that workers with disabilities face barriers in workplace socialization processes that affect job satisfaction, allegiance, performance, motivation and, ultimately, career advancement opportunities (Colella, 1994; Gates, 1993). A performance gap is most likely for these workers if they have frustrated expectations, lack of co-worker and supervisory support, lack of accurate and critical supervisory feedback, and if management's expectations of them are low. The EJRM Survey findings indicate that most disabled workers are credentially qualified to meet job demands. However, most of the disabled workers interviewed still experience job performance mismatches because their organizations fail to use and support their distinct job competencies.

Subjective Underemployment

In a study by the Canadian Council on Social Development in 2002, 27 per cent of disabled workers reported feeling underemployed (see CCSD, 2002). However, Graph 11.1 shows that nearly half of disabled workers in the 2004 EJRM Survey felt underemployed, compared to just a third of the general labour force. Three possible reasons exist for disabled workers' greater sense of underemployment. First, some workers interviewed choose to remain in their jobs because they have adequate impairment-job matches in terms of support. Claire, the administrative assistant, explained:

> I think that someone with college or university education would be fine for this job, but over time I think they would probably want more involvement in other projects.... I think I probably did not move jobs as much as I wanted to because my employment accommodations are excellent and also my work tower itself is basically barrier free. Also, I find a lot of people in my workplace, even though they change quite a bit, I find overall they're very supportive. And so basically I might not be totally satisfied with my job, but you look at everything. I work four days a week and if I move to another position, I'm facing a five-day work week and all the different issues that have to be balanced with the working conditions.

Other disabled respondents in professional occupations feel underemployed but redress these feelings through supplementary employment in other fields because it generates additional income, challenges their abilities, and otherwise interests them. Demitri, the university-educated program analyst, said:

> I'm very overqualified to do this job. I have a lot of skills and abilities that are not being utilized here. I've completed a paralegal program and am currently completing a certified financial planner program.... I want to work in government until I retire and, in the meantime, build up clients in the financial area by doing their taxes or financial planning. So I have financial skills that I don't use here.... I want to advance in that area, but at the same time I want to stay doing what I'm doing because the support I have here is really good. So if you're asking me if I want to get a new job, no.... There are a lot of support networks in government for employees with disabilities.

Similarly, Tom, the senior systems analyst with a doctorate, said:

> I'd say I'm somewhat overqualified. I decided to [return to school] and complete a master's in statistics because I thought it would be good for my professional development.... A number of people have suggested that I do some post-secondary teaching in the evenings.... We have some people here who are older and approaching the age of retirement. These people will not be very interested in upgrading their skills or learning. But I'm not that old. I have a strong academic background in computer information systems... what I'm doing is I'm viewing my [education] as an opportunity to really understand the complexity of my work, and this is why I'm also interested in consulting.

It appears that those with acute impairments sense that they are underemployed because their qualifications surpass job performance requirements; yet they place self-imposed constraints on their career opportunities in an effort to control their work environment. Toula, the teacher with a master's in administration and 32 years of job seniority, spoke frankly about the barriers she confronts networking:

> I feel like I am somewhat overqualified. Not many teachers have a master's. I wanted to be in an administrative position when I started, but realized that there would be too much physical activity and with my disability it would be too hard... you are limited. For instance, when I thought that I wanted to go into the administration field, I attended many of the meetings, but they took place in carpeted hotels that I found very difficult to walk in. My foot would turn and then I would limp... I'd get really tense and could not get from point A to point B without stopping or hanging on to something. I realized I needed to attend these meetings to network and create a high profile.... I don't know about other people with disabilities, but fatigue has been a real issue with me. So I had to make choices, and I just learned to live with them.

Claire, the administrative assistant, pondered her underemployment:

> I do have some physical barriers at work... that may factor into why I haven't been promoted. I also have concerns about stress and other mental health issues.... I don't feel like I could manage a managerial or professional consulting-level position. I couldn't handle that amount of stress. You have to be multifaceted and able to juggle a lot of priorities, and I would find that too exhausting. I don't want to try because I feel it would deteriorate my health.

This case study has shown that disabled respondents have acquired the knowledge and abilities they need to meet their job requirements, even though they have faced workplace barriers that have hindered their career advancement. Clearly they need more enabling opportunities to give them control over their job responsibilities and use of their distinct competencies in the workplace.

CONCLUSION

This chapter has reviewed the work and learning challenges confronting workers with disabilities. Disability employment policies continue to fail because they focus on ways to make people with disabilities employable at the expense of their needs at job entry and beyond. This "supply side" solution to labour problems puts the burden of responsibility for their successful employment on disabled individuals and conveniently ignores the inequities within the workplace (Barnes, 2000; Lunt & Thornton, 1994). To make matters worse, employers now demand that workers continue to upgrade their formal education and job training but provide them only limited opportunity to use their acquired knowledge and abilities. Although underemployment is a feature of the Canadian economy, its various forms and consequences remain unrecognized in official employment records, particularly as it affects workers with disabilities. National occupational classification resources that continue to present performance markers and job taxonomies based on general population standards disregard and disadvantage disabled workers who have distinct needs and abilities.

A new definition of job competence as it relates to workers with disabilities is needed and current labour market researchers should address this. Such a definition should take into account both ethical and cognitive approaches to job performance. The ERJM Survey and case study findings indicate that disabled workers are even more likely than other workers to have little say in workplace policy decisions. Their exclusion from organizational decision-making may explain why disabled workers tend to concentrate on developing their technical abilities. While they have more discretion and creativity in job tasks, many have felt threatened by the rapid change in the social organization of work processes because such change seemed to exacerbate their impairment problems.

Compared to other workers, disabled workers not only attain similar levels of post-secondary education but also engage in similar levels (over 80 per cent) of job-related informal learning activities to meet job requirements. However, even though the case study sample of disabled workers exhibited a similar level of credential underemployment as the general labour force, they were more prone to express feelings of underemployment. This sense of underemployment is most likely attributable to the employment discrimination that disabled workers routinely encounter. Some disabled workers were denied jobs for reasons unrelated to job requirements and faced prolonged periods of unemployment. Others were the last hired in recruitment pools and then placed in positions below their qualifications and abilities. Disabled workers were promoted much less than other workers but stayed longer with their employers. Comments from disabled workers reveal that most of them did not receive the support they needed to succeed. They wanted training to understand workplace accommodation procedures and to manage the on-the-job discrimination that they faced, but none existed. The vast majority reported an absence of mandatory courses on disability awareness and sensitivity training in the workplace.

Most disabled workers developed compensation strategies to manage job tasks and several relinquished their right to reasonable accommodations. They did not request accommodations from a fear of being refused them, or of being perceived as incompetent, or being otherwise dismissed. However, these self-limiting behaviours left some with less energy and time to pursue opportunities for career advancement, which also increased their underemployment estimates.

Disabled respondents spoke frankly about their performance gaps. Some said they had accepted new jobs knowing that they were overqualified for the positions. Others reported feeling fortunate to find and retain a job and were thus reluctant to change jobs despite having knowledge and abilities that exceeded performance requirements. Still others, who developed new impairments while on the job and took sick leave, discovered that their return to work required that they once again prove their competence to their employer. The assumption that disabled workers are incapable of productive work remains widespread. The EJRM survey findings indicate, however, that these workers require the same amount of time as other workers to learn how to perform jobs.

Disabled workers expressed greater feelings of underemployment than most other workers for several reasons. Some respondents chose to remain in their jobs because they had found suitable impairment-job matches. That is, they found supportive employers who modified job requirements to suit their impairment-related needs. Others in professional-level jobs counterbalanced their sense of underemployment with supplementary employment in other fields for the extra income, and because it challenged their abilities and otherwise interested them. Still other respondents with acute impairments felt underemployed but had constrained their career opportunities in an effort to control their work environments.

Prior research on disability workplace management and discussions with case study respondents, employers, and union representatives confirm four basic standards to advance an education-job match. First, include workers with disabilities in workplace decision-making processes. Studies have shown that the presence of people with disabilities in these processes provides practical knowledge to employers that can help resolve the job performance gap (Westmorland et al., 2005; Westmorland & Williams, 2002). Second, establish disability management workplace protocol. Many workplaces have disability manuals and procedures unknown to workers because they are not made readily available. This material should be shared with workers and other employers who have initiated procedures but are in need of assistance. As employers are largely responsible for shaping inclusive workplace cultures, they should facilitate dialogue with workers to address disabling barriers, gaps in communication, and to unearth solutions (Westmorland et al., 2005). The successful employment of disabled persons is determined not only by the function of the impairment but also by the social support provided on the job (see Gates, 2000).

A third standard in support of an improved disability education-job match involves paid work programs from government, employers, and schools that offer genuine opportunities and, equally important, are based on employer accountability. If these organizations coordinate their efforts with employment agencies, which assess, train, and place disabled workers, the probability of finding a suitable impairment-job match will be increased. The fourth standard involves introducing disability awareness training in secondary and post-secondary education settings; such groundwork would be vital to the establishment and success of workplace initiatives.

Finally, the current trend in Canadian federal policy-making is to commit funds to the support of workers with disabilities who are already in paid work rather than to support the development of paid work opportunities. However, in these uncertain times of workplace cutbacks and escalating job demands, disabled workers find it increasingly difficult to find and retain good paid employment. The four measures outlined could modify labour practices so that greater numbers of people with disabilities would have access to employment opportunities. Instead of relying on disabled workers' individual efforts to modify disability-related workplace barriers, cost-conscious employers should opt for universally applicable solutions when feasible because these can benefit all workers. Democratic workplace reform for disabled workers requires government and employers to cooperate in the development of initiatives that remove barriers to paid work and formal training. Such action could create increased opportunity for those within the workplace to creatively apply and develop their storehouse of work-related knowledge.

Part Four
Conclusions

Chapter Twelve
The Relationship between Learning and Work: Empirical Evidence from the Case Studies

K.V. Pankhurst

The empirical evidence from interviews with individual workers modifies the findings from the EJRM random statistical survey by providing insight into how workers learn to perform their jobs. This chapter examines the evidence by applying the theory of the relationship between a job and a worker outlined in Chapter 6. The essence of this theory is that, under an open contract of employment, the uncertain nature of work entails problem solving and discretionary choice that dynamically transform both a job and the incumbent worker. This relationship between a worker and a job is reformulated as one between thought and action and is significantly different from the neoclassical concept of a simple exchange of work for pay. The interview data contain evidence about respondents' cognitive processes during paid and unpaid work and provide a few insights into implicit learning and the reserves of cognitive knowledge and abilities that they acquired.

EDUCATION REQUIRED AND ATTAINED

The Criteria of Matching
The statistical data from the EJRM and WALL surveys, reported in Chapters 4 and 5, are methodologically compatible with those of other studies of the education-job match. The findings for these large-scale random samples confirm patterns of matching and mismatching that have been found in previous research and that are typically skewed toward underemployment. However, the qualitative individual case study data present a different picture. The detailed empirical data about selected

groups of employees — examined in Chapters 7 to 11 and used in this chapter — were obtained by in-depth interviews with a non-random sample (N=105), drawn by sequential and snowball sampling.[1] The intention was to include examples of the main categories of workers and jobs in the Toronto region, that is, people with varying levels and types of education and experience, as well as native-born Canadians and immigrants, workers of both genders, and unionized and non-unionized workers. The sample has a bias toward full-time workers. In this chapter, these non-random data are first examined in terms of how individual respondents experienced the credential, performance, and subjective gaps[2,3] and the relevance of their formal education to their jobs. The data are then[4] examined for more evidence about the nature of work and how cognitive abilities are formed and utilized. The observation of cognitive processes is fraught with difficulty, and the evidence about learning is necessarily incomplete. Nevertheless, the case study data are sufficient to provide deeper insights into the nature of the relationship between a job and a worker.

Respondents' Experience of How Education and Jobs Correspond
The levels of education used in the survey and in the case studies were arranged into five categories.[5] Entry criteria differ among the occupational groups. The incidence of credential matching is high among the teachers (T), for whom a university degree and professional training are required in Ontario. A lower proportion of the computer programmers (CP) has a credential match by level of education because, although the field of work is relatively narrow and technologically advanced, it is changing rapidly and the preparatory fields of study vary. The proportion of clerical workers (CW) with credentials that exceed job requirements is high: Clerical workers perform a multiplicity of support tasks, have subaltern responsibilities, and hold jobs that are often temporary, part-time, contingent, precarious, and low paid. The automobile workers comprise two distinct sub-populations: the qualified trades workers (Auto QT), for whom training by apprenticeship is a formal and practical requirement; and the assembly line workers (Auto PL), whose tasks entail judgment as well as conforming to a planned time schedule. Respondents with a disability (Dis) have education-job matching patterns similar to workers without a disability, although the range of jobs to which they have access is limited. A close examination of the case study data reveals the multiple properties of both a worker and a job. As well as levels of schooling and fields of study, the evidence includes a worker's perception of a job and the effects of technical change on it; further education; learning by experience; unpaid work activities; and personal aims, which do not necessarily coincide with a job and entail a compromise.

The respondents had a variety of perceptions of how their education and their jobs were related in practice. Few thought that the level of their education was significant. Stephen (Auto QT), an air conditioning maintenance electrician whose formal qualifications match his job entry requirements, said he does not know what level of education is needed to perform his job: "You just have to have someone who is interested in learning." Although many respondents had a credential match, for a few the match was quite narrow. Fiona, a computer programmer, said, "I came into user-centred design because my background and my master's was in human-computer interaction; so... my skills fit really well with what they were looking for, and they are actually a difficult skill set to find." Zoey (CP), a technical writer, noted that just "one course showed me what it was like to do technical writing." Conversely, a match can be wide. With credentials in psychology, sociology, and business, Aubrey (CW) found a job in retail-distribution research that matched two of his fields of study, "because research is psych-business and this department is a psych-business place, it became that my education kind of matched, and they just went 'wow—this is great.'" On the other hand, Tora (Auto PL, Dis) has a match according to the level of education required but not by field of study: "I have a diploma in interior design and recreation and leadership." However, a match between field of study and job is unlikely for everyone in all industries. As Rebecca (CP), whose job is to test new software, observed: "There is no formal education for testing in university." Benjamin (Auto PL, Dis) is mismatched by both level and subject: He is underemployed by level and has a diploma in sports administration but works in quality control. In the auto industry there are contrasting examples. James (Auto QT), whose level of education matches his job, is the son of an electrician and has been interested in technical matters since childhood. He chose to become a toolmaker because the pay was high. Charles (Auto PL), with an MBA, has a level and content of schooling that greatly exceeds the requirement of his job, and he, too, chose to work for the relatively high pay on the assembly line. A senior systems analyst with a disability, Tom (CP, Dis) studied in a field that matches his job but, with a PhD, is underemployed by credential. Several respondents made their choice of education according to criteria other than employment: Aubrey (CW), like several others, admitted, "I don't think I really made the connection between school and work at that time. To me school was learning and the job market was doing."

A close match between field of study and job is unlikely for several reasons. A worker may compromise between a job and personal objectives: "My primary motivation in picking a job or a profession was employment... and getting rewarded financially for that employment. My whole life growing up... employment fluctuated so much. My mother is a seasonal worker. My father was lucky enough to a have a full-time job all the time; but my wife's father is an ironworker, so he is working or not working. My uncles are the same way: they work so many months of the year. So ... from about this high, I was told 'get a job that you are going to keep and is secure'" (Simon, CP). If further training has opportunity costs that conflict with family concerns, a worker might be satisfied with a less-than-perfect match: "The kids—I wanted to make sure that I spend as much time with them as I can. They are at a critical age, and you need to spend a lot of time with them, and I could feel that, so I decided instead of doing the [further] education I would concentrate on those two" (Aubrey, CW). It is difficult for a new entrant to know what opportunities there are in a rapidly changing industry. Haiyan (CP), who was doing an internship, said, "I wanted the practical experience to make sure that working in CP was going to be the right path for me.... The last couple of years most of us have done [an internship] just because we saw it as the easiest way to enter the industry." She is aware that closer matching can take time: "I know they are still trying to find a role for me to take over permanently." A particular job is rarely representative of the entire field of work. James (Auto QT) commented, "I am fairly well matched to what I am doing now, but it is such a big field now that there is no end of learning that can go on." Rebecca (CP), who is a team lead, has extensive work experience in the field of testing and several certificates relevant to her work taken during 12 years of night school but no university degree. She has achieved parity of esteem with her colleagues by being an active and committed member of the community, performing extracurricular roles in the workplace as a mentor, and being a member of the fitness committee, which are more visible attributes than her job experience and practical ability.

The existence of a small proportion of workers who reported a level of education less than required (typically of the order of one-sixth of paid workers) raises awkward empirical and conceptual problems. If respondents in this category were in fact employable, the data indicating underqualification are false. If the data are correct, we have to ask if their employers are unaware of having employees unable to perform, or if they are aware but have decided to retain them. Moreover, these respondents are not necessarily incapable or incompetent. Some respondents displayed modest attitudes and an engagement in learning by experience how to do a job. In addition, conventional standards change. A computer programmer who has a degree did not think a degree is essential for performance: "For the job that I am doing now ...my co-worker doesn't have university, I don't even think she has college. She's been with the company 30 years now this year. So she started back in the 70s when IBM didn't require a university degree, and she does the job just fine. I would say that... if you had the knowledge or were able to pick up the knowledge quickly you wouldn't need a degree at all for the job we are doing" (Adnan, CP).

Several respondents expressed a more mature view of the connections between education and doing a job. Although the proportion of education-job match was high for teachers, some provided examples of how a formal credential could be enough to get a job but not to perform it. Julian (T) assessed his education and training as follows: "Intellectually it was good, but not practically. It encouraged me to think about ideas and different ways to approach problems, but it gave me no practical experience." Salma, who teaches French, explained, "With my school knowledge I think I have a general cultural sense. With French, I know general statements, and can explain grammar.... With on the job training, it's all about classroom management, seeing how others handle it. My other learning helps me relate more to the kids." Similarly, Chris, a security specialist computer programmer who has two degrees—one related to his job and the other not—observed: "If you consider the intent of university to be to prepare you for the workforce, it doesn't do that, at least not in my experience. It does teach you to be able to answer questions independently, figure out the answers and so forth, to ask the right questions. It is wonderful for training the mind in terms of the overall quest for knowledge. It is not so good in terms of 'this is what you are going to need to know when you get out there.'"

It is well recognized that labour-market information is far from perfect, so that the expectation of a close correspondence among all the properties of formal education and job requirements is a chimera. Moreover, measures of education attained and required provide a static vision of a relationship that is highly dynamic. The properties of both the job and the incumbent worker develop as a worker acquires by experience an evolving perception of what is required to perform the job, develops personal relationships with colleagues and managers, acquires new knowledge and abilities, makes decisions that modify how a job is done, and forms new understandings of how personal activities and working life fit together. Inevitably, the nature of the education-job relationship evolves.

The Evolving Relationship between Education and Jobs

The data from the case study interviews provide a first crude picture of a progression in time in the distribution of matching and non-matching. Although the data are not statistically significant, the distributions are similar to those of the random sample, and the criteria are identical. According to the credential criterion, 33 workers said they were underemployed, 53 matched, and 10 underqualified, which broadly corresponds to the typical skewed distribution (see Chapter 5). Of the 33 workers who were underemployed on the credential criterion, four later became matched on the performance criterion, and 17 became adequately qualified on the subjective criterion. Of the 53 workers who reported being matched by credential on job entry, 14 were underemployed on the performance criterion, and 38 were matched. Of the 10 workers who were underqualified by credential, four were underemployed by the performance criterion and one was matched. Thus, there are a few indications that on the performance criterion the distribution continues to be skewed toward underemployment, but that the gap can also increase. The interviews provide rich evidence of many ways in which the relationship between a worker and a job evolves after entry. Not only do the respondents have to keep up with changing economic conditions and technology but also they develop their abilities and perceive ways to modify their jobs.

Part of this continuing change in the employment relationship can be ascribed to further formal education and to intentional informal learning in a variety of adult learning projects (Tough, 1971), most of which increase the incidence of underutilization or enable those who are underqualified to do their jobs. The respondents were most conscious of their intentional learning by attending courses, reading manuals, and consulting colleagues—methods that have been described in the previous chapters. While deliberate learning activities can be of practical importance, they are primarily instrumental adjustments of workers' knowledge and abilities to the requirements of their jobs, i.e., of the supply of labour to the demand for it. More important, they are a limited part of individual learning and do not reveal the full dynamic nature of the labour process. Although the notion of self-directed, intentional learning has been instrumental in stimulating research in adult learning, it is too restrictive to represent the full extent of learning and its significance. It fails to reveal learning by experience, which is the generic form of learning and a major source of adjustment in personal knowledge and abilities.

Learning by Experience

In the automotive plant the practice of promotion by seniority implicitly admits that learning by experience is useful, even though a worker has to wait for a vacancy before this experience can be acknowledged. Teachers' pay scales, too, embody a reward for experience. The CP company applies a variant of the same principle by keeping workers long enough in a job to gain experience of it: "When you start a job they give you an availability date and you're not expected to look for a[nother] job before that date" (Chris, CP).

Several respondents were more aware of having learned by experience than of what they had learned in that way. One worker said, "Everything I've learned to this point related to this job has been hands on and passed down" (Maria, Auto PL, Dis). Kamene (CP, Dis) generalized: "This is the way I see it. Life every day will teach you something; every experience you have teaches you something. Every bad thing happens to you teaches you; every good thing teaches you. So I think everyday life is a learning experience for me." Asked how many hours a week she learns, Corrie (CW) referred only to her paid work week: "About the same amount of hours I work a week, about 36 and a quarter, same as work." However, a teacher pointed out that not all learning is perceived: "We learn all the time. Reading the newspaper is a way ...where informal learning goes on.... I think it goes on a lot unrecognized."

Nevertheless, some evidence can be gleaned about the nature of learning by experience, which takes a variety of forms, and is most evident in observation. Several respondents had reflected on the process. "I watched a lot of the older guys do their work. They never got hurt, and they knew how to work. A lot of the younger guys ended up with carpel tunnel. The older guys didn't... because they knew how to do it properly. You're using a pair of tongs, some of them are six feet long, and they're heavy, and they're all made of steel. You're holding steel with steel. So you're handling about 45 pounds with a pair of tongs and the part that you are forming. And you do, like, 1,200 pieces in a shift. There's a way to avoid injury, but the minute you do it wrong you end up with carpel tunnel and your wrists swell. The old guys taught me to do it. And the young guys there, they said 'forget about the old guys,' but that's how you learn, you watch the old guys" (Philip, Auto PL). When one clerical worker observed the bearing of people she admired, she formed the ambition to emulate them: "I remember thinking that these women are so much better than me. They were professional; they were articulate; they look better; they speak better; they know what they are talking about" (Jennifer, CW). A teacher learned by experience things that she did not or could not learn during formal instruction: "discipline, interpersonal relationships with the students, delivery of curriculum in an interesting and engaging way, pacing, questioning techniques — all of that" (Mary, T).

The content of what was learned by experience varied. It might be specific content, such as installing or regulating new equipment: "Every time a new product is introduced, it is a whole learning curve... and there is nobody there to teach you, you have got to... yourself learn all the idiosyncrasies or problems with them" (Ethan, Auto QT). "The company does not give any sort of formal training on the machine.... When new equipment comes, you go and have a look at the blueprints, try to figure out how it works.... That is something you do own your own" (Charles, Auto QT). A worker might learn about new equipment dysfunctions from the operatives: "The guys that are running the equipment are my best source of information" (James, Auto QT). An element of what was learned was often some aspect of personal relations: "We want to work with people that we know and we trust" (Talma, an office manager). Several employees echoed that view. Respondents in all occupational groups were conscious of having learned to adapt themselves to a job or to their colleagues. Irving (CP, Dis) said it is harder to deal with people than with equipment: "Dealing with people, that's the toughest part. The computer stuff is easy. It either works or it doesn't."

Immigrants reported that they had to learn a multitude of differences in culture and customs. Theresa, a receptionist from an eastern European country, described some of them: "I am coming from a communist country. The bookkeeping is totally different. Just the basic stuff. We don't have a profit, just the financial papers." She hesitated to assess her ability to learn, saying, "It's a shame to be talking too nice about yourself in my country, but here it's ok." She was familiar with a simple telephone and found it difficult to manage one with several lines ringing simultaneously. Emily (CW), who learned formal standards of speech, dress, and deportment in a Jamaican business college, had to learn more casual customs in Toronto. An immigrant from Ethiopia explained that "in our culture we don't disagree with older people, and we don't talk back to... a supervisor.... That area, more than the work, took me longer to learn" (Kamene, CP, Dis).

Learning by experience is only partly observable, since the greater part of the process happens unconsciously. The remainder of this chapter is devoted to examining the evidence from respondents about the deeply rooted processes of individual learning by experience during work. To do that, it is necessary first to consider how opportunities to learn by experience arise under the contract of employment.

THE NATURE OF WORK

The Contract of Employment

Respondents described several disjunctions and adjustments between education and work that illustrate the uncertain and unknowable nature of the contract between an employer and a worker, which is more implicit that explicit (Chapter 6). Neither an employer nor a worker can anticipate all the contingencies than might arise in the future. Workers and management alike are uncertain about what to do. An employer hires the ability to work, not a foreseeable quantity or quality of output. One manager in CP acknowledged that she cannot know all the intricacies of a job, or if the team can do something: "She asked me point blank... 'Can you do this in a typical work week, or is it too much?'" (Simon, CP). This inability of an employer to specify in advance what is to be done in a job, or how, creates uncertainty that consequently leaves a measure of discretion to all workers, even in jobs described as unskilled. A receptionist has to "follow instructions," but said, "I have to make priorities" (Theresa, CW). The open contract of employment is an arena of problem solving and decision-making by each worker to a greater or lesser degree. Work is therefore a psychological activity, whether it is described as manual or mental. These considerations apply to unpaid work too.

Few respondents had written contracts. Those who had did report that they provided little or no specific direction about what to do in a job or how to do it. "No, we don't have one. Basically I was trained for about a week and that's all. That's how I learned the job" (Sam, Auto PL). A woman in a government office said, "We have outdated job specs that date back to the 1970s and 60s" (Danielle, CW). Those respondents who had no written contract had to find out for themselves what to do. They had to learn the technical tasks to be performed, the division of labour, and how the workplace functioned. A man in the auto plant said, "I had worked with the previous release engineer, so I had an idea of what he did. So I talked to him about it, but I still didn't realize the exact responsibilities until I started, and I am still feeling that out a little bit in terms of where the lines are" (Simon, CP). The CP workers typically started the day by reading their emails to discover problems or priorities. Predominantly, the respondents had to observe what was going on, although one team leader had reservations about the reliability of observing others: "They didn't provide me with a written job description, but I have worked in the area long enough. I have actually worked on one of the teams, so I have just... moved up to take the team lead position. So I have observed it for enough years that I have an idea of what people have to do; but I think that a lot from observation tends to be biased. You have this perception of what the job is and not necessarily a true understanding of what is expected of you" (Fiona, CP).

A toolmaker in the automobile plant reported that he has "all kinds of choice.

They do not care how I get it done, just as long as I get it done" (James, Auto QT). Ming, a manager, confirmed that "in the CP field generally they are told what to do, not how to do it." He added that he, too, was given an objective, not a detailed description: "I have a revenue target that I have to hit." The teachers' contract was prescriptive in indicating such things as administrative requirements or the length of the school day but, nevertheless, left considerable discretion to each teacher about how to deliver the curriculum. Anthony, a school principal, said, "In terms of the instructional methodology that you're going to use, and certainly the content you are going to engage in, you've got a lot of academic freedom." He went on to explain why a written contract is impossible: "I think you'd have to be an idiot to write one of those things because it would change daily.... During the school day I work hard at keeping my time unscheduled.... I spend an awful lot of time out of this office talking to kids, interacting with staff... you find out much more than if you sit in this room."

The respondents indicated several sources of uncertainty under the open employment contract. Conditions external to the organization were one of them. CP workers could not anticipate how the firm would develop but had to keep up with changes in the technology and its applications: "Things are changing so quickly in technology. You know, we'll be working on one release... and by the time we get it out of the door, some technology has come in and we need to upgrade" (Rebecca, CP). Another CP worker, Mitesh, commented on parallel advances in work requirements and in learning resources: "The job is harder, but it is easier to figure out." Teachers have to adapt to government requirements: "an awful lot of my colleagues have been affected by the new collective agreements and the restrictions that the last Conservative [provincial] government placed on them in terms of becoming very prescriptive with the length of the educational day, how much time had to be spent on TAP,[6] and remediation, and all these other factors" (Anthony, a school principal). Teachers also had to adapt to the local demographic structure: "A third of the community is Greek, and the other two-thirds are recent immigrants" (Rajine, T). An auto worker commented on the demand for automobiles: "I've learned that the automobile industry is very competitive. I didn't realize. I know there's tons of different cars out there in the world, but I never really thought about it. But when you work in a facility that isn't selling very well it gets kind of scary" (Tora, Auto PL).

Within an organization, management decisions were held to be another source of uncertainties in a job. In a poorly organized government department, "nobody knows which head to go to" (Gwenevra, CW). Several qualified trades workers in the automobile plant complained about managers who had degrees but no practical production experience. A typical complaint was inadequate spending, which increased the chance of equipment dysfunctions. According to Martin (Auto QT), management was "abandoning some of the core ways we used to do business, and one of them was to spend money up front to keep the equipment running." Continuing uncertainty in office work arises from several sources, including the range of tasks that has to be performed by each person in a small firm. "There are admins that are working in smaller organizations, let's say maybe under 50 employees... where they are the be all to end all, so they do everything. They do reception, office equipment, maybe the website maintenance" (Owenis, CW). A secretary commented, "In this field, you have to work with different people; you have to understand different things; there are changes every day so you have to have the ability to grasp things easily" (Emily, CW). The production system in the automobile plant is more uncertain than theories of Fordism suggest. A machine operator, Thom (Auto PL), does not know until each morning which machine he will be running or if he has to set it up. Ethan, a qualified tradesperson in the automobile assembly plant, described the variety of tasks, people, and functions his job entails. He has to modify the equipment for changes in a product; deal with dies, pressers of varying sizes, the different makes of the machining centre; and work with electricians and tool and die makers. One teacher, John, created his own uncertainty: "I've changed courses because I like change. A lot of people don't. I like the challenge." Since a job cannot be prescribed in detail and performance is governed by how a worker applies his or her abilities, uncertainty also resides in the minds of the workers about how to go about a complex task: "Family studies... are all called open courses, which means that they throw in the gifted kids, and they throw in academics, and then they throw in the applied kids, and they throw the basic kids all into one class and say here's your curriculum, now teach it, which is a bit challenging" (Maya, T).

These examples demonstrate the continuing interaction between a worker and a job. A worker has to create, or interpret, a job. Jennifer (CW), an executive assistant to a vice-president of human resources, observed, "There was nobody before me. I was the first one in the role." Some workers reported having experimented: "I've been pretty free in being able to say I want to look at this for a while. I tend to just go off and discover new things and bring them back to my boss and say I think we should be doing this, and he says, 'Yes, you are right, we should.' So my job description, I guess you could say, is part troublemaker and part finding out what interests me and seeing if it relates back to the business" Chris (CP). Dynamic change is institutionalized at Chris's company in an annual Personal Business Commitment procedure (PBC), which describes what a worker is going to try to accomplish for the business in the coming year. Chris explained, "At the end of the year you go through with your boss what you actually did to achieve those PBCs. So you are expected not only to set goals, but to keep goals and document how you kept those goals." The need for dynamic change might be recognized by the employer: "I have an open mandate to change it. As the department and I grow, the job changes" (Aubrey, CW). Angus (CP) claimed that he has modified his job, "probably 10 per cent of it I invented... because at least 10 per cent wasn't being done before I was hired."

Discretion

Confronted with these uncertainties, all workers are left with varying degrees of discretion in the way they perform their jobs. Teachers have considerable freedom in deciding how to work. One of them welcomed this freedom because "you deal with stress better when you have a sense of control over it". (Rajine, T). Abe (CP) coordinates the work of a team converting software for use in over a dozen countries. Asked if there is someone who comes in and tells him what to do, he replied, "No, no. It does not work like that. Basically I am doing what has to be done, and I am telling my manager what has to be done." A person who keeps hospital records and also holds office in the union reported having limited discretion in records management but a great deal in her role as union leader (Beatrice, OW). Kamene (CP, Dis) said there is no control over how she works other than having to meet deadlines. Those in ostensibly low-level jobs can have more discretion than might appear at first sight. Thom (Auto PL), who lifts pieces off the assembly line and is one of the least qualified respondents, said he has "more [discretion] than I thought I would ever be given credit for." Another assembly line worker took the initiative to interrupt the line: "I was on the assembly line putting the parts that I forged on the motor into the machine.... I found a lot of parts that I wouldn't have passed... I put them on the floor beside me and all these motors were going by with no parts in them. And the foreman came by and said, 'What the hell are you doing?' I said... 'I'm not going to be responsible for putting this dud part in this motor that I've worked on'... So they put an inspector down at the end of the line, before they would get to me. And he found three skids of these bad parts. I showed him exactly what to look for" (Philip, Auto PL).

Problem Solving

Given the uncertainties that arise from unforeseeable contingencies, neither a worker nor an employer can know in advance precisely what the final product will be. Consequently, the essential nature of work is problem solving (see Chapter 6), which is significant because it is during the process of solving problems that a worker's abilities to make use of subject-matter knowledge are formed. "If you are in a course or at school, you can only learn a language or a specific thing, but when you are actually doing it, the problems that come are far more difficult than what you were doing at school" (Mitesh, CP). Many of the workers interviewed were conscious of this characteristic of their jobs, whether they used the terms *problem solving* or *troubleshooting*, or other language to describe it.

The responsibility of performing a new task begins with identifying what has to be done. An executive assistant said, "If I'm asked to do something, it's up to me to get it done" (Jennifer, CW). A clerical worker, asked to type a letter to 300 people, took the initiative to try to rent a suitable machine: "I said, 'I'm not doing that. It will take me forever.' So I called up Micon and asked them where I can rent a machine for two days" (Renata, CW). "You troubleshoot steadily" (Michael, Auto QT, a millwright). His colleague, an electrician, described the range of problems he encounters in his job: "Troubleshooting—you get a call on a particular machine, go up there, talk to the tool setter, the operator, see if you can work these things out. It could be as simple as an operator error, or a dirty switch, something out of focus. It could be a number of really simple things or something extremely complicated that could take days to figure out with engineering support.... Then it's the next job, then that repeats all the way down the day" (Martin, Auto QT).

Problem solving, which is characteristic of all jobs at all levels, takes different forms. A tool setter said, "My machine that I run has sandpaper in it, and it shines up all these lobes [on a camshaft]. So if parts of them turn out shiny and parts don't, you know there is a problem with the sandpaper" (Katharine, Auto PL). Vanessa, a temporary clerical worker, found that the scope for problem solving was limited because the permanent staff "don't want you to excel." In teaching, the scope of problem solving can be wide. A school principal reported that he wants his staff to be ready to deal with behavioural problems as soon as they arise: "I don't expect you to walk by an incident. I want you to deal with it" (Anthony). According to Guy (vice-principal), "A typical day is solving problems, mediating between students and teachers, trying to set the stage so that students have the best opportunity to advance their education and overcoming roadblocks. The biggest one is attendance, and the next one is not doing what teachers would like. So I'm constantly trying to find solutions that pacify both."

A line worker explained the need for continual problem solving. "There's always something wrong... maybe with the product not being here on time, fear of shutting the plant down, having the product messed up, having to have it reworked, trying to get people in to rework the product or, you know, have onesies and twosies that the operator can't do because something's wrong with it. The onesies and twosies I can take care of, but when we get a whole trailer load then that presents a big problem" (Maria, Auto PL, Dis).

Recognizing that problems exist, and what form they are likely to take, comes with experience and can become habitual. "Most of the problems we have are from suppliers that supply us with parts [the wrong size]" (Ethan, Auto QT). An air-conditioning mechanic has learned that "the machinery's going to have problems... we've had big shafts break because they weren't greased, because the guy who used to grease them retired, and they never replaced him. Things like this" (Stephen, Auto QT). The automobile company is aware that problems are inevitable, have costs, and must be anticipated, and the company provides a course in problem solving. According to Benjamin (Auto PL), "I just took a problem-solving course and actually everyone in our department took it at different stages."

A key stage is problem identification. "The first thing that you do is find out what the problem is. They tell you what they think it is. I take that with a grain of salt, do my own little thing to try to figure it out, and then think of solutions. If I need to go get parts, try this, try that. And then, if it works, we're off" (Martin, Auto QT). A machine operator has learned to anticipate dysfunctions and knows the limits of what she can do. "I will watch the machine and try to find out what the problem is. Some things I can fix and other things I have to determine what tradesperson I need to fix it, like an electrician, or a pipe fitter, or a machine repairer" (Jane, Auto PL). Prior experience helps identify the nature of a problem. George, an information-retrieval assistant (CW), learned to anticipate transcribing errors in the location codes of records; "maybe it was keyed in wrong—instead of 08 it should have been 80."

A few workers were conscious that problem solving entails choices and decision. Problems include having to decide whether to accept a task or not. For example, an auto worker spoke of his dilemma in deciding how to respond to an urgent call when he realized that his decision had staffing implications: "When they call me in the middle of the night, I say I really don't want to come in. They say, 'We need someone who knows what they're doing. You've got to come in.' So I go in there. See, the best policy for me would be to say I'm not coming in, and the more that it happened they'd see that they'd better train more people. I feel responsible—that I should go in—but I see the other side where the company is not doing anything" (Stephen, Auto QT).

For many respondents, problem solving to get a job done also entails managing personal relationships and devising techniques to deal with others, especially among workers in precarious jobs. For example, a recent immigrant who reported having been subjected to harassment learned how to manage personal relations: "I learned how to deal with a difficult situation, with difficult kind of people, how to calm them down, and how to help" (Theresa, CW). She also learned to judge the limits to what she could do and concluded that her best option might be to exit an unpleasant employment situation, despite her need for paid work. Another office worker made the same decision: "If you don't like the people that you are working for, then you don't stay" Renata (CW). A woman in the automobile plant has learned to talk like the men: "I've had to change my attitude. I used to be really quiet and nice. Now I can roll with the best of them. It depends on who I'm talking to, you know. Yes, you have to. I have to adjust my attitude.... I know some guys they like to be talked crazy to—for lack of a better word—crazy and rough—so I have to talk to them like that" (Maria, Auto PL, Dis). An automobile worker on the production line learned to ask leading questions to get managers to see what he wants to get done but then lets them take the credit: "So my role is a facilitator. I have to start asking... them questions in order to get the answers I want, and that is a trick I am just barely getting down" (Thom, Auto PL).

THE ACQUISITION OF COGNITIVE KNOWLEDGE AND ABILITIES

The respondents' accounts of how they deal with mechanical, organizational, and personal dysfunctions in the course of productive activity are evidence of the labour process as a process of thinking during which a worker acquires cognitive knowledge and abilities. Cognition begins with curiosity (Bruner, 1966), which is evoked by the awareness of an incongruity and can be either intuitive and rapid or explicit. "I basically watched and saw what other people did and asked a lot of questions" (Benjamin, Auto PL). Rebecca (CP) explained how curiosity drew her into testing: "I got really intrigued about two things: about the fact that people were not educated properly on computers and the fact that they were not user friendly.... It was just out of my curiosity and my need to help these poor people who could not do their job.... You don't know what they're thinking when they're pushing the buttons, so I got really interested into... figuring out different ways that people will break the system." Some respondents described being aware of an incongruity between what they see has to be done and their own abilities. An archivists' assistant learned by experience that errors in coding are frequent: "I'm always asking questions about this, or questions about that" (George, CW). "That's really one of the things you need in order to do computer security successfully—a very healthy curiosity" (Chris, CP). A teacher observed, "Anything that you learn is when you are going in to do the practical stuff. And sometimes you are going to screw up" (Maya, T). A manual worker is aware that the apparently simple task of taking parts off the assembly line entails learning not to make mistakes during a complex sequence of mental and physical control: "Yes, there are ways of doing the job better you know, better for you ergonomically... like how to handle the parts.... On my job... you pick up a part and turn it around, but it is how you turn it around—your bodily movements are very important because if you move around and pick it up wrong you are going to get hurt" (Jeff, Auto PL). James (Auto QT) recognized the personal worth of problem solving: "Troubleshooting is fine because it gets the grey matter moving again." One CP worker realized that one is likely to learn more by the experience of error than by getting things right. Speaking about how he learned to communicate with colleagues, he said, "I haven't taken courses; I haven't sat down and said, how do I improve my communication skills, or things like that, but... when something does not work perfectly you learn a lot from that experience, and if it does work you learn a little, maybe" (Angus, CP).

Respondents provided evidence of using conceptual and theoretical thinking in their work. A clerical worker observed, "Problem solving—I think people develop their styles, and then you can modify them if they don't work, but basically you do have to have a framework to help you" (Claire, CW). Some respondents were specific. Theresa (CW) insisted that "grammar rules are very important, and personally I cannot learn the language if I don't know the rules." Ethan (Auto QT) saw how theory was relevant to all his tasks: "Every [problem] is slightly different in one way or another, especially if it is on a different machine.... Your axis, sometimes it is a horizontal spindle and sometime it is a vertical spindle, and then you have one that reorients all your X, Y axes around this, and you have to think that way." Nevertheless, not all respondents were conscious of using a theory or principle. Although practical problem solving implicitly makes use of doubt, which is an element of scientific thinking, a few workers gave indirect indications of its importance. Martin (Auto QT) mentioned that he takes others' opinion about the cause of a problem with "a grain of salt." One person, when asked how long it took to investigate a supplier of parts, referred to doubt explicitly: "It depends on how much I doubt the information" (Franca, CW).

Learning from Unpaid Activities

Learning can occur during any form of paid or unpaid activity because both have elements of uncertainty about what to do and how to do it that entail problem solving. One worker saw no connection between his unpaid informal learning and his repetitive task at work: "It keeps my mind alive outside of work, but doesn't help me work" (Felix, Auto PL). Other respondents saw a broad connection, but were only vaguely aware of it: "For me learning is continuous, so I don't stop it except maybe when I'm sleeping" (Aubrey, CW). "I learned more outside of [high] school than in it" (Greg, Auto PL). Mitesh (CP) had a functional view of this process: "Every time I am doing something, it is related to something I have done in the past." According to other respondents, "I think everything flows into my job" (Tora, Auto PL); "You learn something new and different every day... [and] can use it in your daily life, at home, at work, and in your social life" (Gabrielle, CW); "I think that you need to have a lot of outside activities in order to do your job better because it makes you more knowledgeable about the world around you, and having different interests" (Rebecca, CP). "The more you know about figuring out how to solve problems, or how to organize, or how to cook, or how to manage your time or manage your money, you become better at applying those kind of skills at your job, etc. You know, like managing email correspondence, or figuring out how to work with maybe people that are stubborn, or figuring out how to communicate something to your manager like what kinds of strategies to use" (Zoey, CP). Wilma (CW), who is bored by her data entry job, helps in a nursing home and at an animal shelter so that "at the end of the day I feel as if I've accomplished something." Guy, a vice-principal who is also a pilot, is aware that the personal attitudes he learned in flying have influenced the way he works: "It's the material I picked up outside formal education that has put me in better stead for my roles — in piloting, never getting upset and losing control of a situation."

Varied experience is significant because while a person is ostensibly learning one thing other things are being learned collaterally and unconsciously. Although respondents sometimes identified subject matter they had learned explicitly in one domain, and which they have used in paid work, it was harder for them to be aware of habits of thought and action they had acquired by the experience of unpaid work and leisure and had used in paid employment, and vice versa. A CP worker realized that learning happens without her being aware of it: "I find that having different interests relaxes you... but also I find a lot of times if I'm at the gym, or if I'm playing baseball or doing something different, I'll suddenly be able to solve a problem that I could not solve all day long because now I'm relaxed; I'm not thinking about it" (Rebecca, CP). An auto worker had the same perception: "A lot of my interests at home do not involve the kind of work that I do at work, but I apply the same principles to both things" (James, Auto PL). By contrast, Theresa (CW) wants to learn consciously: "I like to learn at home, but I like to know how I'm learning." Although it is possible to be conscious of some aspects of learning, most cognitive processes are unperceived. As Aubrey (CW) said, "Learning goes on all the time even if people deny it." One reason is that highly complex neurological processes happen too fast to be observed. An auto production line worker relies on her auditory sense to be aware of a dysfunction: "I am always in tune to all my machines. I know when my machine is not running, just by listening. I know if the cutter is broken. All I have to do is hear it" (Tara, Auto PL). In the automobile plant, even repetitive assembly tasks performed by Jeffrey or the apparently simple cleaning work done by Grace require rapid cognitive processes of visual observation and physical adjustment of which they are unaware.

A secretary could see the implication of collateral learning. France (CW) described it as an "economy of habitual action. I could be doing my washing, the drying, my exercises, or whatever, all at the same time. My thoughts are all together. I have X amount of time to do it all." A teacher at first denied the relevance of her recreational activity to her work: "I learned how to do pottery, but it doesn't carry over into my work at all." However, on reflection, she discovered she had learned something highly relevant to the function of teaching: "I found that I wasn't as technically able in pottery as I thought I would be.... I had this learning disability, because I had these visions of what the pot should look like, and yet not the motor skills to carry it out. And I think maybe that... not being able to do something that I wanted and being frustrated in that situation... has made me more empathetic to kids who aren't naturally able in languages in the subjects that I teach" (Mary, T). She added, "I learned that teaching is a kind of reciprocal kind of thing, that I could learn a lot about cultures and I could learn a lot about people while I am teaching them something as well." A security specialist described the unconscious process of learning: "I don't think there is a moment to stop learning. Even when I am sleeping, sometimes I will have a dream and I will wake up and think, oh, that's the way to do it. Yes, that's when your brain puts it all together for you" (Liang, CP).

THE NATURE OF HUMAN CAPITAL

What Is Learned

As learning by experience during work of all kinds continues to develop understanding, each worker acquires a reserve of cognitive knowledge and abilities. The entire process of the perception, interpretation, and organization of data is so fast and complex that it cannot be observed, either by the worker concerned or by an external observer. These manifold perceptions are interpreted and organized in the mind into a coherent understanding (Chapter 6), which is more implicit than explicit and constitutes a personal capital that evolves continually. Just as the content of thinking remains partly invisible, so, too, the extent and content of individual human capital remains unknown.

Mental coherence is significant since it enables knowledge and abilities to be combined into smooth, effective, and economical performance. A secretary said, "I manage myself. Time management I'm excellent at, I can be doing five different things at once" (Franca, CW). Similarly, Rebecca (CP) observed, "You've got to be thinking about 50 things, not one straight stream of information." It is unlikely that a worker is aware of this ability until after performing a complex task that he or she did not realize could be done. The expression of surprise is an indicator of having been able to retrieve abilities from an unknown reserve. A government real estate officer remarked, "I'm amazed that I actually got through it because there's just so many variables involved" (Helena, CW). A woman working at a call centre said, "I did surprise myself by learning it, just by doing it. Such as the tables that I am doing. I learned the spreadsheets, and, using the templates created by another person, I had to learn how it was created" (Paulina, CW).

Moreover, each person possesses an ability to retrieve instantly and selectively just those parts of knowledge and abilities needed to perform a task. This retrieval process also occurs too fast for anyone to be aware of it. The process is not well known, and learning is often inaccurately described as an accumulation, rather than as a reformulation. One experienced worker described his reserve as an assemblage of factual knowledge: "I'm 58 now... from time to time I need to draw on every bit of knowledge that I've got to fix a problem on a machine" (Martin, Auto QT). Not all one's knowledge or abilities are utilized for a given problem; the rest remain in reserve. As an automobile worker commented, "I have to be careful because there is so much information out there. I have to glean just the information that I need out of all the stuff" (Thom, Auto PL). Another auto worker said, "The whole thing is focusing on what you are doing" (Ethan, Auto QT).

Polanyi (1958) went further, postulating that to deal with a task for which there is no prior experience a worker can also form new abilities during retrieval (see Chapter 6). To deal with a new and unexpected kind of problem, retrieved abilities may have to be complemented by learning new ones, and the experience of acquiring them further develops the reserve of personal capital. Polyvalence is the ability to perform more than one kind of task, and it derives from this ability to modify one's own cognition. Owenis (see above) described how clerical workers in small organizations have to be polyvalent. The experience of Grace (Auto PL), a cleaner in the automobile plant, demonstrates the process of acquiring polyvalence: having done many jobs in the past, meeting the needs in her present job to learn the intricacies of each machine, keeping in close touch with colleagues, ensuring the workspace is kept clean and uncluttered, and assuming office in her union. A worker in the automobile plant described how he had become polyvalent: "I learned a lot of it... because I got put into so many areas.... I worked in machine shops, shoe factories, clothing factories, sometimes we even got into the food industry" (Ethan, Auto QT). Polyvalence is common among clerical workers at all levels. The secretary to the head of a government department said, "I have to organize my boss so that everything can run effectively. If he's not running this department effectively, then that means that I am not doing my job effectively. Working with senior people you have to have the basic knowledge and skills, the functions of management, you have to have that knowledge to do your work. Managing, meaning even how you manage yourself and your work and your time. If you can't manage yourself, how are you going to manage your boss's time? And the day's gone, and you look back, and you have so much left to do, and in most cases it's when you're not organized, or your boss is not organized, and something is wrong" (Emily, CW).

Although the scope of a job on the assembly line or in an office might be restricted in some respects, several respondents reported being engaged in demanding unpaid work activities during which they formed new abilities. Among the automobile workers, one man had built his own house (Michael, QT) and one woman had built an addition to hers (Carlotta, PL). A lift truck driver (Greg, Auto PL) and a cleaner (Grace, Auto PL) both have union responsibilities that are more demanding than their paid jobs. As Grace observed, "It's a very intense process to even become a board director. You have to put your time in. You have to know the issues." Theresa (CW) explained how her home life gave her confidence: "If you have good communication with your family members, if your household is okay, if you're an organized person and everything at home is how you like it, you can be more confident and better at your job because you are more comfortable." She had also become a member of the board managing her apartment building, "just to see how it works."

The foundation of polyvalence is the possession of an underlying theory or set of concepts that can be adapted to more than one task. An auto worker recognizes what is common among several machines: "As far as my trade goes, a cylinder is a cylinder. Doesn't matter if it's on this machine or on that machine, it's still a cylinder. And it has an action, you know, it goes out or goes back. It has a device affixed to it, you know, whether it's a hidden clevis,[7] or it's threaded into something, or welded to something, or whatever, you know. The mechanics of the job stay pretty much the same from one machine to another; so the idea is to determine what the machine is supposed to do, and what it's not doing" (Michael, Auto QT). Another auto worker explained the need to perceive the relationships between things: "It's hard to fix things if you don't understand how they work. I think what's made it easy for me is, in a sense, I've been able to recognize not the differences, but the similarities between the different manufacturers and the different systems. Because that becomes the common ground from where you work, when you go from what you know to what you don't know" (Martin, Auto QT).

The progression of conceptual and theoretical understanding formed by unconscious learning develops intuition and habit, which permit the economies of thinking that underlie improvements in performance. Kamene (CP, Dis) indicated that she is vaguely aware of this process: "The more you work the more you are experienced, right? The more it's easier to design." A worker in a call centre thinks her informal learning helps her keep up with the pressure of work: "Organizing yourself at home helps you to organize your mind at work. You find a way to develop a habit and do more in the time." (Paulina, CW). A specialist in computer security explained why his job and personal life are interconnected: "If you really want to find the relation between the informal learning at home and my job...I think the...job helps me be more willing to learn new things in my daily life, and vice versa. It's kind of a habit" (Liang, CP). An administrative assistant who taught herself a variety of procedures such as setting up a PowerPoint presentation said, "I have a certain confidence. It's just the familiarity. In the beginning a job might take you an hour to do and then after six months it took you 15 minutes" (Renata, OW). The time she saves enables her to do other work in the time liberated.

Mobility
The evidence of the case studies challenges some cherished notions about the importance of formal instruction. Although occupational groups are defined by current employment, several respondents had previous experience in other jobs and occupations. The polyvalence that enables a worker to move among tasks in one organization also makes it possible to move among jobs. Several respondents from all levels of schooling reported having held a variety of jobs with little or no formal training. A machine operator said, "You would be surprised how many jobs I have done in there with zero training" (Thom, Auto PL). Philip (Auto PL), who works afternoons at the automobile plant, also runs a renovation business. Moishe, now a teacher, has degrees in journalism and English and has worked as a reporter but also "got a job at a psychiatric hospital as a nurse's assistant for about a decade" and worked on a stock exchange. Several respondents provide evidence of having undertaken diverse unpaid tasks. A man who did not complete high school, and was employed on the production line to do work considered low skilled, learned on his own to become a part-time travel agent (Jeffrey, Auto PL). Vijay (CP, Dis) has a major responsibility as president of an organization that houses large numbers of people with disabilities.

Most respondents understood *learning* to mean the acquisition of specific subject-matter knowledge. They were more aware of their opportunities to learn information than of the abilities they had acquired. Ming, a manager in CP, considered that he transfers certain managerial abilities from his job to his voluntary work: "I do come with a set of management skills that are not readily available when you go into a volunteer organization... even basics like how to run a meeting—Do you have an agenda, do you have minutes, do you have action items? and things like that."

Few respondents realized that mobility to other tasks and jobs involved applying the function of problem solving to another domain. One worker did not see the relevance of her education in policing and law to her job in quality control in automobile production, even though the aims of observing discrepancies and securing compliance are common to both: "Oh, not at all, there's no relation... it doesn't really relate to the work that I do" (Ruth, Auto PL). It was an information security specialist who most clearly saw that personal input into learning is important: "When we go on training, it's kind of following their steps, and we are controlled by their thoughts... but if we studied by ourselves we would learn more, and you don't need an instructor" (Liang, CP).

Common Features of Work and Learning
A worker's engagement in learning reflects the underlying nature of the role of labour in the production process. This is illustrated both by workers who have a disability and by those who perform what are often regarded as unskilled jobs.

Respondents with a handicap working in four occupational groups of this study demonstrate the same capacity for cognitive development and use of their abilities as those without a disability. Their attitudes and experience confirm that work is a psychological process: "We can do anything we want to" (Mike, T, Dis). Some workers with a handicap require an adjustment of their working conditions; thereafter, they perform as well as, or even better than, colleagues without a disability. A respondent with a mental disability who has achieved a diploma in business administration and a certificate in human resource management claimed to be good at "time management, more so working under stress and pressure" (Claire, CW, Dis). A blind worker memorizes telephone numbers as an alternative to keeping a written record (Kalam, OW, Dis). Another person takes an aggressive attitude to demonstrating that his disability is not an obstacle to work, as had once been suggested to him. He said, "[Being] impaired means you can't do it the traditional way. You have to make your own way of doing things" (Mike, T, Dis). Two respondents who are in wheelchairs can work normally. One said, "I'm basically like anyone else. I can do things that most people can do" (Vijay, CP, Dis); the other said, "I don't have to move or run away or carry stuff. With a computer you sit in one place, and your mind is in your hands" (Kamene, CP, Dis). Mike (T, Dis) qualified as a teacher not only to show that he had the ability to do so but also so that he might demonstrate to students that it is possible to do a job well when disabled.

The case studies include workers who are typically regarded as unskilled, such as a cleaner, temporary clerical workers, a call centre operator, manual workers on the assembly line, and some underemployed workers in what are regarded as low-level or low-skilled jobs. Some of the respondents had held several jobs but had little or no formal training. "I guess my experience carries over from every job I've ever had. I've never had any training" (Franca, OW). Close inspection of their paid and unpaid work tasks, their learning processes, and their employment histories reveals that each person has acquired a range of knowledge and abilities, and such qualities as courage and mature judgment. Wilma, an office worker, said, "We are learning until we die, no matter where we work." The respondents perform a range of work tasks and manage personal relations with employers and supervisors, sometimes with subtlety.

Immigrants learn not only English but also the customs and conventions of a new culture; many have taken specific occupational courses or studied alone. In a variety of precarious, low-paid, temporary, contingent jobs they have encountered the uncertainty that requires problem-solving ability and have exercised discretion to make decisions. Some have learned to assume new functions: "I started out as a secretary in purchasing, and then as a purchasing officer.... Then I was a programs assistant. I was responsible for different programs. Then when records services came along and they amalgamated... we didn't have an admin person, so I started up the admin portion" (Gabrielle, CW). Uma (CW), one of the lowest-paid workers interviewed, is underemployed. She has a degree in economics and psychology and has had several jobs; she also demonstrated a long list of achievements, ranging from teaching herself a variety of procedures, such as compiling a PowerPoint presentation, to being able to frame and execute a long-term plan to bring her son to Canada. The histories of these respondents confirm Kusterer's neglected judgment (1978) that no job or worker is completely unskilled.

CONCLUSIONS

Measures and Concepts of Matching

Grouped data from the EJRM Survey are compatible with the findings of earlier research on the gaps between levels of education required and attained (Chapter 2). However, the level of education is too simple a measure to represent the details of an employer's requirements. The level of education attained is also an inadequate measure of a worker's cognitive abilities. Taken together, these measures fail to constitute robust evidence of correspondence or absence of correspondence between education and jobs. The individual case study data reveal not only a multiplicity of evolving personal attributes among heterogeneous workers who have personal objectives that do not always coincide with employment aims, but also a multiplicity of characteristics in each and every job. As a result, in each instance, education and job can correspond on some attributes, but not on others.

Underutilization

The common, simple version of the education-job matching paradigm requires restatement in order to distinguish two aspects of underutilization, which raise different implications for policy.

The grouped survey data show discrepancies between the distributions of educational attainment and job requirements, which are typically skewed toward an excess of attained education over job requirement. The overall cross-sectional data do not reveal the temporal adjustments in technology and production or the adjustments that workers make by applying their abilities on the job. Nevertheless, the finding of underutilization raises broad issues of the nature and purpose of schooling and the extent to which it is, or should be, closely related to employment; it also raises issues of employment practices and policies.

New disaggregated findings from the EJRM Survey demonstrate that the incidence of underemployment is unequal within the labour force. Underemployment falls more heavily on some employee classes and specific occupational groups, and particularly on workers with the least working experience and recent immigrants. This aspect of underemployment raises additional issues of social equity in access to jobs.

The detailed case study evidence of paid and unpaid work reveals extensive polyvalence. Each person possesses a large reserve of abilities from which the cognitive abilities required to perform each task are retrieved selectively. A correspondence is established between the requirements of a particular task and the abilities used to perform it, while other abilities remain idle but available for future use. At any time, the partial use of a worker's abilities is a normal state, not an anomaly. This finding raises new and distinct questions about the extent to which the human potential of each worker can be recognized and actively engaged.

Epistemology

One of the more important practical implications of this project is the improvement in understanding when the emphasis is moved from macro-social measures of education to micro-social observation. The data most commonly used in analysis and policy formulation are measures of formal schooling, using indicators of levels of attainment or of the duration of education. The data are commonly differentiated by level, and—although they are sometimes modified by data about socio-economic status or ability—analysis has not yet taken adequate account of individual differences in learning and ability. Such an approach could help develop a critical view of how work and learning are influenced by policies and programs for education and employment that have been conceived "top-down" and have permitted the rhetoric of a simple, one-directional relationship between levels of education and economic performance. This encourages an oversimplification of policies for economic growth, which emphasize the quantity of formal education. In contrast, the EJRM case studies provide detailed evidence of learning outside formal schooling and its detailed distribution among individual respondents by economic class, race, gender, and other social variables. These data make it possible to construct an analysis, from the "bottom up," of the variety and wealth of relationships between individual workers and their job. This analysis can be used to devise new practices and policies that recognize and engage individual thought and initiative.

Work necessarily entails learning, and case studies of workers' accounts of what they do can provide a better insight into workers' abilities than attempts to describe how and what workers learn. Since problem solving takes place in all domains of human activity, any kind of paid and unpaid work is a source of learning. Respondents were less than fully aware of the extent of their abilities, including the ability to learn, or the ability to form a coherent understanding, but they provided evidence of an intuitive perception of principles relevant to their jobs. Few respondents were aware of the process of collateral learning, or of the multiplicity of things learned collaterally. It cannot be concluded that they learned nothing collaterally, but rather that little of their collateral learning could be elicited by the questions as framed. The statements of a few respondents who found they had been able to do something they had not expected to be able to do are fragmentary evidence of the existence of hidden abilities, but not of the content or full extent of those abilities. There is a dilemma in that the difficulty of observing acquired cognitive knowledge and abilities applies to the researcher as well as to the worker being observed. These limitations in the findings are inherent in the design of the study, which was not intended to bring out the subtleties of cognitive acquisition. Thus, the process and its findings have to be seen as a stage in the progressive refinement of research and can be used as a point of departure for a new and different analytical technique.

The Relationship between a Worker and a Job

The multiple attributes of both a job and a worker's abilities interact to form a complex and dynamically evolving relationship between the performance of work and a worker. The formation and utilization of cognitive knowledge and abilities are interdependent. The case study data illustrate the active role performed by a worker and the heterogeneity of the labour force. It is necessary to restate the concept of human capital, not as an accumulation but in qualitative terms that take into account the abilities that people possess, especially the ability to modify one's own cognition and continually improve performance.

All workers are able to learn both formally and by experience, and they have experience of work outside their paid jobs. Although the content of jobs varies among industries and occupations and among production methods and outputs, respondents provided evidence of a common thinking process: cognitive reformulation by experience. The ostensible differences of status between, on the one hand, the teachers, computer programmers, and qualified trades workers in automobile production and, on the other hand, the clerical workers and automobile production line workers conceal essential similarities. To varying degrees they all work under uncertain conditions and use their cognitive knowledge and abilities to identify and resolve problems by exercising discretion. As they learn from both paid and unpaid work activities, they reformulate their reserves of knowledge and ability, become increasingly polyvalent, and modify their jobs.

The empirical evidence from the case studies is at variance with the assumptions of neoclassical theory that workers are passive, homogeneous, and fully controlled by managerial decisions. Instead, the new evidence confirms the propositions of implicit contract theory, which recognize workers as active, heterogeneous, and capable of exercising initiative and judgement. The interview data brings to light what the statistical data otherwise conceal: A person cannot be judged solely by the level of schooling attained or by the job currently being performed.

Notes

1. This non-random sample was drawn independently of the larger random sample survey and is not a sub-set of it.
2. Cf. Chapters 5 and 6.
3. This analysis employs the taxonomy of credential, performance, and subjective matching criteria. As noted in Chapter 1, other taxonomies of matching can be conceived, e.g., Kalleberg (2008).
4. Managers are excluded for consistency with the statistical data, but some managers provide evidence about the work of employees or their own experience as workers.
5. No diploma, high school diploma, college certificate, bachelor's degree, post-graduate degree, and/or professional qualification.
6. The Teacher Advisor Program in Ontario. It is no longer in operation.
7. A pin inserted between the end of one part and an U-shaped bracket at the end of another so as to form an articulated joint.

Chapter Thirteen
Education and Jobs: The Way Ahead

D.W. Livingstone and K.V. Pankhurst

> Just involve the people.... This guy might run this machine every day for years. He will come up with ideas that will make his job easier for him and easier for [management].
> —Ethan, a tool setter on an auto assembly line

In this chapter the empirical findings of the surveys and case studies are summarized, a new paradigm of the relationship between work and learning is outlined, and policies and practices are suggested to enable employees to use their abilities more fully. The objective of improving labour utilization has wide implications for governments, employers, education and training institutions, workers' organizations, and individual members of the labour force. Further research is indicated.

MAIN FINDINGS

From the Surveys
Although the lack of correspondence between the education of the labour force and the requirements of jobs can be described by several criteria, in this study the initial analysis relied on measures of *levels* of formal education attained and required.

The main findings from the general Canadian surveys (Chapter 4) confirm the general findings of a large body of previous international research. That is:

- There is a skew toward underemployment by level of formal education (also described as overeducation or overqualification or underutilization), that is, the proportion of people in the labour force whose levels of education exceed the levels of education required upon entry into a job.

- As higher education continues to raise the attainment levels of the population faster than the formal educational requirements of jobs increase, the incidence of underemployment increases and the incidence of underqualification (or undereducation) decreases.
- The labour force is continually engaged in informal learning, primarily learning by experience, the content of which is not necessarily related to a worker's current job. Learning by experience is not closely related to either the level of formal schooling, the participation in further education courses, or the educational level of job requirements. However, informal learning is at least as useful for improving job performance as further education.
- Longer employment experience is linked with lower subjective underemployment.
- The survey data indicate little evidence of a shortage of computer skills or declining literacy in relation to job requirements.
- Relatively high levels of credential underemployment are found among recent immigrants, people of colour, and disabled people.
- There are persistent inequalities in the extent of underemployment by economic class: professional employees and those with high levels of educational attainment in jobs that require specialized academic credentials have lower levels of underemployment than service workers and industrial workers.
- There is also a lack of close correspondence between the fields of education studied and knowledge required in jobs.

More detailed statistical comparisons (Chapter 5) confirm these patterns and further find that:

- The levels of educational attainment and formal job requirements of teachers are closely matched, while computer programmers have high levels of credential overqualification.
- Clerical workers, with little recognized specialized knowledge and employed in diverse employment settings where educational entry requirements are low, have high levels of underemployment.
- Auto workers on the assembly line, where levels of formal education requirements are low, have a fairly high incidence of underemployment, but the apprenticeship training of qualified trades workers is more closely related to their job requirements.
- For employed workers with a disability, the patterns of matching of education and job requirements are similar to other workers in most respects. However, the data exclude many who are not employed because of disability, while some who are employed are placed in jobs below their level of attainment because of their disability.

From the Case Studies
Evidence from the case studies provides deeper insights into the manifold educational attributes of individual workers and the characteristics of their jobs.

- To greater or lesser degree workers continually learn by experience and adapt the content of their jobs.
- Most participants are engaged in intentional learning activities that are to various degrees directly relevant to their jobs.
- More important, all participants are engaged in problem solving in both paid and unpaid work; they continually acquire and reformulate their cognitive knowledge and abilities, and use them to modify their jobs.
- Most workers are not fully aware of being engaged in autonomous learning or of the abilities they are acquiring.
- Learning activities develop both workers' educational attributes and their jobs and, consequently, modify the gaps that had been measured between their education and job requirements.
- Many workers exercise discretion in performing their jobs. Nevertheless, the opportunities they have to use their abilities are limited by the design of their jobs and by organizational decision-making. This limitation applies especially to clerical and auto workers, as well as to many disabled workers.

IMPLICATIONS FOR THE EDUCATION-JOBS PARADIGM
The stereotypical education-jobs paradigm, which compares measures of levels of workers' formal educational attainment and estimates of the formal education required to perform jobs, needs to be reconceived in two distinct ways. First, at a technical analytical level it is not robust. Cross-sectional surveys are static and provide grouped data that conceal dispersions among individuals. The reliability of workers' self-reports of the educational levels required for their jobs is not known, and expert assessments of job requirements are unreliable. Single integers are too broad and general to measure the complexity and variability of job requirements, and employers' requirement levels are subject to variation if the supply of labour changes. Similarly, the data about education are levels of attainment, and a single measure of this kind is too simple to reveal a worker's cognitive knowledge and abilities. Measures of attainment-requirement gaps are for different intervals between education and entry into a job. Such measures cannot reliably indicate the nature of the correspondence, or lack of it, between education and jobs. The standard deviations of estimates of differences between measures of educational attainment and requirements are probably large. The concept of a definitive gap between schooling and jobs is misleading. Simplistic measures of differences between education and jobs cumulate unreliability and cannot capture the details of changes in workers and in their jobs.

Second, a more critical interpretation of the statistical findings is needed. The terms *overeducation* or *overqualification*, commonly used in education-job requirement analyses to refer to an excess of formal education as measured by level, are misconceived and misconstrued. This usage implies a narrow instrumental and restrictive functional concept of education as a preparation for working life and paid employment. Differences between educational attainments and job requirements are inevitable since formal education and labour markets are quite different systems, with different objectives, functions, and time horizons. More important, the purposes of education are much wider than use in employment, as several respondents observed. The terms *overeducation* and *overqualification* misleadingly suggest that the general cultural purposes of education have little application in employment and that work has no general formative value. These terms also ignore the active role of a worker in performing and modifying a job.

Excesses of formal education over job requirement, or differences between field of study and employment, are not anomalous and cannot be considered as a waste of talent or expenditure on education and training. Instead, they are to be expected and encouraged. The pursuit of knowledge has many benefits for individuals and for society. It is time that the terms *overeducation* and *overqualification* were dropped from serious discourse about the relationship between education and employment. The terms *underutilization* or *underemployment* are more appropriate, since they indicate that better opportunities can be created for workers to use their capabilities and to create better jobs.

Despite conceptual and technical limitations, comparisons of the statistical results of surveys over time suggest that the formal educational attainments of the labour force are growing faster than opportunities to use them in employment. Given the extent of education in excess of requirements, the labour market cannot be expected to reconcile the differences in a timely way, if at all, and major reforms of policy and practice are needed. In the 1960s, inner-city riots and student protests raised concern that underemployment could lead to political upheaval among many whose rising expectations were not being met. Since then the lack of adequate or commensurate jobs has led to pragmatic responses by workers, to seek additional educational credentials, and by employers, to raise formal requirements. However, the design of jobs to make full use of human abilities has not been given sufficient consideration.

Moreover, formal education is likely to be extended. There is some evidence that, among people with increasing levels of formal educational attainment, chronic unemployment and the lack of sufficient employment are growing. Both the employed and the unemployed are engaged in ongoing, extensive efforts to acquire work-related abilities, formally and informally; they do this both unaware and also consciously. Consequently the differences between the education of workers (widely conceived to include the abilities acquired during work) and the requirements of jobs can be expected to continue to rise. This gap is also consistent with estimates of declining rates of return to education. Unless there is a significant improvement in the utilization of workers' abilities in their jobs, this major social inequality can be expected to increase further and to sharpen the contrast between those with a formal credential and those without.

For these reasons, the paradigm of a static relationship between education and jobs needs to be replaced with one that takes into account the interactive nature of learning and work. The detailed case study data provide a more reliable view of the heterogeneous attributes of workers and of the active and dynamic relationship between education and employment at the level of an individual worker. A worker continually learns on and off the job, and modifies the content of the job being performed in ways that are not immediately evident.

IMPLICATIONS FOR POLICY AND PRACTICE

These findings have extensive implications for the policies and practices of all participants in the labour market. The implications, which can only be outlined here, should be examined in greater detail by all those who have interests and responsibilities. A new paradigm also has implications for further research into the relationship between learning and work.

It is time to reverse the dominant assumption in thinking about policies to address the relationship between education and employment. The issue is not too much education or the wrong kind of education. Although formal education is recognized for its intrinsic value, further expansions of formal education are likely to accentuate the apparent differences between levels of attainment and requirements, unless the reliance on credentials for jobs is reduced. The emphasis on greater investment in higher education as a solution to economic problems, or as a means of growth, ignores weaknesses in the organizational structure of jobs and the design of job content. A passive adaptation of educational systems to job requirements fails to recognize the potential of human beings as active agents of their own learning, economic production, and cultural, political, and social development.

The alternative to interpreting an excess of formal education attainment over job requirements as overeducation is to consider that these measures indicate an underutilization of human abilities. The possibility that workers' abilities could be better utilized is confirmed by the empirical evidence provided by the workers interviewed about their active roles in production and dealing with obstacles. Consequently, the emphasis in public policies and in the practices of organizations and individual members in the labour force should be shifted to reforming employment so as to better utilize workers' abilities. Whereas the predominant policy approach emphasizes more investment in education to meet the needs of the economy, the ongoing need for adjustments in the labour market and in jobs can be more effectively achieved by making better use of the existing labour supply. Greater emphasis should be placed on organizing work processes in ways that better utilize human abilities, rather than adapting human abilities to jobs.

GUIDING PRINCIPLES

A key principle is to recognize that human thought and effort is the fundamental resource that enables cultural, economic, political, and social development. Whereas fixed capital assets are passive, human capital that is continually developed by intentional and autonomous learning is the active resource in production. "Who better to ask than the people that are doing the jobs? They are the ones that know" (Shelley, an administrative assistant).

Formal education is an internationally agreed right. The current emphasis on the functional purposes of education, and the assumption that education should be adapted to estimates of economic needs, distort its essential purpose. The value of formal education for the labour market lies in forming character and beginning to develop abilities. However, the expansion of formal education cannot satisfy all the aspirations of the population if a crude reliance on the use of credentials continues.

Experience is a more important source of learning in work than is formal education and training, and it has wide applications. A well-established economic principle is that learning by experience during work has the advantage of zero opportunity costs, which means there is no loss of production as happens during formal training off the job. Moreover, the experience of other kinds of activities from early childhood and throughout adult life enriches, and is enriched by, performing a paid job.

Employees should be given the opportunity to demonstrate and be rewarded for the rich reserves of ability—notably the ability to change cognition—which are continually formed during the experience of all forms of paid and unpaid activity. Human cognitive reserves include polyvalence, which is the ability to move among a wide range of tasks and functions and to make decisions, and a potential to imagine, which extrapolates beyond past experience.

It is an error to judge a worker by his or her current job or occupation. An employee in a job that offers limited opportunities to learn by experience may have acquired extensive abilities during unpaid work activities.

Maintaining employment is a condition of improving it. A job and a worker's experience are enhanced under the following conditions: (1) when levels of employment are stable, (2) when formal education has endowed a student with the abilities for independent, critical thinking, (3) when a job is sufficiently sustained in time and progressive in scope so that the reserve of abilities can develop as fully as possible, (4) and when the organization of employment and the design of jobs allow workers to exercise judgment.

THE FEASIBILITY OF BETTER LABOUR UTILIZATION

Although the empirical analysis of this study has been of workers in paid employment, the aim of improving labour utilization has implications for everyone in the labour force and for a wide range of socio-economic policies. The aim of better utilizing human abilities in employment is compatible with two perennial socio-economic objectives: more efficient, long-term, economic production and equitable life-time opportunities, irrespective of age, gender, race, class, or disability.

It is feasible to improve labour utilization throughout the economy and society. This objective, which is in the interests of employers and employees alike, can enhance productivity and earnings. Several fields of employment offer suitable opportunities. The most evident are those in which the structure of production is changing, employment is expanding, or new types of activity are being introduced in the pursuit of new policy objectives, including the measures being taken for economic recovery and reorganization. In other fields special intervention is needed. In some countries there is already much experience of measures to help improve the development and utilization of human abilities in the workplace, which should be better known. The experience of some countries can be adopted, provided it is adapted with imagination to different conditions and its effectiveness is tested in pilot studies.

For example, the efforts now being introduced to reduce environmental degradation by reducing carbon emissions and capturing and sequestering carbon, and to make greater use of renewable energy resources such as wind, geothermal, solar, and tidal power, entail creating new jobs to apply new technologies. The new jobs will provide opportunities to mobilize the abilities workers possess to confront new and demanding problems. Moreover, new technologies are developed and refined during the experience of using them.

Another example can be found in the fields of education, health, and law enforcement, which are large-scale industries that employ large workforces to meet sustained demands and use advanced technologies that continue to develop. In such industrial sectors that provide opportunities for sustained employment, a condition of good labour utilization would be to ensure that the age structure is regularly renewed by comprehensive succession planning. Government, as a major employer, has an opportunity to influence the practices of private employers.

The right to work is also internationally agreed. It implies the right to use one's abilities in the performance of a job. Many governments have adopted the International Labour Office declaration of the right to a *decent job*, which can be defined as "productive work in conditions of freedom, equity, security and human dignity" (Somania, 1999: v.1, p. x.) This objective can only be achieved if it is recognized that improved performance, sustained employment, and effective international competition depend on organizational arrangements and processes that are better designed to make full use of human abilities. The criteria of a decent job can be enriched and made more effective by including stability of tenure, equitable opportunities to exercise judgment, and opportunities for workers to continue to develop and apply their cognitive and social abilities.

RESPONSIBILITIES FOR IMPLEMENTING A NEW PARADIGM

The aim of better utilizing the current and potential abilities of the labour force has implications for employers, in better designing employment structures and jobs; governments, in modifying national policies for employment; individuals, when making career choices and demonstrating abilities; workers' organizations and employers, in establishing more effective consultation and collaboration between them; and education and training institutions, in addressing the balance between formal instruction and learning by experience.

Employers

In many organizations, employers could make more effective use of the abilities and knowledge of their workforces by good strategic planning, changes in organizational structures, and job redesign; in doing so they could achieve greater productive efficiency. The inclusion in some company annual reports of a statement about the personnel, along with the estimates of fixed assets in balance sheets, is a practice that has potential for improving the overall management of an organization and could be more widely adopted.

The conditions for optimizing output primarily involve continuity of employment coupled with progressive opportunities to learn new tasks and jobs. This entails maintaining the demographic stability or steady growth of a workforce by means of a coherent policy for continuously recruiting, progressively redeploying workers among jobs and tasks, improving orientation and technical training, and planning retirements and successions. For each individual worker, sustained employment entails progressive career development and requires the design of better methods to assess and compensate abilities acquired by experience.

Better management at all levels is essential to good labour utilization. A manager should be aware that in the course of performing a job a worker thinks, is able to make discretionary decisions, and is involved both in the function of management and in the process of redesigning a job. If opportunities are to be given to workers to bring their practical knowledge and abilities into decision-making, managers should be better informed about their employees and the abilities they have acquired in their unpaid work. A manager should have a well-rounded view of what makes a good employee and also understand how to judge a worker's competence, including that of a worker who lacks formal credentials.

Correspondingly, it is essential for managers to be familiar with the details of production and specific jobs in order to ensure that managerial decisions are constructive and positive. Many managers with a formal credential have little practical experience of the details of production and the kinds of work their subordinates do. The experience of enterprises and organizations in countries where a large proportion of managers is recruited from among employees with acquired practical experience should be better known.

Better labour utilization can be achieved by improved practices to mobilize and reward the experience that workers acquire of the minutiae of production and of the quality of the output and services they produce. As Ethan's comment at the head of this chapter suggests, employees are often the most knowledgeable about how well their workplace is designed, equipped, and maintained and how well it contributes to organizational success, or to avoiding mistakes. Suggestion schemes, which have been successfully adopted in some enterprises, can be more widely used as ways to improve organizational management; they should not be used simply as a symbolic gesture or treated merely as an incentive to effort.

The unequal distribution of working time among the population of working age is an impediment to efficient work and learning. Some employees work longer-than-average days and weeks, while others work less than average, and others not at all. Measures for more equitable working time can permit better opportunities to learn on the job, while also reducing stress. A redistribution of working time and employment could be part of succession planning to embrace recruitment, personnel redeployment and development, mentoring by older workers, and retirement. Its benefits can include a better balance between work and leisure, improved employee health, and higher productivity. The experience of the past century, during which the annual hours worked per employed person in most advanced economies were reduced by about one-third by standard hours legislation, extended vacations, and sick leave benefits, suggests that it is feasible to continue to redistribute working time more equitably. Reorganizing work in such ways raises well-known complex issues that have to be carefully examined prior to enabling legislation. The issue needs to be addressed in a more comprehensive and effective way.

Employers could better utilize the abilities of workers with disabilities. Many of them have disabilities that have little or no effect on their ability to work, and are at least as competent as their colleagues. Many of those with serious disabilities can still work well, provided they are given appropriate facilities in the workplace. Sheltered employment is required for those with disabilities that are too serious for them to be employed in regular workplaces.

Governments

The objective of improving labour utilization can be pursued by adjustments to existing national-level policies for efficiency and equity, including macroeconomic measures to deal with the overall employment situation and programs for income support and assistance during unemployment. Macroeconomic policies have been based for some time on a belief that inflation hurts more people, and for longer, than unemployment, but the use of crude fiscal and financial policy instruments is passive, unselective, and places the burden of economic adjustments on the labour force. This view fails to recognize the costs of interrupted employment experience. If the rhetoric of the importance of human capital were embodied in logical policies, more emphasis would be placed on the objective of minimizing changes in levels of aggregate employment. Continuity of employment experience facilitates further workplace learning and the growth of competence in the labour force. More emphasis could be placed on complementary policies, including those for industrial, regional, and scientific development, to stabilize the continuity of employment as a condition of enhancing the reserves of human abilities. Assistance with worker mobility to new and expanding sectors of production is also an effective way to sustain employment experience. The experience of countries that have coherent policies and practices to utilize their labour forces well can be adapted and more widely adopted. Examples include the comprehensive employment policy in Sweden, which aims to balance security and flexibility in the labour market and includes educational leave, parental leave, and anticipatory training for succession planning. Another is the Finnish experience in the employment of older workers.

The present employment situation reflects three major global trends during recent years: the rising indebtedness of governments, enterprises, and individuals that erupted into the financial crisis of 2008; trends in demand and production in the real economy that turned down sharply in 2008; and a continuing degradation of the ecological and human environment that has become very serious. These trends revealed the consequences of too great a reliance on automatic market adjustments and a need for more public intervention and regulation. Governments are taking action that includes inducements for consumption and for private investment, and also public investment in infrastructure, the scope for which is limited in times of full employment but which is greater when capacity utilization is low. The management of the physical environment has become a central economic issue, and significant differences in the extent of environmental degradation among developing and developed countries raise questions of how the long-term costs can be borne and shared internationally; these questions require imagining different modes of life that can be viable in the future.[1] Government measures vary with the economic organization of each country, the size of its external sector, its financial and fiscal structure, and the scope for action permitted by its constitutional and political system. Even when decisions are taken rapidly, their impacts are distributed over time. Unpredictable changes in consumption, production, international trade, and industrial and occupational structures will place new demands on labour forces in the form of changes in patterns of labour utilization and mobility, and they will call into play human ingenuity and the capacity for problem solving in private life as well as in the workplace. However, levels of employment are typically slower to recover than to fall, and further government action will be needed to provide flexible income support, temporary employment, information, and training while members of the labour force seek and change jobs. National economies and labour markets are now sufficiently interconnected globally for there to be many opportunities for international collaboration and exchanges of experience about the design and effectiveness of measures.

The aim of greater social equity can also be pursued by improving labour utilization. Customary and conventional employment structures in the organization of employment, and the design and scope of jobs, assign levels of decision-making responsibility, authority, and pay that fail to take into account what happens during production. Employees who are often more familiar than managers with the minutiae of production and technology make discretionary decisions and participate in the function of management without they or their hierarchical superiors being aware, but their remuneration is inconsistent with their contribution to production. During the 2008–9 international crisis attention has been drawn to the inequitable distribution of net outputs from production among executives, managers, and employees. Large disparities in the rewards from work damage social cohesion. Recent initiatives to end the large separation payments made to senior executives and to reduce their pay implicitly recognize the need for, and the possibility of, comprehensive reform of pay structures in organizations.

Not all employing organizations operate in conditions of stable demand and can provide stable employment or opportunities for development. For workers in organizations where jobs are precarious, public authorities have a residual responsibility to promote the lifetime development of those workers' abilities. Mobility among industries and occupations, which is a vital condition of economic restructuring, rests on greater lifetime mobility and security in the labour force. To that end, legislation is needed to give casual and part-time workers the same entitlements as full-time employees, in proportion to the hours worked, for further education and training, paid vacations, sick leave, and pensions. Comprehensive social insurance can ensure that all those in paid work contribute fairly to financing the income support for those who are unemployed and changing jobs, as well as for dependants such as children, the sick, and retired persons.

Employees

The evolving economic situation enhances the likelihood of employees having to be more mobile among industries and occupations during a lifetime at work. Although this mobility can be assisted by formal training, it rests primarily on making better use of the abilities human beings develop by experience to change cognition and to address new and unexpected problems in different situations. Workers should be more aware of the need for these attributes as well as their abilities to possess them.

Non-managerial employees can be more aware of their abilities than their employers or managers, but many are frustrated by workplace constraints on using these abilities. It would be advantageous for employers to be aware of the benefits to them of developing and utilizing workers' abilities, and they should recognize and reward them. A preoccupation with formal educational credentials, or formal professional or trades certification, obscures the recognition of an employee's abilities. Many workers are not fully aware of their reserves of abilities. Abilities that are not yet sanctioned by a credential, especially the ability to continually develop them, should be better known by employers and workers themselves. Techniques that have been devised for that purpose could be more widely adopted, such as the use of a portfolio of achievements to document abilities that go far beyond an occupational or professional qualification. Such methods are effective only if they are used as an essential part of a human resource development strategy, and if employees can be satisfied that they will be taken seriously.

Workers in each of the case studies complained that there are constraints on the use of their capabilities to redesign their jobs and that management was unaware of the details of production. Production could be enhanced by a more widespread use of arrangements to mobilize the experience that workers have acquired of practical problems of production and dealing with them. Some countries have legislation that requires workers to be involved in the major policy decisions of an organization, which could be extended more widely and adapted to other conditions.

For workers with few or no formal credentials, the assignment to jobs according to the possession of a credential (norm referencing) ignores the abilities they acquired outside paid work and creates increasing social inequality. It is both inequitable and inefficient because many workers are excluded from jobs for which they are quite capable. The recognition of prior experience and competence, and its integration into organizational strategies, is still a major unresolved issue. For workers who have few formal credentials but have acquired abilities through experience, the alternative method for selection, promotion, and compensation is to assess those abilities directly (criterion referencing). Although some employers informally recognize competent employees with potential and promote them, the practice could be more systematically and widely adopted. To that end, a multipartite institution could be given the responsibility to devise methods of assessing abilities and competence acquired by experience and to ensure that those who demonstrate acquired competence shall be given full parity with their formally qualified peers by being awarded the appropriate formal credential.

Collaboration Between Employers and Employees

It is in the interests of both workers and employers to pursue better labour utilization by maintaining stable employment. It is also advantageous to them to recognize that their functions are complementary and entail continual collaboration in problem solving. There is extensive experience of formal and institutional methods, variously known as joint worker-employer councils, participatory democracy, employee-share ownership, or consultative arrangements between the social partners. Collaborative arrangements between workers and employers are an alternative to conflictual relationships, and the experience of countries that have developed them could be better known and appropriately adapted. Collaboration will be effective in improving labour utilization only if stereotypical managerial techniques are changed to mobilize and reward the practical knowledge and abilities of workers engaged in daily or routine operations.

Labour Market Competition

Formal education, which is intended to be an instrument of democracy and social cohesion, has been misused to create a meritocracy of diminishing status. Further investment in education, when coupled with credentialism, will increase income inequalities. At one end of the spectrum, those with higher education attainments still tend to have lower unemployment rates and higher incomes if they are employed, although some highly qualified people are unable to find jobs. At the other end of the spectrum, the costs of credentialism fall most directly on those who lack a higher credential but have demonstrated competence in practice.

The main obstacle to appreciating an individual's employability is the use of credentials to compete for jobs and to select employees. Formal credentials are now used by employers as screening criteria to such an extent that they are important in competing for many jobs. These practices rest on the belief that formal education diplomas and degrees are adequate indicators of job requirements and represent a person's capabilities. Possessing a formal credential can create an advantage for one person in the labour market, but if everyone pursues the same aim, not everyone can be satisfied at a given time. A credential is an ordinal indicator, and its utility for obtaining a job is likely to be diminished if the number of people holding it exceeds the number of jobs for which it is required. The number of people with high credentials has been increasing faster than the opportunities to use them in employment, and this has created a credential inflation and a series of downward displacements of workers to compete for jobs at lower levels. The strong, popular belief in the instrumental value of formal education represents a search by those with a credential for a greater share of economic growth, in the form of access to the goods and services being produced. This view is reinforced by a double fallacy in public rhetoric: the notion that more formal education is necessary for economic growth and that economic growth is inherently desirable.

In practice, credentialism reflects more interest in the process of job competition than in the relevance of education to performance. Formal credentials as well as transcripts and standardized psychological tests are often used by employers as ostensibly low-cost ways of indicating job knowledge or as surrogates for the other less easily defined personal qualities of job entrants. These means are often ineffective and incur the ultimate costs of turnover, new selection, and dismissal. It would be less expensive and more reliable to form a view of a job applicant's motivation, interests, level of achievement in education, experience, and abilities by in-depth interviewing, probationary periods, and regular performance assessments. However, it should be recognized that these practices will remain arbitrary until appropriate methods for personnel selection and performance review can be devised to assess workers' implicit cognitive knowledge and abilities.

Credential inflation undermines the expectation that education will ensure higher income. Since credentialism creates individual expectations that cannot be realized by everyone, the task of changing expectations is a major problem that requires attention. It is possible that in time reduced expectations could bring about a change of attitude among both employees and employers. Many workers know that a simple reliance on credentials is an inadequate indicator of their abilities, and many employers attempt to assess individual abilities. An increasing awareness that rapid economic growth incurs heavy costs for the ecological system and the human environment could strengthen a search for ways to use education to help protect the environment rather than to accumulate wealth. The rhetoric of public policy that emphasizes education as an instrument of economic growth and personal economic success raises unrealistic expectations. If there were a greater awareness that formal education cannot provide economic prosperity for all, this could lead schools to concentrate less on subject-matter instruction and more on an all-round, general education. Changes in expectation may be slow to emerge, but ways can be found to promote public consultation and discussion of the nature and purpose of education in relation to both the economy and individual well-being.

The heavy reliance on credentials for employment selection means that many workers who lack a higher formal credential, and their employers, seriously underestimate what they have learned and are able to do. To greater or lesser degree all workers acquire cognitive knowledge and abilities during the experience of paid and unpaid work, and they have the ability to exercise discretion during the labour process. Just as it is an error to judge a worker by the current job, it is inappropriate to use education attainment as a criterion to judge a person.

Educational Practice

Formal education systems are producing more people with higher levels of education than the labour market can immediately absorb into paid jobs. That does not, however, imply that formal education opportunities should be reduced or that curricula should be more directly related to jobs. Although education can contribute to the economy, it should continue to be expanded as an internationally recognized human right whereby everyone is provided with access to an inherited culture and the means to contribute to it. Many perceive the purpose of education as the acquisition of specific subject-matter knowledge, and employers argue that the cost of education should be borne by governments. These views fail to take into account the extent and significance of learning by experience.

The central implication of this study for educational practice is to be more aware that learning by experience is the generic form of learning. The empirical evidence of this study confirms that learning by experience is more important than formal learning in work, and that is also true of life as a whole. Assisting everyone to learn by experience can be a foundation of cultural life, not solely working life. To bring learning by experience to the centre of school education, several specific measures can be proposed.

- Since early childhood education proceeds primarily by experience, more extensive and equal access to it can lay stronger foundations for subsequent autonomous learning throughout life.
- Mixed ability groupings are valuable in promoting implicit learning. Those with lesser abilities can often do better in mixed classes, while more advanced students can learn by teaching the others.
- Languages, which can be taught from early childhood, are vital means of thinking and communication in all aspects of life, including paid work.
- Subject matter in the curriculum is a vehicle for developing abilities, conveying attitudes and values, and introducing established knowledge; however, testing requirements encourage too much emphasis on formal content. Placing more emphasis on learning by experience—which is not fully observable—reduces the administrative requirement for testing, and can help diminish the fixation on credentialism.
- A social distinction between those presumed to work with their heads and those presumed to work with their hands is a misleading dichotomy, which is not supported by the empirical evidence of the case studies. The practice of assigning those who do not perform well in academic subjects to vocational subjects is discriminatory in stigmatizing those students, while at the same time denying opportunities for practical studies to students who are also good at abstract, academic studies. More opportunities to gain experience of practical problem solving are needed by students with all kinds of abilities.
- Abilities that have wide applicability, including autonomous learning, are formed by aesthetic studies such as music, dance, drama, and the visual arts. These subjects are at least as important for developing practical abilities as technical and other studies, which are often mistakenly assumed to be more directly relevant to working life. The study of the fine arts is particularly valuable in developing coherent perceptions and intuition, which are essential features of thinking during work. However, because their value in cognitive development

is poorly appreciated, reduction in expenditure tends to fall on these subjects.
- Whereas a school curriculum typically introduces students to relatively simple well-defined problems, the problems that occur in adult life are often ill defined and quite dissimilar. The scope of curricula should be extended to include a wider range of opportunities to learn by experience, including field excursions and community service.
- Vocational education and training can perform the essential function of introducing workers to technical subject-matter knowledge, but in practice this kind of education tends to be demand driven. It can be more proactive and reinforced by providing more opportunities of longer duration for practical work experience. It can also be better integrated with formal instruction. There is scope for a more effective integration of training in institutions and in employing organizations to facilitate mobility among organizations and occupations.
- Educational institutions should improve access for those with a disability so that they are not excluded from formal learning opportunities.

The overall implication is that formal education practices should be extended to include a wider range of opportunities for people to learn by experience. At the same time it must be recognized that much of what is learned by experience is collateral and cannot be intended, designed, or observed. A better understanding of how different domains of study and activity provide opportunity to develop cognitive abilities could help diminish the widespread fixation with narrow credentialism and encourage teachers, parents, students, and employers to give greater attention to the essential purposes of schooling. A less instrumental basic education that emphasizes the development of a wide range of abilities, including communication, can provide better preparation for creativity and fulfilment in adult life.

Research

Further surveys of the nature and content of jobs, and learning during paid and unpaid work, can provide valuable data for estimating patterns and trends in a range of activities and formal job requirements. Surveys whose design is progressively adapted can be useful in assessing theories of work and learning and for reconsidering both employment and education policies. Longitudinal surveys of the changing work and learning conditions of specific cohorts would also be welcome.

However, the emphasis in research methods could now more usefully be placed on collecting qualitative data by means of individual case studies. At the level of the individual, the analysis of the relationship between education and employment is different because it permits observations that cannot be made with aggregated survey data. The case study findings demonstrate considerable differences among workers and jobs. The evidence of continual shifts in both workers' abilities and job content enables the static education-jobs paradigm to be more appropriately replaced by that of a dynamic relationship between learning and work. Specific techniques that could be used for further in-depth analyses of learning in work include longitudinal case studies, diaries by workers, and autobiographical recollection.

Since learning is more implicit than explicit, a central research problem is how to observe the processes of learning and the cognitive knowledge and abilities that are acquired. All kinds of learning entail learning by experience, including formally organized courses, because in the process of deliberately and consciously learning one thing, several other things are learned collaterally and unconsciously. Learning also entails combining disparate information and ideas into a coherent understanding, but what is learned is also less than fully observable because the process of learning involves a continual reorganization of prior understanding in the light of the latest experience. To a limited extent, information can be obtained about organized learning opportunities in the form of courses of study, and their curriculum content can be outlined; from this a researcher can infer that a process has taken place, but without being able to know precisely what has been learned. Consequently, the process of learning and the reserves of cognitive knowledge that are acquired can only be described in general terms. Data about modes of learning, such as courses of study that respondents have followed, or mentoring, or the use of libraries and the internet, have limited value for research.

Although the current case studies were not designed to investigate learning by experience, they contain incidental comments about learning in one sphere that are applicable elsewhere and some serendipitous remarks about learning by experience, which require careful interpretation. Nevertheless, the evidence that respondents provided about their work, paid and unpaid, is often more informative about the process of learning than direct questions about learning. This is most notable in their accounts of problem solving. They also provide some insight into the formation of personal reserves of ability. The overall analysis of work and how it is done provides evidence from which inferences can be drawn about how and what people learn, and is a practical alternative to attempting to observe learning directly.

CONCLUSION: A NEW AGENDA FOR DISCUSSION AND ACTION

The chapters in this book have outlined a need to reconceive the relationship between education and jobs as a dynamic interaction between learning and work. Broad principles have been proposed for framing a new policy paradigm; areas of feasible application have been indicated; and initial suggestions have been made about how and by whom this change can be brought about. The scope of the problems raised and the task of achieving them requires comprehensive and sustained efforts, but the potential benefits of a new approach are vast. This study raises more questions than answers.

However, it can draw attention to a major issue for our societies and launch a debate. The analyses in this book and the many implications presented for all political, economic, and social interests can now be seen as the outline of an agenda to be elaborated in detail. The next step will require the engagement of all institutions and individuals who are concerned with the role and importance of human beings in the productive activities of the economy and the continued sustainability of society.

Note

1. See the discussion of alternative modes of production in relation to labour force utilization in Chapter 6 of Livingstone (2004).

Appendices

APPENDIX 1

EJRM Case Study Interviewee Profiles

1. Secondary School Teacher Interviewee Profiles

Pseudonym	Sex	Age	Ethnicity	Job Title	Total Work Experience (Years)	Educational Attainment
Sarah	F	50–54	White	Teacher	31+	Professional degree
Neil	M	55–59	White	Teacher	31+	Master's degree
Rajine	F	35–39	White	Teacher	21–25	Master's degree
Moishe	M	40–44	White	Teacher	16–20	Master's degree
Julie	F	25–29	White	Teacher	0–5	Professional degree
Declan	F	30–34	White	Teacher	6–10	Master's degree
Salma	F	40–44	White	Teacher	11–15	Master's degree
Goranna	F	35–39	White	Teacher	21–25	Master's degree
John	M	55–59	White	Teacher	31+	Master's degree
Signe	F	30–34	White	Teacher	6–10	Professional degree
Anthony	M	55–59	White	Teacher	26–30	Master's degree
Mary	F	25–29	White	Teacher	11–15	Professional degree
Maya	F	25–29	White	Teacher	0–5	Professional degree
Reeva	F	45–49	Southeast Asian	Teacher	21–25	Professional degree
Julian	M	55–59	White	Teacher	31+	Professional degree

2. Computer Programmer Interviewee Profiles

Pseudonym	Sex	Age	Ethnicity	Job Title	Total Work Experience (Years)	Educational Attainment
Chris	M	35–39	White	Security specialist	6–10	Bachelor's degree
Katie	F	35–39	White	Research staff member	6–10	Master's degree
Carolyn	F	35–39	White	Software developer	6–10	Master's degree
Tariq	M	35–39	African	Software developer	6–10	Doctoral degree
Fiona	F	30–34	White	Software developer	6–10	Master's degree
Simon	M	30–34	White	Release engineer	6–10	Bachelor's degree
Carlos	M	35–39	White	Software developer	11–15	Bachelor's degree
Haiyan	F	18–24	Southeast Asian	Tester	0–5	Bachelor's degree
Adnan	M	25–29	South Asian	Software developer	0–5	High school diploma
Rebecca	F	40–44	White	Tester	26–30	Master's degree
Isaac	M	45–49	White	Software developer	21–25	Bachelor's degree
Zoey	F	25–29	White	Technical writer	0–5	Bachelor's degree
Nisha	F	25–29	South Asian	Software developer	0–5	Doctoral degree
Andrew	M	55–59	White	Research staff member	21–25	Bachelor's degree
Susanna	F	25–29	White	Software developer	0–5	Bachelor's degree
Angus	M	50–54	White	Software developer	26–30	Master's degree
Abe	M	40–44	White	Software developer	16–20	Bachelor's degree
Mitesh	M	30–34	South Asian	Software developer	6–10	Master's degree
Liang	M	30–34	Southeast Asian	Advisory IT specialist	11–15	Bachelor's degree
Mayko	F	35–39	Southeast Asian	Tester	11–15	Bachelor's degree

Appendix 1

3. Clerical Worker Interviewee Profiles

Pseudonym	Sex	Age	Ethnicity	Job Title	Total Work Experience (Years)	Educational Attainment
Aubrey	M	25–29	White	Research coordinator	11–15	Bachelor's degree
Beatrice	F	40–44	Caribbean	Medical records clerk	16–20	College or trade certificate
Corrie	F	55–59	Caribbean	Outreach customer service clerk	6–10	College or trade certificate
Danielle	F	40–44	White	Customer service representative	21–25	High school diploma
Emily	F	35–39	Caribbean	Administrative assistant	16–20	College or trade certificate
George	M	40–44	White	Information retrieval assistant	16–20	College or trade certificate
Helena	F	40–44	White	Real estate officer	21–25	High school diploma
Isolde	F	50–54	East African	Administrative assistant	26–30	College or trade certificate
Jennifer	F	45–49	White	Executive assistant	26–30	College or trade certificate
Kara	F	40–44	White	Administrative assistant	16–20	High school diploma
Laura	F	25–29	White	Office legal administrator	6–10	College or trade certificate
Maggie	F	25–29	White	Medical research assistant	6–10	High school diploma
Naomi	F	45–49	Central American	Administrative assistant	26–30	High school diploma
Ophelia	F	40–44	White	Executive secretary	16–20	High school diploma
Paulina	F	30–34	White	Call centre representative	6–10	High school diploma
Renata	F	45–49	White	Administrative assistant	26–30	College or trade certificate
Shelley	F	30–34	White	Administrative assistant	11–15	High school diploma
Theresa	F	55–59	White	Medical receptionist	31+	High school diploma
Uma	F	40–44	South Asian	Constituency assistant	6–10	Professional degree
Vanessa	F	50–54	White	Executive assistant	31+	High school diploma
Wilma	F	45–49	White	Investigations clerk	26–30	College or trade certificate
Gabrielle	F	45–49	South American	Administrative coordinator	26–30	College or trade certificate
Franca	F	50–54	Caribbean	Requisition administrator	21–25	College or trade certificate

4. Auto Industry Worker Interviewee Profiles

Pseudonym	Sex	Age	Ethnicity	Job Title	Total Work Experience (Years)	Educational Attainment
Martin	M	50–54	White	Electrician	21–25	College or trade certificate
Ethan	M	50–54	White	Certified tool setter	21–25	College or trade certificate
Sam	M	50–54	White	Tool delivery driver	31+	High school diploma
Michael	M	50–54	White	Industrial mechanic millwright	26–30	College or trade certificate
Jeff	M	45–49	White	Metalworking machine operator	26–30	No diploma
Tom	M	45–49	White	Metalworking machine operator	26–30	High school diploma
Stephen	M	55–59	White	Electrician	26–30	College or trade certificate
James	M	45–49	White	Toolmaker	26–30	College or trade certificate
Charles	M	45–49	White	Toolmaker	26–30	Professional degree (C.A.)
Grace	F	50–54	White	Plant cleaner (janitor)	26–30	High school diploma
Jane	F	50–54	White	Metalworking machine operator	26–30	College or trade certificate
Tara	F	55–59	White	Metalworking machine operator	31+	No diploma
Katharine	F	45–49	White	Metalworking machine operator	21–25	College or trade certificate
Doug	M	40–44	White	Electrician	21–25	College or trade certificate
Mimi	F	45–49	White	Metalworking machine operator	26–30	High school diploma
Philip	M	60–64	White	Blacksmith	31+	No diploma
Robert	M	55–59	White	Tool and dye maker	26–30	College or trade certificate
Greg	M	45–49	White	Lift-truck driver	31+	High school diploma
Carlotta	M	50–54	White	Assembler	26–30	High school diploma
Bill	M	55–59	White	Assembler	26–30	High school diploma

5. Disabled Worker Interviewee Profiles

Pseudonym	Sex	Age	Ethnicity	Job Title	Total Work Experience (Years)	Educational Attainment	Self-reported Disability
Teacher							
Barbara	F	40–44	White	Elementary	16–20	Master's degree	Dyslexia
Mike	M	25–29	White	Secondary	6–10	Bachelor's ed. degree	Blind
Toula	F	50–54	White	Elementary	31+	Master's degree	Polio
Cynthia	F	40–44	White	Elementary	11–15	Master's degree	Environmental allergies, bi-polar
Chandra	F	60–64	South American	OAC, family studies, secondary	31+	Bachelor's ed. degree	Cardiovascular disease, diabetes
Bethamie	F	25–29	White	Elementary	0–5	Bachelor's ed. degree	Spina bifida, depression
Lourdes	F	55–59	White	High school, dept. head, English	31+	Bachelor's ed. degree	Lung disease
Programmer							
Tom	M	50–54	South American	Senior systems analyst	31+	Doctoral degree	Speech
Demitri	M	40–44	White	Program analyst	16–20	Bachelor's degree	Muscular dystrophy
Irving	M	40–44	White	Systems officer #3	11–15	High school diploma	Cerebral palsy
Ling	F	35–39	East Asian	Software programmer	0–5	College/trade certificate	Polio
Lina	F	35–39	White	Accessibility officer	6–10	Master's degree	Cerebral palsy
Kamene	F	35–39	East African	Program analyst	6–10	College/trade certificate	Scoliosis, polio
Vijay	M	50–54	South Asian	Senior mgr. stats. and analysis	31+	Doctoral degree	Polio
Clerical							
Rivka	F	55–59	White	Receptionist/admin. assistant	31+	High school diploma	Deaf
Claire	F	40–44	White	Employment transition assist.	16–20	College/trade certificate	Cerebral palsy
Ellen	F	35–39	White	Data input operator	16–20	High school diploma	Cerebral palsy
Petra	F	55–59	White	Central registry mail clerk	11–15	High school diploma	Deaf

5. *Disabled Worker Interviewee Profiles* (continued)

Pseudonym	Sex	Age	Ethnicity	Job Title	Total Work Experience (Years)	Educational Attainment	Self-reported disability or difficulties with:
Mercedes	F	30–34	White	Administrative assistant	0–5	High school diploma	Blind
Kalam	F	40–44	Southeast Asian	Receptionist	16–20	College/trade certificate	Blind
Temma	F	40–44	White	File mail clerk	21–25	High school diploma	Cerebral palsy
Automotive							
Maria	F	35–39	Caribbean	Customer quality liaison	11–15	Bachelor's degree	Repetitive strain injury, cancer
Benjamin	M	25–29	White	Quality control technician	11–15	College/trade certificate	Sciatica
Juan	M	50–54	Caribbean	Super-utility assembly line	31+	No diploma	Asthma, plantar fasciitis
Ruth	F	30–34	White	Quality control supervisor	11–15	College/trade certificate	Environmental allergies
Tora	F	25–29	White	Supplier	0–5	College/trade certificate	Environmental allergies
Lewis	M	45–49	White	Incoming quality inspector	26–30	High school diploma	Herniated disk

Appendix 1

6. Manager Informant Interviews

6a. Managers from Secondary School Teachers Case Study

Pseudonym	Sex	Age	Ethnicity	Job Title
Abbas	M	55–59	African	Principal
Soren	M	45–49	White	Vice-principal
Guy	M	55–59	White	Principal
Florence	F	55–59	White	Union leader
Marc	M	55–59	White	Union leader

6b. Managers from Computer Programmers Case Study

Pseudonym	Sex	Age	Ethnicity	Job Title
Anjali	F	40–44	White	Manager
David	M	45–49	White	Manager
Ming	M	45–49	Southeast Asian	Manager

6c. Managers from Clerical Workers Case Study

Pseudonym	Sex	Age	Ethnicity	Job Title
Gwenevra	F	35–39	Non-white	Manager
Talma	F	35–39	Non-white	Principal, temporary agency
Jean	F	40–44	White	Manager, temporary agency
Margriet	F	30–35	Non-white	Manager, temporary agency branch
Finiola	F	50–55	White	Vice-president, human resources
Glynnis	F	50–55	White	Director, office worker retraining centre

6d. Managers from Disabled Workers Case Study

Pseudonym	Sex	Age	Ethnicity	Job Title
Deborah	F	45–49	White	Manager
Henry	M	50–54	White	Manager
Aileen	F	35–39	White	Manager
Patricia	F	45–49	Non-white	Manager
Ruth	F	30–34	White	Manager

APPENDIX 2

Economic Class and Specific Occupational Group, by Intentional Learning Activities, 2004

Table 1 Economic Class by University (and Total Post-secondary) Completion, Further Education, and Incidence of Job-Related Informal Learning, Employed Labour Force, Canada, 1998–2004 (%)

Economic class	University/(Total post-secondary) completion		Taken further education course in past year		Done job-related informal learning	
	1998	2004	1998	2004	1998	2004
Large employers	*	35(76)	*	67	*	87
Small employers	22 (36)	23(55)	52	46	87	88
Self-employed	16 (40)	22(56)	52	46	83	87
Managers	25 (66)	34(72)	72	68	96	92
Supervisors	10 (45)	14(56)	37	54	95	88
Professional employees	49 (73)	46(83)	76	67	88	92
Service workers	9 (31)	10(50)	54	52	83	84
Industrial workers	4 (23)	4(34)	37	41	83	84
All employees	18 (41)	21(56)	49	53	86	87
N	948	5365	945	5436	940	5428

Sources: NALL Survey, 1998; WALL Survey, 2004. * Large employers N in 1998 too small for reliable estimate.

Appendix 2

Table 2 *Employee Class and Specific Occupational Group, by University (and Total Post-secondary) Completion, Further Education, and Incidence of Job-Related Informal Learning, Non-managerial Employees, Ontario, 2004 (%)*

Class/Group	University/(Total post-secondary) completion	Taken further education course in past year	Done job-related informal learning	N
Employee class				
Professional employees	50 (85)	74	93	363
Service workers	15 (50)	55	83	554
Industrial workers	6 (37)	48	87	380
Occupational group				
Teachers	93 (96)	80	98	45
Computer programmers	56 (86)	70	87	60
Clerical workers	19 (54)	66	81	121
Auto workers	4 (26)	46	98	83
All employees	22 (55)	58	87	1283

Sources: EJRM Survey, 2004

Bibliography

Abercrombie, N., and Urry, J. *Capital, Labour and the Middle Classes*. London, UK: G. Allen & Unwin, 1983.

Abramovitz, M. "Resource and Output Trends in the United States Since 1870." *American Economic Review. Papers & Proceedings* 46.1 (1956): 5–23.

Acker, S. *The Realities of Teachers' Work: Never a Dull Moment*. London, UK: Cassell, 1999.

Adelman, P.B., and Vogel, S.A. "Issues in the Employment of Adults with Learning Disabilities." *Learning Disability Quarterly* 16 (1993): 219–32.

Adler, P.S., and Clark, K.B. "Behind the Learning Curve: A Sketch of the Learning Process." *Management Science* 37.3 (1991): 267–81.

Ahamad, B., and Blaug, M. *The Practice of Manpower Forecasting*. Amsterdam, NL: Elsevier, 1973.

Ainley, P. *Class and Skill: Changing Divisions of Knowledge and Labour*. New York, NY: Cassell, 1993.

Akyeampong, E.B. "Fact sheet on unionization." *Perspectives on Labor and Income* 47(7) (2003): 2–25.

Allen, J., and Weert, E. de. "What Do Educational Mismatches Tell Us About Skill Mismatches? A Cross-Country Analysis." *European Journal of Education* 42.1 (2007): 59–73.

Aneesh, A. "Skill Saturation: Rationalization and Post-Industrial Work." *Theory and Society* 30.3 (2001): 363–96.

Anxo, D. *Contribution to the EEO Autumn Review 2006 "Flexicurity."* Sweden. Brussels: European Employment Observatory, 2006. Accessed September 27, 2008, www.eu-employment-observatory.net/resources/reports/Sweden-FlexicurityAR06.pdf.

Anyon, J. "Social Class and the Hidden Curriculum of Work." *Journal of Education* 162 (1980): 67–92.

Archbald, D.A., and Porter, A.C. "Curriculum Control and Teachers' Perceptions of Autonomy and Satisfaction." *Educational Evaluation and Policy Analysis* 16.1 (1994): 21–39.

Archives of Ontario. The Evolution of Education in Ontario—Public School Boards, 2006. Accessed July 18, 2006, www.archives.gov.on.ca/english/exhibits/education/ legislation.htm.

Armstrong, P., and H. Armstrong. *The Double Ghetto: Canadian Women and Their Segregated Work*. Toronto: McClelland & Stewart, 1994.

Aronowitz, S. *False Promises: The Shaping of American Working Class Consciousness*. New York, NY: McGraw-Hill, 1973.

Arrow, K. "The Economic Implications of Learning by Doing." *Review of Economic Studies* 29 (1962): 155–73.

Ashford, S.J., and Black, J.S. "*Self-socialization: Individual Tactics to Facilitate Entry.*" Paper presented at the National Academy of Management Meetings, Las Vegas, NV, 1993.
Attewell, P. "The De-Skilling Controversy." *Work and Occupations* 14.3 (1987): 323–46.
Autor, D.H., Levy, F., and Murnane, R.J. "The Skill Content of Recent Technological Change: An Empirical Exploration." *Quarterly Journal of Economics* 118.4 (2003): 1279–333.
Axtell, R.C. "Skill Reconsidered: The Deskilling and Reskilling of Managers." *Work and Occupations* 16.1 (1989): 65–79.
Aydemir, A., and Skuterud, M. "Explaining the Deteriorating Entry Earnings of Canada's Immigration Cohorts: 1966–2000." *Canadian Journal of Economics* 38.2 (2005): 641–71.
Babson, S. (Ed.). *Lean Work: Empowerment and Exploitation in the Global Auto Industry*. Detroit, MI: Wayne State University Press, 1995.
Baldoz, R., Koeber, C., and Kraft, P. "Making Sense of Work in the Twenty-First Century." In R. Baldoz, C. Koeber and P. Kraft (Eds.), *The Critical Study of Work: Labor, Technology, and Global Production*. Philadelphia, PA: Temple University Press, 2001, 3–17.
Baldwin, M., and Schumacher, E.J. "A Note on Job Mobility Among Workers with Disabilities." *Industrial Relations* 41.3 (2004): 430–41.
Barnes, C., and Mercer, G. "Disability, Work and Welfare: Challenging the Social Exclusion of Disabled People." *Work, Employment and Society* 19.3 (2005): 527–45.
———, Mercer, G., and Shakespeare, T. *Exploring Disability: A Sociological Introduction*. Cambridge, UK: Polity Press, 2000.
Barsalou, L.W. "Perceptual Symbol Systems." *Behavioural & Brain Sciences* 22 (1999): 577–660.
Barton, P.E. *What Jobs Require: Literacy, Education and Training, 1940–2006*. Princeton, NJ: Educational Testing Service, 2000.
Becker, G. "Human Capital and the Economy." *Proceedings of the American Philosophical Society* 136.1 (1992): 85–92.
———. *Human Capital* (1st ed.). New York, NY: Columbia University Press for the National Bureau of Economic Research, 1964.
Bein, J. et al. "Teacher Locus of Control and Job Satisfaction." *Educational Research Quarterly* 14.3 (1990): 7–10.
Bell, D. *The Coming of Post-Industrial Society*. New York, NY: Basic Books, 1973.
———, Brown, K., Buddo, P., Gunderson, M., Rifkin, K., Stager, D., and Vaillancourt, F. *The Information Technology Labour Market: Issues and Options*. Ottawa, ON: Software Human Resource Council, 2002.
Bell, H.M. *Matching Youth and Jobs*. Washington, DC: American Council on Education, 1940.
Berg, I. *Education and Jobs: The Great Training Robbery*. New York, NY: Praeger, 1970.
———. *Education and Jobs: The Great Training Robbery* (reissue with a new introduction by the author). Clinton Corners, NY: Percheron Press, 2003.
———, and Freeman, M. *Managers and Work Reform: A Limited Engagement*. New York: Free Press. 1978.
Berle, A.A., and Means, G.C. *The Modern Corporation and Private Property*. New York, NY: Macmillan, 1933.

Bernstein, B. *Class, Codes and Control, Vol. 4: The Structuring of Pedagogic Discourse*. London, UK: Routledge, 1990.

———. *Pedagogy, Symbolic Control and Identity*. London, UK: Taylor & Francis, 1996.

Betcherman, G., Leckie, N., and McMullen, K. *Barriers to Employer-Sponsored Training in Canada*. Ottawa, ON: Canadian Policy Research Networks, 1998.

———, McMullen, K., and Davidman, K. *Training for the New Economy*. Ottawa ON: Canadian Policy Research Networks, 1998.

Billett, S. *Learning in the Workplace: Strategies for Effective Practice*. Sydney, AU: Allen & Unwin, 2001.

Blackburn, R., and Mann, M. *The Working Class in the Labour Market*. London, UK: Macmillan, 1979.

Blaug, M. "Where Are We Now in the Economics of Education?" Special Professorial Lecture. University of London Institute of Education, London, UK, 1983.

Bloom, M., and Grant, M. *Brain Gain: The Economic Benefits of Recognizing Learning and Learning Credentials in Canada*. The Conference Board of Canada, 2001.

Borghans, L., and de Grip, A. *The Overeducated Worker: The Economics of Skill Utilisation*. Cheltenham, UK: Edward Elgar, 2000.

Bourdieu, P. *Le Sens Pratique*. Paris, FR: Les Editions du Minuit, 1980.

———. *Distinction*. London, UK: Routledge, 1984.

———, and Passeron, J.C. *Reproduction in Education, Society and Culture*. [1970]. London, UK: Sage, 1977.

Bowles, S., and Gintis, H. *Schooling in Capitalist America: Educational Reform and the Contradictions of Economic Life*. New York, NY: Basic Books, 1976.

Bowman, M.J. "The Human Investment Revolution in Economic Thought." *Sociology of Education* 39.1 (1966): 111–37.

Braddock, D., and Bachelder, L. *The Glass Ceiling and Persons with Disabilities*. Washington, DC: U.S. Department of Labor, 1994.

Braverman, H. *Labor and Monopoly Capital*. [1974]. New York, NY: Monthly Review Press, 1998.

Breen, R. "Foundations of a Neo-Weberian Class Analysis." In E.O. Wright (Ed.), *Approaches to Class Analysis*. New York, NY: Cambridge University Press, 2005, 31–50.

———, and Luijkx, R. "Social Mobility in Europe Between 1970 and 2000." In R. Breen (Ed.), *Social Mobility in Europe*. Oxford, UK: Oxford University Press, 2004, 37–75.

Brenner, R. *Turbulence in the World Economy*. London, UK: Verso, 2000.

Briscoe, C. "Cognitive Frameworks and Teacher Practices: A Case Study of Teacher Learning and Change." *The Journal of Educational Thought* 28.3 (1997): 286–309.

Briscout, J.C. "Partnering with the 21st Century Workplace: Leveraging Workplace Ecology." *Work* 21 (2003): 45–56.

———, and Bentley, K.J. "Disability Status and Perceptions of Employability by Employers." *Social Work Research* 24.2 (2000): 87–95.

Brown, C., Reich, M., and Stern, D. *Skill and Security and Evolving Employment Systems: Observations from Case Studies*. Berkeley, CA: University of California, 1990.

Brown, G., and Pintaldi, F. "A Multidimensional Approach in the Measurement of Underemployment." Joint UNECE/ILO/EUROSTAT Seminar on the Quality of Work, Statistical Office of the European Communities Working Paper No. 15, 2005. Accessed June 10, 2007, www.unece.org/stats/documents/2005/05/labour/wp.15.e.ppt.

Bruner, J. *Toward a Theory of Instruction*. Cambridge, MA: Belknap Press, 1966.

Buchel, F., de Grip, A., and Mertens, A. (Eds.). *Overeducation in Europe: Current Issues in Theory and Policy*. Cheltenham, UK: Edward Elgar, 2003.

Burawoy, M. "Review of Beyond Contract: Work, Power and Trust Relations." *American Journal of Sociology* 82.1 (1976): 239–42.

———. *The Politics of Production*. London, UK: Verso, 1985.

Burke, R.J., Greenglass, E.R., and Schwarzer, R. "Predicting Teacher Burnout Over Time: Effects of Work Stress, Social Support, and Self-doubts on Burnout and Its Consequences." *Anxiety, Stress, and Coping: An International Journal* 9.3 (1996): 261–75.

Burnham, J. *The Managerial Revolution*. New York, NY: John Day, 1941.

Burris, B. *No Room at the Top: Underemployment and Alienation in the Corporation*. New York, NY: Praeger, 1983.

———. "Computerization of the Workplace." *Annual Review of Sociology* 24 (1998): 141–57.

Burris, V. "The Social and Political Consequences of Overeducation." *American Sociological Review* 48.4 (1983): 454–67.

Camping on Contingent Work. *What's Wrong With Temp Work? A Report on the Temp Industry in Massachusetts*. (Report). Boston, MA: 1998.

Campolieti, M. "The Correlates of Accommodations for Permanently Disabled Workers." *Industrial Relations* 43.3 (2004): 546–72.

Canadian Auto Workers (CKW-TCA). *Work Reorganization: Responding to Lean Production*. North York, ON: CAW Research and Communications Department, 1993.

Canadian Council on Social Development. "Persons with Disabilities on the Job." Disability Information Sheet, No. 8, 2002. Accessed January 8, 2005, www.ccsd.ca.

———. "Two Themes: Workplace Issues and Personal Security." Disability Information Sheet, No. 10, 2001. Accessed January 8, 2005, www.ccsd.ca.

———. "Workers with Disabilities and the Impact of Workplace Structures." Disability Information Sheet No. 16, 2004. Accessed January 20, 2006, www.ccsd.ca.

Canadian Human Rights Act. Section 15.2, R.S. 1985, c. H-6. Accessed July 15, 2006, www.canlii.org/ca/sta/h-6.

Capan, N., and Kuhn, D. "Logical Reasoning in the Supermarket: Adult Females' Use of a Proportional Reasoning Strategy in an Everyday Context." *Developmental Psychology* 15.4 (1979): 450–52.

Carchedi, G. *Problems in Class Analysis*. Boston, MA: Routledge & Kegan Paul, 1983.

Carnegie Commission on Higher Education. *College Graduates and Jobs, Adjusting to a New Labor Market Situation*. New York, NY: McGraw-Hill, 1973.

Carneiro, P., and Heckman, J. "Human Capital Policy." Institute for the Study of Labor (IZA) Discussion Paper No. 821, 2003. Accessed June 10, 2007, http://papers.ssrn.com/sol3/ papers.cfm?abstract_id=434544#.

Carnoy, M. *Segmented Labor Markets: A Review of the Theoretical and Empirical Literature and Its Implications for Educational Planning*. Paris, FR: International Institute of Educational Planning, 1977.

———, and Levin, H. *Schooling and Work in the Democratic State*. Stanford, CA: Stanford University Press, 1985.

Carter, B. "A Growing Divide: Marxist Class Analysis and the Labour Process." *Capital and Class* 55 (1995): 33–72.

Cavanagh, J., and Mander, J. (Eds.). *Alternatives to Economic Globalization: A Better World Is Possible* (2nd ed.). San Francisco, CA: Berrett-Koehler Publishers, 2004.

Center for Workforce Development. *The Teaching Firm: Where Productive Work and Learning Converge*. Newton, MA: Education Development Center. 1998.

Chen, L., Muthitaacharoen, A., and Frolick, M. "Investigating the Use of Role Play Training to Improve Communication Skills of IS Professionals: Some Empirical Evidence." *The Journal of Computer Information* 43.3 (2003): 67–74.

Chaykowski, R. P. *Non-Standard Work and Economic Vulnerability*. Ottawa, ON: Canadian Policy Research Networks, 2005.

Chickowski, E. "Is There Really an IT Labor Shortage?" *Baseline Magazine*, March 5, 2008.

Childs, R.A., Ross, M., and Jaciw, A.P. "Initial Teacher Certification Testing: Preservice Teachers' Experiences and Perceptions." *Canadian Journal of Education* 27.4 (2002): 455–76.

Church, K., Frazee, C., Panitch, M., and Luciani, T. *Doing disability at the bank: 2006 project's snapshot*. Toronto, ON: Ontario Institute for Studies in Education, University of Toronto, Centre for the Study of Education and Work (CSEW), The Work and Lifelong Research Network (WALL), 2006.

City of Toronto. *Labour Force Readiness Plan. IT Human Resources: Meeting the Challenges of Growth*. Toronto, ON: Toronto Economic Development, 2003. Accessed April 3, 2008, www.toronto.ca/business_publications/tlfrp/labour_force_IT_screen.pdf.

Clement, W., and Myles, J. *Relations of Ruling: Class and Gender in Postindustrial Societies*. Montreal: McGill-Queen's University Press, 1994.

Clogg, C. *Measuring Underemployment: Demographic Indicators for the United States*. New York, NY: Academic Press, 1979.

———. "Mismatch Between Occupation and Schooling: A Prevalence Measure, Recent Trends and Demographic Analysis." *Demography* 21.2 (1984): 235–57.

Coalition of Provincial Organizations of the Handicapped and the National Anti-poverty Organization. *Willing to Work Together*. Winnipeg, MB: 1991.

Coase, R.H. "The Nature of the Firm." *Economica* 4.16 (1937): 386–405.

Cochran-Smith, M. "Sometimes It's Not About the Money: Teaching and Heart." *Journal of Teacher Education* 54.5 (2003): 371–75.

———, and Lytle, S.L. "Relationship of Knowledge and Learning: Teacher Learning in Community." *Review of Research in Education* 24, (1999): 249–305.

———. "Constructing Outcomes in Teacher Education: Policy, Practice and Pitfalls." *Education Policy Analysis Archives* 9.11 (2001): 36–7.

Cockburn, C. *Machinery of Dominance: Women, Men and Technological Know-How.* London, UK: Pluto Press, 1985.

Coffield, F. *The Necessity of Informal Learning.* Bristol, UK: Policy Press, 2000.

Cohen, S.S., and Zysman, J. *Manufacturing Matters: The Myth of the Post-Industrial Economy.* New York, NY: Basic Books, 1987.

Colella, A. "Organizational Socialization of Employees with Disabilities: Critical Issues and Implications for Workplace Interventions." *Journal of Occupational Rehabilitation* 4.2 (1994): 87–106.

———. "The Organizational Socialization of Employees with Disabilities: Theory and Research." In G.R. Ferris (Ed.), *Research in Personnel and Human Resources Management* (Vol. 14). Greenwich, CT: JAI Press, 1996, 351–417.

———, and DeNisi, A.S. "The Impact of Ratee's Disability on Performance Judgments and Choice as Partner: The Role of Disability-Job Fit Stereotypes and Interdependence of Rewards." *Journal of Applied Psychology* 83.1 (1998): 102–11.

———, and Varma, A. "Disability-Job Fit Stereotypes and the Evaluation of Persons with Disabilities at Work." *Journal of Occupational Rehabilitation* 9.2 (1999): 79–95.

———, DeNisi, A.S., Varma, A., and Lund, M. "Evaluations and Personnel Decisions Regarding Persons with Disabilities: The Role of Stereotypical Fit." Paper presented at the National Academy of Management Meetings, Dallas, TX, 1994.

Colley, S., Hodkinson, P., and Malcom, J. *Informality and Formality in Learning.* London, UK: Learning and Skills Research Centre, 2003.

Collins, R. *The Credential Society: An Historical Sociology of Education and Stratification.* New York, NY: Academic Press, 1979.

Conn, R. "Developing Software Engineers at the C-130J Software Factory." *IEEE Software* 19.5 (2002): 25–9.

Connell, R.W. *Teachers' Work.* Sydney, AU: George Allen & Unwin, 1985.

Cooley, C. *Human Nature and the Social Order.* New York: Charles Scribner. 1902.

Corak, M.R. *Are the Kids All Right?: Intergenerational Mobility and Child Well-Being in Canada.* Ottawa, ON: Analytical Studies Branch, Statistics Canada, 2001.

Cortese, C.G. "Learning Through Teaching." *Management Learning* 36.1 (2005): 87–115.

Couger, J.D., Davis, G., Dologite, D., Feinstein, D., Gorgone, J., Jenkins, A.M., Kasper, G., Little, J., Longenecker, H, and Valacich, J. "IS '95: Guideline for Undergraduate IS Curriculum." *MIS Quarterly* 19.3 (1995): 341–59.

Crompton, S. "I Still Feel Overqualified for My Job." *Canadian Social Trends* 67 (Winter) (2002): 23–6.

Curtis, B., Livingstone, D.W., and Smaller, H. (1992). *Stacking the Deck: The Streaming of Working Class Kids in Ontario Schools.* Toronto, ON: Our Schools/Our Selves, 1992.

Czajka, J.M., and DeNisi, A.S. "Effects of Emotional Disability and Clear Performance Standards on Performance Ratings." *Academy of Management Journal* 31 (1988): 394–404.

Cziko, G., and Zhao, Y. "Teacher Adoption of Technology: A Perceptual Control Theory Perspective." *Journal of Technology and Teacher Education* 9.2 (2001): 67–88.

Darling-Hammond, L. "Teacher Quality and Student Achievement: A Review of State Policy Evidence." *Education Policy Analysis Archives*, 8.1 (1999). Accessed September 27, 2008, http://epaa.asu.edu/epaa/v8n1/.

Darrah, C. *Learning and Work: An Exploration in Industrial Ethnography*. London, UK: Garland, 1996.

———. "Workplace Skills in Context." *Human Organization* 51.3 (1992): 264–73.

Darwin, C. *On the Origin of Species*. London, UK: John Murray, 1859.

———, and Wallace, A.R. "On the Tendency of Species to Form Varieties; and On the Perpetuation of Varieties and Species by Natural Means of Selection." *Journal of the Linnean Society of London* 3 (1858): 45–62.

Day, C. *The Life and Work of Teachers: International Perspectives in Changing Times*. New York, NY: Falmer Press, 2000.

de Jong, G.F., and Madamba, A.B. "A Double Disadvantage? Minority Group, Immigrant Status, and Underemployment in the United States." *Social Science Quarterly* 82.1 (2001): 117–30.

de Witte, M., and Steijn, B. "Automation, Job Content, and Underemployment." *Work, Employment and Society* 14.2 (2000): 245–64.

de Wolff, A., and Associates. *National Occupation Classification: Review of Office Support Occupations*. Toronto, ON: Report to Human Resources and Skills Development Canada, 2005.

———. *Job Loss and Entry Level Information Workers*. Toronto, ON: Report of the Metro Toronto Clerical Workers Labour Adjustment Committee, 1995.

———, and Bird, P. *Occupational Analysis: Clerical Occupations in Metropolitan Toronto* (Report). Toronto, ON: Clerical Workers Centre, 1997.

Dei, G., Karumanchery, L.L., and Karumancher-Luik, N. *Playing the Race Card: Exposing White Power and Privilege*. New York, NY: Peter Lang, 2004.

———, and Kempf, A. (Eds.). *Anti-Colonialism and Education: The Politics of Resistance*. Rotterdam, NL: Sense, 2006.

Denison, E.F. "Measuring the Contribution of Education (and the Residual) to Economic Growth." In *OECD Study Group, The Residual Factor and Economic Growth*. Paris, FR: OECD, 1964, 13–55.

Derber, C. "Underemployment and the American Dream—'Underemployment Consciousness' and Radicalism Among Young Workers." *Sociological Inquiry* 49.4 (1979): 37–44.

———. "Unemployment and the Entitled Worker." *Social Problems* 26.1 (1978): 26–37.

———, Schwartz, W., and Magrass, Y. *Power in the Highest Degree: Professionals and the Rise of a New Mandarin Order*. New York, NY: Oxford University Press, 1990.

Descartes, R. *Discours de la Méthode* [1637]. G. Rodis-Lewis (Ed.). Paris, FR: Flammarion, 1966.

Devereaux, M. *One in Every Five: A Survey of Adult Education in Canada*. Ottawa, ON: Statistics Canada and the Department of the Secretary of State, 1985.

Dewey, J. *The Influence of Darwin on Philosophy*. New York, NY: Holt, 1910.
———. *Democracy and Education*. London, UK: Macmillan, 1916.
Diamond, D., and Bedrosion, H. *Hiring Standards and Performance*. Manpower Research Monograph No. 18. Washington, DC: U.S. Department of Labor, U.S. Government Printing Office, 1970.
Doeringer, P.B., and Piore, M.J. *Internal Labour Markets and Manpower Analysis*. Lexington, MA: D.C. Heath and Company, Lexington Books, 1971.
Dolton, P., and Vignoles A. "The Incidence and Effects of Overeducation in the U.K. Graduate Labour Market." *Economics of Education Review* 19 (2000): 179–98.
Domar, E. *Essays in the Theory of Economic Growth*. New York, NY: Oxford University Press, 1957.
Dominion Bureau of Statistics (DBS). *Participants in Further Education in Canada*. Ottawa, ON: Dominion Bureau of Statistics, 1963.
Dorus, S., Vallender, E.J., Evans, D.E., Anderson, J.R., Gilbert, S.L., Mahowald, M., Wyckoff, G.J., Malcolm, C.M., and Lahn, B. "Accelerated Evolution of Nervous System Genes in the Origin of *Homo sapiens*." *Cell* 119.7 (2004): 1027–40.
Drucker, P. *Managing in a Time of Great Change*. New York, NY: Truman Talley Books/Dutton, 1995.
Dutton, J.M., and Thomas, A. "Treating Progress Functions as a Managerial Opportunity." *Academy of Management Review* 9.2 (1984): 235–47.
Eckhaus, R.S. "Economic Criteria for Education and Training." *Review of Economics and Statistics* 46 (1964): 181–90.
Economic Council of Canada. *First Annual Review*. Ottawa, ON: Queen's Printer, 1964.
Educational Quality and Accountability Office (EQAO). Accessed September 27, 2008, www.eqao.com.
Educational Testing Service. "Ontario Teacher Qualifying Test: Registration Bulletin." Toronto, ON: Queen's Printer for Ontario, 2002.
Edwards, R. *Contested Terrain: The Transformation of the Workplace in the Twentieth Century*. New York, NY: Basic Books, 1979.
Eichler, M. "The Other Half (or More) of the Story: Unpaid Household and Care Work and Lifelong Learning." In N. Bascia, A. Cumming, A. Datnow, K. Leithwood, and D. Livingstone (Eds.), *International Handbook of Educational Policy, Part 2*. Bodmin, Cornwall, UK: Springer, 2005, 1023–42.
Einstein, A. *Out of My Later Years*. New York, NY: Philosophical Library, 1950.
Elias, P., McKnight, A., and Kinshott, G. *Redefining Skill: Revision of the Standard Occupational Classification (SOC2000)*. Skills Task Force Research Paper 19. Nottingham, UK: DEE Publications, 1999.
Elliott, J.R. "Class, Race, and Job Matching in Contemporary Urban Labor Markets." *Social Science Quarterly* 81.4 (2000): 1036–52.
Engestrom, Y., Miettinen, R., and Punamaki, R.L. (Eds.). *Perspectives on Activity Theory*. Cambridge, UK: Cambridge University Press, 1999.

———, Engestrom, R., and Kerosuo, H. "The Discursive Construction of Collaborative Care." *Applied Linguistics* 24.3 (2003): 286–315.

Erickson, G., Minnes Brandes, G., Mitchell, I., and Mitchell, J. "Collaborative Teacher Learning: Findings from Two Professional Development Projects." *Teaching and Teacher Education* 21.7 (2005): 787–98.

Erikson, R., and Goldthorpe, J.H. "Intergenerational Inequality: A Sociological Perspective." *Journal of Economic Perspectives* 16.3 (2002): 31–44.

Esping-Anderson, G. *The Three Worlds of Welfare Capitalism*. Cambridge, UK: Polity Press, 1990.

Eyerman, A. *Women in the Office*. Toronto, ON: Sumach Press, 2000.

Fairris, D., and Tohyama, H. "Productive Efficiency and the Lean Production System in Japan and the United States." *Economic and Industrial Democracy* 23.4 (2002): 529–54.

Feldman, D. "The Nature, Antecedents and Consequences of Underemployment." *Journal of Management* 22.3 (1996): 385–407.

Felstead, A., Gallie, D., and Green, F. *Work Skills in Britain 1986–2001*. Nottingham, UK: Department for Education and Skills, 2002.

———, Fuller, A., Unwin, L., Ashton, D., Butler, P., Lee, T., and Walters, S. "Exposing Learning at Work: Results from a Recent Survey." Paper presented to the Work, Employment and Society Conference, University of Manchester Institute of Science and Technology (UMIST), 1–3 September 2004.

Fields, R.D., and Stevens-Graham, B. "New Insights into Neuron-Glia Communication." *Science* 298 (2002): 556–62.

Fine, S.A. "The Use of the Dictionary of Occupational Titles as a Source of Estimates of Education and Training Requirements." *Journal of Human Resources* 3.3 (1968): 363–75.

Finnie, R. *Early Labour Market Outcomes of Recent Canadian University Graduates by Discipline: A Longitudinal, Cross-cohort Analysis*. Statistics Canada, Analytical Studies Research Paper Series No. 164. Ottawa, ON: Business and Labour Market Analysis Division, 2002.

Fleming, P., and Harley, B. "A Little Knowledge Is a Dangerous Thing: Getting Below the Surface of the Growth of 'Knowledge Work' in Australia." *Work, Employment and Society* 18.4 (2004): 725–47.

Fletcher, J.K. *Disappearing Acts: Gender, Power and Relational Practice at Work*. Cambridge, MA: MIT Press. 1999.

Florida, R. *The Rise of the Creative Class: And How It's Transforming Work, Leisure, Community and Everyday Life*. New York, NY: Basic Books, 2002.

Fox, T., Hindi, N., and Remington, W. "Students' Perceptions and Misconceptions of a Career in IS." *The Journal of Computer Information Systems* 42.1 (2001): 83–90.

Freeman, C., and Soete, L. *Work for All or Mass Unemployment: Computerised Technical Change into the 21st Century*. London, UK: Pinter Publishers, 1994.

Freeman, R. *The Overeducated American*. New York, NY: Academic Press, 1976.

Freire, P. *Pedagogy of the Oppressed*. New York, NY: Herder & Herder, 1974.

Frenette, M., and Morissette, R. *Will They Ever Converge? Earnings of Immigrant and*

Canadian-born Workers Over the Last Two Decades. Analytical Studies Branch Research Paper 215. Ottawa, ON: Statistics Canada, 2003.

Frenette, N. "The Overqualified Canadian Graduate: The Role of the Academic Program in the Incidence, Persistence, and Economic Returns to Overqualification." *Economics of Education Review* 23 (2004): 29–45.

Friedan, B. *The Feminine Mystique*. New York, NY: Norton, 1963.

Friedman, A. *Industry and Labour: Class Struggle at Work and Monopoly Capitalism*. London, UK: Macmillan, 1977.

Galarneau, D. "Earnings of Temporary Versus Permanent Employees." *Perspectives on Labour and Income* 6.1 (2005): 5–18.

Gallie, D. "Patterns of Skill Change: Upskilling, Deskilling or the Polarization of Skills?" *Work Employment and Society* 5.3 (1991): 319–51.

Gallivan, M.J. "Examining IT Professionals' Adaptation to Technological Change: The Influence of Gender and Personal Attributes." *ACM SIGMIS Database* 35.3 (2004): 28–49.

———. "Reskilling IS Professionals: Individual and Organizational Adaptation to Software Process Innovations." Proceedings of the 1995 ACM Special Interest Group on Computer Personnel Research, Nashville, TN, April 1995, 103–16.

Garnier, O. "La Théorie Néo-classique Face au Contrat de Travail : de la 'Main Invisible' à la 'Poignée de Main Invisible.'" (1984). In Salais, R., and Thévenot, L. (Eds.), *LeTravail : Marchés, Règles, Conventions*. INSEE. Paris, FR : 1986.

Gates, L.B. "The Role of the Supervisor in Successful Adjustment to Work with a Disabling Condition: Issues for Disability Policy and Practice." *Journal of Occupational Rehabilitation* 3.4 (1993): 179–90.

———. "Workplace Accommodation as a Social Process." *Journal of Occupational Rehabilitation* 10.1 (2000): 85–98.

———, Akabas, S.H., and Kantrowitz, W. "Supervisors' Role in Successful Job Maintenance: A Target for Rehabilitation Counselor Efforts." *Journal of Applied Rehabilitation Counseling* 27.3 (1996): 60–6.

———, Akabas, S.H., and Oran-Sabia, V. "Relationship Accommodations Involving the Work Group: Improving Work Prognosis for Persons with Mental Health Conditions." *Psychiatric Rehabilitation Journal* 21.3 (1998): 264–72.

Geijsel, F., and Meijers, F. "Identity Learning: The Core Process of Educational Change." *Educational Studies* 31.4 (2005): 419–43.

Gindin, S. *The Canadian Auto Workers: the Birth and Transformation of a Union*. Toronto, ON: James Lorimer & Company, 1995.

Gidney, R.D. *From Hope to Harris: The Reshaping of Ontario's Schools*. Toronto, ON: University of Toronto Press, 1999.

Glassford, L. "A Triumph of Politics Over Pedagogy? The Case of the Ontario Teacher Qualifying Test, 2000–2005." *Canadian Journal of Educational Administration and Policy* 45 (3 November 2005). Accessed April 3, 2008, www.umanitoba.ca/publications/cjeap/articles/glassford.html.

Goldthorpe, J.H. *On Sociology: Numbers, Narratives, and the Integration of Research and Theory.* Oxford, UK; New York, NY: Oxford University Press, 2000.

Green, D., and Worswick, C. "Earnings of Immigrant Men in Canada: The Roles of Labour Market Entry Effects and Returns to Foreign Experience." Research paper, *Strategic Research and Review.* Citizenship and Immigration Canada, 2002. Accessed April 3, 2008, www.econ.ubc.ca/green/chrfexp4.pdf.

Green, F. *Demanding Work: The Paradox of Job Quality in the Affluent Economy.* Princeton, NJ: Princeton University Press, 2006.

———, McIntosh, S., and Vignoles, A. *"Overeducation" and Skills — Clarifying the Concepts.* Discussion Paper No. 435. London, UK: Centre for Economic Performance, London School of Economics and Political Science, 1999.

———, McIntosh, S., and Vignoles, A. "The Utilization of Education and Skills: Evidence from Britain." *The Manchester School* 70.6 (2002): 792–811.

Greer, G. *The Female Eunuch.* London, UK: MacGibbon & Kee, 1970.

Groot, W., and van den Brink, H.M. "Overeducation in the Labour Market: A Meta-analysis." *Economics of Education Review* 19 (2000): 149–58.

Grugulis, I. "Putting Skills to Work: Learning and Employment at the Start of the Century." *Human Resource Management Journal* 13.2 (2003): 3–12.

Gunderson, M., Jacobs, L., and Vaillancourt, F. *The Information Technology (IT) Labour Market in Canada: Results from the National Survey of IT Occupations.* Ottawa, ON: Software Human Resource Council, 2005.

Gutek, B.A. "Review of Doing It: Women Working in Information Technology." *Gender, Work & Organization* 13.6 (2006): 621–23.

Habermas, J. *Legitimation Crisis.* (Trans. T. McCarthy). London, UK: Heinemann, 1976.

Hamper, B. *Rivethead: Tales from the Assembly Line.* New York, NY: Warner Books Inc., 1991.

Hampshire, S. *Thought and Action.* London, UK: Chatto & Windus, 1960.

Handel, M. "Trends in Direct Measures of Job Skill Requirements." Working Paper No. 301, Jerome Levy Economics Institute, 2000. Accessed September 27, 2008, www.levy.org/pubs/wp/301.pdf.

———. "Skills Mismatch in the Labour Market." *Annual Review of Sociology* 29 (2003): 135–65.

———. *Worker Skills and Job Requirements: Is There a Mismatch?* Washington, DC: Economic Policy Institute, 2005.

Harbison, F., and Myers, C. *Education, Manpower and Economic Growth.* New York, NY: McGraw Hill, 1964.

Harlan, S.L., and Robert, P.M. "The Social Construction of Disability in Organizations: Why Employers Resist Reasonable Accommodations." *Work and Occupations* 25.4 (1998): 397–435.

Harley, B. "The Myth of Empowerment." *Work, Employment & Society* 13.1 (1999): 41–66.

Harper, D. *Working Knowledge: Skill and Community in a Small Shop.* Chicago, IL: University of Chicago Press, 1987.

Harris, J. "Globalisation and the Technological Transformation of Capitalism." *Race & Class* 40.2/3 (1999): 21–35.

Harris, S. *The Market for College Graduates.* Cambridge, MA: Harvard University Press, 1949.

Harrod, Sir R.F. *Economic Dynamics.* London, UK: Macmillan, 1973.

Hartog, J. "Overeducation and Earnings: Where Are We, Where Should We Go?" *Economics of Education Review* 19 (2000): 131–47.

Hatch, T., Eiler, W.M., and Faigenbaum, D. "Expertise, Credibility, and Influence: How Teachers Can Influence Policy, Advance Research, and Improve Performance." *Teachers College Record* 107.5 (2005): 1004–35.

Hauser, R. "The Measurement of Labor Utilization." *Malayan Economic Review* 19 (1974): 1–17.

Head, J., and Hutton, J. *The Union Makes Us Strong: OSSTF/FEESO 1964–2004.* Toronto, ON: OSSTF, 2005.

Heckman, J.J., and Klenow, P.J. *Human Capital Policy.* Mimeo, Chicago, IL: University of Chicago, 1997.

Helsby, G. *Changing Teachers' Work: The Reform of Secondary Education.* Buckingham, UK: Open University Press, 1999.

Henry, F., and Ginzberg, E. *Who Gets the Work: A Test of Racial Discrimination in Employment.* Toronto, ON: The Urban Alliance on Race Relations and the Social Planning Council of Metropolitan Toronto, 1985.

Henson, K.D. and Rogers, J.K. "'WHY MARCIA YOU'VE CHANGED!': Male Clerical Temporary Workers Doing Masculinity in a Feminized Occupation." *Gender Society* 15(2): 218–38. 2001.

High, S. *Industrial Sunset: The Making of North America's Rust Belt, 1969–1984.* Toronto, ON: University of Toronto Press, 2003.

Hilton, M. "Information Technology Workers in the New Economy." *Monthly Labor Review* 124.6 (2001): 41–5.

Hitt, L., and Brynjolfsson, E. "Information Technology and Internal Firm Organization: An Exploratory Analysis." *Journal of Management Information Systems* 14.2 (1997): 81–101.

Hoddinott, S. (2004). "The Assessment of Workers' 'Basic Skills': A Critique Based on Evidence from the United States, Canada and England." In H. Rainbird, A. Fuller and A. Munro (Eds.), *Workplace Learning in Context.* London, UK: Routledge, 2004, 89–106.

Hodgson, G.M. (Ed.). *The Foundations of Evolutionary Economics 1890–1973* (2 vols.) Aldershot, UK: E. Elgar, 1998.

Hodkinson, P., and Hodkinson, H. "Rethinking the Concept of Communities of Practice in Relation to School Teachers' Workplace Learning." *International Journal of Training and Development* 8.1 (2004b): 21–31.

———, and Hodkinson, H. "The Significance of Individual's Dispositions in Workplace Learning: A Case Study of Two Teachers." *Journal of Education and Work* 17.2 (2004a): 167–82.

Holzer, H. *What Employers Want: Job Prospects for Less-educated Workers.* New York, NY: Russell Sage Foundation, 1996.

Horn, I.S. "Learning on the Job: A Situated Account of Teacher Learning in High School Mathematics Departments." *Cognition and Instruction* 23.2 (2005): 207–36.

Hosmer, D.W., and Lemeshow, S. *Applied Logistic Regression* (2nd ed.). New York, NY: John Wiley & Sons, 2000.

Human Resources and Social Development Canada (HRDC/HRSDC). About NOC (National Occupation Classification). Hull, PQ, 1992, 2001, 2006. Accessed September 27, 2008, www5.hrsdc.gc.ca/NOC-CNP/app/AboutNOC.aspx?lc=e.

———. Participation and activity limitation survey: Employment. Hull, PQ, 2006. Retrieved August, 15, 2009, from www.statcan.gc.ca/ daily-quotidien/080724/dq080724a-ebg,gtm.

Human Resources Development Canada (HDRC). National Occupational Classification, NOC. Hull, PQ, 2006. Retrieved June 15, 2006, from www23.hrdc-drhc.gc.ca.

———. Advancing the inclusion of people with disabilities: A government of Canada report. Hull, PQ, 2004. Retrieved January, 10, 2005, from www.hrdc-drhc.gc.ca/hrib/sdd-dds/odi/menu/home.shtml.

Hurst, A. "The Dearing Report and Students with Disabilities and Learning Difficulties." *Disability & Society* 14.1 (1999): 65–83.

Huws, U. *The Making of a Cybertariat: Virtual Work in a Real World*. New York, NY: Monthly Review Press, 2003.

IBM. IBM Canada website. Accessed March 18, 2005, www.ibm.com/ca/.

Ilavarasan, P.V., and Sharma, A.K. "Is Software Work Routinized? Some Empirical Observations from Indian Software Industry." *Journal of Systems and Software* 66 (2003): 1–6.

Industry Canada. *Cars on the Brain: Canada's Automotive Industry 2007*. Ottawa, ON: Industry Canada, 2007.

Information and Communications Technology Council (ICTC). "The Canadian IT Labour Market Initiative: Labour Force Survey—December 2007." Accessed March 20, 2008, www.ictc-ctic.ca/en/Content.aspx?id=80.

Ingersoll, R.M. "Teacher Turnover and Teacher Shortages: An Organizational Analysis." *American Educational Research Journal* 38.3 (2001): 499–534.

———. *Who Controls Teachers' Work? Accountability, Power, and the Structure of Educational Organizations*. Cambridge, MA: Harvard University Press, 2003.

International Labour Office (ILO). "Resolution Concerning the Measurement of Underemployment and Inadequate Employment Situations (adopted by the Sixteenth International Conference of Labour Statisticians)." Geneva, CH: International Labour Office, October 1998. Accessed June 10, 2007, www-ilo-mirror.cornell.edu/public/english/bureau/stat/res/underemp.htm.

———. *Decent Working Time: New Trends, New Issues*. Geneva, SE: ILO, 2006.

International Monetary Fund (IMF). "The Globalization of Labor." In *World Economic Outlook, April 2007: Spillovers and Cycles in the Global Economy*. Washington, DC: International Monetary Fund, 2007, 161–92.

Jamieson, B. "State of the Teaching Profession 2006." *Professionally Speaking* September, (2006): 45–53.

Jaques, E. *The Measurement of Responsibility*. London, UK: Tavistock Press, 1956.

———. *A General Theory of Bureaucracy*. London, UK: Heinemann, 1976.

Jensen, L., and Slack, T. "Race, Ethnicity, and Underemployment in Nonmetropolitan America: A 30-Year Profile." *Rural Sociology* 67.2 (2002): 208–33.

———, and Slack, T. "Underemployment in America: Measurement and Evidence." *American Journal of Community Psychology* 32.1/2 (2003): 21–31.

Jevons, S. *The Theory of Political Economy*. [1870]. Harmondsworth, Middlesex, UK: Penguin Books, 1970.

Job Futures. Service Canada, 2007. Accessed September 27, 2008, www.jobfutures.ca/.

Jones, G.E. "Advancement Opportunity Issues for Persons with Disabilities." *Human Resource Management Review* 7.1 (1997): 55–76.

Kabat-Zinn, J. *Full Catastrophe Living: Using the Wisdom of Your Body and Mind to Face Stress, Pain and Illness*. New York, NY: Delacourt Press, 1990

Kahneman, D., Slovic, P., and Tversky, A. *Judgment Under Uncertainty: Heuristics and Biases*. New York, NY: Cambridge University Press, 1982.

———, and Tversky, A. "On the Reality of Cognitive Illusions" *Psychological Review* 103 (1986): 582–91.

———, and Tversky, A. *Choices, Values, Frames*. New York, NY: Cambridge University Press, 2000.

Kalleberg, A. "Linking Macro and Micro Levels: Bringing the Workers Back Into the Sociology of Work." *Social Forces* 67.3 (1989): 582–92.

———. "The Mismatched Worker: When People Don't Fit Their Jobs." *Academy of Management Perspectives* 22.1 (2008): 24–40.

Karmarker, U.R., and Buonomano, D.V. "Temporal Specificity of Perceptual Learning in an Auditory Discrimination Task." *Learning & Memory* 10 (2003): 141–47.

Katz, M. *Class, Bureaucracy and Schools*. New York, NY: Praeger, 1971.

———. *Multivariable Analysis: A Practical Guide for Clinicians* (2nd ed.). Cambridge, UK: Cambridge University Press, 2006.

Keep, C. "The Cultural Work of the Type-Writer Girl." *Victorian Studies* 40.3 (1997): 401–26.

Kerbo, H. "Review of the Classless Society." *Contemporary Sociology* 31.3 (2002): 267–68.

Keynes, J.M. *A General Theory of Employment, Interest and Money*. London, UK: Macmillan, 1936.

Kilmoski, R., and Donahue, L. "HR Strategies for Integrating Individuals with Disabilities into the Workplace." *Human Resource Management Review* 7.1 (1997): 109–38.

King, A. *Building the Ontario Education Advantage: Student Achievement*. Toronto, ON: Ontario Ministry of Education, 2003.

Kingston, P.W. *The Classless Society*. Stanford, CA: Stanford University Press, 2000.

Klein, N. *The Shock Doctrin: The Rise of Disaster Capitalism*. Toronto, ON: Knopf Canada, 2007.

Kleinman, D.L., and Vallas, S.P. "Sciences, Capitalism, and the Rise of the 'Knowledge Worker': The Changing Structure of Knowledge Production in the United States." *Theory and Society*, 30.4 (2001): 451–92.

Koffka, K. "Perceptions: An Introduction to the Gestalt-Theorie." *Psychological Bulletin* 19 (1922): 531–85.

Kolbasuk McGee, M. "IBM offers employees new 'learning accounts' and global training programs." *Information Week:*, July 26, 2007. Accessed March 9, 2009 from http://informationweek.com/news/global-cio/training/showArticle.jhtml?articleID=201201391.

Kraft, P. *Programmers and Managers: The Routinization of Computer Programming in the United States.* New York, NY: Springer-Verlag, 1977.

———, and Dubnoff, S. "Job Content, Fragmentation, and Control in Computer Software Work." *Industrial Relations* 25.2 (1986): 184–96.

Krahn, H., and Bowlby, J.W. *Education-Job Skills Match: An Analysis of the 1990 and 1995 National Graduates Surveys.* Applied Research Branch, Strategic Policy, Human Resources Development Canada and Centre for Education Statistics, Research Paper No. R-00-1-1E. Ottawa, ON: Statistics Canada, 1999.

Kumar, P., and Holmes, J. "Canada: Continuity and Change." In T. Kochan, R.D. Lansbury, J.P. MacDuffie (Eds.), *After Lean Production: Evolving Employment Practices in the World Auto Industry.* Ithaca, NY: Cornell University Press, 1997, 85–108.

Kusterer, K. *Know-How on the Job: The Important Working Knowledge of "Unskilled" Workers.* Boulder, CO: Westview Press, 1978.

Labaree, D. "Power, Knowledge, and the Rationalization of Teaching: A Genealogy of the Movement to Professionalize Teaching." *Harvard Educational Review* 62.2 (1992): 123–54.

Lamarck, J.P.B.A. *Philosophie Zoologique.* [1809]. Codicote, Herts, UK: H.R. Englemann and Wheldon & Wesley, Ltd., 1960.

Landsbergis, P.A., Cahill, J., and Schnall, P. "The Impact of Lean Production and Related New Systems of Work Organization on Worker Health." *Journal of Occupation Health and Psychology* 4 (1999): 108–30.

Lapointe, M., Dunn, K., Tremblay-Côté, N., Bergeron, L.-P., and Ignaczak, L. *Looking Ahead: A 10-Year Outlook for the Canadian Labour Market (2006–2015).* Ottawa, ON: Human Resources and Social Development Canada, 2006.

Lareau, A. *Home Advantage: Social Class and Parental Intervention in Elementary Education.* New York, NY: Falmer Press, 1989.

———. "Invisible Inequality: Social Class and Childrearing in Black Families and White Families." *American Sociological Review* 67.5 (2002): 747–76.

Lave, J. *Cognition in Practice.* New York, NY: Cambridge University Press, 1988.

Lavoie, M., and Roy, R. *Employment in the Knowledge-Based Economy: A Growth Accounting Exercise for Canada.* Research Paper No. R-98-8E. Ottawa, ON: Applied Research Branch, Human Resources Development Canada, 1998.

Le Bas, C., and Mercier, C. *Le Savoir-faire et l'Innovation : Une Problématique du Système Industriel, Formation-Emploi.* La Documentation Française, Paris, FR : 1988.

Leckie, N. *On Skill Requirements Trends in Canada, 1971–1991.* Ottawa, ON: Canadian Policy Research Networks, 1996.

Lee, D. "Information Seeking and Knowledge Acquisition Behaviors of Young Information Systems Workers: Preliminary Analysis." Proceedings of 5th Americas Conference on Information Systems, Milwaukee, WI. August 13–15, 1999, 856–58.

———, Trauth, E., and Farwell, D. "Critical Skills and Knowledge Requirements of IS Professionals: A Joint Academic/Industry Investigation." *MIS Quarterly* 19.3 (1995): 313.

Lee, S., Koh, S., Yen, D., and Tang, H. "Perception Gaps Between IS Academics and IS Practitioners: An Exploratory Study." *Information & Management* 40.1 (2002): 51–61.

Lee, Y-J., and Roth, W-M. "The (Unlikely) Trajectory of Learning in a Salmon Hatchery." *Journal of Workplace Learning* 17.4 (2005): 243–54.

Leontaridi, M.R. "Segmented Labour Markets: Theory and Evidence." *Journal of Economic Surveys* 12.1 (1998): 63–101.

Leslie, D., and Butz, D. "'GM Suicide': Flexibility, Space, and the Injured Body." *Economic Geography* 74.4 (1998): 360–78.

Levin, B. "Remarks by the Deputy Minister of Education to the Ministry of Education/Faculties of Education Forum 2006." OISE, University of Toronto, 16 May 2006.

Lewchuk, W., Roberts, B., and MacDonald, C. *The CAW Working Conditions Study: Benchmarking Auto Assembly Plants*. Willowdale, ON: CAW Canada, 1996.

Li, C., Gervais, G., and Duval, A. "The Dynamics of Overqualification: Canada's Underemployed University Graduates." Analytical Paper. Statistics Canada, 2006, 1–18.

Lieberman, A. *Teachers—Transforming Their World and Their Work*. New York, NY: Teachers' College Press, 1999.

Lindbeck, A., and Snower, D. "Multi-task Learning and the Reorganisation of Work: from Tayloristic to Holistic Organisation." *Journal of Labour Economics* 18.3 (2000): 353–76.

Linhart, D. *L'Appel de la Sirène*. Paris, FR : Le Sycomore, 1981.

Littler, C.R. (Ed.). *The Experience of Work*. London, UK: Gower, 1985.

Livingstone, D.W. "Job Skills and Schooling: A Class Analysis of Entry Requirements and Underemployment." *Canadian Journal of Education/Revue Canadienne de l'Education* 12.1 (1987): 1–30.

———. "Upgrading and Opportunities." In D.W. Livingstone (Ed.), *Critical Pedagogy and Cultural Power*. South Hadley, MA: Bergin and Garvey Publishers, Inc., 1987, 125–36.

———. *The Education-Jobs Gap: Underemployment or Economic Democracy*. Toronto, ON: Garamond Press, 1999a.

———. "Exploring the Icebergs of Adult Learning: Findings of the First Canadian Survey of Informal Learning Practices." *Canadian Journal for the Study of Adult Education* 13.2 (1999b): 49–72.

———. *Working and Learning in the Information Age: A Profile of Canadians*. CPRN Discussion Paper No. W16, Ottawa, ON: Canadian Policy Research Network, 2002.

———. "Introduction: Mapping the Forest of Underemployment." In D.W. Livingstone, *The Education-Jobs Gap: Underemployment or Economic Democracy*. Aurora, ON: Garamond Press, 2004, xvii–xxxii.

———. "The Learning Society: Past, Present, Future." Jackson Memorial Lecture, Toronto, ON, 2004.

———. "The State of Workplace Learning in Canada: Findings of a 2004 National Survey." Presentation for Plenary Panel on State of the Industry: Workplace Learning and Performance. Canadian Society for Training and Development Knowledge Exchange, 2005.

———. "Informal Learning: Conceptual Distinctions and Preliminary Findings." In Z. Bekerman, N.C. Burbules, and D. Silberman-Keller (Eds.), *Learning in Places: The Informal Education Reader*. New York, NY: Peter Lang, 2006, 202–26.

———. "Re-exploring the Icebergs of Adult Learning: Comparative Findings of the 1998 and 2004 Canadian Surveys of Formal and Informal Learning Practices." *The Canadian Journal for the Study of Adult Education* 20.2 (2007): 1–24.

———, and Antonelli, F. "How Do Teachers Compare to Other Workers?" *Professionally Speaking*. March 2007. Accessed May 10, 2008, www.oct.ca/publications/professionally_speaking/march_2007/how_do_teachers_compare.asp.

———, and Antonelli, F. (forthcoming). "Professional Occupations, Class Structure, Workplace Control and Learning." In H. Smaller, F. Antonelli, R. Clark, D.W. Livingstone, K. Pollock, J. Strachan, and P. Tarc (Eds.), *Teachers' Work and Learning: Challenges for Professional Control*.

———, and Mangan, J.M. "Men's Employment Classes and Class Consciousness: An Empirical Comparison of Marxist and Weberian Class Distinctions." In D.W. Livingstone and J.M. Mangan (Eds.), *Recast Dreams: Class and Gender Consciousness in Steeltown*. Toronto, ON: Garamond Press, 1996, 15–51.

———, and Pollock, K. "No Room at the Top: Gender Limits to the 'Managerial Revolution,'" WALL Working Paper, 2005. Available at www.wallnetwork.ca.

———, and Raykov, M. "Workers' Power and Intentional Learning: A 2004 Benchmark Survey." *Relations Industrielles/Industrial Relations* 63.1 (2008): 30–54.

———, and Sawchuk, P.H. *Hidden Knowledge: Organized Labour in the Information Age*. Aurora, ON: Garamond Press, 2004.

———, and Scholtz, A. "Contradictions of Labour Processes and Workers' Use of Skills in Advanced Capitalist Economies." In W. Clement and V. Shalla (Eds.), *Work in Tumultuous Times: Critical Perspectives*. Montreal: McGill-Queen's University Press, 2006, 131–62.

———, and Scholtz, A. *Work and Lifelong Learning in Canada: Basic Findings of the 2004 WALL Survey*. Toronto, ON: CSEW, Ontario Institute for Studies in Education, 2006.

———, and Stowe, S. "Class Mobility and University Education: The Inter-generational Talent Gap in Canada." In A. Scott and J. Freeman-Moir (Eds.), *The Lost Dream of Equality: Critical Essays on Education and Social Class*. Rotterdam, NL: Sense Publishers, 2007, 29–46.

———, and Stowe, S. "Work Time and Learning Activities of the Continuously Employed: A Longitudinal Analysis, 1998–2004." *Journal of Workplace Learning* 19.1 (2007): 17–31.

———, Hart, D., and Davie, L.E. "Public Attitudes Toward Education in Ontario: The 14th OISE/UT Survey." Toronto, ON: OISE, University of Toronto, 2003.

Loasby, B.J. "Cognition, Imagination and Institutions in Demand Creation." *Journal of Evolutionary Economics* 11 (2001): 7–21.

Locke, J. *An Essay Concerning the True, Original, Extent and End of Civil Government.* [1690]. Reprinted in *The Social Contract: Essays by Locke, Hume and Rousseau.* London, UK: Oxford University Press, 1947.

Lorenz, K. *Trois Essais sur le Comportement Animal et Humain.* Paris, FR : Editions du Seuil, 1970.

Lowe, G. *Women in the Administrative Revolution.* Toronto, ON: University of Toronto Press, 1987.

Lucas, R. "On the mechanics of economic development." *Journal of Monetary Economics* 22, (1988): 3–42.

Ma, X., and Macmillan, R.B. "Influences of Workplace Conditions on Teachers' Job Satisfaction." *The Journal of Educational Research* 93.1 (1999): 109–17.

Maas, I., and van Leeuwen, M.H.D. "Intergenerational Mobility in Sweden." *Acta Sociologica* 45.3 (2002): 179–94.

Machlup, F. *The Production and Distribution of Knowledge in the United States.* Princeton, NJ: Princeton University Press, 1962.

———. *Knowledge, Its Creation, Distribution and Economic Significance.* Princeton: Princeton University Press, 1980.

Maguire, E.A., Gadian, D.G., Johnsrude, I.S., Good, C.D., Ashburner, J., Frackowiak, R.S.J., and Frith, C.D. "Navigation-Related Structural Change in the Hippocampi of Taxi Drivers." *Proceedings of the National Academy of Sciences of the United States of America* 97.8 (2000): 4398–403.

Manpower and Immigration. *Canadian Classification and Dictionary of Occupations (CCDO).* Vol. 1 and 2. Ottawa, ON: Manpower and Immigration, 1971.

Manpower Report of the President. Washington, DC: Government Printing Office, 1967.

Maroy, C., and Doray, P. "Education-Work Relations: Theoretical Reference Points for a Research Domain." *Work, Employment & Society* 14.3 (2000): 173–89.

Marshall, A. *Principles of Economics* (8th ed.). London, UK: Macmillan, 1920.

Marshall, R., and Tucker, M. *Thinking for a Living: Education and the Wealth of Nations.* New York, NY: Basic Books, 1994.

Marx, K. *Capital* (Vol. 1). [1867]. New York, NY: International Publishers, 1967.

———. *Wages, Prices and Value Added.* Paris, FR: La Pleiade, 1865.

Mason, G. "Graduate Utilisation in British Industry: The Initial Impact of Mass Higher Education." *National Institute Economic Review* 156 (1996): 93–103.

Maynard, D.C., Joseph, T., and Maynard, A. "Underemployment, Job Attitudes and Turnover Intentions." *Journal of Organizational Behavior* 27.4 (2006): 509–36.

McGuiness, S. "Overeducation in the Labour Market." *Journal of Economic Surveys* 20.3 (2006): 387–418.

McIntyre, F. "Transition to Teaching Report 2007." *Professionally Speaking* (December 2007): 28–41.

McKinlay, B. *Characteristics of Jobs That Are Considered Common.* Columbus, OH: Center for Vocational Education, 1976.

McLean, E.R., Smits, S.J., and Tanner, J.R. "The Career Dynamics of Information Systems Professionals: A Longitudinal Study." *ACM SIGCPR Computer Personnel* 17.4 (1996): 3–26.

McMullen, J., Cooke, M. Downie, R. *Labour Force Ageing and Skill Shortages in Canada and Ontario*. Research Report W24. Ottawa, ON: Canadian Policy Research Networks, 2004.

Mead, M. *Culture and Commitment: A Study of the Generation Gap*. Garden City, NY: Natural History Press, 1970.

Medlin, D., Dave, D., and Vannoy, S. "Students' Views on the Importance of Technical and Non-technical Skills for Successful IT Professions." *The Journal of Computer Information* 42.1 (2001): 65–70.

Metz, M. "How Social Class Differences Shape Teachers' Work." In M. McLaughlin, J. Talbert, and N. Bascia (Eds.), *The Contexts of Teaching in Secondary Schools: Teachers' Realities*. New York, NY: Teachers College Press, 1990.

Mezirow, J. "Perspective Transformation." *Adult Education* 28 (1970): 100–10.

Miller, A.R., Treiman, D.J., Cain, P.S., and Roos, P. (Eds.). *Work, Jobs and Occupations. A Critical Review of the Dictionary of Occupational Titles*. Washington, DC: National Academy Press, 1980.

Mincer, J. "The Distribution of Labor Incomes: A Survey with Special Reference to the Human Capital Approach." *The Journal of Economic Literature* 8.1 (1970): 1–26.

Mincer, J. *Schooling, Experience and Earnings*. New York, NY: National Bureau of Economic Research, 1974.

Moore, A. "Teaching, School Management and the Ideology of Pragmatism." *International Studies in Sociology of Education* 15.3 (2005): 195–212.

Morley, L. "Producing New Workers: Quality, Equality and Employability in Higher Education." *Quality in Higher Education* 7.2 (2001): 131–8.

Murphy, J.B. *The Moral Economy of Labour: Aristotelian Themes in Economic Theory*. New Haven, CT: Yale University Press, 1993.

Murphy, S.A. *What To Do Before the Well Runs Dry: Managing Scarce Skills*. Report 285-00. Ottawa, ON: Conference Board of Canada, 2000.

Myles, J., and Fawcett, G. *Job Skills and the Service Economy*. Working Paper No. 4. Ottawa: Economic Council of Canada, 1990.

———, and Turegun, A. "Comparative Studies in Class Structure." *Annual Review of Sociology* 20 (1994): 103–24.

National Advisory Commission on Civil Disorders. *Report of the National Advisory Commission on Civil Disorders*. New York, NY: Bantam Books, 1968.

National Center on Education and the Economy. *Tough Choices, Tough Times: The Report of the New Commission on the Skills of the American Workforce: Executive Summary*. Washington, DC: National Center on Education and the Economy, 2007.

National Institute of Disability Management and Research, NIDMAR. *Code of Practice for Disability Management: Describing Effective Benchmarks for the Creation of Workplace-based Disability Management Programs*. Port Alberni, BC, 2000.

National Research Council. *The Changing Nature of Work: Implications for Occupational Analysis*. Washington, DC: National Academy Press, 1999.

Neilson, D. "Formal and Real Subordination and the Contemporary Proletariat: Re-coupling Marxist Class Theory and Labour-Process Analysis." *Capital and Class* 91 (2007): 89–123.

Nelson, R.R., and Winter, S.G. *An Evolutionary Theory of Economic Change*. Harvard, MA: Harvard University Press, 1982.

Nisbett, R., and Wilson, T. "Telling More Than We Can Know: Verbal Reports on Mental Processes." *Psychological Review* 84 (1977): 231–59.

Noll, C.L., and Wilkins, M. "Critical Skills of IS Professionals: A Model for Curriculum Development." *Journal of Information Technology Education* 1.3 (2002): 140–54.

Nyhan, B. *Developing People's Ability to Learn: A European Perspective on Self-Learning Competency and Technological Change*. Brussels, Belgium: European Interuniversity Press, 1991.

O'Connor, B.C. "A Successful Pathway for All Students: Final Report of the At Risk Working Group." Toronto, ON: Ontario Ministry of Education, 2003.

Ontarians with Disabilities Act, 2001. Bill 125, Chapter 32. Statutes of Ontario, 2001. Accessed August 11, 2006, http://sph-planning-consulting.ca/documents/ODA%202001.pdf.

Ontario College of Teachers. "State of the Teaching Profession 2005 Annual Survey." Toronto, ON: Ontario College of Teachers and COMPAS Inc., 2005.

———. "The Standards of Practice of the Teaching Profession." 2006a. Accessed July 20, 2006, www.oct.ca.

———. "The Ethical Standards for the Teaching Profession." 2006b. Accessed July 20, 2006, www.oct.ca.

———. *Standards of Practice for the Teaching Profession*. Toronto, ON: Ontario College of Teachers, 1997.

Ontario Ministry of Education. *Ontario College of Teachers Act*. Toronto, ON: Queen's Printer, 1997.

———. "Teacher Graduates to be Tested." News Release, Accessed March 14, 2001, www.edu.gov.on.ca.

———. *Creating an Education Partnership*. Toronto, ON: Queen's Printer, 2004a.

———. *Teacher Excellence—Unlocking Student Potential Through Continuing Professional Development*. Toronto, ON: Queen's Printer, 2004b.

———. Education Act. Toronto, ON: Queen's Printer, 2005a, 2008.

———. *Early School Leavers: Understanding the Lived Reality of Student Disengagement from Secondary School*. Toronto, ON: Queen's Printer, 2005b.

———. Education Act. Toronto: Queen's Printer, 2008.

Ontario Public Service Employees Union (OPSEU/SEFPO). *Table Talk*. June 1, 2004. Toronto, ON: Ontario Public Service Employees Union, 2004.

Ontario Secondary School Teachers' Federation. *Executive Report*, No. 4. Toronto, ON: District 12 OSSTF, 2007.

Oppenheimer, M. "The Proletarianization of the Professional." *Sociological Review Monograph* 20 (1973): 213–27.

Organisation for Economic Co-operation and Development (OCED). *The Residual Factor and Economic Growth.* Paris, FR: OECD, 1964.

———. *Selection and Certification in Education and Employment.* Paris, FR: OECD, 1977.

———. *Lifelong Learning for All: Meeting of the Education Committee at Ministerial Level.* Paris, FR: OECD, 1996.

——— "Calls for Rethink of Governments' Opposition to School Systems, Teacher Recruitment." 2004. Accessed May 8, 2008, www.oecd.org/document/43/0,3343,en_2649_34487_30385387_1_1_1_1,00.html.

———/IEA. *Experience Curves for Energy Technology Policy.* Paris, FR: OECD, 2000.

O'Toole, J. *Work, Learning, and the American Future.* San Francisco, CA: Jossey-Bass, 1977.

Pankhurst, K.V. "Education and Employment: Overview of Research and Policy Issues." In T. Wallace, N. Murphy, G. Lépine, and D. Brown (Eds.), *Exploring New Directions in Essential Skills Research.* Ottawa, ON: Public Policy Forum, 2005, 22–40.

———, and Livingstone, D.W. "The Labour Process: Individual Learning, Work and Productivity." *Studies in Continuing Education* 28.1 (2006): 1–16.

Parnes, H. *Forecasting Educational Needs for Economic and Social Development.* Paris, FR: OECD, 1962.

———"Relation of Occupation to Educational Qualification." In H. Parnes (Ed.), *Planning Education for Economic and Social Development.* Paris, FR: OECD, 1963, 147–57.

Parsons, T. "The School Class as a Social System: Some of its Functions in American Society." *Harvard Educational Review* 29 (1959): 297–318.

Pavlov, J.P. "The Scientific Investigation of the Psychical Faculties or Processes in the Higher Animals." *The Lancet* 168.4336 (1906): 911–5.

Payne, N. "Job Accommodations: What Works and Why." In P.J. Gerber and D.S. Brown (Eds.), *Learning Disabilities and Employment,* Austin, TX: Pro-ed, 1995, 255–73.

Pazy, A. "Cognitive Schemata of Professional Obsolescence." *Human Relations* 47.10 (1994): 1167–99.

Peat Marwick Stevenson and Kellogg. *Software and National Competitiveness.* Ottawa, ON: HRDC, 1992.

Pentland, B. "Bleeding Edge Epistemology: Practical Problem Solving in Software Support Hotlines." In S. Barley, and J. Orr (Eds.), *Between Craft and Science: Technical Work in U.S. Settings.* Ithaca, NY: Cornell University Press, 1997.

People for Education. *About Us.* 2006. Accessed 14 July 2006, www.peopleforeducation.com/aboutus.

Perry, E., Simpson, P., NicDomhnaill, O., and Siegel, D. "Is There a Technology Age Gap? Associations Among Age, Skills and Employment Outcomes." *International Journal of Selection and Assessment* 11.2/3 (2003): 141–9.

Perry, E.L., Hendricks, W., and Broadbent, E. "An Exploration of Access and Treatment Discrimination and Job Satisfaction Among College Graduates With and Without Physical Disabilities." *Human Relations* 53.7 (2000): 923–55.

Piaget, J. *Psychologie et Pédagogie.* Paris, FR: Denoël, 1969.

Piore, M. "Labour Market Segmentation: To What Paradigm Does It Belong?" *American Economic Review* 73.2 (1983): 249–53.

Polanyi, M. *Personal Knowledge*. London, UK: Routledge & Kegan Paul, 1958.

———. *The Tacit Dimension*. Garden City, NY: Doubleday, 1966.

Popper, K. *The Logic of Scientific Discovery*. New York, NY: Basic Books, 1959.

———. *All Life is Problem Solving*. (1972). London, UK: Routledge, 1999.

Pratzner, F.C., and Stump, R.W. *Occupational Change and Transferable Skills: An Empirical Analysis*. Paris, FR: OECD, 1978.

Prescott, C.P. *Employment and Handicap*. London, UK: Social and Community Planning Research, 1990.

Pruijt, H. "Teams Between Neo-Taylorism and Anti-Taylorism." *Economic and Social Democracy* 21.1 (2003): 71–101.

Rabban, D.M. "Is Unionization Compatible with Professionalism?" *Industrial and Labor Relations Review* 45.1 (1991): 97–112.

Rainbow, H., Fuller, A., and Munro, A. (Eds.). *Workplace Learning in Context*. London, UK: Routledge, 2004.

Rajan, D., and Penafiel, T. *Job Integration for Persons with Disabilities from Ethnocultural Communities*. Final Report. Roeher Institute. Toronto, ON: York University, 2003.

Raykov, M. (2008). "Underemployment and Health-related Quality of Life." Unpublished doctoral dissertation. Toronto: Ontario Institute for Studies in Education, Centre for the Study of Education and Work, University of Toronto, 2008.

Reid, A. "Understanding Teachers' Work: Is There Still a Place for Labour Process Theory?" *British Journal of Sociology of Education* 24.5 (2003): 559–73.

Reich, R.K. *The Work of Nations: Preparing Ourselves for 21st-Century Capitalism*. New York, NY: Vintage Books, 1991.

Reitz, J. "Immigration Success in Canada, Part II: Understanding the Decline." *Journal of International Migration and Integration* 8.1 (2007): 87–62.

———. *Warmth of the Welcome*. Boulder, CO: Westview Press, 1998.

Richardson, J. "Teaching Teachers About Learning." *The Education Digest* 70.3 (2004): 49–50.

Rifkin, J. *The End of Work: The Decline of the Global Labor Force and the Dawn of the Post-Market Era*. New York, NY: Tarcher/Putnam, 1995.

Rifkin, K. *Case Study Results: Implications for IT Managers and HR Professionals*. Ottawa, ON: Software Human Resource Council, 2002.

Rigby, M., and Sanchis, M. "The Concept of Skill and Its Social Construction." *European Journal of Vocational Training* 37.1 (2006): 22–33.

Rikowski, G. "Education for Industry." *Journal of Education and Work* 14.1 (2001): 29–49.

Robinson, T. "IBM Discloses 15,000 Layoff." 2002. Accessed February 6, 2006, www.technewsworld.com/story/19014.html.

Romer, P. "Economic Growth and Investment in Children", *Daedalus* 123.4, (1994): 141–54.

Rose, M. "The Working Life of a Waitress." *Mind, Culture and Activity* 8.1 (2001): 3–27.

Rosen, S. "Learning by Experience as Joint Production." *Quarterly Journal of Economics* 86 (1972): 366–82.

Rosenberg, N. *Inside the Black Box: Technology and Economics*. Cambridge, UK: Cambridge University Press, 1982.

Roth, R. "Auto Workers: Lean Manufacturing and Rich Learning." In D.W. Livingstone and P. Sawchuk, *Hidden Knowledge: Organized Labour in the Information Age*. Toronto, ON: Garamond Press, 2003, 71–100.

Roulstone, A. *Enabling Technology Disabled People, Work and New Technology*. Buckingham, UK: Open University Press, 1998.

———. "Disabling Pasts, Enabling Futures? How Does the Changing Nature of Capitalism Impact on the Disabled Worker and Jobseeker?" *Disability & Society* 17.6 (2002): 627–42.

———. "Employment Barriers and Inclusive Futures?" In J. Swain, S. French, C. Barnes, and C. Thomas (Eds.), *Disabling Barriers—Enabling Environments*. London: Sage Publications, 2004, 195–200.

Rozanski, M. *Investing in Public Education: Advancing the Goal of Continuous Improvement in Student Learning and Achievement*. Toronto, ON: Queen's Printer, 2002.

Rumberger, R. "The Growing Imbalance Between Education and Work." *Phi Delata Kappan* 65 (1984): 342–46.

Runte, R. "The Impact of Centralized Examinations on Teacher Professionalism." *Canadian Journal of Education* 23.2 (1998): 166–81.

Ryle, G. *The Concept of Mind*. Chicago, IL: University of Chicago Press, 1949.

Sattinger, M. "Assignment Models of the Distribution of Earnings." *Journal of Economic Literature* 31 (1993): 831–80.

Sawchuk, P. "Theories and Methods for Research on Informal Learning and Work: Towards Cross-fertilization." *Studies in Continuing Education* 29.3 (2007): 295–312.

Sayer, P. "Workers Protest IBM 'Layoffs on Demand.'" 2005. Accessed April 3, 2008, www.infoworld.com/article/05/03/14/HNprotestibmlayoffs_1.html.

Schrag, P. "Schoolhouse Crock: Fifty Years of Blaming America's Education System for Our Stupidity." *Harper's Magazine* 315.1888 September (2007): 36–44.

Schranck, R. *Ten Thousand Working Days*. Cambridge, MA: MIT Press, 1978.

Schugurensky, D., and Mundel, K. "Volunteer Work and Learning: Hidden Dimensions of Labour Force Training." In N. Bascia, A. Cumming, A. Datnow, K. Leithwood, and D. Livingstone (Eds.), *International Handbook of Educational Policy, Part 2*. Bodmin, Cornwall, UK: Springer, 2005, 997–1022.

Schultz, T.W. "Capital Formation by Education." *Journal of Political Economy* 67.6 (1960): 571–83.

Schumann, M. "New Concepts of Production and Productivity." *Economic and Industrial Democracy* 19.2 (1998): 17–32.

Scott-Dixon, K. *Doing IT: Women Working in Information Technology*. Toronto, ON: Sumach Press, 2004.

Scribner, S. "Thinking in Action: Some Characteristics of Practical Intelligence." In R. Sternberg and R. Wagner (Eds.), *Practical Intelligence*. New York, NY: Cambridge University Press, 1986, 13–30.

Seccombe, W., and Livingstone, D.W. *'Down to Earth People': Beyond Class Reductionism and Post Modernism*. Toronto, ON: Garamond Press, 1999.

Seltzer, K., and Bentley, T. *The Creative Age: Knowledge and Skills for the New Economy*. London, UK: Demos, 1999.

Senge, P., Kleiner, A., Roberts, C., Ross, R., Roth, G., and Smith, B. *The Dance of Change: The Challenges of Sustaining Momentum in Learning Organizations*. New York, NY: Doubleday/Currency, 1999.

Service of Canada, Job Futures. "Secondary School Teachers (4141) at a Glance." 2006. Accessed August 1, 2006, www.jobfutures.ca/noc/4141.shtml.

Shaw, M. "Software Engineering Education: A Roadmap." In A. Finkelstein (Ed.), *The Future of Software Engineering*. New York, NY: ACM Press, 2000, 371–80.

Shaw, W.S., and Feuerstein, M. "Generating Workplace Accommodations: Lessons Learned from the Integrated Case Management Study." *Journal of Occupational Rehabilitation* 14.3 (2004): 207–16.

Sheak, R. "The Chronic Jobs' Problem in the United States: No End in Sight." *Free Inquiry in Creative Sociology* 22.1 (1994): 23–32.

Shields, J. "Flexible Work, Labour Market Polarization, and the Politics of Skills Training and Enhancement." In T. Dunk, S. McBride, and R.W. Nelsen (Eds.), *The Training Trap: Ideology, Training and the Labour Market*. Halifax, NS: Fernwood Publishing, 1996, 53–72.

Shiffrar, M., Li, X., and Lorenceau, J. "Motion Integration Across Differing Image Features." *Vision Research* 35 (1995): 2137–46.

Shiffrin, R.M. "Attention." In R.C. Atkinson, R.J. Herrnstein, G. Lindzey, and R.D. Luce (Eds.), *Stevens' Handbook of Experimental Psychology, Vol. 2: Learning and Cognition*. London, UK: Wiley, 1988.

——, and Schneider, W. "Controlled and Automatic Information Processing: II. Perceptual Learning, Automatic Attending, and a General Theory." *Psychological Review* 84 (1977): 127–90.

Sicherman, N. "Overeducation in the Labor Market" *Journal of Labour Economics* 9.2 (1991): 101–22.

Simon, B. *Studies in the History of Education* (Vols. 1–3). London: Lawrence & Wishart, 1974.

Simon, H.A. "A Formal Theory of the Employment Relationship." *Econometrica* 19.3 (1951): 293–305.

——. "Theories of Decision-Making in Economics and Behavioural Science." *American Economic Review* 49 (1959): 253–83.

——. *Administrative Behaviour*. New York, NY: Free Press, 1965.

——. *Models of Man*. New York, NY: Wiley, 1957.

Simpson, I.H. "The Sociology of Work: Where Have the Workers Gone?" *Social Forces* 67.3 (1989): 563–81.

Siskin, L. "Departments as Different Worlds: Subject Subcultures in Secondary Schools." *Educational Administration Quarterly* 27.2 (1991): 134–60.

Sjogren, D.C. *Occupationally Transferable Skills and Characteristics: Review of Literature and Research*. Columbus, OH: Center for Vocational Education, 1977.

Sloane, P. "Much Ado About Nothing? What Does the Over-education Literature Really Tell Us?" In F. Buchel, A. de Grip, and A. Mertens (Eds.), *Over-education in Europe*, Cheltenham, UK: Edward Elgar, 2004, 11–45.

Slonim, J., Scully, S., and McAllister, M. *Outlook on Enrollments in Computer Science in Canadian universities*. ICTC, 2008. Accessed March 9, 2009, www.ictc-ctic.ca/uploadedFiles/ Labour-Market_Intelligence/Outlook-on-enrollments.pdf.

Smaller, H., Clark, R., Hart, D., Livingstone, D., and Noormohammed, Z. *Teacher Learning, Informal and Formal: Results of a Canadian Teachers' Federation Survey*. NALL Working Paper 14. Toronto, ON: OISE/UT, 2000.

———, Hart D., Clark R., and Livingstone, D. *Informal/Formal Learning and Workload Among Ontario Secondary School Teachers*. NALL Working Paper 39. Toronto, ON: OISE/UT, 2001.

Smith, A. *An Inquiry into the Nature and Causes of the Wealth of Nations*. [1776]. E. Cannan (Ed.). (6th ed.). London, UK: Methuen, 1904.

———. *The Theory of Moral Sentiments*. [1759]. New York, NY: A.M. Kelly, 1966.

Smith, T.M., and Rowley, K.J. "Enhancing Commitment or Tightening Control: The Function of Teacher Professional Development in an Era of Accountability." *Educational Policy* 19.1 (2005): 126–54.

Smulyan, L. "Who Controls Teachers' Work: Power and Accountability in America's Schools: A Review." *Social Forces* 82.2 (2003): 845–47.

Solow, R.M. *Learning from "Learning by Doing": Lessons for Economic Growth*. Stanford, CA: Stanford University Press, 1997.

Somania, J. 1999 Introduction. In "Globalising Europe. Decent Work in the Information Economy. Report of the Director General." Sixth European Regional Meeting, ILO. Vol. 1, p. X. Geneva, SZ: 2000.

Spataro, S.E. "Diversity in Context: How Organizational Culture Shapes Reactions to Workers with Disabilities and Others Who Are Demographically Different." *Behavioural Sciences and the Law* 23 (2005): 21–38.

Spenner, K. "Deciphering Prometheus: Temporal Change in the Skill Level of Work." *American Sociological Review* 48.6 (1983): 824–37.

———. "The Upgrading and Downgrading of Occupations: Issues, Evidence, and Implications for Education." *Review of Educational Research* 55.2 (1985): 125–54.

———. "Skill: Meanings, Methods, and Measures." *Work and Occupations* 17.4 (1990): 399–421.

Staines, G., and Quinn, R. "American Workers Evaluate the Quality of Their Jobs." *Monthly Labor Review* 102.1 (1979): 3–12.

Stam, M., and Molleman, E. "Matching the Demand For and Supply of IT Professionals: Towards a Learning Organization." *International Journal of Manpower* 20.6 (1999): 375–87.

Statistics Canada and Council of Ministers of Education Canada. *Education Indicators in Canada: Report of the Pan-Canadian Education Indicators Program: 2005.* Ottawa/Toronto, ON: Statistics Canada, 2006.

———— and Organisation for Economic Co-operation and Development (OECD). "Learning a Living: First Results of the Adult Literacy and Life Skills Survey." Ottawa, ON; Paris, FR: Statistics Canada and OECD, 2005.

————. "General Social Survey: Cycle 4: Education and Work." [Computer file]. Ottawa, ON: Statistics Canada. [Producer]. Toronto, ON: University of Toronto Data Library [Distributor], 1989.

————. "General Social Survey: Cycle 9: Education, Work, and Retirement." [Computer file]. Ottawa, ON: Statistics Canada [Producer], Toronto, ON: University of Toronto Data Library [Distributor], 1994.

————. "General Social Survey: Cycle 14: Access To and Use of Information Communication Technology." [Computer file]. Ottawa, ON: Statistics Canada. [Producer]. Toronto, ON: University of Toronto Data Library [Distributor], 2000.

————. *A Report on Adult Education and Training in Canada: Learning a Living.* Ottawa, ON: Statistics Canada, 2001a.

————. *Adult Education Participation in North America: International Perspectives.* Ottawa, ON: Statistics Canada, 2001b.

————. *National Occupational Classification 2001.* Ottawa, ON: Ministry of Supply and Services, Statistics Canada, 2001c.

————. *The Labour Market at a Glance.* Minister of Industry. Catalogue No. 71-222-XIE. Ottawa, ON: Statistics Canada, Labour Statistics Division, 2004a.

————. *Women in Canada: Work Chapter Updates 2003.* Catalogue No. 89F0133XIE. Ottawa, ON: Ministry of Industry, 2004b. Accessed August 27, 2008, www.statcan.ca/english/freepub/89F0133XIE/89F0133XIE2003000.pdf.

————. *General Social Survey on Time Use: Overview of the Time Use of Canadians.* Ottawa, ON: Statistics Canada, 2005.

————. Labour Force Survey. [Computer file]. Ottawa, ON: Statistics Canada. [Producer]. Toronto, ON: University of Toronto Data Library [Distributor], 2006a.

————. *Women in Canada: A Gender-based Statistical Report* (5th ed.). Ottawa, ON: Minister of Industry, 2006b. Accessed September 27, 2008, www.statcan.ca/english/freepub/89-503-XIE/0010589-503-XIE.pdf.

————. Latest release from the Labour Force Survey. *The Daily* (May 9, 2008). Ottawa, ON: Statistics Canada, 2008. Accessed August 27, 2008, www.statcan.ca/english/Subjects/Labour/LFS/lfs.pdf.

Stein, M.A. "Labor Markets, Rationality, and Workers with Disabilities." *Berkeley Journal of Employment and Labor Law* 21.1 (2000): 314–34.

Steinberg, R.J. "Social Construction of Skill: Gender, Power, and Comparable Worth." *Work and Occupations* 17.4 (1990): 449–82.

Sternberg, R.J. *Practical Intelligence in Everyday Life*. New York, NY: Cambridge University Press, 2000.

Stiglitz, J. "The Theory of Screening, Education, and the Distribution of Income." *American Economic Review* 65 (1975): 283–300.

Stone, D.L., and Colella, A. "A Model of Factors Affecting the Treatment of Disabled Individuals in Organizations." *Academy of Management Review* 21 (1996): 352–401.

Stone, E.F., Stone, D.L., and Dipboye, R.L. "Stigmas in Organizations: Race, Handicaps, and Physical Unattractiveness." In A. Kelly (Ed.), *Issues, Theory, and Research in Industrial and Organizational Psychology*. New York, NY: Elsevier Science Publishers B.V., 2002, 385–457.

Stroobants, M. *Savoir-Faire et Compétences au Travail*. Bruxelles, BE: Editions de l'Université de Bruxelles, 1993.

Sturgeon, T., Van Biesebroeck, J., and Gereffi, G. "Value Chains, Networks and Clusters: Reframing the Global Automotive Industry." *Journal of Economic Geography* 8.3 (2008): 297–321.

Suchman, L.A. *Plans and Situated Actions: The Problem of Human-Machine Communication*. Cambridge, UK: Cambridge University Press, 1987.

Tåhlin, M. "Skill Change and Skill Matching in the Labor Market: A Cross-national Overview." EQALSOC Network. 2006a. Accessed June 10, 2007, www.equalsoc.org/9.

———. "Class clues." Manuscript. Swedish Institute for Social Research (SOFI), Stockholm: Stockholm University, 2006b.

Talbert, J.E., and McLaughlin, M.W. "Teacher Professionalism in Local School Contexts." *American Journal of Education* 102.2 (1994): 125–53.

Taylor, F.W. *Scientific Management*. [1911]. London, UK: Harper & Row, 1964.

Terborg, J.R. & Ilgen, D.R. "A Theoretical Approach to Sex Discrimination in Traditionally Masculine Occupations." *Organizational Behavior and Human Performance* 13 (1975) 352–76.

Terkel, S. *Working: People Talk About What They Do All Day and How They Feel About What They Do*. New York, NY: Pantheon Books, 1972.

Thibodeau, P. "IT Unemployment Hits 'Unprecedented' Level." *Computerworld* 37.38 (2003): 6.

Thomas, A.M. "Prior Learning Assessment: The Quiet Revolution." In A.L. Wilson, and E.R. Hayes, (Eds.), *Handbook of Adult and Continuing Education*. San Francisco, CA: Jossey-Bass, 2000, 508–22.

Thomas, L. *The Occupational Structure and Education*. Eaglewood Cliffs, NJ: Prentice Hall, 1956.

Thompson, P. *The Nature of Work: An Introduction to Debates on the Labour Process*. London, UK: Macmillan, 1989.

———. "Fantasy Island: A Labour Process Critique of the 'Age of Surveillance.'" *Surveillance and Society* 1.2 (2003): 138–51.

Thurow, L. *Generating Inequality*. New York, NY: Basic Books, 1975.

Tinker, T. "Spectres of Marx and Braverman in the Twilight of Postmodernist Labour Process Research." *Work, Employment and Society* 16.2 (2002): 251–81.

Tough, A.M. *The Adult's Learning Projects: A Fresh Approach to Theory and Practice in Adult Learning*. Research in Education Series No. 1. Toronto, ON: Institute for Studies in Education, 1971.

Tsai, H.P., Compeau, D., and Haggerty, N. "A Cognitive View of How IT Professionals Update Their Technical Skills." *SIGMIS '04*, April 22-24, 2004.

United States Employment Service. *Dictionary of Occupational Titles* (rev. 4th ed., vols. 1–2). Washington, DC: U.S. Department of Labor, Employment and Training Administration, U.S. Employment Service, 1991. (National Center for O*NET. *O*NET Database*. U.S. Department of Labor. Accessed September 27, 2008, http://online.onetcenter.org/.)

Usalcas, J. "Hours Polarization Revisited." *Perspectives on Labour and Income* 9.3 (2008): 5–15.

Vadasz, L.L. "Computing Professionals: Changing Needs for the 1990s: A Workshop Report." Washington, DC: National Academy Press, 1993.

Vaisey, S. "Education and its Discontents: Overqualification in America, 1972–2002." *Social Forces* 85.2 (2006): 835–64.

Vallas, S.P. "The Concept of Skill: A Critical Review." *Work & Occupations* 17.4 (1990): 379–98.

Varma, A. "An Investigation of the Impact of Subordinate Disability and Ingratiation on Performance Evaluations Using an LMX Framework: An Organizational Simulation and Field Study." Unpublished doctoral dissertation. Rutgers University, NJ: 1996.

———, Colella, A., and DeNisi, A. "Performance Evaluation of Individuals with Disabilities: The Role of Ingratiation." Paper presented at the Conference of the Society for Industrial and Organizational Psychology, San Diego, CA, 1996.

Veblen, T. *The Theory of the Leisure Class. An Economic Study in the Evolution of Institutions*. New York, NY: The Macmillan Company, 1899.

Verdugo, R., and N. Verdugo, 1989. "The Impact of Surplus Schooling on Earnings." *Journal of Human Resources* 24(4): 629–43.

Verhaest, D., and Omey, E. "Measuring the Incidence of Over- and Undereducation." *Quality and Quantity* 40 (2006): 783–803.

Verton, D. "Anything BUT IT." *Computerworld* 38.48 (2004): 41.

Vosko, F.L. "Precarious Employment and 'Lifelong Learning': Challenging the Paradigm of 'Employability Security.'" In D.W. Livingstone, K. Mirchandani, and P. Sawchuk (Eds.), *The Future of Lifelong Learning and Work*. Rotterdam, NL: Sense Publishers, 2008, 157–70.

Vygotsky, L. *Mind in Society: The Development of Higher Psychological Processes*. Cambridge: Harvard University Press, 1978.

———. *The Collected Works of L.S. Vygotsky*. (Vol 1). R.W. Rieber and A.S. Carton (Eds.). New York, NY: Plenum Press, 1987.

———. *The Collected Works of L.S. Vygotsky*. Vol. 4: *The History of the Development of the Higher Mental Functions*. R.W. Rieber (Ed.). New York, NY: Plenum Press, 1987.

Wald, S. "The Overqualification of Canadian Workers." Unpublished doctoral dissertation. Toronto: Centre for Industrial Relations and Human Resources, University of Toronto, 2004.

Waring, M. *If Women Counted: A New Feminist Economics*. San Francisco, CA: Harper and Row, 1988.

Weale, M. "A Critical Evaluation of Rate of Return Analysis." *Economic Journal* 103.418 (1993): 729–37.

Weber, M. *Economy and Society: An Outline of Interpretive Sociology*. [1928]. New York, NY: Bedminster Press, 1968.

Webster, J. *Shaping Women's Work: Gender, Employment and Information Technology*. London, UK and New York, NY: Longman, 1996.

Webster. *New World Dictionary*. D.B. Guralnik (Ed). New York, NY: World Publishing, 1972.

Weeden, K., and Grusky, D. "The Case for a New Class Map." *American Journal of Sociology* 111.1 (2005): 141–212.

Weir, E. "The Manufacturing Crisis." Ottawa, ON: Social and Economic Policy Department, Canadian Labour Congress, 2007. Accessed September 27, 2007, http://canadianlabour.ca/updir/03-27-07ManufacturingCrisisNote.pdf.

Wershler-Henry, D. *The Iron Whim: A Fragmented History of Typewriting*. Toronto, ON: McClelland & Stewart, 2005.

Wertheimer, M. "Experimentelle Studien uber des Sehen von Bewegung." *Zeitschrift fur Psychologie* 61 (1912): 161–265.

Westheimer, J. *Among School Teachers: Community, Autonomy and Ideology in Teachers' Work*. New York, NY: Teachers College Press, 1998.

Westmorland, M.G., and Williams, R. "Employers and Policy Makers Can Make a Difference to the Employment of Persons with Disabilities." *Disability and Rehabilitation* 24.15 (2002): 802–9.

Weststar, J. "Worker Control as a Facilitator in the Match between Education and Jobs." (forthcoming). *British Journal of Industrial Relations* (2009).

White, J. *Sisters & Solidarity: Women and Unions in Canada*. Toronto, ON: Thompson Educational Publishing, Inc., 1993.

Wihak, C. and Hall, G. *Work-related Informal Learning: Research and Practice in the Canadian Context*. Ottawa, ON: Work and Learning Knowledge Centre, Canadian Council on Learning, 2008.

Williams, C. "Disability in the Workplace." *Perspectives on Labour and Income* 7.2 (2006): 59–67.

Williamson, O.E. *The Economic Institutions of Capitalism*. London, UK: Macmillan, 1985.

Wilson, S.J. *Women, Families & Work* (4th ed.) Toronto, ON: McGraw-Hill Ryerson Limited, 1996.

Wolbers, M.H.J. "Job Mismatches and Their Labour-Market Effects Among School-leavers in Europe." *European Sociological Review* 19 (2003): 249–66.

Wolff, E. "Technology and the Demand for Skills." In L. Borghans and A. de Grip (Eds.), *The Overeducated Worker? The Economics of Skill Utilization*. Cheltenham, UK: Edward Elgar, 2000, 27–56.

Wolfson, W. *Analysis of Labour Force Survey Data for the Information Technology Occupations*. Ottawa, ON: Software Human Resource Council, 2003.

Womack, J., Jones, D.T., and Roos, D. *The Machine that Changed the World*. New York, NY: Macmillan, 1990.

Wong, H.K. "New Teacher Induction: The Foundation for Comprehensive, Coherent and Sustained Professional Development." In *Teacher Mentoring and Induction: The State of the Art and Beyond*. Thousand Oaks, CA: Corwin Press, 2005, 41–58.

Wood, S. *The Degradation of Work? Skill, Deskilling and the Labour Process*. London, UK: Hutchinson, 1982.

Wooten, L.P., and James, E.H. "Challenges of Organizational Learning: Perpetuation of Discrimination Against Employees with Disabilities." *Behavioral Sciences and the Law* 23 (2005): 123–41.

Wright, E.O. "The Class Structure of Advanced Capitalist Societies." In E.O.Wright, *Class, Crisis and the State*. London, UK: Verso, 1978, 30–110.

———. "Class and Occupation." *Theory and Society* 9 (1980): 177–214.

———. (Ed.). *Approaches to Class Analysis*. Cambridge, UK: Cambridge University Press. 2005.

Yalnizyan, A. *The Rich and the Rest of Us: The Changing Face of Canada's Growing Gap*. Toronto, ON: Canadian Centre for Policy Alternatives, 2007.

Young, A.A. "Increasing Returns and Economic Progress." *Economic Journal* 38 (1928): 527–42.

Zimbalist, A.S. *Case Studies on the Labor Process*. New York, NY: Monthly Review Press, 1979.

Zuboff, S. *In the Age of the Smart Machine: The Future of Work and Power*. New York, NY: Basic Books, 1988.

The Authors

Dr. D.W. Livingstone is Canada Research Chair in Lifelong Learning and Work and professor in the Department of Sociology and Equity Studies in Education at the Ontario Institute for Studies in Education of the University of Toronto (OISE/UT). He is director of the Centre for the Study of Education and Work at OISE/UT and leader of the Social Sciences and Humanities Research Council–funded research network on the Changing Nature of Work and Lifelong Learning (WALL) (see www.wallnetwork.ca). His recent books include *Working and Learning in the Information Age: A Canadian Perspective* (CPRN, 2002); *The Education-Jobs Gap: Underemployment or Economic Democracy* (Garamond Press, 2004, 2nd edition); *Hidden Knowledge: Organized Labour in the Information Age* (with Peter Sawchuk, Garamond Press and Rowman & Littlefield, 2004) ; and *The Future of Lifelong Learning and Work: Critical Perspectives* (with Peter Sawchuk and Kiran Mirchandani, Sense Publishers, 2008). Addresses: email: dlivingstone@oise.utoronto.ca; phone/fax: 905-271-2755; mail: D.W. Livingstone, SESE, OISE/UT, 252 Bloor St. W., Toronto, ON M5S 1V6.

Dr. Meredith Lordan received her doctorate in 2008 from the Department of Sociology and Equity Studies at OISE/UT. Her doctoral research focuses on education as a human right within the United Nations. She has been a teacher educator, program coordinator, and secondary school teacher, having served as the co-coordinator of the Students at Risk: Learning Pathways and co-coordinator of the School, Community, and Global Connections cohorts at OISE/UT. She is extending her research of teachers' work and learning to include youth at-risk programming and new teacher mentoring.

Sandria Officer received her doctorate in 2009 in the Department of Sociology and Equity Studies at OISE/UT. She is currently an instructor at OISE in the Academic and Cultural Support Centre. Her research interests include disability; links between school, work, and learning; policy-making; and social justice. She is a member of government-sponsored and non-profit organization committees involved in social inclusion, employment, and disability.

Dr. K.V. Pankhurst, Visiting Scholar at the Centre for Studies in Education and Work, has retired from a career combining appointments in universities, government departments, and international institutions, and was for many years a senior official of the OECD. Recent articles include "Education and Employment: Overview of Research and Policy Issues," in T. Wallace, N. Murphy, G. Lépine, and D. Brown, *Exploring New Directions in Essential Skills Research*. (Public Policy Forum, 2005, 22–40) and "The Labour Process: Individual Learning, Work and Productivity." with with D.W. Livingstone in *Studies in Continuing Education*, 28.1, March 2006.

Marion Radsma is a doctoral candidate in the Department of Sociology and Equity Studies at OISE/UT. Her work career spans more than twenty-five years of varied work assignments with major Canadian corporations and includes a decade of experience as an independent consultant. In this current phase, she helps organizations enhance their employee development initiatives by identifying learning needs, building learning programs, and assessing program effectiveness.

Milosh Raykov is the main statistical research analyst for the Education-Job Matching Survey research, including the Changing Nature of Work and Lifelong Learning (WALL) project. He holds a graduate degree in the methodology of socio-psychological research and has contributed to several studies on the methodology of empirical research, and studies on work, labour organizations, and lifelong learning. Currently, his main research focus is on informal learning about workplace health and safety, and the impact of underemployment on workers' health-related quality of life.

Dr. Johanna Weststar is an assistant professor of Management in the Sobey School of Business at Saint Mary's University. She received her doctorate in 2007 from the Centre for Industrial Relations and Human Resources at the University of Toronto. Her doctoral research focused on workplace learning, qualification, and worker control. She has contributed to several labour studies publications. Weststar is currently extending her research of the IT industry to include the electronic games industry and new media.

Olivia Wilson completed her BA and MA in sociology at the University of Toronto. Her MA thesis focused on the effect of economic changes on automotive workers and their families in a small town in Ontario. She completed her LLB at the University of Ottawa in 2008 and is pursuing a career in public interest law.

Index

A

Adult Education and Training Survey (AET), 84, 86–87, 89
adult learning, 51, 82, 85, 117. *See also* further education; lifelong learning
aesthetic studies (music, dance, drama, visual arts), 323
    arts-based teaching across the curriculum, 174
apprenticeship programs. *See* certification or licensing
assembly line workers. *See* production workers
authority structures, 11, 26, 57. *See also* job control
    economic class-based, 57
    public schools, 168–71, 174, 177
    relation to education-job matching, 26
auto sector, 238–40
    changes, 255 (*See also* lean production)
    global industry, 239
auto workers, 7, 61, 104, 237–56. *See also* production workers; trades workers
    abilities unrecognized, 255
    age, 240, 253, 255–56
    changing nature of work, 241
    closeness of field of study to job, 120
    demographic characteristics, 240
    education-job matches, 8, 252–54
    formal education, 106
    further education, 249
    hours of work, 245
    informal learning, 117, 252, 255
    job control, 243–47
    need to learn new skills, 249
    participation in decision-making, 110
    post-secondary education, 117, 249
    task discretion, 108
    trade certification, 113, 248
    underemployment, 122, 253–54
    underqualification, 253
    veteran work force, 255
auto workers case study (GM plant), 240–41
autobiographical recollections of workers, 324
automation, 17, 33
    computer software, 222, 228, 249–50, 264
    computerized machinery, 241
    self-service, 71
autonomous learning, 323
autonomy in decision-making, 39, 186. *See also* job control
    teachers, 176–77, 179

B

Bachelor of Education (BEd), 158, 175, 177–78
balance between work and leisure, 317
Bill 160, 161
breakfast programs, 160
British Skills Survey time series, 40, 43

C

Canada
    inter-generational class mobility, 23
    literacy rates, 85
    proportion of labour force with post-secondary degrees, 41, 83, 114
Canada's Information and Communications Technology (ICT), 207
Canadian Automotive Workers (CAW), 239, 241, 249
    position on lean production, 240
Canadian Class Structure (CCS) Project Survey, 7, 71, 78, 81
Canadian National Institute of Disability Management and Research, 261
Canadian National Occupational Code (NOC), 38
capital investment, 12–13
casual, seasonal, and short-term contract jobs, 68

certification or licensing, 24, 113, 187, 263
   production workers, 248
   trades workers, 248
changing employment conditions, 68–78, 255
   time required to learn job, 78–79
   women's entry into paid employment, 68
changing job requirements, 78–82, 111
class analysis. *See* economic class analysis
class mobility, 23
classical economic theory, 12
   labour force as homogeneous and passive, 26
clerical sector, 39, 217, 227
clerical workers, 7, 104, 211–34
   age profile, 217
   call centre work, 222
   case study site profile, 218–19
   changes effecting, 214–16, 218, 220, 222
   closeness of field of study to job, 120
   collaborative support behaviours, 233–34
   continual, self-directed learning, 216
   continuing education, 226
   contradictory class situation, 212–13
   control over workdays, 220
   creativity, 109, 220, 223
   credential requirements for job entry, 113
   declining availability of jobs, 216, 232
   divergent work situations, 212
   earnings, 217, 224
   education-job match, 8, 229–30
   employer sponsored education, 216
   fear of job loss, 217–18, 232–33
   formal education, 106, 117, 216, 224, 231
   further education, 227
   human relations abilities, 234
   informal learning, 228–29, 234
   intensification of work, 215
   job descriptions, 220
   job duties, 219–22
   learning by experience, 8
   literacy, 225
   nineteenth century, 213
   organizational and policy decision-making, 110, 222–23
   in public service, 218
   skills, 215–16, 234
   supplementary and subordinate work, 106
   task discretion, 108, 220, 223
   temporary labour, 216
   time required to learn job, 112, 225
   twenty-first century, 214–16
   underemployment, 122–23, 310
   unemployment, 217
   unionization, 212–14, 218
   women, 212–14, 217–18
co-curricular programming, 160
co-worker mentoring, 86–87
cognition
   ability to change, 314
cognitive knowledge and abilities, 148
   acquisition of, 144–46, 297–99
   assessment, 321
   formation during work, 143–45
   reserve of, 9, 28, 148, 152, 199, 300–301, 306, 314, 319, 325
cognitive processes (in different societal contexts), 18
cognitive psychology, 144
cognitive reformulation, 148, 307
collaboration between employers and employees, 320
collateral learning, 145, 154, 165, 300, 307
"Common Sense Revolution" era, 161
competence (or personal competence), 147, 153
competency gaps in Canadian labour force (debate), 186
computer programmers, 5, 7–8, 38, 104, 123, 185–208
   closeness of field of study to job, 120
   continual learning, 186
   demographic characteristics, 187
   diverse backgrounds, 191
   education-job match, 124, 190–93, 195
   emerging profession, 106
   formal schooling, 106, 117, 187
   job creativity, 109
   job stress, 193
   learning new skills, 114, 193
   need for interpersonal relations abilities, 193–94
   overqualification, 310
   participation in decision-making, 110
   permanent full-time jobs, 187
   post-secondary education, 117, 187
   self-taught, 192
   specialized knowledge, 106
   task discretion, 108, 202–3, 207

training time to do job, 112
underemployment, 121, 123, 131
unemployment, 187
computer skill match, 91
computer software
  auto workers and, 249
  clerical workers and, 222, 228
  disabled workers and, 264
  trades workers and, 249–50
computerized machinery
  production workers (auto), 241
contingent part-time and temporary jobs, 22, 69, 216
continual learning, 58–60, 146, 186, 255
continual learning and continual job redefinition, 199
continuing education. *See* adult education; further education
control in jobs. *See* job control
creativity, 108, 127, 129, 179
  clerical workers, 220, 223
  computer programmers, 201–2, 204, 207
  disabled workers, 270–73
  teachers, 174–76
  trades workers, 247, 254
credential gap, 19, 23–24, 30, 52, 93
credential inflation, 35, 37, 39–40, 121, 125, 131, 208, 273, 321
  to control access, 81
credential match, 42–43, 120–22, 129
  clerical workers, 231–32
  disabled workers, 274
credential mismatch
  computer programmers, 191–92
  disabled workers, 274–75
credential proliferation, 192
credential requirements, 35, 94, 151. *See also* job requirements
  certification or licensing, 113
  for job entry, 34, 39, 43, 81, 112, 194, 224, 263
  learning new skills, 114
credential underemployment, 127, 310
  clerical workers, 231
  computer programmers, 191
  employment experience and, 129
  industrial workers, 93
credentialism, 11, 18–19, 175, 314, 321
criterion referencing, 320

curiosity, 150, 298
curriculum reform, 169, 323

D

decent job, 315
decision-making
  teachers, 176
demand-centred theories, 17
deskilling, 17, 33, 39, 78, 138, 144, 227, 238
Dewey, John, 141, 150
  "collateral learning," 145
diaries by workers, 324
disability employment policies, 279–80
  formal disability-based competency training, 262
disability management workplace protocol, 281
disability rates, 257–58
disabled workers, 5, 8, 106, 241, 257–82
  barriers to workplace socialization, 277
  better use of abilities, 317
  certification or licensing, 263
  compensation strategies, 267–68, 270–71, 280
  creativity, 270–73
  credential mismatch, 274–75
  early retirement, 264
  education-job match, 273–79, 310
  employer-sponsored training, 264–65
  employment trends, 258–59
  ethnic minorities, 263
  further education, 263–65
  hours of work, 259
  intensification of work tasks, 270
  job control, 269–73
  job entry requirements, 263
  job-related informal learning, 265–69
  job requirements, 261–63
  organizational and policy decision-making, 269
  people of colour, 259
  performance gap, 275–77, 280
  post-secondary education, 263, 280
  relevance of field of study to job, 273
  social abilities, 268
  social discrimination in workplace, 269
  stereotypical thinking about, 258, 266, 274, 276, 281
  technical changes in work (requiring new skills), 260

underemployment, 258, 272, 274–75, 277–81, 310
unemployment, 258, 280
use of vacation and sick days, 270–71
women, 259, 263
working conditions, 260–61
workplace accommodation, 259–60
discretion, degree of. *See* task discretion
disparities in rewards from work, 319
displacement or bumping hypothesis, 58
division of labour, 55–56, 238
doubt, 299
Durkheim, Émile, 139, 144, 149–50

E
early childhood education, 21, 323
early retirement, 264
economic class, 7, 26, 46, 52, 57, 105. *See also* employee class
  in *The Education-Jobs Gap*, 53, 55–56
  in public school system, 23
  relation to education-job matching, 47, 51, 58
  skill and, 61–62
  social distinctions, 323
economic class analysis, 51–58
economic class recomposition, 69–73
economic forecasting (1950s and 1960s), 14
economic growth. *See also* education and economic growth
  costs to ecological and human environment, 318, 321
  inherently desirable (fallacy), 321
economic power, 62
education. *See also* employer-sponsored education
  aesthetic studies, 174, 323
  "Common Sense Revolution" era, 161
  and competency gaps in labour force, 186
  curriculum reform, 169, 323
  declining educational standards (claim), 41, 310
  declining rates of return, 313
  deficits in relation to changing labour market, 17, 90, 311
  dominant educational ideology, 28, 314
  early childhood education, 21
  education and learning, 15 (*See also* learning)
  formal (*See* formal education)
  "hidden curriculum," 176
  internationally recognized human right, 322
  languages, 323
  mixed ability groupings, 323
  need for "skill upgrading," 78
  occupational preparation, 13
  politicized as public good, 160
  post-secondary (*See* post-secondary education)
  private schools, 161
  purposes of (wider than employment), 12–13, 306, 312, 314, 321, 324
  rapid growth of, 40
  upward social mobility from, 28
Education Act, 159–60, 166, 169–70
education and economic growth, 11, 13–16, 321
education and jobs survey profile I (1983-2004), 67–100
education-job match, 7, 11, 17, 26, 30, 90–98, 104, 118–25, 204
  authority structure and, 26
  auto-workers, 8, 252–54
  case study respondents' experience, 286–89
  clerical workers, 8, 229–30
  computer programmers, 124, 190–93, 195
  credential match, 42–43, 120–22
  demographic variables and, 127–28
  employee class and, 127, 129–31
  employment experience and, 125–26, 130–31
  evolving relationship, 289–90
  field of study match, 42, 45, 91, 119–20
  immediate job control factors, 127
  immigration status and race, 126–27
  knowledge match, 97
  non-white groups, 126
  on-the-job learning, 127
  performance match, 42–45, 94, 122–23
  prior empirical research on, 33–49
  professional and technical employees, 48
  social background factors, 125
  subjective match, 42, 45–46, 96, 123–25
  teachers, 124, 166–68, 310
  trades workers, 254, 310
  union or association membership and, 127
education-job mismatches, 47, 59
  effects on workers' health, 130
  political radicalizing effects, 130

social background factors, 46
The Education-Jobs Gap (Livingstone), 4, 6, 47–48, 51–63
  economic class structure, 53, 55–56
education-jobs paradigm, 311
Education-Jobs Requirements Matching Project (EJRM), 4–7, 22, 30, 34, 46, 49, 51, 62, 103–32, 165–66, 173, 188, 201–2
  auto workers, 238, 240, 243, 248–49, 252
  clerical workers, 217, 223, 225
  computer programmers, 186–87
  disabled workers, 258
  focus on non-managerial employees, 103
  knowledge match, 97
  teachers' general-knowledge learning, 180
  teachers' roles, 158
education of girls and women, 152
Education Quality And Accountability Office, 164
Education Quality Improvement Act (1996) (Bill 160), 161
educational discrimination (race, gender), 23
educational practice, 322–24
educational requirements. *See* credential requirements
Employability Assistance for People with Disabilities, 259
employee class, 105. *See also* economic class
  in education-job matching, 127, 129–31
  job design and control, 99
  and learning practices, 88–90
  university degree and, 88–89
employee-share ownership, 320
employer-sponsored education, 216, 249
  computer programmers, 195–96
  disabled workers, 264–65
  managerial and professional employees, 89
employers' role in better utilizing labour, 316–17
employment-based informal learning, 86
employment change (Canada)
  economic sector change and economic class recomposition, 69–73
  worker involvement, 73–78
employment experience, 6, 46, 129. *See also* learning by experience; on-the-job learning
  and education-job match, 125–26, 130–31
employment policy reform, 9
entrepreneurial initiative, 62

epistemology, 306
EQAO, 164
ethno-cultural diversity, 160
  teachers' responsiveness to, 159
everyday learning, 142
"experience curves," 142
expert analyst ratings of job requirements, 34
expert-based measures of overeducation, 44
expert-based skill ratings of occupational titles, 38
expert specific vocational (SVP) scale estimates of training time, 79
explicit reasoning, 146
explicit thought, 147, 149
extrinsic incentives, 137

F
field of study matching, 42, 45, 91–92, 119–20, 273
financial crisis (2008), 318
"folk culture," 149
Ford, Henry, 137
foreign control of Canada's manufacturing sector, 70–71
formal education, 27, 29, 54, 83, 145, 248. *See also* credential requirements
  clerical workers, 216, 224–24
  computer programmers, 106, 117, 187
  economic class influence in, 23
  higher than previous generations, 42, 114
  importance challenged by case studies, 303
  inadequate measure of cognitive abilities, 42, 305–6, 311
  internationally agreed right, 314
  irrelevance of, 195
  as measure of quality of labour, 13
  as measure of workers' capabilities, 16, 40, 48, 319
  required for job entry, 7, 9, 79, 123
  required to perform job, 7
  self-reports on, 41
  teachers, 106, 113, 117, 159, 164–66
  used as screening device, 24, 33, 225, 321
  used by applicants to compete for jobs, 33
formal education / further education relationship, 85
formal learning through employer-sponsored courses. *See* employer-sponsored education
formal schooling. *See* formal education

formal *vs* informal learning, 194–97
free market assumptions, 16
Friedan, Betty, 214
further education, 27, 84–86, 115, 142, 167, 226. *See also* adult education
   access to training, 227–28
   clerical workers, 227
   teachers, 165, 179

G
Gates, Bill, 62
gender, 46, 62. *See also* women
gender bias, 38
general educational development (GED), 34, 37, 39, 44, 47
   estimates of technical skill requirements, 36
   performance match ratings, 95
general labour, 47
General Motors (GM), 239
   case study, 240–41
general working-knowledge gap, 23
"generic skills," 153
gestalt, 144
global market competition, 69
Goldthorpe, J.H.
   occupational classifications, 53
government. *See* role of modern state
Greer, Germaine, 214
Gross National Product, 14

H
habit or habitual action, 146–48, 296, 299–300, 303
Hay Associates, 39
health and safety, 250
   repetitive strain injuries, 240–41, 243
health and safety certification, 248–49
heterogeneity and differentiation of labour, 29, 141, 151–52, 307–8, 313
hidden abilities, 307
high school diploma, 81, 113
high school teachers. *See* teachers
hours of work, 68, 233, 317. *See also* part-time employment
   auto workers, 237, 241, 245
   clerical workers, 221
   computer programmers, 187–88
   disabled workers, 259
   irregular shifts, on call, or casual, 69
   long hours, 69
   unequal distribution of, 317
household work, 27
human capital, 151–52, 300–305, 307, 314
   importance of, 317
   through learning by experience, 153
human capital investment, 15–16
human capital notion of skill development, 186
human capital theories, 11, 20, 41, 52, 263
   earnings related to levels of education, 21
   investment in education will lead to economic growth, 16
human resource development strategies, 320

I
IBM Canada case study, 186, 188–89
   formal training and upgrading initiatives, 196
   matrix management system, 188
immigration status and race
   education-job match, 126–27
impairment-job match, 281
implicit contract of employment. *See* open contract of employment
implicit contract theory, 308
industrial workers, 5, 56, 62, 104. *See also* production workers
   credential requirement for job entry, 81, 112
   decline, 71–72
   employer support for further education, 89
   entry and performance requirements (increase), 82
   field of study match, 92, 119
   formal education requirements, 106
   further education, 117
   match between capabilities and job requirements, 58
   participation in decision-making, 110
   post-secondary credentials, 81, 88, 115
   skill composition, 39
   skill-upgrading trend, 40
   supervisory roles, 75
   task discretion and policy decisions, 73, 76, 78
   underemployment, 7, 93, 121, 123, 129
informal education. *See* informal learning
informal job-related learning, 49, 86, 100, 117

informal learning, 11, 24, 26–28, 41, 51, 87, 115, 179, 251, 303
- auto workers, 117, 251, 255
- clerical workers, 228–29, 234
- importance of, 90, 310
- importance to computer programmers, 194–97
- intentional, 61, 86–87, 146, 311
- production workers, 250
- recognition for, 61
- teachers, 117, 164–65, 178
- trades workers, 250
- transforming abilities and modifying jobs, 9

Informational Technology (IT) sector. *See* IT industry
innovation, 15, 59, 70, 208
integration of learning and work, 149–50
intensification of work, 73, 239, 256
- auto workers, 238, 255
- disabled workers, 270
- health consequences, 243
- pressure on trades workers, 242

intentional informal learning, 61, 86–87, 311
- habits of, 146
- trades workers, 250

intentional learning, 27, 82–90
intentional learning practices, 114–17
inter-firm competition, 60
International Association of Administrative Professionals (IAAP), 215
International Labour Office, 315
International Standard Classification of Occupations (ISCO), 53
intuition, 145–47, 149, 303
- economy of time, 146

involuntary part-time employment, 68
IT industry, 3, 73, 187, 207. *See also* computer programmers
- diversity of work in, 191–92
- learning new skills, 193
- move to standardized credentials, 208
- need for interpersonal and business skills, 193–94
- undefined job descriptions, 204

J

"Japanese model," 239
job control, 177, 200

auto workers, 243–47, 254–55
computer programmers, 202, 204
disabled workers, 269–73
role in moderating underemployment, 186
teachers, 177
job control, effects of differences in, 6
job control by education job-match, 98–99
job creativity. *See* creativity
job entry requirements, 34, 39, 43, 81, 112, 194, 224, 263
job performance requirements, 39
job-related informal learning, 49, 86, 100, 117
job requirement-worker capacity matches, 29
job requirements, 33
- auto workers, 248–49
- credential requirements, 35–36 (*See also* job entry requirements)
- disabled workers, 261–63
- expert analyst ratings, 34
- incremental gains, 111
- learning new skills, 113–14
- licensing or certification, 111, 113, 248
- performance requirements, 35–40
- self-reports, 34, 38, 73
job rotation, 69, 99, 238
job security, 68–69, 78

K

Keynes, John, 12, 151
"know-how," 39, 149
"knowing that" *vs.* "knowing how," 208
knowledge-based economy (KBE), 16–17, 21, 36, 52
- literacy rates, 86
- need for "skill upgrading" for, 78
knowledge-based occupations, 71
knowledge class, 54
knowledge-deficits, 11
knowledge gap, 25
knowledge match
- education-job matching, 97

L

labour
- deficient in knowledge and ability, 11, 17
- demand for in post-industrial society, 16–17
- in economic theory, 12–14
- global labour pool, 68

375

heterogeneity and differentiation of, 29, 151–52, 307
routinization, 17, 33 (*See also* deskilling)
specialized forms of, 47
surplus of qualified labour, 17, 58
thought to be passive, 12
wasted abilities, 20
labour mobility, 153
labour scarcity, fears of, 13, 207
labour surpluses, 39, 159
labour utilization, 309, 313–17, 319–20
employers' role, 316–17
large employers, 56, 58, 62, 71, 88
lean production, 238, 247, 256. *See also* auto sector
Canadian Automotive Workers' views on, 240
repetitive strain injuries from, 240
work intensification, 239, 243
learning, 15, 142
attempts to locate within an organization, 142
autonomous, 323
continual, 58–60, 146, 186, 199, 255
endogenous in any kind of activity, 150
human beings as active agents of, 313
informal (*See* informal learning)
lifelong (*See* lifelong learning)
on-the-job (*See* on-the-job learning)
personal input, 304
as reformulation, 301
reliance on intuition, 146
reserve of personal knowledge (*See* reserve of knowledge and abilities)
learning and knowledge, 151, 249–52
learning and work, 7, 26–27, 49
common features, 304–5
connections between, 199
empirical evidence from case studies, 285–308
integration of, 149–50
interactive nature of, 28, 313
research into, 138, 154
teachers, 180–81
underlying relationship, 150
learning by experience, 7, 16, 28, 149–50, 153, 290–91, 310, 314, 322–23
computer programmers, 189–90, 197
empirical evidence of, 142–43
learning for work, 27
learning from unpaid activities, 299–300

learning outside formal schooling, 307
licensing. *See* certification or licensing
lifelong learning, 21, 49, 90, 158, 180
literacy rates, 41, 90, 225, 310
Canadian adults, 85
knowledge-based economy, 86
younger *vs.* older workers, 41
Livingstone, D.W., 26, 367
The Education-Jobs Gap, 6, 47–48, 51–63
longitudinal case studies, 324
Lordan, Meredith, 367
lumpenproletariat, 53

M
maintaining employment, 314, 318
management work, 71
managerial and professional jobs. *See* professional and managerial jobs
managerial authority, 53, 55–57
computer programmers, 201, 207
delegation of, 75
managerial decisions, 140
managerial division of labour, 56
managerial employees, 54, 81, 89, 91, 93, 99
increase, 71–72
match between capabilities and job requirements, 58
managers, 56–57, 73
levels of schooling, 88
mandatory retirement, 51
manual labourers, 16
manufacturing sector, 39, 69–71
market economics, 3, 318
Marx, Karl, 26, 47, 53, 144
Marxist class analysis, 18
matrix management structure, 188
measures and concepts of matching, 305
mentoring, 86–87, 158, 165, 178
Mill, John Stuart, 17
Ministry of Education, 173–75, 179
mobility, 188–89
mobility and job modification, 153
mobility to other tasks and occupations, 15, 303–4
multi-skilling, 69, 78
multi-tasking, 241–42
Multilateral Framework for Labour Market Agreements for Persons with Disabilities (LMAPD), 258–59

N

National Occupations Codes (NOC), 158, 219, 261
"neo-Taylorism," 238
neoclassical theory, 12, 15
    labour as homogeneous and passive, 26, 140, 151, 308
New Approaches to Lifelong Learning Project (NALL), 7, 60–61, 69, 82, 86, 89–90
"new economy," 4
New Teacher Induction Program (NTIP), 165, 178
non-managerial employees, 4–5, 62

O

occupational class models, 53
occupational distribution, changes in, 35
occupational projections (manpower requirements), 14–15
Office Workers' Career Support Centre, 219
Officer, Sandria, 219, 367
on-the-job learning, 8, 20–21, 59, 165
    adjustment of abilities and jobs, 9
    computer programmers, 193, 197
    teachers, 158, 178
on-the-job training, 22, 41, 166
Ontario College of Teachers (OCT), 161, 174
    certification, 159, 164
    instrument of state authority, 163
    Standards of Practice, 162–63
Ontario high school teachers. *See* teachers
Ontario Public Service Employees Union (OPSEU), 218–19
Ontario Secondary School Curriculum, 159
Ontario Secondary School Teachers' Federation (OSSTF), 161–62, 164
open contract of employment, 7, 9, 19, 60, 137, 139–41, 151, 292–94
Organization for Economic Cooperation and Development, 14
organizational and policy decision-making, 104, 109–10, 127, 129
    auto workers, 243–44
    clerical workers, 110, 222–23
    computer programmers, 201
    disabled workers, 269
    industrial workers, 243
    trades people, 244

out-sourcing and off-shore labour, 69
"outdoor psychology," 149
overeducation, 3, 6, 11, 42–44, 48, 309
    expert-based measures of, 44
    Flemish school leavers (2001), 44
    and human capital theory, 20–22
    narrow and restrictive concept of education, 312
    self-reports of, 44–45
    Swedish Survey data, 45
overqualification, 3, 43, 309
owner classes, 71
owners (enterprise owners), 54
ownership, 55–57
ownership of production, 60
ownership of property, 47, 53

P

Pankhurst, K.V., 368
part-time employment, 3, 51, 68–69, 99
participant observation, 5
participation in decision-making. *See* organizational and policy decision-making
participatory democracy, 320
people of colour
    credential underemployment, 310
    exclusion from decision-making, 77
performance gap, 19, 23, 25, 30, 52
    computer programmers, 192
    disabled workers, 275–77, 280
    production workers, 254
    trades workers, 254
performance match, 43–45, 123
    clerical workers, 231–32
    expert ratings, 94–95
    self-reports, 94–95
performance requirements, 34–40, 82
personal knowledge, 148–49
personnel selection, 322
"pink ghetto," 212
Polanyi, M., 40, 139, 141, 144–45, 148–49, 151, 301
polyvalence, 301–3, 306, 308, 314
portfolios of achievements, 320
post-industrial social theories, 11
post-industrial society
    demand for labour, 16–17
post-secondary certification

computer programmers, 187
post-secondary education, 41, 167, 224
   access to, 23–24
   clerical workers, 117
   computer programmers, 106
   disabled workers, 263
   expansion of, 24
   increase in, 43, 83, 85, 92
   requirement for job entry, 81
   requirement for service and industrial jobs, 81
   university (*See* university degrees)
power relations, 23
"practical common sense," 149
practical guidelines, 147–48
"practical intelligence," 149
practical or tacit knowledge, 149
"practical wisdom," 148
"precarious employment," 69
prior experience, 148, 320
probation, 151
problem solving, 39, 137, 140, 142–43, 147, 149–50, 298, 304, 311
   choices and decisions, 297
   essential nature of work, 295
   making use of doubt, 299
   managing personal relationships, 297
   problem identification in, 296
   progressive learning by experience, 141
   work as, 141
production workers, 5, 62, 238–40, 244–51, 254–56, 297, 300, 303–4, 307–8. *See also* auto workers; industrial workers
   certification or licensing, 248
   computerized machinery, 241
   intensification of work tasks, 243
   multitasking, 241
   task discretion, 245–46, 255
   underemployment, 310
   upskilling, 39
productivity, 153–54
professional and managerial jobs, 81, 89
   field of study match, 91
   growth of, 71
   increase, 99
professional and technical workers, 16, 40, 48, 62
professional employees, 5, 56–57, 62, 104
   closeness of field of study to job, 119–20
   education-job match, 48, 124

formal education requirements, 88, 106
further education, 117
   increase, 71–72
   job creativity, 108
   match between capabilities and job requirements, 58
   participation in decision-making, 73, 110
   post-secondary credential for job entry, 112
   task discretion, 73, 107–8
   underemployment, 7, 121
   underqualification, 121
   university degrees, 115
professional learning community (PLC), 179
professional occupations, 35
   self-regulation, 54
   specialized body of knowledge, 47, 53–54
professional regulation of teaching, 162–63
Progressive Conservative government (Ontario, 1995–2003), 161
   creation of OCT, 163
propositional thinking, 144
public employment services, 12–13
public intervention and regulation, 318
public school teachers. *See* teachers
purposive action, 149–50

R
race and immigration status, 46–47, 62
racial minorities, 18
Radsma, Marion, 368
Raykov, Milosh, 368
recent immigrants
   credential underemployment, 129, 310
   entry into labour market, 68
   underemployment, 127, 131, 205–6
reflective learning, 145
relevance gap, 23–25, 30, 191
relevance of field of study to job, 45, 91, 119–20, 273
repetitive strain injuries, 240–41, 243
representations (or mental representations), 146
reserve of knowledge and abilities, 9, 28, 148, 152, 199, 300–301, 306, 314, 319, 325
retired people, 22, 51, 68
right to work, 315
role of modern state, 60
   educational and employment planning, 13
   employment in, 70

income support, 317–18
public employment services, 12–13
public intervention and regulation, 318
responsibilities to workers in precarious employment, 319
role in improving labour utilization, 317–19
social welfare, 14, 60

S
school completion, 41. *See also* education
school dropouts, 21
school leaving age, 13
schooling. *See* education
schools
    authority (or hierarchical structure), 168, 171, 174
scientific thinking, 144, 147
second wave feminists, 214
segmentation of work, 200
segmented labour market theories, 11, 16–19, 26
self-employed, 56, 69, 71–72
self-reported entry credentials, 81, 122
self-reported training time, 78–79
self-reports of job requirements, 34, 38, 73
self-reports of overeducation, 44–45
self-reports of skill levels, 40
self-reports on formal education attainments, 41
sensorimotor abilities, 145
service sector employment, 16, 105
    increase, 71
    shift to, 69–70
    upgrading (or upskilling), 39
service workers, 5, 40, 56–57, 62, 104
    credential underemployment, 129
    decline, 71–72
    employer support for further education, 89
    entry and performance requirements, 81–82, 106, 112
    field of study match, 92
    formal education requirements, 106
    further education, 117
    match between capabilities and job requirements, 58
    supervisory roles, 75
    task discretion and policy decisions, 73, 76, 78, 110
    underemployment, 7, 94, 121, 123
    university degrees, 115

sexual harassment, 249
skill, 138, 305
    ambiguity and multiple meanings, 139
skilled worker, 138
small employers, 56, 71
small parts manufacturing, 61
Smith, Adam, 17, 139, 143, 152
social background profiles, 5
social equity, 319
Social Sciences and Humanities Research Council of Canada (SSHRC), 4
social variables, 307
social welfare, 14, 60
sociology of work, 138
specialized knowledge, 47, 53–54, 56–57
specific vocational preparation (SVP) scale, 37, 39
    gradual skill upgrading, 78
State of the Teaching Profession (2006) Survey, 159
subemployment, 20
subjective gaps, 23, 25, 30
subjective match
    education-job match, 7, 96, 123–25
subjective underemployment, 19, 45, 52
    computer programmers, 198–99
    disabled workers, 277–79, 281
succession planning in employment, 315, 317
supervisors, 56–57
Sweden, 39
    class mobility, 23
    post-secondary completion, 83
symbiosis of thought and action, 150, 153

T
"tacit knowledge," 148
talent use gap, 23–24, 52
task discretion, 9, 73–78, 104, 107–11, 140–41, 220, 295, 311. *See also* job control
    clerical workers, 108, 220, 223
    computer programmers, 108, 202–3, 207
    industrial workers, 243
    production workers, 245–46, 255
    teachers, 160, 163, 173–74, 176–77
    trades workers, 246–47, 255
teachers, 5, 7–8, 104, 157–82
    alliance building, 158
    authority structure, 168–71, 174, 179
    autonomy, 173–74

Bachelor of Education (BEd), 158, 175, 177–78
"burnout" and stress, 159, 166, 175
closeness of field of study to job, 120
continuing learning, 164, 167
discretion, degree of, 160
education-job match, 124, 166–68, 310
formal credentials required, 113, 164–66
gender and racial homogeneity, 159
graduate work, 158
high level of thought and attention, 107–8
informal learning, 117, 164–65, 178
job creativity, 109
job stability, 158
learning new skills, 114
lifelong learners, 158
market oversupply of, 159
OCT certificate of qualification, 165
on-the-job learning, 8
participation in decision-making, 110
performance criteria, 177
post-secondary attainment and certification, 167
practicum, 177
professional induction, 178
professional regulation of, 162–63
teacher education programs, 177–79
teaching certification, 113
time required to learn job, 78, 112
underqualification, 121
university degree requirement, 106, 117, 164–65
Teachers' Days of Action (1997), 161
teachers in technological studies, 164
teachers' professionalism
lack of public awareness, 162
teachers' work, 168–72
continually changing, 181
impediments, 172, 177
teaching in Ontario
organizational context, 158–60
technological change, 68
technological innovation, 15, 59
temp agencies, 227
temporary, part-time jobs, 22, 69, 216
theoretical thinking, 147
Tough, Allen, 86
"Toyotism," 238

trades workers, 5, 241
apprenticeship programs, 248
certification or licensing, 248
computer software (need for continuous learning), 249–50
creativity, 247, 254
education-job match, 254, 310
formal job requirements, 248
informal learning, 250
job control, 254–55
multi-tasking, 238, 242
performance gap, 254
specialized bodies of knowledge, 55, 254
task discretion, 246–47, 255
training time, 248
work intensification, 242
training time, 37, 78–79, 111–13, 193, 225, 248

U
"the unconscious," 148
unconscious learning, 303
undereducation, 21
underemployment, 3, 6–8, 10n4, 11, 19–21, 42, 48, 58, 120, 127, 129, 306, 309–10, 312. See also overeducation
age of worker and, 46
auto workers, 122, 253–54
blacks and Hispanics in US, 47
clerical workers, 122–23, 231
computer programmers, 121, 191
disabled persons, 100, 272, 274–75, 280
by economic class, 310
education or skill-based, 51–52
employment experience and, 129
industrial workers, 7, 93
job control and, 186
non-white persons, 100
professional employees, 7, 121
recent immigrants, 100, 127, 205–6
revolutionary political consciousness from, 20, 45, 312
service workers, 7, 121
skill or education-based conceptions, 22
time-based dimension, 22, 46, 51
underemployment and lack of adequate jobs, 19–20
underemployment/overeducation a persistent problem, 48

underqualification, 21, 59, 121, 253, 288
underutilization, 306, 309, 312–13. *See also* labour utilization
unemployment, 3, 17, 22, 59, 158, 187
   clerical workers, 217
   structural, 51
unemployment insurance, 12
union or professional association membership, 46, 104, 123. *See also names of unions and associations*
   auto workers, 61, 104, 239, 241, 249–50
   certification requirements and, 113
   clerical workers, 212–14, 218
   computer programmers, 187
   credential matching and, 129
   education-job match, 127
   and further education, 89
   teachers, 161–62
university degrees, 88–89, 106, 115, 117, 164–65, 224
   clerical workers, 117, 231
   computer programmers, 117
   rates of return, 20
unpaid work, 11, 26–27
   job-related learning, 27
"upskilling," 39, 138
US Department of Labor, 38
US labour force
   mismatch (overeducation) studies, 47
   overqualification, 44
   post-secondary completion, 83
   underemployment of blacks and Hispanics, 47
US National Research Council, 40
US Working Conditions Survey (1969), 130

V
vocational education and training, 324
voluntary community labour, 27

W
Weber, Max, 26, 47
   economic class scheme, 53
welfare provisions. *See* social welfare
Weststar, Johanna, 368
Wilson, Olivia, 368
women, 18
   continuing low representation in some fields, 24
   entry into paid employment, 68
   exclusion from decision-making, 77
   labour-force participation and occupational advancement, 100n1
   low-paid part-time jobs, 47
   married women in paid work force, 99
   overeducation, 47
   unpaid housework, 47
work and learning. *See* learning and work
Work and Lifelong Learning (WALL), 4–7, 69, 82, 89, 130, 216
   computer use, 91
   on economic class recomposition, 71–72
   education-job match, 90
   educational requirements for job entry, 81
   on job design control, 98
   job-related informal learning, 90
   on level of skill required, 78
   on literacy skills, 86
   on mentoring, 86
   task discretion and policy decisions, 77
   on teacher job tenure, 159
work as economy of thinking and acting, 146. *See also* labour
work as heterogeneous, 141
work as problem solving, 141
work experience. *See* employment experience
work intensification. *See* intensification of work
worker attributes, 139
worker-employer councils, 320
worker involvement in major policy decisions
   legislation on, 320
worker-job relationship, 307
"worker trait requirements" (WTR), 38
workers, 311
   active and heterogeneous, 308, 313
   control of, 137
   as homogeneous and passive, 138
   "resistant to change" assumption, 137
   Taylor's assumptions, 137
workers' capabilities. *See also* cognitive knowledge and abilities
   better use of, 313 (*See also* labour utilization)
   formal education as measure of, 40
   measures of, 40–41
   neglect of, 15, 17, 55
workers' rights, 249–50

"working-class capital," 24
Working Class Learning Strategies (WCLS) project, 61
working conditions, current national profiles, 7
working knowledge (auto workers) about to be lost, 256
workplace restructuring
challenge to disabled workers, 260, 270, 272
written contracts, 292

Y
youth cognitive skills, 41
youth underemployment, 19
youth unemployment, 130